China's
Forty
Millions

Harvard East Asian Series 87

The East Asian Research Center at Harvard University administers research projects designed to further scholarly understanding of China, Japan, Korea, Vietnam, Inner Asia, and adjacent areas.

Minority Nationalities and National Integration in the People's Republic of China

June Teufel Dreyer

China's Forty Millions

Harvard University Press
Cambridge, Massachusetts
and London, England
1976

Preparation of this volume has been
aided by a grant from the
Ford Foundation
Printed in the United States of America
*Library of Congress Cataloging in
Publication Data*
Dreyer, June Teufel, 1939–
    China's forty millions.
    (Harvard East Asian series : 87)
    Bibliography: p.
    Includes index.
    1. Minorities—China.   I. Title.
    II. Series.
DS730.D73   323.1'51   76-19032
ISBN 0-674-11964-9

To

Edward and Elizabeth

Contents

ACKNOWLEDGMENTS

I am grateful for the support of the Harvard East Asian Research Center and the Faculty Research Committee of Miami University. Portions of this book have previously appeared in Problems of Communism *and* Elites in the Peoples' Republic of China, *edited by Robert Scalapino (Seattle: University of Washington Press, 1972).*

China's Forty Millions

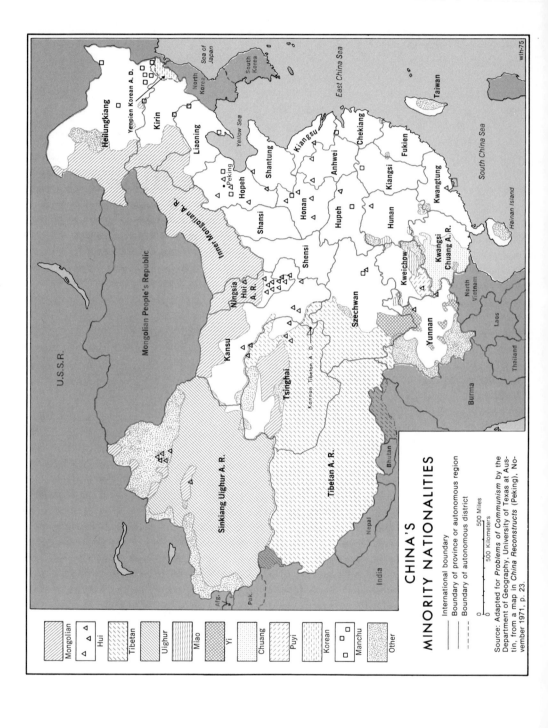

CHINA'S
MINORITY NATIONALITIES

International boundary
Boundary of province or autonomous region
Boundary of autonomous district

Mongolian	
Hui	△ △
Tibetan	
Uighur	
Miao	
Yi	
Chuang	
Puyi	
Korean	
Manchu	□ □
Other	

0   500 Miles
0   500 Kilometers

Source: Adapted for *Problems of Communism* by the Department of Geography, University of Texas at Austin, from a map in *China Reconstructs* (Peking), November 1971, p. 23.

wih-75

Introduction

Integration may be defined as the process whereby ethnic groups come to shift their loyalties, expectations, and political activities toward a new center, whose institutions assume jurisdiction over, and responsibility for, said groups.[1] Theoretically, integration can take place among an infinite number of equal ethnic groups. In practice, however, it typically involves a majority-minority group(s) situation. Minority groups may be characterized as:

subordinate units of complex state societies;
having physical and/or cultural characteristics that set them apart from the majority and that the majority hold in low esteem;
self-conscious units bound together by these special characteristics and by the disabilities these involve;
hereditary in membership—through choice or necessity, minority-group members tend to intermarry.[2]

The techniques by which minority groups may be integrated into a state have come to be of increasing interest in recent years. The condition of the Ibo in Nigeria, Negro in America, and Bengali in Pakistan are but the most newsworthy examples. Methods of integration may be arranged along a spectrum, the opposing ends of which are pluralism and assimilation. In an archetypal pluralistic system, integration is achieved with minority groups retaining their respective cultures and other distinguishing characteristics, presumably with the full approval of the majority group. At the opposite end of the spectrum, assimilation implies that members of minority groups have absorbed the characteristics of the dominant group to the exclusion of their own and become indistinguishable from members of the majority. In essence, they have ceased to exist as groups. Ranged between these extremes are a variety of intermediate positions, which may be collectively referred to as accommodation. Within the parameters of this term, minority groups may accept certain characteristics from the dominant group, such as language or style of clothing, while still maintaining many elements of their traditional cultures and varying degrees of ethnic identification.

Though studies of integration have generally been associated with the modern nation-state, the problems connected with incorporating diverse ethnic groups into a single political entity are as old as human history. The bondage of Israel in Egypt, the millet system of the Ottoman Empire, and the dual monarchy of Austria-Hungary represent three solutions that antedate the nation-state.

Minorities problems have indeed been exacerbated by the rise of nationalism. Many of the new nation-states have been formed on the ruins of multigroup empires. Instrumental in the demise of these empires has been pressure from without—for example, the British takeover of India from the Moghuls and the crumbling of the Ottoman Empire as a result of World War I. Aggression from outside a country's borders tends to produce a defensive form of nationalism that is extremely sensitive to ethnic differences. Outstanding examples are Gandhi's insistence on returning to Indian ways vis-à-vis those brought by the British Raj and the pre–World War II attempt to purify Japanese by removing words of foreign origin. At the same time, the very defensiveness of this nationalism makes it reluctant to confine the nation to a single ethnic group. With Kemal Atatürk a major exception, nationalist leaders have considered it imperative to retain the boundaries of the old multigroup empire. At the same time, the component parts thereof have generally themselves been affected by nationalist feelings, and separatist movements based on ethnic origin grow in strength. In other states, geographical dispersion of minority groups and/or economic considerations have made separate political units for ethnic groups impractical, but tensions remain.

Despite Karl Marx's prediction that the victory of the proletariat in a state would end nationality problems, the socialist states have not constituted exceptions to this continuation of tensions among nationalities. Josip Tito has declared that he feels the major accomplishment of his life has been the abatement, not the ending, of such tensions in

Yugoslavia,[3] and it is generally conceded that they will be revived after his death.[4] The birth of the Soviet Union was accompanied by a bitter struggle to incorporate as much of czarist Russia as possible, regardless of the wishes of the groups concerned. The People's Republic of China has been equally determined to retain the territories governed by Ch'ing dynasty China.

In the opinion of this writer, the Chinese have made a concerted and, within the boundaries set by Marxist-Leninist ideology, a creative effort to deal with their minorities problem. While it would be unrealistic to suppose that any one nation's attempt to deal with such a problem could be generalized to another, China's problems with her minorities—for instance, their poverty and backwardness, the legacy of domestic imperialism and external colonialism—are shared by many nations. It is therefore hoped that a study of China's policy toward her minority nationalities will be of more than specific interest.

China's minorities constitute a bare 6 percent of her total population, and none are more advanced technically than the Han majority. Yet they receive the attention of the central government to a degree unwarranted by mere numbers. The reasons are not difficult to find.

The first and perhaps foremost reason is strategic. Most minority groups live on the land frontiers of China. In many cases the borders as presently demarcated divide a minority group between two or more states. There are, for example, Shan peoples in Thailand and Burma as well as in China, and Mongols in Russia, China, and the Mongolian People's Republic. If hostile to the Peking government, such minorities could weaken border defense, increase the danger of attack by a foreign power, and result in loss of territory for the Chinese People's Republic (CPR). Conversely, an enthusiastically Communist Chinese minority group not only strengthens border defense, but provides potential for infiltrating a neighboring state's borders and for increasing the territory of the CPR. Maps in these areas are notoriously subject to change. The Sino-Soviet and Sino-Indian border disputes have both included differences of opinion over cartography. Thailand has persistently complained of infiltration by Yao tribesmen trained in guerrilla tactics in Yunnan; for her part, China regularly protests infiltration by Kazakhs and Tibetans instigated by "neorevisionists," "imperialists," and their "running dogs."

Second is the fact that most minority areas are underpopulated in comparison with the rest of China. According to Chinese sources, this 6 percent of the population occupies 60 percent of the land area of China. While this figure is somewhat misleading in that it simply assigns to nearby minorities large portions of inhospitable mountainous or desert terrain not inhabited by Han, there is no doubt that many parts of this 60 percent are capable of absorbing emigrants from over-populated Han areas.

Third is the matter of resources. Minority areas contain large quantities of unworked mineral deposits, the majority of China's forestland, and over 80 percent of her meat-, milk-, and wool-supplying animals. Effective exploitation of these could result in a marked improvement of the Chinese standard of living.

Fourth is the propaganda factor. A prosperous, contented minority population is living proof of the successes the Chinese model of socialism can have for non-Han peoples. On the other hand, rebellious minority groups protesting oppression can only lend credence to the claims of the enemies of the CPR.

Thus, what Chinese Communist Party (CCP) spokesmen invariably call "the minorities problem" has occupied an important place in Chinese policymaking. Essentially, it is a problem of integration: for reasons of defense, economic and social well-being, and national pride, the present government attaches considerable importance to obtaining the loyalties of minority peoples and to assuming jurisdiction over them. This book will examine the steps taken to achieve integration. Subsidiary considerations include the questions what, in the Chinese Communist view, constitutes a minority nationality, and how have these groups been classified in the Chinese People's Republic? How has the CCP's policy toward minority groups differed from that of previous Chinese governments and from that of the Soviet Union? Who have been the executors of this policy, and through what mechanisms has it been carried out? How has policy changed over the past quarter century, and what have been its enduring features, if any? Have the changes in policy been associated with differences of opinion among any particular groups or factions, and, if so, how have these differences been resolved? How have minorities reacted to the communist system? Are there significant differences in the rate at which various groups have adapted to the system? How has policy toward minorities differed from policy toward the Han majority? Finally, the book will attempt to assess the success of the Chinese government in its efforts to "solve" the nationalities problem.

Part One
Chinese Mold and Soviet Model

When I walk with two others, they may serve as my teachers. I will select their good qualities and follow them, their bad qualities and avoid them.

Analects, Book VII, Chapter 21

1
The Imperial Legacy

Chinese historical records have since earliest times made reference to peoples considered different from the men of Han.[1] Wolfram Eberhard has found more than eight thousand separate groups mentioned over a period of almost three thousand years.[2] Often, as a kind of shorthand, these were referred to as the "Man, Yi, Jung, and Ti"—the barbarians of the four directions.

In earliest times, the "Chinese" state occupied a rather small area on the north China plain. The rest of what we know as China today was ruled by other ethnic groups called barbarians by the Han. At this time these groups were not necessarily culturally or technologically inferior to the Han, and some of their members held high positions in Han Chinese states.[3]

During the period known as the Warring States (403–221 B.C.) the geographic area now known as China was more a Thai empire than a Han one.[4] The founding of the Ch'in dynasty (221–206 B.C.), with its unification of Han Chinese states and absorption of non-Han states, may be taken also as beginning the evolution of the Chinese state in its modern form. Through military conquest and cultural influence its sphere of political control gradually widened. Non-Han groups were obliged to move from areas under its sway or be assimilated. This process of expansion was generally easier in the southerly direction than toward the north, which was populated by warlike tribes inhabiting cold, in-hospitable terrain. In addition to the greater physical difficulty of Han expansion to the north, its rewards were fewer. The Han, always primar-ily an agricultural people, found agriculture decreasingly profitable as they progressed northward. That this expansion was by no means steady is attested by the number of non-Han dynasties that ruled the Han Chinese state or parts thereof: the Northern Wei (Topa, A.D. 386–534), Liao (Khitan, 907–1125), Chin (Jurched, 1115–1234), Yüan (Mongol, 1260–1368), and Ch'ing (Manchu, 1644–1911).

It should be noted that all of these were northern groups, and that with the exception of the Yüan they ruled the Chinese state not so much on the basis of their own governing organization but through adaptation to the already existing system. Modifications might, how-ever, be made. In the Ch'ing system, for example, the Six Boards had not one head each, as had been the case in previous dynasties, but two: one Han and one bannerman. These modifications cannot, however, be considered major in scope. Han culture was not coterminous with Han political control, and most of these barbarian dynasties, already sinified[5] to a certain degree before assuming power, became more so in the process of governing.

Though some degree of sinification may have been considered de-sirable by the "barbarians," political control by the Han Chinese state was generally not so esteemed. While the king of Tibet requested T'ang emperor T'ai-tsung's (r. 627–650) permission for his sons and younger brothers to be educated in China, and asked for information on seri-culture, papermaking, and other matters, this did not prevent the Tibetans from waging war on the Han Chinese state. When the Nan-chao state, established in Yunnan by a group now known as the Pai or Min-chia, captured Ch'engtu in 892, it was then, as now, the major city of Szechwan. The victorious Nanchao seized thousands of captives, including artists, craftsmen, and scholars. These people, together with their books and tools, were transported en masse to the Nanchao capital. Some talented Han also voluntarily gave their allegiance to Nanchao, thus further contributing to the "barbarians'" sinicization without loss of their independence. These invasions were repeated.[6]

Thus the "barbarian problem" occupied an important place in Han Chinese policymaking. One solution, set forth in a memorial to the Hui Ti Emperor in 299, proposed strict boundary control and the ex-clusion of barbarians from the empire. Entitled "The Necessity of Ex-cluding the Jung and Ti from China Proper," it noted that

In the time of Ch'in Shih Huang-ti [246–222 B.C.] there were no bar-barians in the Middle Kingdom. Then the Han dynasty chose Ch'angan as its capital city . . . in the middle of the Chien-wu era [40–41] Ma Yüan . . . subjugated the rebellious Ch'iang and moved the rest of the tribes inside the boundary of China Proper . . . thus mixing them with the Hua-jen (Chinese). . . . Ever since then this element has been a constant source of trouble. . . . China Proper is not the place for these barbarians—they should therefore be ordered back to their original homes so that the grounds of future trouble may be nipped.[7]

However, this advice was ignored, and the empire continued to expand to include ever larger numbers of peoples.

Another solution, applied to the Tibetans and Pai mentioned above, was to play one group off against the other. Since this "divide and rule" policy could be—and was—practiced by the barbarians as well, results were not always successful. In many areas, including Mongolia, Tibet, and the so-called "Western Regions" (now referred to as Sinkiang), Han control was sporadic, depending upon the strength of the dynasty relative to the strength of native resistance.

With increased contact between Han and non-Han came increased friction. This, often exacerbated by periodic economic crises, encouraged rebellion. Though the exact measures taken to encourage the barbarians differed somewhat from dynasty to dynasty, all employed the same basic techniques to varying degrees. The Ch'ing system, which refined previous techniques to a high degree, may serve as the best example of such practices while providing the immediate background for the period under study.

Ch'ing Policy

The Ch'ing employed a full range of coercive and persuasive methods to control China's barbarian population. Coercive methods included direct military force—used most notably against the seventeenth-century Yi rebellion in Yunnan and the two Muslim rebellions of the nineteenth century—and the military agricultural colony (*t'un-t'ien*) system. The latter, traceable as far back as the Han dynasty, provided animals and a plot of land to each soldier for his private use. This was meant to solve both supply and defense problems simultaneously. Though ingenious in theory, the military agricultural colonies had their practical drawbacks. Officials often cheated soldiers out of their land, and the bellicose native population frequently made farming so difficult that production was inadequate to the colony's needs. Soldiers tended to marry local women and become assimilated to the very peoples they had been sent to pacify.[8] Even when they brought their families with them, the men eventually became more farmers than soldiers.

Persuasive methods included, first, the tribute system proper; second, a system of relations between the barbarian areas and the Ch'ing court handled by the Court of Colonial Affairs (*Li-fan yüan*); and, third, the native official (*T'u-ssu* or *T'u-kuan*) system. To these may be added encouragement of Chinese imigration to barbarian areas and the incorporation of these areas into the regular Chinese administrative system.

With regard to the tribute system, certain states presented tribute under a system managed by the Board of Rites (*Li-pu*).[9] Since the areas covered by the tribute system subsequently became independent nations or component parts thereof, they need not concern us here.

The Court of Colonial Affairs dealt with the powerful peoples to China's north and west: Mongols, Tibetans, Hui, and Turkic peoples. The hereditary elite of these were integrated into the imperial system through the granting of court titles consonant with their ranks in their respective groups. The more important of the *jasak* (hereditary Mongol chiefs) ranked equally with princes of the Ch'ing imperial house. In return for confirmation of their titles to rule their own peoples and/or the granting of imperial noble titles,[10] this hereditary elite was responsible for the taking of censuses, the collection of taxes, and the keeping of peace. The tendency was to avoid interfering with local affairs unless developments directly threatened imperial control of the area. The Mongols, for example, were not only allowed but encouraged to retain their traditional clan organizations. In traditional divide-and-rule tactics, support was given to this decentralized system in order to take advantage of clan rivalries. The Ch'ing system also supported the Lamaist hierarchy common to both Mongolia and Tibet. In exchange, the lamas decreed that the Ch'ing emperor was an incarnation of the Buddha of Wisdom.[11] In Tibet the temporal as well as the spiritual rule of the Dalai Lama was recognized. The Court of Colonial Affairs was responsible for relations with these peoples, including the translation of documents, the solution of disputes regarding succession to titles, and the presentation of tribute. It also directed the activities of such officials as the *amban*,[12] stationed in such areas as Tibet, Mongolia, and Sinkiang to ensure the keeping of peace. While the well-known banner system incorporated people of three different nationalities, it was not designed to integrate non-Han peoples to Han culture.[13]

The native official system dealt with the smaller and in general more primitive groups of the south and southwest. Under the *T'u-kuan* system, leaders of these groups were absored into the government hierarchy on its lower levels; they were given ordinary official titles save that they were preceded by the character "t'u," meaning "native" or "earth." In the closely related *T'u-ssu* system, applicable to the same areas, local chieftains received one of a hierarchy of titles separate from the ordinary administrative hierarchy, many translatable as "Pacification Commissioner" or some variant thereof.[14] There seems to have been no systematic basis for using one set of titles in some areas and the other set in other areas. Ethnic groups brought under these systems were referred to as "cooked" or "ripe" (*shu*), while those who remained outside it were termed "raw" (*sheng*).

Like the military agricultural colony, the native official system had its origins in certain practices of the Han dynasty wherein conquered native rulers were given hereditary official titles in return for their maintenance of peaceful relations. A rationalization for this, said to be found many times in Chinese history, goes: "The barbarian peoples take advantage of their difficult geographic area to strengthen their independence and use it for defense. The Imperial Court, not wishing to raise armies, which would burden its people, has established native tribal officials to control their own peoples." [15] The Ming dynasty saw the systematization of the congeries of customs that had grown up for dealing with such peoples, and this came to be known as the native official system. The Ch'ing took over the Ming system and added a few refinements, such as the requirement of detailed genealogical tables for claimants to a title.[16]

Aiming at no more than control, the imperial system did not include any provision for inspection of the affairs of the native officials whom it confirmed in power. By the middle of the Ch'ing dynasty a sufficient number of those officials so appointed had come to misuse their power to an extent that aroused doubts as to the efficacy of the system. In many areas, moreover, emigration had brought large numbers of Han under the rule of native officials. The Han were contemptuous of things native, while the native officials feared that their power base was being undermined. In some areas progressive sinification of the minority peoples had rendered native officials unnecessary. To deal with such situations, the Ch'ing instituted a change from native to regular government called the *kai-t'u kuei-liu*.[17] However, the policy was said to have been successful only in Hunan, Hupei, Kweichow, and Kwangsi.[18] In other areas, an effort was made to weaken the power of individual native officials by increasing their numbers and thus decreasing the size of the area presided over by each.

In Tibet, reforms were imposed to curb the power of the noble families, who had previously used their estates as bases of resistance to the Dalai Lama. It was stipulated that henceforth nobles were to hold these estates only on condition that they render service to the government as officials and not, as previously, by hereditary right. Since powerful families had often sought to have the Dalai Lama declared reincarnated in their own family, the problem of choosing the reincarnation had been surrounded by power politics. Ch'ing reforms in this area required that the Dalai Lama be reincarnated in a commoner family. The resident amban was made responsible for supervising these regulations.[19] Although the amban's power to influence events was often limited, the net effect of these reforms was to begin bureaucratization of the Tibetan administration and to increase the power of the Dalai Lama vis-à-vis the noble families while simultaneously increasing the power of the Ch'ing over the Dalai Lama.

From the mid-nineteenth century onward, the Ch'ing became increasingly conscious of the encroachments of Western powers. The British had dealings with the tribes of Yunnan through Burma and with Tibet through India; the Russian empire also had ambitions in Tibet and toward the lands of north China. French missionaries entering south China through Tonkin began proselytizing the peoples there. In the northwest an independent Turkistani Muslim state was set up under Yakub Beg. The tacit approval of Britain and Russia helped to maintain it.[20]

The Ch'ing response was to try to tighten control over the threatened areas. One manifestation of this policy was the creation of a new province, Sinkiang, in 1884, after the defeat of Yakub Beg's state. Another was the invasion of Tibet in 1910 and an effort to revive the moribund amban system there. A third involved reversal of the past policy that had restricted Han emigration to Manchuria and Mongolia. Previously formally illegal and only tacitly allowed, it was now not only permitted, but actively encouraged.[21] A number of railway construction projects were undertaken in these areas as well,[22] in an effort to counter the railway construction projects of foreign countries perceived as having territorial interests there.

In 1909 the Mongolian and Tibetan School (*Chih-pien hsüeh-t'ang*) was founded in Peking to train officials to serve in these areas. A radical departure from the previous assumption that a Confucian generalist education would provide the best background for official service anywhere, the school's curriculum included lectures on politics and finance plus courses on the language, literature, history, and geography of Mongolia and Tibet.[23] The assumption on which it had been founded was, of course, that better-prepared officials would result in Mongols and Tibetans more amenable to imperial rule.

These reforms achieved some results despite the progressive weakening of the dynasty, but their effects were largely nullified by the fall of the Ch'ing in 1911.

In sum, the goal of Ch'ing, and of other dynasties', policy toward ethnic minorities was a pluralistic form of integration that aimed at little more than control. Abstention from aggression and a vague commitment of loyalty to the emperor and the Confucian values he embodied were sufficient to attain this level of integration. Traditional customs, languages, and governing systems were not interfered with so long as they did not pose a threat to the Chinese state. The imperial bureaucracy extended its influence no further down than the *hsien* (county) level, if that far. Barring the rise of a major threat to the peace of the territory under their jurisdiction, most officials had little further interest in the events of these areas.

Absorption of Han Chinese culture and values did occur and minority areas did come under the regular Chinese administrative system, but this was more a by-product of Han emigration than the result of any conscious effort at assimilation. The late nineteenth- and early twentieth-century reforms discussed above do not represent a change in this policy of control, but simply a shift in the means through which it was to be obtained.

There were, of course, exceptions. Tso Tsung-t'ang, famed for his role in putting down the great nineteenth-century rebellions, is described by Mary Wright as "dedicated to the ideas of sinicization." [24] Feeling that the barbarians failure to understand the Confucian ethic had been the cause of rebellion,[25] he wished to prevent future troubles by turning barbarians into Han.[26] To this end, he arranged for the Imperial Edict to be read to Han and Hui communities alike[27] and set up scholarships to educate Mongols, Hui, and Miao[28] according to Confucian principles.

However, the general attitude was summarized by an American missionary: "The Chinese have never taken a great deal of trouble to find out about the history of these different tribes, and while willing that the aboriginals shall come to them, learn of them, and share their privileges, they have never been keen on learning from the aboriginals." [29] His impressions would have been confirmed by reading the views of Ming dynasty philosopher-statesman Wang Yang-ming:

Barbarians are like wild deer. To institute direct civil service administration by Han Chinese magistrates would be like herding deer into the hall of a house and trying to tame them. In the end they merely butt over your sacrificial altars, kick over your tables, and dash about in frantic flight. In the wilderness districts, therefore, one should adapt one's methods to the character of the wilderness. . . . On the other hand, to leave these tribal chiefs to themselves to conduct their own alliances or split up their domains is like releasing deer into the wilderness . . . To fragment their domains under separate chiefs is to follow the policy of erecting restraining fences and is consonant with the policy of gelding the stallion and castrating the boar . . . To set up independent chiefs without supervisory aides is like herding deer in enclosed gardens. Without watchers to guard the fences and prevent their goring and battling, they will leap the fences, bite through the bamboo screens, and wander far to trample the young crops. The presently established civil service aides are such guardians of the parks and fences.[30]

It would have appeared unseemly to most Han to seek out these barbarian deer to convince them of the superiority of Chinese culture. Its virtues were considered to be so obvious that all who were capable of understanding it and worthy to receive it would come of their own volition. For those unworthies who did not come, policy aimed at no more than control.

2
The Republican Era

Because of the diffusion of power among warlords, the Kuomintang (KMT), and foreign powers, the assessment of minorities policy during the republican period presents peculiarly difficult problems.

The republic's troubles began immediately after the fall of the Ch'ing. Tibetans, still smarting from the dynasty's attempt to reassert control in 1910, set upon Chinese garrisons and in some cases annihilated them completely.[1] In Mongolia there were massacres of Han residents,[2] and the British continued to encroach upon Yunnan from Burma.[3]

In several other provinces native warlords, professing nominal allegiance to the central government but actually acting independently thereof, took over. Yunnan, with its large minority population, came under the control of Lung Yun,[4] a sinicized Yi. Ma Pu-fang and Ma Hung-k'uei, both Hui, ruled in Ch'inghai and Ninghsia respectively.[5] In Sinkiang, Yang Tseng-hsin, a Han who commanded native Turkic Muslim troops, assumed power first, then had himself appointed governor by the central government. Though remaining loyal to it, he received no military and almost no financial support from Peking and made his own decisions perforce.[6] His successor, Sheng Shih-ts'ai, was Soviet-oriented through most of his career.

In this situation, minorities affairs, like most other aspects of government, were left to the provinces to handle as they saw fit. While this arrangement had the advantage of flexibility, in that the lower administrative level was more often able to deal with a particular situation in its area on the basis of direct knowledge, it had the disadvantage of allowing "policy" to be interpreted into a scarcely recognizable image of what had been decided upon in the capital. The KMT was not even nominally in power until after the Northern Expedition in 1928, and by then much damage had already been done.

Kuomintang Theory

Whereas the Ch'ing had been a multigroup empire legitimized on the basis of loyalty to the emperor and the Confucian principles he embodied, the republican leaders who succeeded the Ch'ing had been heavily influenced by Western-style nationalism and sought to use it as the foundation for the creation of a new Chinese state. However, because a primary goal of this nationalism was the strengthening of a China heretofore deteriorating under the pressure of foreign aggression, they were understandably unwilling to confine the new nation to a single ethnic group. Writing shortly after the birth of the republic, Sun Yat-sen asserted that, in contrast to the situation in other countries, the terms "state" and "nation" meant the same thing in China, because there alone a single state was developing from a single race. As for those who did not belong to that race, they should be kept within the state by all means and be urged to merge themselves with that race: "Although there are a little over ten million non-Han in China, including Mongols, Manchus, Tibetans and Tatars, their number is small compared with the purely Han population. . . . China is one nationality." [7] He further explained that "The name 'Republic of Five Nationalities' exists only because there exists a certain racial distinction which distorts the meaning of a single republic. We must facilitate the *dying out* of all names of individual peoples inhabiting China, i.e., Manchus, Tibetans, etc. . . . we must satisfy the demands of all races and unite them in a single cultural and political whole." [8]

Sun thus recognized the existence of four distinct minority groups. It will be noticed that three of these were the same peoples who had received special treatment by the Ch'ing dynasty; the fourth was the Manchus themselves. As for the omission of the numerous southwestern peoples, Sun either did not know about them or felt they were so close to "dying out" as to be unworthy of attention. He also did not mention the Hui, apparently assuming that they were a religious rather than an ethnic minority. As will be seen, this was denied by both the Hui and subsequent KMT policy. Sun also seems to have subsumed all Turkic Muslims under the term "Tatar." Tacit acceptance of his classification by the warlord government in Peking is implicit in the design of the flag of the Chinese republic. Its five stripes of equal width symbolize the equality of the five groups.

Phrases such as "dying out of names of individual peoples" and "uniting in a single political and cultural whole" clearly imply integration through assimilation, and this must be assumed to exemplify Sun's views on minorities policy at the time. A few years later, however, Sun came under the influence of the Soviet Union. Under the terms of the Sun-Joffe Manifesto of January 1923, the KMT was reorganized with the help of Comintern advisers, and new ideas, principally self-determination and autonomy, were added to its minorities policy. The Manifesto of the KMT's First National Congress in 1924, said to have been formulated by Sun himself, stated inter alia that "The Government should help and guide the weak and small racial groups within its national boundaries toward self determination and self government." [9] The assimilation implied in Sun's earlier statements would hardly seem to be furthered by encouraging self-determination and self-government. However, Sun, more orator than logician, never bothered to reconcile these two sets of views. The Communist government of China may be said to have inherited a policy of trying to facilitate the demise of nationality identities through granting self-government to minorities. It has in fact been struggling with the consequences to this day.

While Sun Yat-sen is unequivocally on record as favoring the equality of all groups in China and would surely have denied favoring coercive measures to attain the "single cultural and political whole" he advocated, there can be no doubt that he regarded the continued existence of non-Han groups as hindrances in the path to its attainment. His successor, Chiang Kai-shek, went one step further in the pursuit of unity, proclaiming the common ancestry of all inhabitants of China: "... our various clans actually belong ... to the same racial stock (*tsung-tsu*) ... that there are five peoples designated in China ... is not due to differences of race or blood but to religion and geographical environment. In short, the differentiation among China's five peoples is due to regional and religious factors, and not to race or blood." [10] That this statement has no scientific support whatever does not seem to have bothered its author. After the completion of the Northern Expedition the KMT substituted its own white sun banner for the national flag of five equal stripes. The unconscious symbolism inherent in this substitution was underlined by the adoption of an explicitly assimilationist policy.

Implementation

Administrative Changes

After the demise of the Ch'ing dynasty, the Court of Colonial Affairs was replaced by a Mongolian and Tibetan Affairs Bureau (*Meng-tsang shih-wu chü*). In 1914 the bureau became a separate ministry (*Meng-tsang yüan*), but in 1927, under the KMT's direction, it was downgraded to a commission (*Meng-tsang wei-yüan hui*) subordinate to the executive *Yüan* (ministry). The Mongolian and Tibetan School was retained.[11] Recognition of a special status for Mongolia and Tibet is implicit in the fact that they were always called territories rather than provinces.[12] Education was adopted as the chief vehicle of assimilation, and to this end a Mongolian and Tibetan department was established under the Ministry of Education in 1930.[13]

Aside from periodic declarations that all ethnic groups belonged to the same racial stock as Han, the KMT devoted little attention to minority peoples other than Mongolians and Tibetans until World War II forced it from its urban coastal bases of strength and into rural areas where minority groups were more prominent. At that time the Mongolian and Tibetan department of the Ministry of Education was given charge of all "Border Education." A network of schools was to be set up to give primary-level instruction in "modern education, citizenship, Han language, vocational skills and hygiene." Secondary schools were also to be founded, with emphasis on the development of technical abilities and "clear understanding of the Chinese race and nation." [14] In official documents the variety of terms denoting barbarians was replaced by more neutral terms that reflected the influence of Western anthropology—for example, *chung-tsu* (ethnic group) and *jen-chung* (race).

It was agreed that once psychologically prepared for assimilation through this new system of education, members of minority ethnic groups should be treated as Han. There was also general acceptance of the idea that minority areas should come under the regular administrative system of China.[15] Since the implementation of these policies differed considerably according to local conditions, a look at the main areas involved may be helpful.

The Northeast

Most Mongols regarded their ties with China as being of the nature of a personal union under the Ch'ing emperor. They thus believed these ties had been severed by the demise of the dynasty and considered their subordination to the government of China at an end. In northern Mongolia, relatively untouched by the Han emigration that had been a feature of late Ch'ing policy, most Han were driven out or killed in 1911–1912, and the area achieved de facto independence. This separate status was made more secure after the Russian Revolution of 1917, when the victorious Bolshevik government backed Outer Mongolia's claims to nationhood. Thus supported, the new Mongolian People's Republic (MPR) was able to withstand Chinese pressure. Its internal policy took a prosocialist and antireligious direction heavily influenced by the Soviet Union.

As to the areas where Han emigration had been more pronounced, "Chinese policy in regard to the Mongols of Manchuria and Inner Mongolia had been singularly well adapted to further Japanese designs." [16] In 1914 the Peking government declared that all Mongol lands belonged to China and that consequently all Mongol land titles were invalid unless ratified by its local authorities. The legal authority for this decision was said to be an imperial edict of 1748 that forbade Mongol princes to allocate land for cultivation to either Han or Mongols without imperial sanction. Although the imperial edict had been intended to stop Han colonization as well as to prevent the spread of agriculture among Mongols, it was not now applied to lands held by Han, and the net result of the 1914 decision was to deprive Mongols of their land. This led to the land booms of 1916–1919 and 1926–1928, at the end of which Han had come to outnumber Mongols in the Mongols' own homeland.[17]

After the Northern Expedition had brought the KMT to power in 1928, a Mongol delegation visited Chiang Kai-shek to request the creation of an Inner Mongolian autonomous area. Chiang's answer was the division of Inner Mongolia into the four nonautonomous provinces of Chahar, Jehol,[18] Ninghsia, and Suiyuan. This was interpreted by many politically conscious Mongols as a clear case of divide and rule, and it dashed whatever hopes they may have entertained for better treatment by the KMT vis-à-vis the warlord government it had replaced.

It was not difficult to find others who were more sympathetic to the Inner Mongols' grievances. A delegation sent to the Mongolian People's Republic was well treated, but the Outer Mongols, afraid to compromise their precarious international position, could offer their ethnic kin from across the border little more than spiritual comfort. Hopes for an alliance were further limited by the fact that Inner Mongols, more conservative and religious than their northern brethren, were somewhat scandalized by the attitudes toward Lamaism and the social order then taking place in Ulan Bator.

The Japanese, however, were willing to offer both spiritual comfort and material aid. The propaganda that accompanied a Japanese-sponsored independence movement assured not only Mongols but Manchus,

Koreans, Hui, and White Russians as well that ethnic and economic wrongs would be set right in the new state. Japanese efforts culminated in the founding of Manchukuo on March 1, 1932. A proclamation of independence issued at that time banned discrimination among ethnic and national groups, and a Law of Civil Rights, promulgated soon after, guaranteed equality for all.[19]

A five-colored flag symbolized the cooperative efforts of the five "races," [20] and a mural of five attractive, smiling young women in different national dress, walking arm in arm, adorned the lobby of the capital building at Hsinking.[21] Not nationalism but *"wantao"* [sic], the "way of the benevolent ruler," was to be the basic philosophy of the state.[22]

Within Manchukuo the Japanese created a special Mongol region called Hsingan, carefully demarcating the boundary in order to include areas where the Mongol population predominated. Mongolian language schools were set up and the Lamaist religion supported. Similar encouragement was given to the customs and religions of other minorities in Manchukuo. These were not always successful. For example, an effort to encourage the use of the Manchu language was abandoned when it received little support from the people it had been intended to benefit.[23]

The success of Japanese efforts to gain support among Mongols, which led to the founding of Hsingan, did not induce the KMT to change its position toward Mongols still nominally under its jurisdiction. During the winter of 1933–34, Chiang Kai-shek received a delegation that asked, essentially, for three things: a single Mongol autonomous area, enlargement of powers of autonomy, and the return of pasturelands that had been taken from Mongols for use as cropland. If this last proved impossible, the delegation would accept a guarantee that pasturelands would not be confiscated from Mongols in future. All three demands were flatly refused, on the grounds that (1) local autonomy would be more efficient if decentralized than if centralized, (2) enlargement of the scope of autonomy was "not feasible at present," and (3) nomadic life was not conducive to strong border defense.[24]

Charges and countercharges continued to be made until Japan made its next move, the setting up of another Mongol autonomous area in 1932. Called Mengchiang, it encompassed the Mongol areas to the west of Hsingan.

Mongol leaders in Manchukuo had been hoping that the Japanese would unite Hsingan with Mengchiang to form the basis of a greater Mongolian state, with themselves as rulers. They were therefore disappointed when Mengchiang, headed by Tê Wang,[25] hereditary ruler of the Silingol League, continued to exist as a separate entity. The Japanese, too, it seemed, were practicing divide-and-rule techniques. There were also complaints that Japanese, not Mongols, had the final say in decision making.

Though Tê Wang has been accused of being a Japanese puppet, there is strong evidence to the contrary. Owen Lattimore considers him a sincere nationalist,[26] and a Japanese official in Mongolia during the 1930's has spoken of the great efforts necessary to "persuade Prince Tê to even *see* our point of view." [27] Tê Wang's later conduct substantiates his independence. After Japan's defeat he steadfastly refused to cooperate with Chiang Kai-shek until he received Chiang's pledge of autonomy for a unified Mongolian state. Though Chiang remained equally adamant and threatened to convict Tê Wang of collaboration with the Japanese, no charges were actually pressed.

In addition to not giving the Mongols the large autonomous area they desired, Japanese efforts to convince Mongols to abandon their traditional methods of stockbreeding for more productive scientific techniques (which would, incidentally, better serve the needs of Japanese manufacturers) were carried out with something less than tact, annoying many conservative Mongols.[28] This did not, however, mean that any discernible segment of Mongol opinion favored the return of the KMT. A Kuomintang agent sent to Mongolia in 1942 to assess the popularity of his government reported the following conversation: "I asked these men what kind of government they hoped to see in China. One of the men, inquiring about the ups and downs of Wu P'ei-fu [a once powerful warlord,] said that the Mongols preferred to have him victorious, the emperor restored to the throne and the Panchen Lama reinstated rather than see the KMT triumphant." Reflecting the KMT's feeling that a little education would solve all problems, he concluded: "Such talk is both ridiculous and pitiful. But for this sort of mentality one must blame only the Chinese government, which hitherto has paid too little attention to educating and civilizing the Mongol people." [29]

Interestingly, the policy of assimilation through education does not seem to have been followed in the few Nationalist-held Mongol areas. A visitor to the Alashan Banner in 1948 was surprised by the absence of schools. On inquiring, he was told by Mongols that they considered education "bothersome." [30]

The most positive action taken by the KMT toward Mongolia during this period seems to have been the removal of Genghis Khan's bones from Ikechao League in Suiyuan to Kansu "to frustrate the Japanese attempt to steal them as a means of securing the allegiance of the Mongols." [31] Since this was done in June 1939, well after the establishment of Hsingan and Mengchiang, it amounted to closing the coop after most of the chickens had flown away.

Though believing that they were better off under Japanese rule than under the KMT, the Mongols were far from happy with the Japanese. In the final analysis, the Chinese Communists may have won Inner Mongolia simply because they arrived on the scene last. First, profiting by their predecessors' mistakes, they promised the Mongols one united autonomous area, and second, since they were not yet in power, their promises, unlike those of the Japanese or the KMT, could not be declared at variance with their actions.

The Northwest

Sinkiang Unlike Mongolia, Sinkiang has a large majority of non-Han peoples. The most numerous of these is the Uighur group, which comprised approximately 75 percent of the population prior to 1949. Many of Sinkiang's ethnic groups are, like the Uighurs, of Turkic stock and Muslim faith. Their capacity for effective cooperation however, has generally been shown less in a positive sense than in opposition to a common enemy, such as Han colonization. In addition, anti-Han movements were often crosscut by pan-Muslim and pan-Turanian sentiments. The term nationalism is thus not strictly applicable to the Sinkiang situation.

China's largest province and one of its least densely populated, Sinkiang was ruled from 1911 through 1928 by Yang Tseng-hsin.[32] By judicious apportioning of offices among the more able and ambitious members of Sinkiang's many ethnic groups, and by playing one group off against another, Yang was able to maintain Han dominance in an area where Han numbered less than 6 percent of the total population. Yang's tactics were essentially Ch'ing methods applied with skill and, in the words of one scholar, "for Sinkiang, time stood still." [33] Yang was assassinated in 1928. His unpopular successor, Chin Shu-jen, was toppled from power by a Muslim holy war led by Ma Chung-ying, a member of the same Hui family who provided the warlords of Ninghsia and Ch'inghai. Not Ma, however, but a young Manchurian officer named Sheng Shih-ts'ai took power in Sinkiang. He was to hold it from 1933 through 1944.

Sheng, commanding troops who had been chased out of Manchuria by the Japanese, obtained Soviet support against Ma Chung-ying. This was given in the belief that Ma was being aided by Russia's enemy, Japan.[34] At a later date Ma received political asylum in the Soviet Union, where he was presumably being kept in readiness should the USSR ever decide that Sheng needed a replacement. Well aware of this, Sheng maintained Sinkiang's formal subordination to the KMT government, in case he should need its support.

While Sheng's ties with the Soviet Union constituted an alliance of convenience rather than of friendship, heavy Soviet influence on Sinkiang was the result. In addition to accepting economic and military "assistance," Sheng also adapted Soviet minorities policy to Sinkiang's situation. One of his "Six Great Policies" was the equality of nationalities.[35] The Marxist concept of nationality, translated into Chinese as *min-tsu*, was given prominence for the first time. Uighurs and Kazakhs were appointed to high posts in their own areas; all nationalities were allowed to promote education in their own languages and attend their own schools. Numbers of schools and students increased rapidly. Several hundred young members of Sinkiang's nationalities were sent to the Soviet Union for advanced training in medicine and technology. The Sinkiang daily newspaper was published in seven languages, and cultural associations were set up for Uighurs, Kazakhs, Tungans, Tatars, Russians,[36] and Han.[37]

However, when Russia, seemingly losing its battle with Germany, was forced to discontinue subsidies to Sinkiang, Sheng began to strengthen his ties with the KMT government, then located in Chungking. Part of the price Chiang Kai-shek exacted for this involved Sheng's taking repressive measures toward the nationality groups whose autonomy he had heretofore encouraged. Thus, when Chiang appointed Sheng Minister of Forestry and Agriculture in the KMT government, his departure for Chungking was not mourned in Sinkiang. His successor, Wu Chung-hsin, the first governor of Sinkiang in half a century to be actually selected by the Chinese central government, had been chairman of the Mongolian and Tibetan Affairs Commission for the previous six years. According to Owen Lattimore, his two notable achievements in that office were a "personally profitable mission to Tibet" and a "land grabbing colonization policy which did much to turn Inner Mongolian nationalism against China." [38]

The pattern of Han immigration followed by government-abetted wholesale expropriation of the indigenous peoples' lands is a recurring one. Both central governments and Han in general displayed an astonishing lack of sensitivity to the consequences of their actions. The following excerpt from a journal published in Chungking in 1939 exemplifies the prevailing attitude:

Against [the minorities'] apparent advantage [prior occupancy] in this acute struggle for land possession, it should be remembered that most of the lands ... considered fit for cultivation are the best pastures, which they jealously guard for their own use ... we find the Northwestern farmers slow and even a little lazy, while the Mongol and Tibetan way of living border on the primitive ... in the Northwest, "exactness" is pitifully neglected, and many nomads are even unable to count the numbers of their own animals correctly.[39]

In other words, since the Han felt themselves better able to utilize the "best" lands, the "slow," "lazy" minorities with their "inexact" ways were expected to relinquish their pasturelands.

This, then, was the background against which minority groups saw Sheng's switch to the Nationalist government. Their fears seemed justified when in 1942 Chiang Kai-shek announced plans to transfer ten thousand officials and their families to Sinkiang. Shortly thereafter, outsiders began replacing local people in positions of influence, and an artificial exchange rate was established that allowed merchants from the interior to ship local products out of Sinkiang at great profit to themselves.[40] Corruption soon increased to an extent described by a popular saying as "one Sheng Shih-ts'ai went out, but two came in." [41]

In November 1944, on the anniversary of the Bolshevik Revolution, a revolt accompanied by anti-Han rioting and massacres broke out in the Ili Valley. It quickly became apparent that this was more than a localized expression of grievances. The rebel leaders voiced their desire for independence from China, and to this end set up an "East Turkistan Republic" (ETR) with its capital at Kuldja (Ining). It will be remembered that Yakub Beg's state had also had its capital there, and indeed the rebels claimed to be his spiritual heirs. The three top leadership posts in the new ETR were held, respectively, by a Uighur, a Kazakh, and a resident White Russian. The extent of material aid supplied by the Soviet Union is difficult to ascertain, but its spiritual backing was considerable and included both supportive propaganda and the loan of trained advisers. Among the advisers was a Moscow-educated Uighur named Saifudin. The mainstay of the ETR's military power at this time was the troops of Osman Bator, who was something of a Kazakh folk hero. He later defected, protesting against the ETR's leftist orientation. A. Doak Barnett, who interviewed him, states that Osman eventually fought on the side of every important faction in Sinkiang, and that despite his professed anti-Communist feelings he was basically motivated not by ideology, but by a love of fighting and a desire to keep his group's autonomy intact.[42]

The rebels defeated not only the normal garrisons of central government troops, but also the crack troops of General Hu Tsung-nan, who had been sent into Sinkiang especially to deal with them. In the fall of 1945, with the rebels holding down an estimated 100,000 troops whom Chiang Kai-shek might have been using against the Communists, the central government agreed to negotiate. The highly respected General Chang Chih-chung was appointed chief representative for the government.

By mid-1946, after much hard bargaining, three agreements had been reached between Chang and Akmedjan Kasimov, chief spokesman for the ETR (often called the "Ili group" by those not recognizing the ETR as a legitimate government). Had the measures contained in these agreements been implemented, they would have provided a high degree of autonomy for Sinkiang. Lower-level officials were to be elected rather than appointed by the central government, and the provincial government was to be partly elected and partly appointed by the central government. In the army, Uighur and Kazakh were to be the languages of command. Non-Han were to be allowed to use their own languages in primary school, but the study of the Han language would be compulsory in middle schools.[43] In July 1946, General Chang replaced the unpopular Wu Chung-hsin as governor, and relations between the KMT government and Sinkiang seemed to improve.

Subsequent events showed this to be a deceptive facade. In reality, neither the Ili group nor the central government trusted each other, and the uneasy alliance soon cracked. Specific issues that aroused mutual suspicions concerned railroads, currency, and control of military units. The central government considered the building of a rail line into Sinkiang to be a logical step linking China proper with a frontier province; the Ili group saw it as the Trojan horse of Han colonization. With regard to currency, the central government naturally wanted Sinkiang to use its own issue. Local leaders, however, saw adoption of the central government's currency as a ruse through which the province's wealth would be drained away. In both this currency question and in the matter of Han colonization they had had ample justification for their fears.[44] As for military control, the central government saw the ETR army as a sword held over its ties with Sinkiang and wished to disperse the Ili troops among its own units. The Ili group, surely aware of the fate of those whom the shrewd Chiang had been able to maneuver away from their source of military support,[45] wished to keep its military units intact lest it lose the mainstay of its bargaining power. In addition, of course, the troops Chiang would send in to dilute the Ili units would have to be fed, clothed, and housed, thus imposing an extra tax burden on Sinkiang. This would aggravate the financial problems Sinkiang was experiencing because of cessation of its trade with the Soviet Union and the withdrawal of Soviet technical advisers.

Chang Chih-chung and his Han staff, though credited by all observers[46] with sincere efforts to run an honest, efficient government, were hampered on one side by the Ili group's intransigence and on the other by the central government's stalling techniques, which even extended to not implementing measures it had already agreed upon. The last straw was the central government's apparently unpremeditated announcement in May 1947 that it had appointed Masud Sabri governor of Sinkiang. An elderly upper-class Uighur who had been in China proper for the preceding twelve years, he was considered a protégé of the conservative wing of the KMT, the so-called CC Clique. Those in favor of local autonomy believed that the KMT was trying to undermine their authority by appointing a man completely subservient to it. Opposition was widespread; by July there was open Uighur revolt. This revolt and other dissident movements were suppressed, though the KMT troops sometimes showed scant regard for innocent bystanders or adequate ascertainment of the complicity of those they suppressed. The secret police, which the central government had agreed to dissolve, were much in evidence.[47]

In August the Ili group left the coalition that had been set up with the central government, returned to Kuldja, and sealed the border between Ili and the rest of Sinkiang. Not until December 1948, when the KMT had all but lost the civil war with the Chinese Communists, did the KMT agree to drop Masud and replace him with Burhan, a compromise candidate. Burhan, who came from a wealthy Tartar family, had managed to maintain himself in every regime since that of Yang Tseng-hsin. Barnett, who interviewed Burhan prior to his appointment, prophetically described him as "apparently playing the subtle game of keeping in the good graces of all sides in the hope of becoming governor." [48] The KMT's "Sinkiang problem" appeared to have been solved at last.

Kansu-Ninghsia-Ch'inghai   These three provinces are linked together both by geographical proximity and because they had a substantial Muslim minority, reaching 40 percent in Ch'inghai according to some sources. Chinese Muslims are generally called Hui or Hui-Hui. This term refers to either pure Han Muslims or those of Arabic-Han mixture; Turkic and Mongolian Muslims are know by other names.

Hui with Arab blood may be descendants of the four-thousand-man Arab mercenary army that arrived in China in 756, sent by the Caliph to help T'ang emperor Ming Huang suppress the An Lu-shan rebellion. For their services, they were rewarded with Han wives and substantial land grants in the relatively underpopulated northwestern areas of China.[49] Other Hui are descendants of Arab traders who went to China and settled there. Hui are found all over China, but are most numerous in what Barnett refers to as the "Muslim belt" of Kansu, Ninghsia, and Ch'inghai.[50] Though intermarriage and proselytization have diluted the Arab strain, observers agree that most Hui are physically quite distinct from Han.[51]

Since Hui regarded marriage between Muslim and infidel with the greatest misgivings, intermarriage has been quite rare and fraught with danger. Chin Shu-jen, governor of Sinkiang from 1928 through 1933, was ousted from power by a revolt begun by rumors that a Han tax-collector was demanding the hand of a pretty Muslim girl.[52] The rebels called in fellow Muslim Ma Chung-ying from Kansu, opening a hornet's nest of troubles for the central government. It should be emphasized that the Han-Hui cleavage was not the only source of tension in the area. Disputes arose also among Han, Tibetans, and Mongols; among Hui, Tibetans, and Mongols; and between Tibetans and Mongols.

The Hui, though not as strict as, for example, the Wahabi of Saudi Arabia, have been considered "good" Muslims. They do not eat pork; if literate, they read in Arabic. Hochow, in Kansu, has traditionally been known as "China's Mecca" because of its large Hui population and fine mosques. The hereditary first family of Hochow, surnamed Ma like most Hui, included Ma Pu-fang, governor of Ch'inghai, Ma Hung-k'uei, governor of Ninghsia, Ma Chung-ying[53] and Ma Pu-ch'ing, who for a time controlled the Kansu corridor and hence the most accessible route to Sinkiang. Ma Fu-hsiang, father of Ma Hung-k'uei, had been a military leader during the late Ch'ing dynasty. Other family members held important positions in various parts of the Muslim Belt.[54]

Convinced of their superiority and traditionally a restive minority, the Hui had been handled, according to Robert Ekvall, with great lack of tact except when the Han, equally convinced of their own superiority, feared a Hui rebellion.[55] These rebellions came often: one source quotes a Han popular saying as "every thirty years a small rebellion, every sixty years a large one;"[56] another source quotes the proverb as "every ten years a small rebellion, every thirty years a large one."[57] Renowned for their military prowess under normal circumstances, the Hui became formidable when engaged in holy war against the infidel—into which most of their grievances seem to have escalated. Outnumbered and armed only with swords, they had been known to charge Han machine-gun barrages and win.[58] Not surprisingly, the Han wished to keep their distance from such people, and it was noted in the 1930's that the degree of segregation between Hui and Han was becoming progressively greater. Whole villages tended to become either Hui or Han, and even where the two peoples lived in close proximity the children of one group were not permitted to play with those of the other.[59]

The advantages of having such a group as an ally, and the disadvantages of having it as a foe, were not lost on the various parties involved in the international power struggle being waged in Asia during the 1930's. Though the Soviet Union scored some successes with Ma Chung-ying, Communist attempts to capitalize on Hui discontent were hindered by the extreme distaste with which most Muslims viewed its atheistic principles. The Comintern, of course, did not publicize this particular tenet of Communism to the Hui. Such information was obligingly supplied by the KMT and the Japanese.

Unhampered by atheism, Japan had somewhat more success with the Hui. Sponsored by extremist groups including the Ronin, Kokuryukai, and Young Officers' Clique, recent Japanese "converts" to Islam took exploration trips to Hui communities throughout China. In between prayers, they compiled data and made contacts. A nephew of former Caliph Abdul Hamid, among others, was invited to Tokyo. Ma Chung-ying was given aid, and various Chinese Islamic associations were set up to establish Japan's newly decided-upon role as "Protector of Islam." Schools were set up that emphasized Hui independence and anti-Communism.[60]

The KMT was quick to recognize the implications of these Japanese activities. Whereas in the 1920's the central government's intransigence seemed to be driving the Hui to revolt, in the 1930's their demands were accommodated. KMT propaganda to the Hui made much of the fact that two of its best generals Li Tsung-jen and Pai Ch'ung-hsi, were hui.[61] Pai was made chairman of the China Muslim National Salvation Association,[62] which had been founded as a counterforce against similarly titled Japanese-sponsored groups, and agreements were reached with the governors Ma.

Ma Pu-fang was contacted by Japanese agents in 1937 and 1938. While receiving them cordially, he made the price of his support Japan's conquest of KMT armies elsewhere in China, and Nippon's readiness to fight Russia. The Japanese, taking the hint, gave up on him.[63]

The many references made during this period to the economic progress and political stability of Ninghsia and Ch'inghai relative to the rest of China attest to the efficiency of their governors. However, as in many other parts of the world, efficiency was maintained by the ruthless suppression of dissent. In addition, the taste of the two governors for luxurious living has become legendary. While detractors have viewed their extravagance as derived from the toil of the peasants and hence reprehensible, supporters see it as the accepted style of living for a Muslim potentate. Barnett, frankly impressed with the new roads, schools, hospitals, and afforestation projects of both provinces, summed up the difference between them as "in Ninghsia the good is not quite as good [as in Ch'inghai] and the bad is considerably worse." [64] He felt that the reason for Ch'inghai's greater emphasis on reconstruction vis-à-vis Ninghsia's on law and order might be Ninghsia's proximity to Communist-held areas.[65] There were said to be no Communists in either of the provinces, and both governors had a reputation for personal incorruptibility and for treating Hui and Han with equal fairness. In addition, Ma Pu-fang had gone so far as to learn Tibetan, the better to deal with Ch'inghai's Tibetan population.[66]

Since neither the regimes of the Mas nor that of wartime Chungking were conducive to the frank expression of views, the extent and focus of Hui complaints against the KMT is difficult to pinpoint. One brave Hui published an article in the Chungking *Ta kung pao*, ostensibly on Japan's propaganda overtures to world Islam, but expressing his views on KMT policy as well. While affirming his fellow Muslims' loyalty to the central government, he added that "private conversations" had indicated that they were "not fully satisfied with present conditions." Among the complaints he had heard were the allegations that few Hui received command positions in the armed forces and that the government was following a policy of lining up conservative Hui "big names" when what was needed was mobilization of Hui youth with modern education and ideas. They resented the fact that educational proposals made by General Pai in his capacity as chairman of the Hui National Salvation Association, and approved by the central government, had not been carried out. "If the government approves," Hui wanted a Muslim political party. The government, pleading a need for unity in wartime, did not approve.[67]

South-Southwest

The area of the South-Southwest was the location of the KMT's closest control after the Japanese invasion. Since only in Yunnan did republican-era politics figure importantly in Communist-period developments among the minorities, Yunnan's political situation will be discussed separately, to be followed by an overview of policy in the South-Southwest generally.

Yunnan   From 1911 to 1928 Yunnan was ruled by T'ang Chi-yao, who took advantage of the province's isolated position and the strong localist sentiments of its populace, one-half of whom were non-Han, to maintain only tenuous connections with the central government. Beginning in 1928 several factors occurred to change this power balance. First, T'ang died and was succeeded by Lung Yun, a sinicized Yi. Second, the Northern Expedition placed the KMT in nominal power in China. Third, tensions with Japan increased.

Though Lung's relations with the KMT government were no more cordial than his predecessor's had been with the warlord governments in Peking—Yunnan maintained a separate army and a separate currency—both Lung and his province seemed genuinely anti-Japanese and joined Chiang Kai-shek to oppose the Japanese invasion. One example of anti-

Japanese sentiments in Yunnan may be seen in the flight of many Pai families northward on hearing the news of Burma's fall in 1942.[68]

This alliance did not mean, of course, that either Lung or Yunnan had become loyal to Chiang personally, and when the war was over Chiang devised a plan to bring the province definitively under central government control. He ordered the Yunnan army, commanded by Lung's half brother and chief lieutenant Lu Han, into Indochina to receive the Japanese surrender. This left Lung virtually without military protection. He was quickly disarmed by Chiang Kai-shek's troops and sent to Nanking as a "guest" of the central government. By prior arrangement, Lu Han became governor in his half brother's place.

The assumption behind this move was that Lu, in office through Chiang's maneuver, would henceforth support his benefactor. In fact, Lu's support waned in proportion to the KMT government's loss of power vis-à-vis the Communists. While talking of autonomy and enacting measures conducive to it, he seemed actually to be creating a position from which he could negotiate with either side.[69] To make Chiang Kai-shek's problems worse, Lung Yun escaped from Nanking and surfaced in Hong Kong, where he made contact with leftist groups and began to support pro-Communist movements in Yunnan. Barnett found that the populace, in contrast to their hostility to the Japanese, had no fear of a Communist takeover, even when it was linked to a movement led by the Soviet Union. What they feared most was the evacuation of Nationalist troops into Yunnan, regarding them as mouths to feed rather than as defenders.[70]

South-Southwest   The early republican era saw few changes in policy toward, or in the lives of, ethnic minorities. Since most lived in areas difficult to reach by existing communications systems, and since their lands were poor and often malaria-infested, they were not sought out by government administrators. Though their total population may have approached ten million, no one group was large enough or troublesome enough to command government attention. The several reincarnations of "Mongolian and Tibetan Affairs" bureaus under successive governments are sufficient to show where the republic perceived its interests to lie. The Chuang, living primarily in western Kwangsi, were the largest group numerically, totaling perhaps six million, but were heavily sinicized. The Miao, of whom there were approximately two million, were divided into several different groups, including Black, White, and Flowery, based on the preferred costume of the women. The majority were village centered and not easily mobilized into large groups under most circumstances. The Yao, of whom there were approximately half a million, inhabited the same upland areas as the Miao and spoke a closely related language, but apparently felt little common cause with the Miao. Other groups included the Yi, Tai, Akha, Lisu, Lahu, and many more. A wide variety of languages, customs, and religions coexisted in a complicated ecology which, in the absence of major grievances, seemed relatively peaceful as compared with the situation on the northern borders of China.[71]

There was, however, general agreement that the southern minority peoples should be brought under the regular administrative system of China and the native official system abolished.[72] Despite a clear consensus on the subject, no great effort was expended on dismantling the system, and it would not have been easy to do in any case. However corrupt or averse to progress, the hereditary native elite had been entrenched in office for generations, and it was sometimes absolutely necessary to rely on their administrative expertise and/or private military forces. As one hsien magistrate pleaded to his superiors, "If we wish this chieftain to help in frontier protection, how can we ask her help without providing her subsistence and restoring her position of power and prestige?" [73]

Border-area native officials were also aware that the British government in Burma provided them with a point of leverage in their dealings with the Chinese government. In fact, since road and telephone communications in Burma were infinitely superior to those in rural southwest China, it was often easier to negotiate with the British government than with the Chinese. In one instance, headmen who felt victimized by a corrupt Chinese official called their tribe together and obtained a consensus on petitioning the British to add the area to their domains. The British agreed to do so.[74]

Thus, little progress was made. In some areas native officials were simply confirmed in their former titles. In others, they were made heads of *pao* and *chia* in the regular KMT administrative system. This enabled the abolition of the native official system in name if not in essence. In a third variation, Han officials were appointed to these areas, but they remained only on sufferance of the native officials, who retained all powers. In any case, the differences between late Ch'ing and early republican policy were almost imperceptible.

After 1927 some impetus for change was provided by the Rural Reconstruction Movement, which included slogans admonishing youth to work in rural areas and on the frontiers. Idealistic young volunteers gave minority groups a chance to see Han other than the soldiers, profit-conscious traders, underpaid grasping officials, and land-hungry exiles who had too often been their only previous acquaintances. Medical teams were subsidized by Rockefeller Foundation grants channeled through Peking Union Medical College.

The real impetus for change, however, was the war with Japan. Japan's occupation of the Chinese seacoast provoked a mass migration inland, which led to increased emphasis on heretofore virtually ignored provinces.[75] The extent of this shift in emphasis as it concerns minorities' education may be noted in a sentence from the *China Handbook*: "While there was only one border school under the Ministry of Education before the war, 44 frontier schools of various grades were established or taken over by the Ministry after 1938." [76] The Regulations Governing Admission of Mongolian and Tibetan Students to Schools in the Interior were revised to include applicants from all border regions, and the number of scholarships was increased. Some universities added Border Affairs Departments (e.g., West China Union University) or established Frontier Research Institutes (e.g., National Yunnan University).

Defense needs led to the building of modern roads through once-isolated minority areas, and land surveys revealed the presence of mineral deposits in some minorities' mountain strongholds. Previously such lands had generally been ignored, because they were unsuitable for agriculture.

In short, the war years brought many changes in the lives of south and southwestern minorities. Not all changes, however, were for the better. The influx of refugees inland meant more confiscation of tribal lands than ever before, often on the pretext of war needs. J. E. Spencer, a Caucasian employee of the Chinese salt administration, felt that Kweichow was being "exploited like a colony" [77] and noted that practically all rice lands had fallen into Han hands. Much of this was owned by absentee landlords and lay unused while the minority peoples lived in misery. Notwithstanding the fact that the living standard of the ordinary Han peasant in Kweichow was worse than that of his counterparts elsewhere, "poorest of all are the tribespeople." [78] Writing in 1940, he predicted that if present trends continued, the minorities would be deprived of even their present poor lands. He suggested that a campaign to better the minorities' economic position should precede the planned immediate attempt at assimilation through education.[79]

Assimilation through education simply did not appeal to minorities living on the margins of subsistence. Better roads, on the other hand, were regarded as a real threat. People traditionally occupied in their own small communities saw new roads as paving the way for tax collectors, and their suspicions were often proved correct. Not only tax collectors came on the new roads. For example, the most immediate effect of the Burma Road on Pai areas was the disastrous cholera epidemic it brought northward.[80]

As for the medical teams, anthropologists, and Rural Reconstruction workers, the best of intentions did not always produce the best of results. Francis Hsü, who worked in Pai areas during the cholera epidemic mentioned above, found doctors and missionaries severely berating patients at an inoculation center for attending ceremonies to appease the Plague God. Knowing they were going to be scolded, the people stayed away from inoculation centers, and the plague continued to spread. Missionaries and young intellectuals who had received a modern education would not try to understand the people's traditional beliefs and despised them for their ignorance and lack of sanitation. Thus they could achieve no rapport with the people, a rapport which could have been used as a basis from which to begin reforms.[81]

Anthropologists, though agreeing on the need for field study, were too often content to stay in their offices and theorize.[82] One such scholar, though stating that the tribesmen must first be understood on their own terms and treated as equals before assimilation could take place, suggested that "they need a true religious faith to lean on for strength and guidance." [83] He applauded the end of the native official system and the substitution of taxation of tribespeople for the subsidies they had heretofore received from the central government, feeling that both represented important steps in the direction of the equal treatment he advocated.[84] It is not difficult to imagine that the tribesmen may have seen the removal of their headmen from office and their new fiscal responsibilities in a somewhat different light.

Another anthropologist, while lamenting the fact that assimilation could not be achieved quickly because "there has been nothing but neglect, prejudice and extermination by the Han," consistently used the dog radical in writing ethnic group names. He also urged his fellow Han to hasten to cultivate these lands in order to bring enlightenment to the area.[85] The fact that the inhabitants might be predisposed against the joys of civilization if it meant losing their lands seems not to have occurred to him.

Tibet

The imposition of Chinese administrative forms had generally followed substantial Han immigration to an area, and Tibet was no exception. Despite the fact that Han migration into Tibetan areas was not heavy prior to 1949, the boundary between newly colonized Han lands and Tibetan territory is virtually impossible to fix at any given point in time: often the indigenous peoples were not so much pushed back by the colonists as engulfed by them. Lines of administrative jurisdiction tended to be drawn at easily identifiable markers—a river, a mountain range, or a certain town, for example—while immigration patterns were rarely so neat. Advance parties of Han traders might form an important segment of the population of a town, while the surrounding countryside was solidly Tibetan and the nearest actual Han settlement was many miles to the east. In addition, the population was not simply Han up to one village and Tibetan thereafter: the Han population tapered off gradually but irregularly from east to west.

To complicate matters still further, the indigenous peoples of these marginal lands, though theoretically acknowledging the theocratic rule of the Dalai Lama, were fiercely independent in nature. Those known as the Khambas spoke a different dialect of Tibetan from that used in Lhasa, dressed somewhat differently, and had slightly different customs. Excellent, though undisciplined, soldiers and keen traders, they resented authority from any quarter. This was particularly true of those Khambas who made their living as caravan thieves. Though clearly Tibetans rather than Han, the Khambas had been known to ally with a weak Han government to fight a strong Lhasa one, the price being some sort of autonomy for themselves.

Thus, fixing a boundary between Tibet and China proper was an extremely vexing question. The Ch'ing dynasty at the height of its power in the eighteenth century had incorporated Tibetan areas up to the Chin-sha River, but had never imposed Chinese administrative forms on them.[86] As the dynasty declined, so, of course, did its ability to control these areas.

Britain, considering Tibet desirable as a buffer state against possible Russian designs on India, had tried to secure Ch'ing approval to preliminary measures to this end. The Tibetans, however, refused to honor the resultant Trade Treaty of 1893, since they themselves had not been party to it. Britain next tried direct negotiations with Tibet, but the Lhasa government also rebuffed these, on the grounds that the imperial government in Peking would not allow it.

Diplomatic methods having failed, Britain dispatched a military expedition under Colonel Francis Younghusband. The pathetically weak Tibetan army was easily defeated and the Lhasa Convention of 1904 forced [87] on the Dalai Lama's ministers. The Dalai Lama himself was not present, having fled at the approach of British troops. The Ch'ing held the Dalai Lama responsible for this defeat nonetheless and later declared him deposed. Annoyed with the British, the Tibetans became infuriated with the Ch'ing court for what they regarded as unwonted interference in their internal affairs. Not only Tibetan pride but religious sensibilities as well had been offended. Since the God-king of

Tibet holds his position not as an official with duties to perform, but as the reincarnation of a certain Living Buddha, the only way he can legitimately be deposed is by declaring him a false reincarnation. There being absolutely no evidence that this was the case, the injustice appeared all the more striking.

Meanwhile, the British had proved not nearly so bad as at first impression, and the Lhasa government began to see the uses to which cooperation with Britain might be put. Trade with India grew, British advisers were welcomed in Lhasa, and the Tibetan government began to insist that when the Chinese amban[88] requested an audience, the British consul be present as well.

In 1910 the Ch'ing, understandably worried at increasing British influence in Tibet, sent an army under Chao Erh-feng to reassert its influence. This he did, in such a manner as to earn the nickname "Butcher Chao" in Tibetan history. Among other atrocities committed by the expedition, the great monastery at Batang was burned and its Buddhist scriptures used to sole the soldiers' shoes.[89] While Chao was able to take the area as far west as Gyamda, a few days' march from Lhasa, and even sent a contingent on to Lhasa, the area was garrisoned rather than governed in the administrative sense. Chao's brutality also forced Tibet closer to Britain.[90]

The 1911 revolution enabled the Tibetans to free themselves of Ch'ing troops, and in 1914 Britain, hoping that the new republican government in China would be more amenable to the idea of a buffer state in Tibet than the imperial one had been, called a conference at Simla, in India, to discuss the matter. It was agreed that the Tibetan delegate would have equal status with the Chinese and British plenipotentiaries, which may be seen as a victory of sorts for the British plan.

After a good deal of bargaining, the three representatives initialled a convention which divided Tibet into inner and outer zones. The outer zone, including the Lhasa, Shigatse, and Chamdo areas, was to administer its own internal affairs. An amban with no more than 300 soldiers would reside in Lhasa, but no other Chinese troops were to be sent and no colonists would be allowed. In the inner zone, China might send troops, set up administrative areas, and plant colonies. It comprised a large portion of eastern Tibet (Kham), including Patang (Paan), Litang (Lihua), and Tachienlu (Kangting).

The republican government, however, refused to acknowledge the actions of its representative. The point at issue was the boundary between the inner and outer zones of Tibet, the republican side insisting that the line be drawn at Gyamda by virtue of Chao Erh-feng's conquests.[91] This was too close to Lhasa for the Tibetans' comfort, and the negotiations became stalemated. The outbreak of World War I a few weeks later drew Britain's attentions elsewhere, and the matter was dropped.

In 1917 the Han general in charge of western Szechwan decided to attack Tibet. He chose the time carefully: during a great prayer festival when attentions would be preoccupied with religious matters. The surprise attack produced initial success, but the Tibetans quickly regrouped and drove the Chinese almost completely out of eastern Tibet. It was clear that they would have been able to go farther had not Sir Eric Teichman, then British consul in Kangting, persuaded the predominantly Khamba force that it could not continue to hold areas so close to Han population and troop centers. This advice was accepted.[92] The Lhasa government, having recovered the Khamba areas, then committed a major blunder by trying to collect back taxes for the years they had been under Chinese rule.[93] Needless to say, the right to pay taxes was not what the Khambas had been fighting for, and relations with Lhasa became severely strained.

In 1917 also, for obscure reasons, the British government began an embargo on arms to Tibet.[94] At the cost of lessening her own prestige with the Lhasa government, this did help to stabilize the eastern border situation. The ammunition-short Tibetans were obliged to sign an agreement making Kangting the official post at which duty was collected on goods entering China from Tibet. They also acquiesced in the matter of Chinese administrative forms being introduced in eastern Tibet. Theoretically these forms reached as far west as the Chin-sha River and as far down as the *pao-chia* level. However, local government continued to function as it had for centuries past. Local leaders chosen according to local customs simply accepted nominal posts as *pao* or *chia* leaders. Republican troops kept order, and Han administrators were appointed as far down as the hsien level. But, like its imperial predecessor, the republican administration was scarcely noticeable below it.

As mentioned above, this area of nominal control extended as far west as the Chin-sha. But when the Kuomintang government created the province of Sikang in 1939,[95] they extended its boundaries much further west; the Chin-sha, in fact, bisected the province from north to south. The new territory seems to have been added more as a statement of aspirations than of immediate intent to govern: not even a fictional administration was present. The Lhasa government gave only a few Han traders permission to cross the river, and at Chamdo, west of the Chin-sha, officials collected customs dues on Chinese goods entering Tibet.[96] It also administered the many monasteries on both sides of the river, though the Nationalist government, like the Ch'ing before it, gave subsidies to the abbots in order to create good will.

East of the Chin-sha, under the warlord-style government of General Liu Wen-hui, a Nationalist Pacification Commissioner applied the policy of assimilation through education. Though the official attitude optimistically envisioned that within ten to twenty years people would have forgotten even the names of minority groups, the people this would affect were reported to be sullen and resentful of what they considered unjustified Han culture conceit. Barnett and Patterson, in observing this situation, noted that since upper-class Tibetans have traditionally looked down on education as training for menial clerical positions, all who could afford to hired substitutes to spare their children the indignity of going to school. The lower classes, who could not afford to buy themselves out of this unpleasant duty, saw no clerical positions to which they might put their education to use.[97] Adding insult to education, Han administrators and settlers of all classes treated Tibetans as barbarians and social inferiors, thus hardening their resistance to assimilation.[98]

During the 1920's and early 1930's contacts between the Lhasa government and the Chinese central government had been minimal, though not from lack of interest on the part of the latter. When the pro-British thirteenth Dalai Lama died in December 1933, the Nationalist government held a memorial service in Nanking. It also appointed General Huang Mu-sung Special Commissioner to Tibet and ordered him to deliver a eulogy at the lama's funeral in Lhasa.[99] A man of great personal charm, Huang seems to have favorably impressed the initially hostile Tibetans.[100] On his return to Nanking, General Huang proved to have made good use of his spare time: he presented the Nationalist government with a detailed proposal for a network of highways linking Tibet with China.[101] He also left a radio transmitter behind.[102] The Tibetans, in line with their past policy of using Britain as a counter to China, asked the British to install a transmitter of their own. This was done.

Another Nationalist delegation attended the inauguration of the fourteenth Dalai Lama in 1940; it was headed by Wu Chung-hsin, soon to be named governor of Sinkiang.[103] Wu was unable to obtain Lhasa's acceptance of a Nationalist High Commissioner, which the Tibetan government regarded as a return to the amban system. However, the Tibetan government does not seem to have protested when, without Lhasa's approval, Wu announced that the radio station would henceforth serve as headquarters for the Tibet branch of the Mongolian and Tibetan Affairs Commission.[104]

The Nationalist government also treated the second-highest Tibetan reincarnation, the Panchen Lama, with great care. The institution of Panchen Lama had been created by the fifth Dalai Lama as a way to honor his elderly tutor. Since, according to the Tibetan practice of

Buddhism, the Dalai Lama is the reincarnation of Avalokitesvara, the fifth Dalai Lama proclaimed the Panchen Lama the reincarnation of Amithaba, who was the teacher of Avalokitesvara. Amithaba is higher in the Buddhist pantheon than Avalokitesvara, and some have argued that thus the Panchen Lama is spiritually superior to the Dalai Lama. However, the Panchen Lama's temporal powers have been minimal, while those of the Dalai Lama are recognized as supreme. The Dalai Lama granted to his elderly teacher the revenues from three Tibetan districts centering around the city of Shigatse and himself retained the revenues from twelve districts. Unfortunately, future reincarnations did not get along as well as the fifth Dalai Lama and his tutor, and relations between them were often tense. The thirteenth Dalai Lama had used his alliance with Britain to strengthen the hold of his government over its many semifeudal component parts, including the areas of the ninth Panchen Lama. This led the Panchen Lama to turn to the Chinese government to aid him against their common enemies, the Dalai Lama and Britain. At one point in this contest the Panchen Lama fled to China and eventually died there, under circumstances which were peculiarly convenient for KMT strategy. The pro-Chinese advisers of the deceased then chose a young reincarnation, who was kept in the large Kumbum monastery in Ch'inghai (regarded by Tibetans as their province of Amdo) under close Nationalist supervision. The Lhasa government refused to accept him as the true reincarnation and chose its own candidate for the tenth Panchen Lama. The child was, needless to say, surrounded with pro-Lhasa government advisers. The Lhasa government had also taken advantage of the ninth Panchen Lama's exile in China to extend its control over his domains.[105]

Wishing to accommodate the Chinese when it did not compromise Tibet's independence, the Lhasa government made cash contributions to the Nationalist government's war effort against Japan.[106] However, the Nationalists' request to build an Assam-Szechwan road across Tibet, ostensibly to transport war supplies, was flatly refused.[107]

This uneasy modus vivendi was able to continue through the 1940's for several reasons: first, Britain and China were too preoccupied with World War II to come seriously into conflict over Tibet. Second, the governor of Sikang, Liu Wen-hui, perhaps because he had few friends in the Nationalist government, made a real effort to win acceptance by his Tibetan constituents.[108] Third, British interest in a Tibetan buffer state had waned. Any Tibetan hopes of reviving it must have diminished as Britain prepared to grant India its independence. Thus, the Lhasa government was induced to take a more conciliatory position vis-à-vis China.

The Treatment of Minorities during the Republican Era:
An Assessment

Any assessment of policy during the republican era confronts difficulties posed by diffusion of the decision-making process among sundry warlords, several foreign powers, and numerous KMT factors. When several-score ethnic groups are added to these factors, the interaction of the whole produces a situation of enormous complexity.

It has by now become a cliché for opponents of the Kuomintang to argue that the Chinese Communists won because the KMT was corrupt, self-seeking, and generally evil. Similarly, Kuomintang sympathizers point out that the KMT never did have firm control over China and that a necessary preoccupation with fighting the machinations of rapacious warlords and foreign meddlers—and, in particular, the war with Japan—prevented it from properly implementing its policies. With regard to minorities policy, evidence can be marshaled to support either side. The expropriation of minorities' lands was sanctioned by the highest levels of government, and their attitudes carried on down to local officials. KMT intransigence in dealing with dissident minorities' pleas for autonomy and a stop to Han colonization strengthened the impression that the Kuomintang's promises of equality and self-determination were lies. Acts of political treachery such as that carried out by Chiang against Lung Yun could only result in increased distrust of government promises.

On the other hand, the KMT record is not without successes. The Kuomintang effectively made use of Hui distaste for atheism in drawing that important minority to its side. Though belatedly and after much blundering, it did seem to have achieved a workable solution to the complicated Sinkiang problem. The marked improvement in Sino-Tibetan relations whenever Britain withdrew from the scene shows that foreign meddling was to a significant extent responsible for the KMT's problems there. The Soviet Union's support of Outer Mongolian independence and aid to dissident groups in Sinkiang unquestionably had the same effect. The personal successes of men like Chang Chih-chung in Sinkiang and Huang Mu-sung in Tibet show that talented diplomats were not absent from the KMT group assigned to minorities work. In Francis Hsü's and Li An-che's criticisms of the rural improvement program can be seen concerned individuals working hard to raise standards in these areas. It is not difficult to imagine that with a little more experience the defects of the program might have been corrected.

But the argument that warlords prevented the implementation of policies that would have proved the KMT's idealistic intentions must be rejected—first, because the record of many warlords in minorities administration [109] is a good deal better than that of the KMT, and, second, because the KMT's policies themselves were not in general wisely conceived. Despite their ruthlessness, warlords such as the governors Ma in Ch'inghai and Ninghsia, Sheng Shih-ts'ai in Sinkiang,[110] Lung Yun in Yunnan, and Liu Wen-hui in Sikang had a reputation for equal treatment of minorities and for making an honest attempt to deal with their grievances. In comparison, the KMT's inept handling of Mongolian demands for autonomy and its failure to implement reforms it had already promised in Sinkiang and toward the Hui appear at best unwise.

Moreover, even under ideal conditions—full control of China and a loyal, honest bureaucracy—there is doubt that the policies adopted were the best of all possible choices. The assimilation of minorities who considered assimilation desirable—for instance, the Chuang and Pai— proceeded much as it had during the Ch'ing dynasty: with no conscious help from the government. Among those who considered it undesirable —for example, the Uighurs, Kazakhs, Tibetans, and a number of Mongols—the KMT's emphasis on rapid assimilation had exactly the opposite effect from that intended. Minorities' resentment was aroused, and they tended to cling to traditional customs and forms with greater tenacity.

There is doubt, too, that education was always the best way to achieve assimilation. Education may well reduce cultural differences, but at the cost of making ethnic tensions more severe. Moreover, as has been noted, a significant number of Mongols considered education bothersome, and many Tibetans felt it was either an affront to their social status or useless in terms of their daily lives. In Sinkiang, the issue was antagonism at being taught in the Han language. Spencer's suggestion that the government consider making economic improvements in minorities areas before implementing its assimilation through education programs is well taken. The educational program might have been more successful had it been combined with economic opportunities for those who had completed the course of instruction. Teachers would have been more effective if cautioned to avoid actions that might be construed as haughty or arrogant. In short, the superiority of Han ways should have been demonstrated in action rather than taught in theory.

In working toward its stated goal of assimilation, the Kuomintang was hampered by poor transportation, inadequately trained officials, and a policy that placed too much emphasis on education and threats of force, a policy it was often unable to back up. Judged by its own goal of assimilation, Kuomintang minorities policy was a failure. Judged by that of keeping Ch'ing boundaries intact, its record is a good deal better.

With the exception of Outer Mongolia, territories either remained within the boundaries of the Chinese state or its claim to them was kept alive. In the light of future developments, the Nationalists' eleventh-hour compromise may have been the decisive factor in Sinkiang's remaining in China.

Neither very good nor wholly bad, the Kuomintang's minorities policy might best be described as weak.

3

Marxist–Leninist Prescriptions and the Soviet Example

The growth of nationalism in the nineteenth century was accompanied by heightened awareness of ethnic differences, and it raised questions about the methods by which diverse ethnic groups might be incorporated into state systems. Whether and how much freedom minority groups should have to use their own languages and customs, what positions they should be allowed to occupy in social and administrative hierarchies, and how to deal with ethnic protest movements, all received increasing attention. One of the first to try to put these problems into a theoretical framework was Karl Marx. His writings and the emendations thereof provided by the leaders of the Soviet Union gave the Chinese Communist Party the basis for its own theories and practice on the management of ethnic problems. Thus, a brief overview of Marxist-Leninist prescriptions and the Soviet example will be helpful to an understanding of Chinese Communist perceptions of ethnic problems in their own country.

Karl Marx and Nationalism

According to Marx, what is called national consciousness is merely a manifestation of the bourgeois state of society. Nationalism is a tool of the bourgeoisie: by allowing them to mask class differences and encourage tensions with the proletariat of other countries, nationalism enables the bourgeoisie to perpetuate their own rule.

Nationalism itself can be either progressive or reactionary, depending on the stage of society. When society is feudal, nationalism is progressive; when society has reached a highly developed bourgeois-capitalist phase, nationalism is reactionary. However, nations and nationalities will remain after the revolution against bourgeois capitalism. Marx does not make clear either how long they will remain or to what extent they will disappear: the *Communist Manifesto* says only that the supremacy of the proletariat will cause national differences and antagonisms between peoples to vanish "still faster" than they had been under capitalism.

Since Marx did not explicitly say that *all* nations and nationalities would disappear *completely*, the *Manifesto* may be interpreted as calling either for complete assimilation or for the abolition of only sharp or "antagonistic" contradictions.[1] The timetable for abolition, whether partial or complete, is also in doubt. Given the desire of most socialist states for at least the appearance of Marxist orthodoxy, the official interpretation of Marx's views on when and how completely nationality characteristics are to be erased will greatly affect such a state's nationalities policy.

It has been pointed out many times that Marx never systematically defined his concept of "nation," but uses the term interchangeably with, or as synonymous with, "society," "state," "country," and "ruling class." In addition, his belief in the primacy of economic factors led him to underestimate the power of historic, linguistic, and cultural factors. Thus he held an exaggeratedly high view of the existence of international class consciousness and an unrealistically low view of the attraction of ethnic ties.

Through his belief that national consciousness is a manifestation of economic ties, Marx came to the conclusion that minority ethnic groups ought to be, and actually felt themselves to be, part of the nation whose economy they shared. Economic ties, not differences in language, customs, or history, determined citizenship in the large nation.

Thus Marx was not a proponent of national liberation movements per se, but judged their right to exist in terms of whether or not independence would be conducive to economic progress. As a corollary to this, national liberation movements which led to the progress of worldwide revolutionary movements would also be judged correct. However, since a worldwide revolutionary movement is by Marx's definition conducive to economic progress, it is possible to argue that an essentially reactionary ethnic nationalist movement, in that it weakens the more advanced capitalist large nation of which it is a part, is progressive in terms of world revolution. One might with equal Marxian orthodoxy, if considerably less impatience for the coming of the revolution, argue that not until the minority group has thoroughly "constituted itself part of the nation"—that is, not until its economy has caught up with that of the more advanced group—is the large nation as a whole ready for revolution. Thus Marxists can legitimately disagree on policy toward the backward-looking national liberation movements, that is, toward those nationalities seeking to rid themselves of a more economically advanced large nation so that they can retain their traditional ways in peace. It should be noted, however, that Marx generally opted against national liberation movements. He opposed Indian liberation because he felt British colonialism would lead to economic progress, pan-Slavism because it might strengthen czarism, which he wished to destroy, and Czech liberation because he believed the group was too small to allow the development of a modern economy.

Marx allowed strategy to take precedence over ideology in the case of the Irish liberation movement, however, reversing his earlier conviction that the movement was "wrong" because an independent Ireland would be too small to be economically progressive. Since English workers and Irish workers in England had clashed violently on the independence issue, the independence movement was "destroying" class solidarity, which should properly have been directed against bourgeois rule. Since the bourgeois rulers were clearly English, the interests of the unity of the working classes demanded support for the Irish movement. Marx believed, though, that when independence had been achieved and the attendant furor had died down, the Irish would realize where their economic interests lay and would voluntarily seek union with Britain.[2]

Perhaps because of a growing realization of the importance of ethnic group factors implicit in his decision on the Irish independence movement, Marx was later moved to declare a "right to self-determination." This statement is included in the Declaration on the Polish Question approved by the London Conference of the First International in 1865[3] and again in the Geneva Conference of the International in 1866.[4] Though the Polish independence movement could have been judged progressive simply because it would weaken czarist Russia's power, the decision on Poland was justified instead on the basis of an abstract right, which by definition any group could invoke. The right of self-determination was also included in the Programme of the Second International in 1896.[5] But no precise definition of self-determination was included, thus again allowing at least two interpretations to flourish —that is, that self-determination (a) always meant the right to total independence, or (b) might sometimes mean only the right to some degree of autonomy within the large nation. We may presume that Marx considered it unnecessary to spell out the concept of self-determination more precisely, since he believed that eventually economic self-interest and the proletariat's growing realization of its basic unity would bring all national groupings together again. Walker Connor suggests another explanation: that Marx conceived of self-determination "not as a principle but as a slogan which could be used to weaken enemies and attract allies." [6] Whether or not this is true, there is no doubt that the concept of self-determination did come to be used as a slogan rather than as a principle.

Lenin and the National Question

The program of the Second Congress of the Russian Social Democratic Workers' Party in 1903, drafted by Lenin, included the "right of self determination for all nations comprising the state." [7] In 1916 Lenin made clear that he interpreted self-determination as the right to political independence: "The right of nations to self determination implies exclusively the right to independence in the political sense, the right to free political separation from the oppressor nation." [8]

He expected, however, that granting the *right* to complete independence would result in few nationalities' exercising it, thus achieving his desired goal of a few large states with a minimum of physical coercion. Like Marx, Lenin believed that minorities' perception of economic self-interest would lead them to decide against independence:

This demand [for the right of self-determination] therefore is not the equivalent of a demand for separation, fragmentation, and the formation of small states. . . . The closer a democratic state system is to complete freedom to secede, the less frequent and less ardent will the desire for separation be in practice, because big states afford indisputable advantages, both from the standpoint of economic progress and from that of the interests of the masses. . . . It was from this standpoint that Marx, who was a centralist, preferred even the federation of Ireland and England to the forcible subordination of Ireland to the English. [9]

In the case of a revolt against a feudal state, Lenin originally favored aid to the bourgeoisie, since they were the progressive force in this situation. Where capitalism had not yet developed to any great extent, peasants and such proletarians as existed were too weak to spearhead a liberation movement. However, at the Second Congress of the Comintern in 1920, Lenin's view was challenged by M. N. Roy, a young Indian Communist who believed the working class was already strong enough to lead the movement. After considerable debate, the Comintern approved a compromise program, the so-called "Theses on the National and Colonial Question," which allowed that Soviet aid *might* enable backward peoples to escape the bourgeois-capitalist state of development: "If the victorious revolutionary proletariat conducts systematic propaganda among them, and the Soviet governments come to their aid with all the means at their disposal, in that event it will be mistaken to assume that backward peoples must inevitably go through the capitalist stage of development." As to how this might be accomplished, "The necessary means for this cannot be indicated in advance. These will be prompted by practical experience. It has, however, been definitely established that the idea of the Soviets is understood by the mass of the working people in even the most remote nations, that the Soviets should be adapted to the conditions of a pre-capitalist social system, and that Communist parties should immediately begin work in this direction." [10]

When such help could not be given, "The Comintern must enter into a temporary alliance with bourgeois democracy . . . but should not merge with it and under all circumstances uphold its independence, even if in its most embryonic form." [11] As may be guessed, whether or how much help to give a fledgling proletarian party vis-à-vis a bourgeois democratic one was to become a vexing question, as was the meaning of a "temporary" alliance in which the proletarian party members did not surrender their "independence, even in its most embryonic form."

Support of liberation movements was made mandatory, with one important qualification: "If we do not want to betray socialism, we must support every revolt against our chief enemy, the bourgeoisie of the big states, provided it is not the revolt of a reactionary class." [12] The decision on what constituted reaction—that is, which movements to support—was left to the individual Communist party. This, of course, did little to clarify Marx's ambiguity on the subject.

Surprisingly, Lenin was less equivocal on the right of self-determination of minorities in a socialist state: it was to be supported, with no qualifications about reactionary classes added. Lenin angrily refuted several Polish Communists' contention that the right of self-determination was not applicable to a socialist society: "It would be a betrayal of socialism not to implement the self-determination of nations under socialism." The Poles' reasoning had been that socialism would abolish the class interests which led to national oppression; thus the socialist revolution automatically conferred "freedom" on a nationality and there was no reason for self-determination. Lenin pointed out that the Polish argument considered economic factors only, and that the forcible retention of one nation within the state frontiers of another was "one form of political oppression." [13] It will be noticed that Lenin, unlike Marx, made a clear distinction between economic oppression and political oppression. In Marx, the latter would have been merely a manifestation of the former.

Lenin also denied that all nationality problems would be ended by the revolution: "By transforming capitalism into socialism, the proletariat creates the *possibility* of abolishing national oppression; the possibility becomes a reality only—'only!'—with the establishment of full democracy in all spheres, including the delineation of state frontiers in accordance with the 'sympathies' of the population, including complete freedom to secede." [14]

On the question of a timetable for the transformation of nationality differences into proletarian harmony, Lenin was again unequivocal: it would take a long time. "The socialist revolution is not a single act, it is not one battle on any one front, but a whole epoch of acute class conflicts, a long series of battles on all fronts." [15] Lenin believed that the aim of socialism was not only to bring nationalities closer together, but to integrate them. However, this also was expected to be in the far future: "The fusion of nations will be completed when the state withers away." [16]

Meanwhile, the battle for democracy was to be waged on all fronts. During this transition period, those nationalities who opted to stay within the large state would be given a wide variety of rights, including

The general situation of equal rights—the division of the country into autonomous and self governing territorial units according—among other things—to nationality (the local population determines the boundaries, the general parliament confirms them)—the limits of the administration of the autonomous districts and regions as well as the self governing local units; the illegalization of any departure from equality of nations in the decisions of autonomous districts, *zemstvos*, etc.; general school councils democratically elected, etc.; freedom and equality of languages —the choice of languages by the municipal institutions, etc. The protection of minorities: the right to a proportional share of the expenditures for school buildings (gratis) for students of "alien" (non-Russian) nationalities, for "alien" teachers, for "alien" departments in museums and libraries, theaters and the like; the right of each citizen to seek redress (before a court) for any departure from the corresponding equality of rights, for any "trampling upon" the rights of national minorities; a census of population every five years in the multi-national districts, a ten year census in the country as a whole, etc. . . .

The draft might be worked out by Marxists of *all*, or of very many, of the nations of Russia.[17]

While it may seem odd to promote the fusion of nationalities by encouraging their points of difference, Lenin's belief was undoubtedly that minorities, if not forced to adopt the characteristics of the majority group, would do so voluntarily. Thus both the need for coercion and the charges of Great Russian chauvinism occasioned by coercion would be avoided:

The Russian tongue would be for a number of unfortunate and backward peoples of progressive significance—no doubt about it. But do you not see that it would be of still greater progressive significance if there were no compulsion to use it? ... We are in principle against federation; it weakens the economic connection and is inappropriate for a unified state. Do you want to separate, we say. Then go to the devil and cut yourself off altogether if you can break the economic connection or, rather, if the yoke and friction of "living together" are such that they spoil the economic relationship. You don't want to separate? Then, please, don't decide *for me*, don't believe you have the "right" to federation. ... The right of self determination is an *exception* from our general premise of centralism. This exception is absolutely necessary in view of Great Russian arch-reactionary nationalism and the slightest renunciation of this exception is opportunism, it is a simple minded playing into the hands of Great Russian arch-reactionary nationalism.[18]

On the subject of equality of nationalities within the USSR, Lenin advocated going beyond mere equality per se: one must prove one's good intentions by going beyond equality to atone for past sins:

Not only formal equality. It is necessary to compensate one way or another by one's attitude or one's concessions to the non-Russians for the lack of trust, the suspicion, the insult of which they were the object in the past by the government of the 'dominant' nation ... as far as the Georgian nation is concerned, flexibility being necessary on our side for a genuinely proletariat attitude to the matter ... in this case it is better to overdo it in the way of flexibility and leniency towards the national minorities than underdo it ... we [must] never adopt a formal attitude to the national question but always take into account the specific attitude of the proletariat of the oppressed (or small) nation to the oppressing (or great) nation.[19]

Lenin also cautioned that special care would have to be taken to investigate in detail the observation of rules on the use of native languages, there being "no doubt that there is bound to be ... on the pretext of unity in the railway service, unity in the fiscal service and so on, a mass of really Russian abuses." [20]

Stalinist Emendations

It was, however, Stalin who, as Commissar of Nationalities and successor to Lenin, was the decisive force in Soviet nationalities policy. Refuting "revisionist" contentions that the peasant class, to which the majority of minority nationalities belonged, was inherently the enemy of revolution, Stalin argued that minorities, being doubly oppressed—by the capitalists since they were part of the toiling masses and by Great Russian chauvinists since they were minorities—would be all the more revolutionary.[21] He agreed with Lenin that they should have the right of self-determination, though insisting that the civil war made such a choice clear cut: "*Either* [nationalities] join forces with Russia and then the toiling masses of the border regions will be emancipated from imperialist oppression *or* they join forces with the Entente and then the yoke of imperialism is inevitable . . . the interests of the masses of the people render the demand for the secession of the border regions at the present stage of the revolution a profoundly counter-revolutionary one." [22]

With regard to the nationalities who "elected" to join the Soviet Union, Stalin held forth a broad program of national autonomy combined with economic opportunities and freedom to develop individual cultures. In making clear that he favored a territorial rather than purely cultural basis for autonomy,[23] Stalin also left no doubt that, when he spoke of freedom to develop national characteristics, the emphasis was to be placed on "development" rather than "freedom":

. . . the national programme of the Austrian Social-Democrats enjoins a concern for the "*preservation and development* of the national peculiarities of the peoples." Just think: to "preserve" such "national peculiarities" of the Transcaucasian Tatars as self-flagellation . . . or to "develop" such national peculiarities of the Georgians as the vendetta . . .[24]

What would be the results of national cultural autonomy? . . . to organize [the Tatars] into a national cultural union would be to . . . deliver them to the mercies of the reactionary mullahs, to create a new stronghold of spiritual enslavement of the Tatar masses to their worst enemy. . . . The national problem can be solved only by drawing the backward nations and peoples into the common stream of a higher culture. It is the only progressive solution, and the only solution acceptable to Social Democrats.[25]

Like Lenin, Stalin advocated going beyond legal equality in order to redress the grievances caused by czarist oppression. Aware that the minorities might perceive "new Soviet man" as the same old Great Russian chauvinist with a new name, he railed against the czarist type of oppressions and even advocated returning to certain minorities the lands which had been taken from them by Great Russian colonizers.[26]

He judged that much minority agitation was caused not by lack of independence but by restrictions on the use of minority languages, schools, and freedom of conscience. Removal of these restrictions would, he felt, go a long way toward removing minority distrust of the Bolsheviks.[27] On this new basis of trust, the solidarity of the proletariat of all nationalities could be built. Stalin believed, however, that in the immediate postwar period the development of this solidarity would be hindered by the economic backwardness of nationality areas, the numerical weakness of local proletariats, lack of suitable Marxist literature in native languages, weakness of party educational work, and survivals of radical nationalist traditions.[28]

These same factors would also encourage local nationalist tendencies, which would surely be strengthened by the "New Economic Policy" then coming into force.[29] It was thus imperative to train Communist cadres among the nationalities.[30] For this purpose, the University of the Peoples of the East and its branches must be strengthened and party educational work intensified. Studies of minority economic conditions, social life, and culture were to be carried out, the better to understand them.[31]

There should be cooperation with bourgeois-democratic elements, too. In this and in other aspects of carrying out nationalities policy, both right and left deviations were to be resisted: the rightists erred in being too susceptible to local nationalist influences; the leftists, in being inflexible and unwilling to maneuver bourgeois-democratic elements into supporting the Soviet government. The leftists made no effort to enforce the party line of drawing all reliable elements into state institutions, and, instead, they insisted on mechanically transplanting Russian experience to local areas.[32]

While maintaining that "the Great Russian proletariat must not be placed in a position of inequality with regard to the formerly oppressed nations," [33] Stalin consistently rejected what he called "cavalry raids of pure communism" in the non-Russian areas. Particularly the thirty million people who had not yet reached the stage of industrial capitalism, and who, it was hoped, could skip from feudalism directly into socialism, must be treated with understanding and care. The Soviet government must, he repeated, be made comprehensible to local people. Thus, the government would have to take into account local customs and forms and national peculiarities.[34] In a scathing indictment of those who thoughtlessly applied Russian models to minority areas, he observed tartly, "I do not stoop to mention the elimination of such incongruities as, for example, the demand made by the People's Commissariat of Food ... for the delivery of pigs in Kirghizia where the Mohammedan population have never possessed them." [35]

Stalin's remarks raise some interesting questions. Would not respect for national peculiarities and the fostering of native languages run counter to the "withering away" of the national question? If, as Marx observed, national culture is merely a manifestation of bourgeois culture, how could respect for national culture be made compatible with the socialist duty of fostering a common proletarian culture? Would this not amount to delivering the people up to their reactionary mullahs, a sin of which Stalin had previously accused the Austro-Marxists? Lenin, too, had explicitly differentiated between the "two cultures"—bourgeois and socialist—saying that the former was a reactionary demand of the bourgeoisie, which was striving to infect the minds of the workers with the virus of nationalism. Linguistic and other concessions were granted essentially as a means to an end: once given they would come to be perceived as undesirable and be rejected, thus facilitating the withering away of nationalist cultures and the emergence of a proletarian culture.

Stalin denied the necessity of a contradiction between proletarian and nationalist culture: proletarian culture that was socialist in content would assume different forms and methods of expression among different peoples. "Proletarian culture does not cancel out national culture but lends it content. National culture, on the other hand, does not cancel proletarian culture, but lends it form." [36] For Stalin the crucial point was not *whether* differences in culture existed, but the social system *under which* they existed: "The demand for national culture was a bourgeois demand as long as the bourgeoisie was in power and the consolidation of nations proceeded under the aegis of the bourgeois system. The demand for national culture became a proletarian demand, when the proletariat came into power and the consolidation of nations began to proceed under the aegis of the Soviet government." He considered the idea that a universal socialist language would emerge and all others die out extremely unlikely.[37]

Answering questions as to how assimilation was to take place under such circumstances, Stalin replied:

Undoubtedly certain nationalities may, and even certainly will, undergo a process of assimilation. Such processes have occurred before. But the point is that the process of assimilation of certain nationalities does not preclude, but rather presupposes, the opposite process of reinforcement and development of nationalities. It is because of this that the possible assimilation of individual nationalities does not weaken, but on the contrary confirms, the proposition, an absolutely correct proposition, that universal proletarian culture does not preclude, but rather presupposes and fosters national culture, just as national culture does not nullify, but rather supplements and enriches, universal proletarian culture.[38]

Perhaps the only salient fact to emerge from this classic example of Orwellian doublethink is that Stalin, while not denying that total assimilation *might* take place, appeared unwilling to commit himself to saying that it would *always* be so. Whether this was because he interpreted Marx's statement on the disappearance of national differences to mean only the disappearance of antagonistic differences, because he considered it tactically unwise to admit to minorities that they were scheduled for assimilation, or simply because he believed that Marx and Lenin had been a bit too visionary remains open to question.

Soviet Minorities Policy in Practice

The Provisional Government that came to power after the outbreak of the Russian revolution abolished all czarist restrictions on the minorities[39] and proclaimed the equality of all citizens. Insofar as possible, members of minority groups were appointed to govern minority areas, and the beginnings of autonomous governments were set up.[40]

Feeling that, because a constitution had not yet been approved, it could do nothing which might infringe on popular sovereignty, the Provisional Government took no action on land reform. Unfortunately these ethically admirable scruples proved politically unwise and played into the hands of the Bolsheviks. Their impatience with the Provisional Government reinforced by Bolshevik propaganda, peasants tried to seize for themselves the lands the government denied them. In minority areas this often took the form of natives attempting to expropriate Russian colonists. Frequently these were nomads who wished to reclaim what had formerly been their pasturelands. As might be expected, their efforts met with fierce resistance, and a bloody "national struggle" ensued.

The Provisional Government felt constrained to side with law and order, which put it on the side of the Russian colonists. Thus the Bolsheviks' contention that the Provisional Government was just as Great Russian chauvinist as the czarist regime had been fell on receptive ears. So did their promises of self-determination.[41] More than a dozen minority groups declared themselves independent, and many of the new governments were recognized by the Bolsheviks. Their decision to recognize the secessionist states was, of course, supported by Lenin's argument that those given independence would voluntarily reject it, but there was another reason as well: most of the minority areas were not in fact independent, but were held by either Whites or foreign powers. Recognition of independence thus not only would hurt the Soviet cause, it might also encourage minorities to seek Soviet help in overthrowing foreign or White domination.

Independence was short-lived. Utilizing native Communists, the Red Army, and often Great Russian colonists or other elements hostile to what most minorities believed to be their best interests, the Bolsheviks had imposed their rule on most areas by 1921.[42] The methods used to attain this went well beyond Lenin's appeal to economic self-interest, and savage struggles marred the reunification process. It was during this period that Stalin made his statement that the war had made any demands for self-determination "profoundly counterrevolutionary." Lenin, obviously pleased with the resultant reunification, did not, however, wish to be associated with the less savory means by which it had been attained. After the particularly bloody conquest of Georgia he sharply criticized the handling of the campaign, pleading that poor health had kept him away from party business. Stalin in particular was held responsible:

If matters had come to such a pass that Orjonikidze[43] could go to the extreme of applying physical violence . . . we could imagine what a mire we had got ourselves into. Obviously the whole business of "autonomization" was radically wrong and badly timed . . . the "freedom to withdraw from the union" by which we justify ourselves will be a mere scrap of paper unable to defend the non-Russians from the onslaught of that really Russian man, the Great Russian, the chauvinist, in substance a rascal and lover of violence . . . there is no doubt that the infinitesimal percentage of Soviet and sovietized workers will drown in that sea of chauvinistic Great Russian riff raff like a fly in milk. . . . Were we careful enough in taking these measures to give people of other nationalities real defense against the genuine Russian *Derzhimorda*? [44] I do not think we took such measures although we could and should have done so.

I think that Stalin's haste and enthusiasm for pure administration, and also his spite against the notorious "social nationalism" played a fatal role here. Spite is a bad thing in politics . . . it is common knowledge that people of other nationalities who are russified overdo the real Russian frame of mind.[45]

As to specific measures to curb such behavior, Lenin recommended exemplary punishment of Orjonikidze, though "the political responsibility for all this really Great Russian nationalistic campaign must, of course, be laid on Stalin and Dzerzhinsky." [46] However, far from retreating from the consequences of these actions, which he deplored, Lenin went on to state that the task for the future would be to strengthen this union which force had created.[47]

Soviet minorities policy after unification was effected may be divided into three periods. The first spanned the years from 1922 to 1928, the second from 1929 through Stalin's death in 1953, and the third covers the post-Stalin era.

The first period was characterized by efforts to integrate nationality areas into the socialist state. Relatively benign in nature, its chief features were embodied in the policy known as *korenizatsiia* or "indigenization." [48] A conscious attempt was made to encourage non-Russians to assume responsibilities and power; conversely, Great Russians were restrained from monopolizing important positions. Though local nationalism was frowned upon, Great Russian chauvinism was considered the major danger. The result of this indigenization would be a true friendship of peoples (*druzhba narodov*), which, it was hoped, would lead to a drawing together (*sblizhenie*) and eventual merging of peoples (*sliianie*).

The Constitution of 1924 granted certain powers of autonomy to the republics, including the right to secede and the right to be educated in the native language of the area. Though the right to secede continued to be regarded as "profoundly counterrevolutionary" even after the threat of war had ceased to exist, a genuine effort was made to implement the linguistic provisions of the constitution. Not only were non-Russian children educated in their native languages: Russians were actually encouraged to learn the languages of the republics in which they lived.[49] Investigations of the less well-developed languages were carried out; if deemed necessary, a standard dialect was decided upon and a written language created. The Latin alphabet, not the Cyrillic, was used as the basis for these new written languages and also replaced the Arabic script in the languages of the Muslim minorities. This step should not be seen as an attempt to create a barrier between Soviet Muslims and their Arabic fellow believers. Many of the Soviet Muslims are Turkic-speaking, not Arabic-speaking peoples, and this switch to the Latin alphabet was, moreover, carried out at the same time Kemal Atatürk was implementing a similar change to the Latin alphabet in neighboring Turkey.

Indigenous cadres and native leaders were carefully nurtured. In Kazakhstan, for example, whereas at the beginning of 1921 only 4.4 percent of the Kazakh Communist Party organization were Kazakhs, by January 1, 1937, Kazakh members totaled 48.8 percent.[50] Though it is true that often minorities' leaders held the highest positions in their republics only nominally, with actual power being exercised by a Russian occupying a formally lower-ranking position, there can be little doubt that the effort to train native leaders was sincere.[51]

Particularly after 1928, vigorous attempts were made to modernize the more primitive nationalities. While the Soviet government depicted these efforts as evidence of its great solicitude for the well-being of its less fortunate peoples, many examples can be cited to support the contention that more than humanitarian considerations were involved. As early as 1920, Comintern Chairman Zinoviev had stated in a speech to the Petrograd Soviet that "we cannot do without the petroleum of Azerbaijan or the cotton of Turkestan. We take these products, which are necessary for us, not as the former exploiters but as older brothers bearing the torch of civilization." [52] An effort was made to avoid the appearance of Great Russian chauvinism by having members of other advanced nationalities—principally Armenians, Jews, and Ukrainians—act as "tutors," but since Great Russians made up the great majority of technicians and managers, the intended multinational appearance may have been lost on those for whom it was intended.

With the clarity of hindsight, it can be seen that *korenizatsiia* gave indirect encouragement to local nationalism. Industrialization and collectivization caused inevitable tensions, which aggravated these particularist sentiments. By the late 1920's many native leaders had begun to argue that *korenizatsiia* was a poor substitute for real political and cultural autonomy and to question the motives of the party center. Some complained openly that the replacement of the tyranny of the czar by the dictatorship of the proletariat meant "only the signboard has been changed." [53] Dissent was not merely confined to words but took more damaging forms as well. In Kazakhstan, for example, herdsmen slaughtered their animals rather than surrender them to cooperatives: the number of cattle there dropped from 7.4 million in 1929 to 1.59 million in 1934, the number of sheep and goats from 27.2 million to 2.26 million in the same period. Many Kazakhs fled to China or Afghanistan, the population decreasing by nearly 900,000 between 1926 and 1939.[54] Stalin became increasingly disillusioned with the idea of creating socialist society through native leaders and gradualist means, and the period came to an end.

The second period of Soviet minorities policy, dating roughly from 1929 to 1953, was in many ways the antithesis of the preceding period. Local nationalism was no longer to be lulled out of existence; it would be ruthlessly suppressed. The carefully nurtured nationalities elite began to be eliminated. First to be purged was the Tatar leader Sultan Galiev,[55] then Ukrainians Shumskyi and Skrypnik.[56] In the wake of the purge trials of the late 1930's, thousands of "local nationalists" representing all ten of the non-Russian republics were liquidated. The net effect, of course, was to wipe out the indigenous elite. They were replaced with Russian, and to a lesser extent Georgian and Armenian, personnel.

Union republics' powers were curtailed and the policy of "national in form, socialist in content" more strictly interpreted. As part of a glorification of all things Russian, there was a new emphasis on learning the Russian language.[57] It was further decided that Cyrillic would replace the Latin alphabet as the basis for non-Russian scripts; non-Russian words were also purged of foreign loan words, with Russian vocabulary substituted.[58]

Given this sort of repression, it is hardly surprising that many minority peoples welcomed the invading German army as liberators. This simply confirmed Stalin's convictions of their unreliability, and vengeance was swift. Seven entire nationality groups—the Crimean Tatars, Volga Germans, Kalmyks, Chechens, Ingushi, Karachai, and Balkars—were deported en masse to Central Asia and Siberia. Khrushchev later revealed that Stalin also considered deporting the 28 million Ukrainians, but had to give up the idea since insufficient transportation was available.[59] The deportees made the long trip eastward packed in cattle trucks; on arrival they were put in labor camps. No one knows how many died of starvation, cold, and typhus, but estimates run as high as 40 percent.[60]

Germany's occupation of the USSR's western territories led to increased emphasis on the development of the eastern areas, and the economy of these areas actually prospered during the war years. This development was, however, accompanied by a large influx of Russian personnel, which further diluted the national character of the areas.[61]

The Soviet Union's victory in World War II did not appreciably lessen Stalin's suspicion of the nationalities, and the glorification of things Russian continued. While all the nationalities suffered to some extent, Stalin reserved particularly harsh measures for the Jews. His increasingly blatant anti-Semitism reached its height in the so-called Doctors' Plot, which was "discovered" on the eve of his death.[62]

Stalin's demise resulted in a significant liberalization of policy toward all non-Russian groups except for the Jews. The crucial factor in this decision to liberalize lay partly in the mechanics of Khrushchev's rise to power: facing opposition in the Moscow party organization, Khrushchev established close ties with the non-Russian republics and later rewarded local leaders, particularly Ukrainians, with responsible positions in Moscow. His policy of economic decentralization also gave the non-Russian republics more freedom over their own affairs. At the famous Twentieth Party Congress of 1956, a number of powers were transferred from the federal government to the republics.[63] To ensure a certain minimum of non-Russian representation in the power structure, a quota system was established for university entrance and for filling political offices.[64] Six of the seven deported nationalities were absolved of collaboration charges in 1956.[65]

Beginning in 1958, however, Khrushchev began to reverse the more liberal aspects of his nationalities policy. One important reason for this was that, having eliminated the most vocal of his critics, he was no longer so dependent on the support of the non-Russian republics. Another may have been the realization that a little liberalization seemed to stimulate demands for more; Khrushchev undoubtedly wished to keep disturbances such as those in Poland and Hungary from occurring inside the borders of the Soviet Union. In 1959, when Latvian Communists tried to place quotas on the number of non-Latvian members, its leadership was purged en masse.[66] Khrushchev's virgin lands program led to the large-scale colonization of the Central Asian republics, and by the mid 1960's, Russians constituted 52 percent of the population of Kazakhstan.[67]

In addition, the Education Laws of 1958–1959 decreed that students in Russian language schools, whatever their nationality, need no longer study the language of the republic in which they lived.[68] A program of "interrepublic exchange of personnel" was instituted, ostensibly to aid economic development and "to contribute toward a harmonious fusing together of nationalities and thus hasten the advent of communism." [69]

Under the present Soviet leadership there has been little change in policy toward the non-Russians, with Mssrs. Brezhnev and Kosygin still trying to steer a middle course between repression on the one hand and encouragement of local nationalism on the other. While the virgin lands program has been regarded as a failure and discontinued, the Sino-Soviet dispute has continued its colonization effect: increasing numbers of Russians have been resettled in border areas of the Central Asian republics to aid in defense. Although the Sino-Soviet dispute has thus resulted in further dilution of the indigenous cultures of the area, it has, on the other hand, led to increased Soviet attention to the traditional music and art of the non-Russian nationalities. The USSR's alleged encouragement of nationalities' cultural and economic development vis-à-vis the alleged Chinese repression of such development has formed the major theme of Soviet broadcasts to nationalities on both sides of the border. The seventh deported nationality, the Crimean Tatars, was officially exonerated in 1967.[70]

While Ukrainian power in the central party organs has been reduced since the fall of Khrushchev, there has been a rise in Belorussian representation. The "exchange of personnel" policy is still in effect, though, as before, it becomes less noticeable in the higher and more powerful governmental positions.[71]

In surveying the course of Soviet nationalities policy over the past fifty years, perhaps the two most striking accomplishments are in economic development and language. Living standards in nationalities areas —in Central Asia as well as in originally well-developed areas such as the Baltic states and the Ukraine—are equal to and sometimes surpass those of purely Russian nationality areas.[72] The Russian language has become the accepted lingua franca of the Soviet Union. However, despite the attainment of a considerable degree of economic equality and the establishment of a common medium of communication, there is no evidence of the disappearance of the national consciousness. On the contrary, many scholars have noted an increase in non-Russian nationalism. Particularly prominent among the Muslim peoples, it is by no means confined to them,[73] and has been recorded among the Jews,[74] Armenians, and Estonians,[75] among others.

Richard Pipes has pointed out that national frustrations and animosities are in many ways more acute than when the Communists came to power over half a century ago and that "unless the Soviet rulers face up to it and begin the process of decentralization voluntarily, it is likely someday to explode in a most destructive manner." [76] Recently, a young Soviet writer has predicted that the non-Russian nationalities will withdraw from the Soviet Union within the next fifteen years, their secession being facilitated by a war between Russia and China.[77]

While Soviet propaganda continues to speak of *druzhba narodov*— the friendship of peoples—and still phrases its goals in terms of the drawing together (*sblizhenie*) and eventual merging (*sliianie*) of all national cultures, this goal seems to be getting further away instead of nearer. Increasing dissatisfaction with communism's economic failures and the recent revelation that the Soviet Union's minorities now total a majority of the population can be expected to decrease the possibility of the emergence of a common socialist culture based on the Russian model. Not the emergence of a common proletarian culture but an integration based upon a balancing of nationality interests with Russian forms as common coin would seem the most likely future.

Relevance for the Chinese

As a blueprint for minorities policy, the Marxist-Leninist canon presented the Chinese with considerable leeway for interpretation. Particular ambiguity existed concerning the definition of nationality characteristics and the rate and thoroughness with which they could be expected to disappear. The questions whether and under what circumstances to support national liberation movements and the rights of self-determination and secession were also hedged with doubt, as were the circumstances under which a "backward" nationality might be enabled to skip the capitalist stage and the matter of when and for how long socialists might form alliances with "progressive" members of the bourgeoisie. There is no clear guideline on which minority group characteristics or forms must be erased in order to achieve a truly socialist content. Nor had any precise definition been worked out of which minority rights to support and to what extent.

Ambiguities and differences of emphasis among Marx, Lenin, and Stalin were further compounded by a considerable disparity between socialist theory and Soviet practice, as well as differences within Soviet practice itself over a period of time.

The only enduring features of Marxist theory and practice concerning the minorities question are an insistence on the equality of all nationalities, a vaguely defined commitment to self-determination, and a linkage of nationality characteristics with class structure. The last, explicit in Marx, became progressively more vague as Lenin and Stalin came to grips with the Soviet situation, in which nationalities' special characteristics seemed more firmly imbedded in the toiling masses than in the bourgeoisie. The ultima ratio in this is Stalin's pronouncement—"national in form, socialist in content."

As Soviet experience began to show the weaknesses of a theory that linked social class and nationality characteristics, Marx's references to self-determination and federation were developed into the concept of nationality autonomy. However, when the leadership deemed it necessary to stamp down nationality characteristics, those considered to have erred were attacked as "bourgeois," and the exercise of local autonomy has always been completely circumscribed by the decisions of the strictly hierarchical, centrally directed party. Soviet experience has also demonstrated the difficulties inherent in a policy that aims at erasing ethnic differences by allowing them free rein.

The socialist scriptures could, then, be used to support either nationality diversity or proletarian conformity, nationality autonomy or strict central control. In short, the Chinese could formulate minorities policy in a wide variety of ways and still remain ideologically orthodox.

Part Two

The Chinese Communist Experience

The Chinese Communist Party has consistently recognized the nationalities question as being one of the major questions of the Chinese revolution and the liberation of the national minorities as being a part of the liberation of the Chinese . . . what has been called nationality struggle is in reality a question of class struggle.

Mao Tse-tung

4

Chinese Communist Policy Prior to 1949

Minorities Policy up to 1935

In its earliest years, the Chinese Communist Party appears to have accepted unquestioningly Marxist-Soviet pronouncements on minorities with little regard to how they should be adapted to the Chinese milieu. This was not due to any obtuseness on the part of the members, but reflects the fact that other concerns seemed far more urgent. Faced with a less than enthusiastic proletariat on the one hand and an overly interested government police force on the other, the infant party's lack of attention to minority group problems is understandable. Adapting Marx, with his urban-industrial emphasis, to the Chinese situation must have seemed a formidable enough task without adding consideration of the country's most backward 6 percent.

Thus, minorities were promised self-determination and autonomy, just as they had been by the Russian Communist Party. The manifesto of the party's second congress in 1922 proclaimed Mongolia, Tibet, and Turkistan to be autonomous states (*pang*) and envisioned their voluntary unification with China proper in a Chinese Federated Republic.[1] In May 1930 a conference of delegates from the soviet areas met and agreed on a document called the Ten Great Political Programs, in which item five gave minority nationalities the right to secede or federate.[2]

In November of the next year a

"Constitution of the Soviet republic," the so-called Kiangsi Constitution, was agreed upon. Closely modeled on the 1924 constitution of the USSR, it called for equality of nationalities, freedom of religion, and recognition of

... the right of self determination of the national minorities in China, right to complete separation from China, and to the formation of an independent state for each national minority. All Mongolians, Tibetans, Miao, Yao, Koreans and others living on the territory of China shall enjoy the full right to self determination, i.e., they may either join the Union of Chinese Soviets or secede from it and form their own state as they may prefer. The Soviet regime of China will do its utmost to assist the national minorities in liberating themselves from the yoke of imperialists, the KMT militarists, *t'u-ssu* [native officials], the princes, lamas and others, and in achieving complete freedom and autonomy. The Soviet regime must encourage the development of the national cultures and the national languages of these peoples.[3]

In sharp contrast to these documents, designed to appeal to the nationalistically minded and allay fears of assimilation, the earliest minorities converts to communism were in general highly assimilated and often from that very same decadent aristocratic class which the party sought to destroy. This apparent paradox is explained by the fact that knowledge of communism in China as a whole at this time was confined to a small urban elite. Early minorities communists were members of the same urban intellectual group that produced Han communists, and their ties to that group overrode ethnic considerations.

Children of families with the financial means and inclination to send their offspring to be educated in Peking or Moscow, these individuals tended to have weak ties to their own nationalities and to be of wealthy, or even noble, background. Often they were the sons of that hereditary elite that had cooperated with both imperial and republican governments. Outwardly they appeared little different from Han, and in fact it is probable that they did not see themselves as different in any significant way. Regarding China's problems as their own, they saw the victory of the Bolshevik party in Russia as a possible model for China, a view that was of course encouraged by the Soviet Union. Scholarships for the young leftists—typically they had not yet become Communists —were made available at such places as the University of the Peoples of the East and Sun Yat-sen University, and it was probably there that most of them, minorities and Han alike, made their first acquaintance with "the minorities problem" per se. On their return to China, they could be assigned to enlist support for the party among those of their ethnic group, utilizing an appeal to minority group feeling that they did not in fact share. Ironically, the party was in the position of promoting ethnic group feelings in order to bring about a system of government that was expected to hasten their demise.

The career of Ma Chün, the earliest-known Chinese Communist of minority nationality, illustrates well the pattern described above. Ma, a sinified Hui, was born in Kirin province in 1895. Since there are few concentrations of rural Hui outside the Northwest, it is probable that his family were, like most so-called "scattered Hui," urban merchants or craftsmen serving a Han community and well adjusted to its ways. While a student in Peking, Ma become a political activist and was a participant in the patriotic May Fourth movement. With Chou En-lai, he was a member of the leftist "Awakening Society" (*Chüeh-wu she*). Ma was also one of thirty-odd delegates from Peking and Tientsin chosen to present student grievances to warlord Hsü Shih-ch'ang, then head of the Peking government.

This much is fact. However, since the CCP has subsequently designated Ma as chief minority martyr to the cause of people's revolution, the more extravagant details of his biography become suspect. For example, Hsü Shih-ch'ang is said to have refused to see the students. Under Ma's leadership, the young people maintained a vigil on his front steps until Hsü, realizing their determination, agreed to admit two of them, of whom one was Ma. We are told that the forcefulness and eloquence with which Ma presented the students' petition so impressed Hsü that, speechless with admiration, he wired their instructions to the Paris Peace Conference.

Up to this time Ma appears to have been a leftist rather than a Communist. Soon thereafter he went to Moscow, where, "after long study and research," he became convinced that the solution to "the nationalities problem" and the liberation of the Hui was firmly bound up with the success of the proletarian revolution. On his return to China, he became influential in propagandizing patriotism among the Hui, holding meetings in mosques, and even getting the traditionally conservative clergy to participate. When Shantung police began shooting participants in patriotic demonstrations, presumably on the orders of provincial governor Ma Liang,[4] Ma Chün denounced the governor, a fellow Hui, as a traitor to his people. Later captured by secret police and tortured, he is alleged to have shouted to the passersby en route to his execution, "Hui and Han peoples arise, oppose imperialism and its running dogs the Chinese warlords," and "Only through the Communist party can China be saved!"[5]

The same pattern of recruitment can be seen in the case of the first Mongol converts to communism. Significantly, all were from Tumet Banner in southern Suiyuan, one of Inner Mongolia's more sinified areas. In 1923 four recent arrivals at the Mongolian and Tibetan School became attracted to the left-wing student movement. An introduction to Li Ta-chao, one of the founders of the CCP, was soon arranged, and by 1925 all had joined the party. Three of the group—Li Ta-chien,[6] Chi Ya-t'ai, and K'uei Pi—then returned to Suiyuan to begin agitation for a constituent assembly. Li took the lead in this work. The fourth, Yün Tse, was a Mongol prince whose family had received its noble title through allegiance to the Ch'ing. Despite this flawed class background and the fact that he was so sinified as to be unable to speak Mongolian, Yün Tse seems to have been singled out as especially promising and was sent to Sun Yat-sen University in Moscow. There he adopted the pseudonym Ulanfu,[7] under which he was to become famous.

Another student at the Mongolian and Tibetan School, Tê Wang,[8] was also a prince, but from the more northerly and less sinified Sunid Banner in Chahar. He was to become the leading anti-Communist Mongol. Since the Chinese Communists do not claim to have converted even a single Tibetan at the school, it may safely be assumed that they did not successfully recruit any.[9]

In 1924, in accordance with the policy set forth in the Theses on the National and Colonial Questions, a United Front had been established between the KMT and CCP. Its vehicle in Inner Mongolia was the Inner Mongolian People's Revolutionary Party (IMPRP), which had a military arm called the Inner Mongolian Revolutionary Army. Both were commanded by one Buyantai (Chinese name, Pai Yun-ti), yet another Mongol graduate of the Mongolian and Tibetan School.[10] A separate Communist party with its own military organization also existed, under the aegis of Li Ta-chien.[11] Under the terms of the Sun-Joffe Manifesto, members of the CCP could join KMT-sponsored organizations as individuals.

The alliance did not last long. According to the Communist version of the split, Buyantai, acting on Chiang Kai-shek's orders, carried out a purge in which Li Ta-chien and many other CCP members were murdered.[12] Another version has it that the Communist group, with Comintern support, planned a coup against Buyantai and other pro-KMT members of the Inner Mongolian People's Revolutionary Party and that Buyantai fled to Nanking in the dead of night to escape it. Having made his report to Chiang, he took up residence in Nanking. In the spring of 1928 warlord Feng Yü-hsiang moved against the IMPRP, attacking and disbanding both pro-Communist and pro-KMT factions alike.[13]

Whoever was responsible, the IMPRP effectively disintegrated, with the surviving Communists escaping from the area or continuing their work underground. How much was accomplished during this period is difficult to assess; clearly, however, a great deal of activity would arouse attention and increase the risks of detection. Nonetheless, the movement did not simply languish. Ulanfu's and K'uei Pi's organizing activities in Suiyuan led to their narrow escape to Yenan in 1937 with Fu Tso-yi's secret police at their heels.[14]

As for other early minority group recruits, Chao Pao-chung, of Pai nationality, was converted to communism while attending the prestigous Yunnan Military Academy, from which he graduated in 1923.[15] Chu Te-hai, the son of a well-to-do Korean family apparently native to Kirin province, is reported to have joined the Korean Communist Party in 1929 and to have become a member of the Chinese Communist Youth League a year later. After serving as secretary of a local league branch, he was sent to study in the Soviet Union. On returning to his home in the Yenpien area of Kirin, Chu made his fellow Koreans the focus of his propagandizing.[16]

Influence of the Long March and Yenan Periods

While young activists like Ulanfu and Chu Te-hai were contrasting the CCP's promise of self-determination with the KMT's alleged attempts at forcible assimilation, the vaunted privilege was quietly disappearing from party plans. Speaking at the Sixth Plenary Session of the Sixth Central Committee on November 6, 1938, Mao Tse-tung stated that Mongols, Hui, Miao, and "Fan" [17] were to be given equal rights with the Han. Their cultures, religions, and customs must be respected. Their peoples not only must not be forced to study the Han language and script, they must be encouraged to develop their own languages, cultures, and education. All would be given the right to administer their own affairs *while at the same time establishing a unified state together with the Han.*[18]

Though the CCP has never publicly mentioned what caused it to change its stand on the right of secession between 1931 and 1938, it seems probable that it was the experiences of the Long March. Having broken out of the tightening KMT encirclement of their Kiangsi Soviet, the CCP was at pains to avoid centers of KMT control on their flight north. This forced them into the inhospitable terrain often inhabited by minorities. Typically, the minorities did not live there by choice, but had been forced into the areas by Han colonization or invasion. Not surprisingly, many nourished a deep grudge against their expropriators and, fighting on their own terrain, proved to be formidable enemies. The comparatively small Communist group had no choice but to convince these peoples that they were Han of a different sort: not the greedy land thieves of past acquaintance, but the bearers of a new life of freedom and equality for all.

Party hagiography now depicts this aspect of the Long March as an unbroken series of triumphs for the Red Army, which is alleged to have been traveling north not to escape the KMT, as was actually the case, but in order to fight the Japanese. The minority nationalities are said to have welcomed the Red Army with open arms, begged them for deliverance from the rapacious KMT and/or Japanese bandits, and waited with bated breath for liberation. However, interviews given to Western journalists at Yenan soon after the Long March give quite a different impression. For example, in Yunnan the Marchers encountered the Yi (Lolo) [19] who, though primitive in most aspects, were skilled warriors and savage in their hatred of the Han. What may have proved the decisive factor between survival and annihilation was the presence of an ex-KMT officer, Liu Po-ch'eng, who had previously served in Yi areas and knew something of their language and customs. Knowing that Yi society was rent by blood feuds, Liu was able to persuade the leader of one faction that just as there were good Yi groups and bad, there were good Han groups and bad. He then argued that the Yi and Communists had a common cause in opposing the "bad" KMT faction. Liu and the chief concluded an alliance, very much on Yi terms, by drinking the blood of a chicken. Nym Wales quoted a participant in the Long March, Hsü Meng-ch'iu, as saying:

These Lolo were first class confiscators and we were not too much amused to find someone who could do this much better than ourselves. The whole body of troops was mobilized to hand over gifts to the Lolos to buy our way through, but the tribesmen were never satisfied and took more and more. They looked into the pockets of our soldiers and even pulled off their clothing very rudely. In fact they took everything portable that the Red Army had to spare. But we had no way to save our lives but to grin and forbear." [20]

Nonetheless, the Communists freely admitted that they were lucky to have escaped with their lives. A few Yi joined the Marchers, and the group passed through their territory safely.[21]

In eastern Tibet, also, the Communist group faced a hostile population. Here negotiations proved impossible, for the enemy[22] was nowhere to be seen. The inhabitants removed everything of use from their homes and disappeared with their possessions. They would snipe at the Long Marchers from a safe cover and roll rocks down upon them from mountain passes. Those who went to forage for food often never returned. Able to confiscate only a meager amount of vegetables from the natives' fields, the Marchers were ill equipped for their trek through the hazard-filled grasslands, and they even had to resort to hunting out and capturing the natives themselves in order to find guides through the terrain.[23] Ever since liberation, the CCP leadership, worried about preserving the *élan vital* of their cause, has used the experiences of the grasslands to illustrate the ennobling hardships of revolution to a generation of Chinese youth. A Caucasian missionary who was a long time resident of China wrote,

When I traveled along portions of their route on the plateau three years after their attempted passage, I saw the record of those losses. The trail westward from Sung-p'an was still plainly and unbrokenly marked by bones and skulls, white against the green grass. The upland meadows which they labeled empty and uninhabited normally support a good sized nomadic population, but the chiefs and warriors of those nomadic tribes told me how they shifted their camps by night and evaded every effort of the Chinese to make contact. Their evasion was successful enough to warrant the boast that they did not lose "even a single sick sheep," while the Chinese starved in their camps and dropped along the trail.[24]

The experience was so devastating that years later in Peking the Communist leaders still spoke of it with horror.[25]

At one point a large part of the Communist group was driven back from the grasslands and forced to remain at this spot for the duration of the winter. In apparently only one place did they manage to establish friendly relations with a Tibetan group, setting up the Po-pa Soviet and persuading a few natives to join the Long March.[26] Among them were Sang-chi-yüeh-hsi (Chinese name, T'ien Pao) and Cha-hsi-wang-hsü, soon to become important figures in minorities policy.

On finally reaching Kansu after severe loss of life and morale, the group was nearly wiped out by Hui cavalry.[27] Madame Chu Tê admitted what has been denied ever since: that the Red Army had not approached the Hui properly and had been unable to establish good relations with the masses.[28]

The survivors of this ordeal who arrived in Yenan had proved beyond the shadow of a doubt their ability to deal with crises, whether caused by nature, minorities, or the KMT. They had probably also come to a new understanding of the nationalities problem: that the minorities, if given a choice, would probably not choose to join China voluntarily. Perhaps then, it would be preferable to deny them that choice.

Though post-Kiangsi-period propaganda might have been interpreted as promising the right to secede, it was never again promised in the unequivocal language of the Kiangsi constitution. Edgar Snow, on a mid-1936 visit to the headquarters of a Hui training regiment, recalls seeing a poster advocating "realize the independent government of the Hui people." [29] Snow also noted, however, that the party promised to help the Hui to form an autonomous government.[30]

In December 1935, in the midst of the Long March, Mao Tse-tung issued an appeal to the people of Inner Mongolia to fight together with the Communists to "preserve the glory of the epoch of Genghis Khan, prevent the extermination of their nation, embark on the path of national revival, and obtain the freedom and independence enjoyed by peoples such as those of Turkey, Poland, the Ukraine and the Caucasus." [31] There being a great difference between the freedom and independence enjoyed by the Turks and the Poles on the one hand and the inhabitants of the Ukraine and Caucasus on the other—not to mention the situation under Genghis Khan—this statement was open to various interpretations.

Another factor in the decision to drop the right of self-determination may have been growing realization of the Soviet Union's designs on Sinkiang. Chang Kuo-t'ao, then a high-ranking figure in the CCP, has stated that the Long Marchers were not informed by the Soviet Union of its foothold in Sinkiang, and it has been suggested that this may have been done deliberately so that the CCP would not decide to settle there.[32] It is also known that Mao bitterly resented the separation of Outer Mongolia from China,[33] and, when finally apprised of the USSR's influence in Sinkiang, he may have felt that Stalin, from whom he had received precious little help in the past, might try to instigate a Mongolian-style secession in Sinkiang.

If further reasons for dropping the right of self-determination were needed, surely the establishment of Japanese-backed states in the so-called homelands of the Manchus and Mongols provided them. These states must have shown the inadvisability of making it any easier for an outside power to ally with a minority group in order to diminish the authority of the Chinese central government over what it considered its territory.

Taking all these factors into consideration, it must have seemed best to quietly discard the self-determination clause, which had probably been copied without much thought from the Soviet Union's constitution during a rather idealistic period that the party had long since outgrown. The phrase "self-determination," defined as "forming a union with the Han people on a voluntary basis," does reappear once more, in Mao's report to the party's seventh congress in 1945.[34] Ironically, however, Mao made this pronouncement at the same time that the CCP was energetically suppressing those minorities who had thoughts about independence. Party theorist Chang Chih-i admits that by 1940 the party was interpreting demands for independence or "narrow nationalism" as imperialist plots to use contradictions among China's nationalities to stir up dissension. To overcome this "tendency toward narrow nationalism" he suggests that a number of rights be granted to the minorities, including "let[ting] them manage their own internal affairs." [35] Note that the right to separate is not among them.

Even after they were safely ensconced in Yenan, the Communists still considered minorities relations to be of the utmost importance. In order to establish communications between their Shensi-Kansu-Ninghsia (Shen-Kan-Ning) Border Government and the Soviet Union and Mongolian People's Republic, from whom they hoped to obtain crucial supplies and ammunition, the Communists would have to secure passage through Hui and Mongol areas. Since the Hui were both the more numerous and the more militant of the two groups, establishment of good relations with them was considered a task of the first order.

Previous experiences on the Long March had shown that the establishment of good relations would not be easy. In addition, Liu Tzu-tan, original organizer of the base area before the group from Kiangsi arrived, had failed to convert more than a handful of Hui despite the existence of considerable unrest brought on by famine. One reason for Liu's lack of success may have been that he appealed to the Hui as general members of the downtrodden masses, and not with reference to what they regarded as their special status as Muslims.[36]

Lenin's policy of regional autonomy must have seemed eminently suitable for a situation in which some sort of concession short of separatism had to be made to Hui exclusivism. In view of oft-expressed Mongol desires for some sort of self-government, the policy was applicable to them as well. Thus the 1941 outline for the government of the Shen-Kan-Ning Border Region called for the setting up of Mongol and Hui autonomous areas and proclaimed the equal rights of minorities in government, economics, and culture. In accordance with these stipulations, Hui autonomous areas were set up in parts of Kuan-chung and Ting-pien hsien, and a Mongol area in Ch'eng-ch'uan hsien. A Nationalities Affairs Commission was set up by the Border Region government to handle problems arising in connection with the administration of the autonomous areas.[37]

Coupled with the policy of regional autonomy was that of the united front, which allowed not only peasants but religious figures and wealthier elements of the community to join forces with the party as well. Yang Ching-jen, originally a high *imam* (Muslim prayer leader) in Kansu province, was one of those attracted to communism by this policy. After joining the party he became chief of staff of a Hui cavalry brigade and held various posts in minorities work administration in the Shen-Kan-

Ning Border Region government. After 1949 he was to serve as a vice-chairman of the Nationalities Affairs Commission of the Chinese People's Republic and First Secretary of the Ninghsia Hui Autonomous Region's Party Committee.[38] Another Hui of upper-middle-class background, Ma Yü-huai, also joined the party in the mid 1930's and had an early career in party-backed Hui organizations in the Shansi-Chahar-Hopei (Chin-Ch'a-Chi) Border Region government. After 1949 he too became a vice-chairman of the central government's Nationalities Affairs Commission.[39]

The united front policy was expedient from many points of view. Religious figures, generally among the very few educated people of the area, were held in high esteem by the Hui community. Thus, winning them over would be an important step in winning over the population. Proven friendships with men of religion would also soften the image of militant atheism, which Muslims and many Lamaists found so distasteful. As for cooperation with landlords, the northwest was not seriously overpopulated, and land redistribution did not require drastic confiscation. Snow reports that in many areas the lands of resident landlords were not confiscated at all, but wasteland and land of absentee owners were reallocated, with occasional division of the better-quality land.[40] As befitted a united front, class enmity was diverted into anti-Japanese channels, a sentiment to which all classes, religions, and nationalities in the area could subscribe.

The initial step in the implementation of these policies was the capture by force in 1936 of the city of Yu Wang Pao in Ninghsia. The defending militiamen were given a dollar apiece by the victorious Red Army and sent home. Ma Hung-k'uei's defeated troops were given two dollars apiece and apparently some propaganda as well, since it is reported that several hundred of them decided to throw in their lot with the CCP.[41] Using Yu Wang Pao as a model for the implementation of their policies, the party began to expand outward. In recognition of Islamic exclusiveness, the Hui soldiers were allowed to remain as distinct units rather than being dispersed among units of the Red Army. The cadres of what would, it was hoped, become the nucleus of a Hui army were trained in a building containing the special baths customarily used by Muslims, and they were allowed special food to conform to the tenets of their faith.[42]

Among both Hui soldiers and Hui populace the CCP again proved its ability to exploit enemy weaknesses to the fullest extent. One of the most unpopular aspects of Ma Hung-k'uei's rule was the conscription system, under which all young men save the first son had to join the army. Conscripts' families were responsible for their sons' food, clothing, and firewood. Communist denunciations of this practice were vigorously seconded by the populace, who could hardly fail to contrast Ma Hung-k'uei's system with the CCP's own volunteer army. An effort was made to learn Hui customs, and orders issued accordingly that soldiers were not to:

enter the home of a Hui without his consent;
molest a clergyman or harm a mosque in any way;
say "pig" or "dog" before Hui;
ask Hui why they do not eat pork;
call Hui "small faith" and Han "big faith." [43]

The CCP was also able to take advantage of a Muslim doctrinal dispute to further its own ends. The base-area Muslims were divided into three sects: old, new, and modern. The modern sect advocated adoption of modern scientific knowledge, abolition of certain traditional ceremonies and customs, and the reduction of clerical power in the temporal sphere—all principles with which the Chinese Communists were heartily in agreement. The modern sect was, however, also favored by Ma Hung-k'uei. Thus, the party allied itself with the conservative old and new sects to oppose what it considered the greater enemy. [44]

Hui troops were indoctrinated, when possible, by Hui instructors. Discussion groups were held on the *Communist Manifesto*, the theory of class struggle, and Marxian analyses of the problems of the Hui. The armymen, having absorbed these lessons to the satisfaction of their instructors, then formed their own propaganda corps and went from house to house explaining CCP policies to the civilian population. The party's program promised abolition of all surtaxes, help in the formation of an autonomous Hui government, prohibition of conscription, cancellation of old debts and loans, protection of Islamic culture, religious freedom, help in the creation of an anti-Japanese Hui army, and help in unifying the Islamic peoples of China, Outer Mongolia, Sinkiang, and the USSR. [45]

There was much in this to appeal to Hui and little to which they could object, with the possible exception of the alliance against Japan. Though the population was certainly not pro-Japanese, China's struggle with Japan was utterly remote from the self-contained Hui world. Snow reports that almost no one he interviewed had ever seen a Japanese. A poster on the wall of a Red Army Lenin Club depicted the enemy as having an enormous nose, just as the Chinese generally caricature Caucasians. The chief value of the "anti-Japanese alliance" seems to have been to provide a raison d'être for Communist presence in the area at a time when the party was still too weak to implement the economic program that was its actual fundamental reason for being. Unable to make a frontal attack on the economic structure of the area, the CCP could ally with some of the structure's important elements under the united front program to do what it could while preserving the existence of the party. To the extent that communism was successful among the Hui, its chief appeals seem to have been due to the moderate economic reforms it was able to implement with the aid of cooperative members of the "upper strata" and to its support of Hui nationalism. Though the alliance against Japan was later to be used as the basis on which to build patriotism, it could not have been used to win the initial loyalty of a people who considered that their first loyalty belonged to Mecca and to whom Japan presented no threat. Conversely, party support of the Islamic unification movement could and did win converts. Chalmers Johnson's theory that the CCP's success during the Yenan period was due to its appeal to Chinese patriotism is clearly not applicable here.[46]

In terms of converting a large number of Hui, the CCP effort was not a success: the vast majority remained loyal to the Ma administration. Snow, normally most receptive to the party's point of view, opines that even those who cooperated with the CCP may have been doing so for their own purposes rather than sincerely accepting the ideology it taught.[47] The Hui, having received party help in forming their own government and army, could always turn against their mentors when it seemed advisable. However, numbers and sincerity of converts aside, the mere fact that the party could continue to survive in such initially hostile terrain could not be solely due to the presence of the Red Army and must be considered a success. That they were able to turn active hostility into even feigned enthusiastic cooperation in their immediate area is also to the party members' credit, as is their ability to take advantage of whatever opportunities existed to further their cause.

As for those members of minority nationalities who had joined the CCP on the Long March, they were entered in the Higher Party School founded at Yenan soon after the Reds' arrival there. Minorities numbered 33 of a total of 300 students and represented four nationalities: Tibetans, Mongols, Hui, and Yi. None of the Miao who had accompanied the Chinese Communists attended the school, which was restricted to party members. The regular curriculum included political economy, history of the Communist party of the Soviet Union, Leninism, problems of China, world politics, philosophy, dialectical materialism, mass work, and military training. Most of the minority students, however, because of their unusually low educational background, had a special class of their own and were limited to four subjects: romanization, Han language, "common sense political science," and natural science. This special class must not be regarded as an attempt at educational segregation. It simply reflects the fact that those minorities who had joined the CCP on the Long March came from an entirely different background than the sinified urban elite group which made up the bulk of earlier minorities' converts. Members of the later group had spent their lives in remote rural areas and, in addition, tended to represent the "have not" group of even their own communities.

No work was done in the minorities' own languages; the students first mastered the principles of romanization and then learned Chinese. According to Li Wei-han, then head of the school, none except the Yi, who were the most backward of the group, had any trouble with their language work. But, doubt is cast on their progress by Nym Wales' reports of the great difficulties involved in interviewing them. She recalls that although the men were most eager to talk, the interpreters could not understand them.[48]

The founding of the Nationalities Institute in September 1941 relieved the Higher Party School of this burden on its academic standards and provided minorities students with a school better suited to their needs. The avowed purpose of the Institute was to train nationalities cadres to implement the party's policies in their areas and to serve in the war against Japan. Han students as well were to be trained at the Institute, for eventual service in minorities areas.

In the first years of the school's operation, students, faculty, and staff together totaled nearly one hundred and included eight nationalities: Han, Manchu, Mongol, Hui, Tibetan, Miao, Yi, and Tunghsiang. The great majority of non-Han had either joined the Long March when it passed through their areas or were residents of the Shen-Kan-Ning area. A few Mongols had accompanied Ulanfu and K'uei Pi when they fled to Yenan; several others had been referred to the school by a Mongol "progressive personage" of Ikechao League in Suiyuan. Most of the Han were from Suiyuan also.

The original head of the Institute was Kao Kang, concurrently secretary of the party's Northwest Bureau and long a resident of that area. Ulanfu was head of the education department, and Liu Ch'un, a Han who had become prominent in united front work, was made head of the research department. In 1943 Liu replaced Kao Kang as director of the Institute, and Ulanfu became his assistant. Other faculty came from the party's Northwest Bureau, from the original cadre training school set up by Mao in 1924, and from a small college in north Shensi.

As originally set up in 1941, the Institute had three administrative divisions: education, research, and general affairs. The next year, in line with the party's policy of "fewer and better troops, simpler and more efficient administration," [49] the research department was turned into a research section under the education department. Since research work seems to have greatly expanded during this period, it is probable that the reduction and simplification achieved by this change was minimal. In addition to education and research functions, the education department had charge of registration records, the library, and an exhibition room. The general affairs department dealt with accounts, production statistics, and health work, in addition to having charge of the gymnasium.

The formal course of study was six years, divided into three grades of two years apiece. In practice, the plan was somewhat more flexible, with no rigid requirements for promotion or graduation. One was promoted when one's teachers felt that the required material had been mastered; there were few demotions. Graduation might occur abruptly when a certain student or group of students was needed for party work. Language competence was the most important requirement for passing from one level to the next. As in the party school, all instruction was in Han. This was undoubtedly because instructors versed in both nationality languages and Communist ideology simply were not available, rather than because the party wished to suppress the use of nationality languages.

The heart of the curriculum was political ideology; the unity of all nationalities under party rule was the basic message imparted throughout, even in basic language lessons. Students learned the importance of patriotism, internationalism, and Marxist-Leninist theory on the nationalities question. The party line on equality of nationalities, freedom of religion, mutual respect for nationalities customs, and opposition to both Great Han chauvinism and local nationalism was to be thoroughly absorbed by all students. Stalin's "Marxism and the National Question" was basic discussion material.

The last stage of the Institute's curriculum, the research class, was said to be on a level with the basic course at an average university. Here students were introduced to the systematic study of Marxist-Leninist theory, political economy, nationalities problems, historiography, problems of the Chinese revolution, and government policy. Teachers were instructed to relate the curriculum content to the students' actual lives, to socialist development, and to the war with Japan. Nonfaculty comrades were invited in from time to time as guest lecturers in their special fields. Research was done on three topics and in three areas: the history, economy, and sociopolitical situation of the Hui, Mongols, and southwestern minorities.

Students attended classes for over nine months each year, did productive labor for two months, and were given a "very short" vacation. The emphasis was on self-sufficiency. Students planted tomatoes and watermelons, spun cotton and wool, and made charcoal. They were provided with food, most articles of clothing, and a small amount of spending money.

Judging from the fact that the Yenan Institute's basic principles of organization were adopted by the network of nationalities institutes founded after 1949, and also from the number of Institute graduates who eventually attained important positions in minorities areas, its work was most successful.[50] The Institute was destroyed in 1947 when Chiang Kai-shek's troops captured Yenan, but not before it had, in Communist parlance, "fulfilled its historical duty." [51]

The Yenan period saw the application of Lenin's theory of regional autonomy to China's minorities, the extension of the united front policy to cooperation with minorities as groups (including so-called "progressive personages" of the upper strata of society), and the development of a system for educating cadres for service in minorities areas. Valuable experience had been gained in the techniques of mass work in these areas, and a start had been made on research to overcome the party's admittedly still abysmal ignorance regarding China's minorities. In his 1945 report to the Seventh Party Congress, Mao Tse-tung had high praise for the party's work with Mongols and Hui and stressed the importance of this work for future policy.[52]

What had been achieved at Yenan was essentially a working model for future enlargement, a project which it was hoped could be expanded. Not many years were to pass before these hopes were to be realized.

The Path to Victory

In 1943 a new mood of confidence became noticeable in the party-held areas. In retrospect, this optimism was not unjustified. The Yenan base area had been securely established, the tide had turned in favor of the Soviet Union in her war with Germany, and Japan had definitely been placed on the defensive in the Pacific. It was at this propitious moment that the Li nationality of Hainan Island staged an uprising against the KMT government, and a young party organizer named Feng Pai-chü began his rise to prominence.

The island of Hainan, situated off the southern coast of Kwangtung province, has been called one of the least developed and most neglected areas in China.[53] KMT control had been limited to a small area outside the major centers of populations and had only sporadically touched the mountainous interior, which was considered to be the preserve of the aborigines. The island was known to have had a Communist group since 1927, and Feng had been the leader of its guerrilla force since 1929. When Japan invaded the island in 1939, there was a mass movement of the coastal population inland, much to the distaste of the Li.[54] Heretofore spared the burden of tax collectors and colonists, they were not disposed to acquiesce gracefully. Their efforts at resistance seem to have been brutally dealt with by the Nationalists, and in July 1943, on the anniversary of the Nationalists' massacre of a group of Li in Pai-sha *hsiang,* a rebellion broke out. Generally referred to as the Pai-sha rebellion, it was led by Wang Kuo-hsing, a young Li who had been appointed a village "elder" by the KMT. One KMT hsien magistrate was killed and two hsien cities[55] captured before the rebels were finally defeated. The surviving insurrectionists retreated to caves in the interior to plan their next move.

Somehow, Wang Kuo-hsing and the Communist guerrillas managed to make contact. According to a 1957 reminiscence by Feng Pai-chü, Wang first dreamed that he was standing atop Hainan's most prominent landmark, Wu-chih Shan (Five Finger Mountain). There he saw five red clouds, in each of which a red flag was fluttering. He then noticed that the banners were being held by a troop of soldiers who were singing and beckoning to him to come join them. On waking, he told his comrades about the dream, and they recognized it as a manifestation of their mountain spirit. All knew of the existence of the Red Army and, being given this sign from the mountain spirit, resolved to go find the Communists. They quickly succeeded in this endeavor. In Feng Pai-chü's account, the Li representatives were brought to him by an armyman. They then fell to the ground, bowing and begging to join the Red Army.[56] In a less poetic version published in 1961, not Feng but the detachment leader who first encountered the Li spokesmen is given credit for guiding them into the Communist party.[57] The Li here are portrayed not as groveling suppliants but as dispassionately relating the KMT's atrocities and asking the Red Army's help in expelling them. The detachment chief is said to have commiserated with the Li on the failure of their uprising, which he said he had heard of, and then to have declaimed "Our Ch'iung-ya[58] People's Anti-Japanese Independence Army, formerly the Red Army, is the army of all the fraternal nationalities. Led by the Communist Party we shall certainly help you!" [59]

What would seem more likely is that the Communist guerrillas, having heard of the Li uprising, sensed the possibility of an alliance and sought out the Li. The 1961 version of the incident continues that party "higher levels" (surely Feng, though he, having been demoted during the antirightist campaign of 1957, is never mentioned by name) immediately dispatched a work team to the Li areas in order to "understand the situation, encourage the masses and become familiar with their behavior." This done, troops were sent to help the Li establish a base area. These men were strictly admonished to respect the party's nationalities policy at all times, since only by their conduct would the Li be able to judge the Communist party's trustworthiness. Though the party was not usually fortunate enough to find a rebellious and anti-KMT nationality anxious to form an alliance with them, this pattern of first sending in a People's Liberation Army (or PLA, as the Red Army was later called) work team to investigate the situation, then dispatching regular troops to help set up a base area (and, incidentally, to discourage resistance to the party's administration) was to become a model for future work at the basic level.

By the end of the civil war with the KMT, Feng had some 50,000 troops under his command, and an estimated 15,000 Li were participating in a widely publicized "Li column." This is thought to have been the largest single organized armed minority group serving in an officially recognized unit of CCP forces prior to the Communist victory.[60] Withal, the island was not liberated by the guerrilla group, but by an army from the mainland commanded by Lin Piao. This may have been due to the fact that since the KMT had used Hainan as an evacuation point for defeated troops from the mainland, a much larger liberating force was necessary.

In the spring of 1945, while this work of establishing a Li base area was proceeding, Ulanfu and several Mongol students were detached from the Yenan Nationalities Institute and sent to Inner Mongolia to resume the propaganda and agitation which had been broken off eight years before. The surrender of Japan in August introduced a new element of fluidity into the situation there. Most Mongols were agreed on the desirability of a single, united self-governing region and, with Tê Wang apparently an exception, agreed that the area would have to lean on one or another of the established powers for support. Pro-Soviet Union, pro-KMT, pro-Mongolian People's Republic, and pro-Chinese Communist factions existed. In addition, since there were remnants of the two separate Mongol governments that had existed under Japanese sponsorship, of the four provinces that had been created by the KMT government, and of the variety of league and banner governments that had existed under the Ch'ing system, administrative chaos was added to ideological confusion. Tê Wang, the most prestigious Mongol leader at this time, was in Peking under KMT surveillance.

The Soviet Union initially appeared to have the upper hand in eastern Mongolia, since it received the Japanese surrender at Kalgan. A "Provisional Government of the Inner Mongolian Republic" was set up under Soviet tutelage and with Buyantai, the same person who had carried out the "White Terror" in Mongolia fifteen years before, as head. When the Soviet Union withdrew from the area, it reportedly took with it several thousand Mongols, including Tê Wang's sons and one of his divisional commanders, for indoctrination. However, this left the Provisional Government in a weakened position. Ulanfu's group was able to move in, dissolve the Provisional Government, and set up a United Association of the Inner Mongolian Self-Government Movement. It was rumored that members of the Provisional Government were liquidated on Ulanfu's orders.[61] Despite this inauspicious beginning, Ulanfu's government, which advocated autonomy and abolition of the special rights of princes, proved relatively popular.

In western Inner Mongolia, a "Great Mongolian Republic" had been established with its capital at Wangyehmiao. The new government sent delegations to the KMT government, to the Mongolian People's Republic, and to the Chinese Communists to discuss terms. The KMT, consistent as ever, refused to accede to its demand for a single Mongol autonomous area and would not allow the delegation to proceed beyond Peking. The Mongolian People's Republic also reacted just as it had in 1928, receiving the delegation sympathetically but offering no help for fear of compromising its own independence. The Chinese Communists were able to offer both sympathy and the promise of a single autonomous area. Ulanfu himself went to Changte, capital of Jehol, to negotiate, and the Chinese Communist news agency subsequently announced that eastern and western Mongolian people's autonomy movements had been united. In April 1947, "since the masses had accepted the leadership of the Chinese Communist Party," an Inner Mongolian People's Congress was held in Wangyehmiao. During this congress Ulanfu, defeating "feudalistic upper-class elements"—whether by ballots or bullets was not made clear—emerged as leader, and the Inner Mongolian Autonomous Region (IMAR) was formally established.[62]

Mao Tse-tung's telegram of congratulations conveniently swept all ethnic and ideological differences under the rug of anti-Japanese imperialism. Praising the Mongolian people for the trials they had gone through with the Han in the war against Japan and for the victories they had achieved, he held forth a vision of "a bright future the Mongols would create for themselves in their own area, closely allied with the Han." [63] Here again, as with the Hui, was an attempt to create unity by attributing the Communist victory to an anti-Japanese alliance with people who had not in fact been anti-Japanese.

Despite the great popularity claimed for the new government, it would appear that the "feudalistic upper-class elements" routed by Ulanfu had been only temporarily defeated. Communist sources themselves admitted that the regional party and People's Government began immediately to "resolutely struggle" against traitors who were planning to establish "isolated self-government" and were advocating "neutrality and withdrawal from the civil war." [64] Barnett, writing in January 1948, reported a rumor that the IMAR was having a hard time maintaining stability and that Ulanfu's popularity had waned considerably.[65]

Nor did the new government, despite its title of Inner Mongolian Autonomous Region and its boast of having unified eastern and western Mongolian autonomy movements, control all of Inner Mongolia. Another independent government had been set up in northern Inner Mongolia by a man named Irkim Bator; it maintained its own currency and had diplomatic relations with both Ulanfu's government and the Mongolian People's Republic. Southwest of the IMAR's capital of Wangyehmiao, several groups of Alashan Mongols remained loyal to the KMT, and to the east the Barga Mongols, under their Soviet-oriented leader Hafengga, also resisted incorporation.[66]

The precise steps by which these holdouts were incorporated into the IMAR may never be known, but, generally speaking, the pattern was to combine a show of force with an offer to negotiate. Raids were carried out on the territory of a holdout area with an invitation to talk standing open. Arms for the separatists were in short supply, because the Soviet troops had disarmed the local populace in 1945–1946, and appeals to the KMT were generally unsuccessful, since Chiang Kai-shek feared that the guns might be used against his troops as well. Thus, the separatists usually eventually agreed to negotiate. Depending on the strength of one's bargaining position, the rewards could be considerable. Hafengga, who capitulated in January 1948, bringing the important Barga region under Communist control, was made a vice-chairman of the IMAR government. Sain Bayar (Pao Yüeh-ch'ing), Tê Wang's divisional commander who had been taken to Moscow for indoctrination, became a deputy chairman of Cherim League. Temourbagan, Moscow-educated former chairman of the Japanese-backed Hsingan government, became chief justice of the IMAR People's Court. Missing no chances, Ulanfu also conducted negotiations with Tê Wang.[67] Though the exact details of these negotiations are not known, Ulanfu must have offered Tê Wang, then a leader of much greater stature than himself, some sort of position in the IMAR government, and Tê Wang must have refused.

While the bargaining proceeded, stabilization of Communist rule in Inner Mongolia was being greatly helped by the gradual withdrawal of KMT troops under General Fu Tso-yi from the civil war. Fu, who had been badly treated by Chiang Kai-shek, surrendered Kalgan to the Red Army without a fight and withdrew his armies toward Peking. In January 1949, after more than a month of secret negotiations with the Communists, Fu announced his decision to join with them. A considerable part of Inner Mongolia was thus bounded on the east and south by Chinese-Communist-held areas. In addition, troops once used to march on Peking could now be employed in support of the IMAR. The Mongolian People's Republic and Soviet Union had already shown themselves unwilling to provide help to its opponents.

Ulanfu was to face one last contest with his long-term adversary, Tê Wang. The latter suddenly reappeared in the Alashan area, and by mid-August 1949 he had established an independent anti-Communist state with its capital at Tingyuanying (then a part of Ninghsia province). The KMT voiced support for the new republic and announced that its foreign affairs and defense would be controlled by the Nationalist government.[68] It would thus seem likely that the KMT, in a belated burst of creative thinking, had backed Tê Wang's venture as a last-ditch effort to prevent the complete communization of Inner Mongolia.

But the defection of General Tung Ch'i-wu, governor of neighboring Suiyuan, in late September sealed the new "nation's" fate. The Alashan government was soon conquered by his units,[69] and Tê Wang fled to the Mongolian People's Republic. He was later returned to the Chinese Communist government and imprisoned, thus attaining the dubious distinction of being incarcerated by both the KMT and CCP governments.[70] In order to reduce Tê Wang's popularity, the party mounted an energetic denunciation campaign in which he was accused of being a traitor to his people and held responsible for nearly all the misfortunes to befall Mongolia during the preceding two decades. However, possibly because it was deemed foolish to create a martyr to the cause of Mongolian nationalism, Tê Wang himself was not harmed. He was formally pardoned in 1963.[71]

Thus, despite the IMAR's formal creation in 1947 and the existence of a well-organized Chinese-Communist-oriented core group, Inner Mongolia was secured for the party only at the time of the Communist conquest of China as a whole. Still, it would be erroneous to assume that Inner Mongolia's coming under CCP control was simply a consequence of the CCP victory in China proper. A large part of the party's success in Mongolia was undoubtedly due to Ulanfu's ability to organize negotiations as well as military strategy, and to his knowledge of which to use in a given situation.

Fu Tso-yi's defection had also cut off Nationalist access to the Northwest. First to be affected were the Hui areas under governors Ma Hung-k'uei and Ma Pu-fang, both of whom had relied heavily on KMT-supplied ammunition and war materiel. Now dependent on what little could be brought in by former U.S. General Clair Chennault's Civil Air Transport, the two governors faced the choice of allowing their supplies to dwindle steadily or taking some decisive action to alleviate their situation. With the Communist capture of Sian, capital of neighboring Shensi, they apparently decided on the latter course and moved their armies out of their home provinces. The combined Ma attack was repulsed in late June,[72] and a few weeks later the Communist *Liberation Daily* announced a major offensive against Ma Hung-k'uei.[73]

In preparation for this assault on the Muslim belt, the Red Army received lectures on behavior and speeches on advancing the party's policies and on the importance of gaining the support of minority peoples. Ten rules of behavior had to be memorized. These were an expanded version of the five rules Edgar Snow had noted, reflecting several years of sometimes bitter experience in the Ninghsia border areas. Soldiers were warned never to mention the word pig or ask Muslims why they did not eat pork. They were not to watch Muslim religious ceremonies or to make a noise nearby. No one was to paste propaganda posters on mosques or to throw ritually polluted water back into a Muslim well. In Muslim homes, soldiers were never to smoke, drink wine, or eat pork, mule meat, or unblessed mutton or beef. No one was to speak to young Muslim women, bathe in a Muslim bath house, or use derogatory words for Muslim.[74]

At the end of August 1949, after six weeks of bitter fighting, Lanchow, the capital of Kansu, fell to Communist forces. This was a major victory in both psychological and strategic terms. Access had been gained to the important Kansu corridor with its oil fields at Yümen and easy passage to Sinkiang. The Ma armies' supplies had been dwindling steadily, and the capture of Lanchow made them still more difficult to obtain. In addition, the defeated army of Ma Hung-k'uei had retreated east toward its home province of Ninghsia, while that of Ma Pu-fang had withdrawn westward toward its base at Sining, capital of Ch'inghai. The Communists had thus divided the two forces. Realizing their desperate plight, the two Mas left the Northwest to plead in vain for support from Chiang Kai-shek.

It soon became clear that the capture of Lanchow had broken the back of Hui resistance. Sining, its defenders short of ammunition and backed up against mountains that left little scope for maneuver or retreat, surrendered less than a week later.[75] The young Nationalist candidate for Panchen Lama fled from his monastery near Sining and appealed for a military escort to take him across the mountains to Tibet.[76] Since it would have been next to impossible to fulfill this request, he too soon came under Communist control.

After the fall of Sining, Ma Pu-fang announced his withdrawal from the civil war and his plans to make a pilgrimage to Mecca.[77] Ma Hung-k'uei, suffering from severe diabetes and with virtually no supplies, managed to hold out until the end of September, when his brother and chief lieutenant Ma Hung-ping surrendered with a majority of the Ninghsia troops. Ma Hung-ping was rewarded with a post in the Northwest Military and Administrative Commission (NWMAC), which the Communists subsequently established.[78] The remaining troops, commanded by Ma Chi-yuan, eldest son and heir apparent of Ma Pu-fang, fell back into the Kansu corridor and staged a heroic attempt to stem the Communist advance. Though reportedly a brilliant tactician and idolized by his troops, Ma could do little more than slow down the Red advance. The Yümen oil fields were in Communist hands by early October and the way to Sinkiang open.

The Nationalist government had been aware from the beginning of the isolation of the Northwest caused by Fu Tso-yi's surrender. Within days of his capitulation it was announced that General Chang Chih-chung[79] would go to Tihwa (Urumchi) for talks with the Soviet Union. While Chang at his departure from Nanking airport would say only "you remember Sheng Shih-ts'ai's treaty with the Soviet Union," unofficial KMT sources elaborated a plan, said to have been devised by Chang, which would offer the Soviet Union sweeping concessions in the Northwest. A treaty between the Nationalist government and the Soviet Union granting the latter desired privileges in northwest China would pit Soviet against Chinese Communists and increase the bargaining power of the Nationalists. The Nationalists apparently believed that Stalin's fear of Mao's becoming a "Chinese Tito," plus the potential strength of his government in ruling a unified China, would make the Soviet Union more willing to deal with a weaker Nationalist state than a stronger Mao.[80]

Judging from the speed with which negotiations were set up, the KMT contention had been correct. The exact extent of the concessions offered to the Soviet Union is not known. Some rumors said they included the entire Northwest—Sinkiang plus the Muslim belt areas of Kansu, Ninghsia, and Ch'inghai—others, that they concerned Sinkiang only. The latter appeared more plausible, particularly considering the historic ties of the Muslim belt to China and the fanatic anticommunism of its Hui population. Although the Uighurs and Kazakhs of Sinkiang were Muslims also, the influence of their ties to fellow Turkic peoples in the Soviet Union and their less rigid practice of Islam seem to have diluted their abhorrence of communism's atheistic materialism.

Though the talks were secret, unofficially "leaked" information revealed that the Nationalists had offered the Soviet government a:

1. forty- to fifty-year mining monopoly in Sinkiang;
2. trade monopoly in Sinkiang;
3. virtual air monopoly through a joint Sino-Soviet airline.[81]

The Nationalist government proposed, however, that all ventures be staffed by an equal number of Chinese and Soviet nationals. Since this, as KMT officials privately confirmed, was precisely the situation that already obtained—except in the airline, where most personnel were already Soviet nationals—the Soviet Union refused to agree. Negotiations became stalemated while competing factions in the KMT government bickered over how much to concede to the Soviet Union. Meanwhile, Chang Chih-chung became increasingly impatient for permission to settle the terms of an agreement, and the Chinese Communists continued their stunning military successes. Finally, with the Mas, who had provided a buffer for Sinkiang, utterly defeated and Chinese Communist troops advancing quickly, the Sinkiang provincial government, including the East Turkistan group, Nationalist garrison commander T'ao Chih-yüeh with 60,000 troops, and Chang Chih-chung himself, issued a declaration of loyalty to Mao Tse-tung.[82]

These actions did not go unrewarded. Burhan, the KMT-appointed governor of Sinkiang, became governor of Sinkiang under the Chinese People's Republic, and T'ao Chih-yüeh was only slightly demoted, becoming deputy commander of the Sinkiang Military District. Saifudin was sent to Moscow to help negotiate the Sino-Soviet Treaty. The anti-Chinese riots that he had been instrumental in fomenting could, after all, be explained as anti-KMT government rather than anti-inclusion in a Han Chinese state. While Saifudin was in Moscow, it was announced from Peking that he had resigned from the Communist party of the Soviet Union and been accepted as a member of the CCP.[83] The other leaders of the former East Turkistan Republic were killed in a mysterious plane crash on their way to attend the Chinese People's Political Consultative Conference (CPPCC) in Peking. News of the crash was not made public until many months later, leading to speculation that the CCP had arranged a convenient way to rid itself of a potentially troublesome group. While not totally implausible, this allegation ignores the fact that the party had made peace with others who had equal potential for causing trouble, but who remained perfectly healthy and accident-free.

What is more significant is that whereas Inner Mongolia, which had a substantial native CCP-oriented group, had been won by the party only after four years of bitter fighting, Sinkiang, with no native Chinese-Communist-oriented group worthy of note, surrendered without a fight. The explanation for this discrepancy lies, of course, in the deterioration of the KMT's power position between the founding of the IMAR and the capitulation of Sinkiang. There is a common denominator in the CCP's route to power in the two areas: a crucial factor in the party's success in both was the KMT's insistence on bargaining as if it possessed power, which it did not in fact have. Unwilling to agree to autonomy for Inner Mongolia, it pushed that area toward the CCP, which was willing to grant autonomy. Unwilling to grant to the Soviet Union more concessions than that power already possessed, the Nationalists lost their position in Sinkiang as well. Dissatisfied with half the loaf, the KMT ended up with nothing at all.

While these developments were taking place in the Northwest, the conquest of the South was proceeding. The Red Army crossed the Yangtze River in April 1949 and continued its sweep southward. With each CCP success, Governor Lu Han of Yunnan became more concerned to assert his independence of the KMT, and he was urged by his half brother Lung Yun to take the final step and declare his allegiance to Mao Tse-tung. However, each time Lu seemed to be on the verge of doing so, Chiang Kai-shek was able to send troops to Yunnan to "persuade" Lu to remain in the KMT fold. The universities would then be closed for rectification, some members of the provincial government purged as leftists, and a campaign to root out local Communists would begin. After a short period of enforced calm, during which Communist elements were officially declared nonexistent, guerrilla bands and student demonstrators would spring up again, and Lu would again move toward establishing relations with the CCP.[84]

This comic opera lasted until mid-December 1949, when the KMT was too weak to exercise persuasive tactics and CCP personnel began to arrive to supplement Yunnan's local guerrillas. Lu Han's declaration of allegiance to Mao followed soon after. He was appointed acting governor of Yunnan's new Communist administration, and Lung Yun was named a member of the Government Affairs Council (forerunner of the State Council) and a vice-chairman of the Southwest Military and Administrative Commission (SWMAC).[85]

Of the remaining minority areas, Kwangsi, under the control of generals Li Tsung-jen and Pai Ch'ung-hsi, was considered most important. The generals' armies, numbering over 200,000 men, were not used to full potential because of Chiang Kai-shek's persistent attempts to undercut their power. Li Tsung-jen had been elected vice-president of the KMT government in April 1948 over Chiang's opposition and later became acting president, when Chiang resigned after Fu Tso-yi surrendered Peking to the CCP. Both Li and Pai, though unequivocally anti-Communist, were also substantially independent of Chiang Kai-shek, and Chiang was anxious that they not become even more so, even at the cost of reduced effectiveness against the Red advance.

The Kwangsi forces, having been refused supplies by Chiang, were forced progressively south, eventually retreating to Hainan or into Indochina. In the latter case, they were disarmed by the French. Pai Ch'ung-hsi attempted to secure aid from Chiang Kai-shek for the starving remnants of his troops on Hainan, but it was not forthcoming. Attacked simultaneously from behind by Feng Pai-chü's guerrillas and from the mainland by Lin Piao's forces, the demoralized group soon surrendered.[86]

It was at first envisioned that a token segment of the KMT government and forces that had retreated from Sining, briefly the capital of the peripatetic Nationalist government, would take refuge in Sikang in order to argue that at least a part of the Nationalist government remained on the mainland. The defection of the Sikang governor, Liu Wen-hui, made this rather difficult, however,[87] and the CCP's New China News Agency (NCNA) subsequently announced that the token group had fallen into a trap on the way to Ya-an.[88] On December 31, 1949, the final conquest of China except for Taiwan and Tibet was proclaimed. The capture of Sikang had opened the way to Tibet.

The Chinese Communists did not march on Tibet immediately, but stopped at Sikang in December. Meanwhile, their mass media repeatedly stated the Chinese claim to possession of Tibet. Those periods of history when China actually did exercise some control over the area were carefully documented; the periods when it had not were conveniently ignored. However, nothing was done to make the claim effective. This failure to back up words with immediate deeds may be traced to several causes.

First, army supply-lines were badly overextended. Nationalist troops had retreated so quickly during the latter half of 1949 that Communist forces were hard pressed to keep up with them. Some soldiers jokingly referred to this as "the battle with the feet." Second, it was winter and the mountainous, highway-less approaches to Tibet, difficult under the best of circumstances, would be nearly impassable now. Lack of food supplies and warm clothing would have made the undertaking still more hazardous.

Third, the Korean War had just begun, and China, already ravaged by war for many years, had to allocate limited resources where the need seemed most urgent. Time seemed to be on the Chinese side in Tibet to a greater extent than in Korea. Fourth, the international status of Tibet was at best uncertain. Chary of Western intervention, the CCP had no desire to provoke a military confrontation with a foreign power, particularly when its rule had not yet been consolidated domestically.

Finally, there was not a single Communist party member in Tibet proper.[89] There were no guerrilla bases to link up with and few who could advise the party on how best to proceed.

On the other hand Tibet, already de facto independent for forty years, had recently formally declared its independence. Simultaneously it cut the telegraph line to China and expelled the Nationalist representative with his wireless set. The Tibetan army, which had been allowed to de-

teriorate since the death of the thirteenth Dalai Lama in 1933, began
to drill again. Arrangements were made to send "trade missions" abroad
to ascertain how much help Tibet could expect in support of its independence. The initial mission was unable to proceed to Hong Kong,
since Britain feared for its colony's continued existence and had no desire to provide the Chinese with a *casus belli*, but the message was clear
to Peking. From this point of view, the sooner Tibet was brought under
Chinese Communist control, the better.

Radio Peking began a massive propaganda barrage in which the
Tibetan government was informed that its declaration of independence
had been forced by British and American imperialists who had infil-
trated the country. With the exception of a short visit by U.S. explorer-
journalist Lowell Thomas, there were, however, apparently no Americans in Tibet. According to Robert Ford, there were only three Britons,
one of whom had become a Tibetan citizen many years before. In poor
health, he left for India, where he died soon afterward. Of the remaining two, Ford had been assigned by the British army to train Tibetan radio operators. While possibly not a spy in the conventional sense of the
word, all Britons in Tibet were ipso facto imperialists in Chinese eyes,
and Ford's actions were clearly designed to help Tibet retain its independence. The third Englishman, a nineteenth-century-style missionary
named, appropriately enough, Bull, was identified by NCNA as an
Englishman in the Tibetan army.[90]

This paucity of resident imperialists notwithstanding, a Chinese car-
toon depicted John Bull on the Indian side of the border with a scarf
draped over his arms in the traditional Tibetan gesture of greeting.
Beneath the scarf, his clawed hands were poised to seize Tibet. From
the Chinese side of the border a stalwart PLA man raised his rifle in de-
fiance.[91]

Chinese mass media assured Tibetans that there was no cause for
alarm, however, since the People's Liberation Army would soon drive
the imperialists out of Tibet, which would then rejoin the ancestral
land. Tibetan "democratic personages" were summoned to a widely publicized meeting in Peking, which dutifully repeated the party line on
liberation.[92] Typically, these were elderly scholars who had been studying Buddhism in Peking under a system established by the Ch'ing. Often
they or their monasteries had received subsidies from Ch'ing and republican governments in order to create good will with Tibet. Whatever
their views on godless communism, these men could hardly object to a
political relationship between the government of China and Tibet, and
their knowledge of their people and willingness to echo the party line
were to prove of great use to the CCP.

For the present, however, the People's Liberation Army settled down in eastern Sikang and made preparations. Eastern Sikang was Khamba territory,[93] and here again the CCP showed its mastery of the skill of exploiting existing dissensions. The Pangda brothers, exceedingly wealthy Khamba traders who regarded eastern Tibet almost as their private fief, proved willing to negotiate with the Communists, while also sending one of their number to negotiate with the Lhasa government. Though the respective bargaining positions have remained a well-guarded secret, it would seem probable that the Pangdas offered the support of their private Khamba army to both sides in return for some degree of privileges for themselves. The Pangda brother sent to Lhasa was apparently still en route there when the PLA attack came.

In October 1950, just as the Tibetans had concluded that the arrival of winter[94] would protect them for another year, PLA troops crossed the Chin-sha River and marched on Chamdo. Ford, an eyewitness, reported that Tibetans greeted the horrifying news with a veritable frenzy of prayer and not much else.[95] Ngapo Ngawang Jigme, a high-ranking noble and minister who had been transferred from Lhasa to eastern Tibet (primarily to remove him from the capital because of his agitation for cabinet reforms) was appointed to head the Tibetan force opposing the PLA. The mainly Khamba army, though outnumbered five to one, apparently fought well. The PLA claimed victory only after nine days of fighting, including twenty engagements, and did not release its casualty figures.[96]

Ngapo Ngawang Jigme was captured and seems to have become convinced of the correctness of the CCP cause from that moment on. Ford reported that Ngapo had considered trying to fight the PLA futile from the beginning, but that Lhasa had refused him permission to surrender.[97] While it is possible to contend that Ngapo's sudden conversion was a result of his pique at the Lhasa government, Ford describes him as extremely anxious to avoid being captured by the PLA, and the resistance put up by his troops was apparently genuine. Rather than arranging a sham battle to cover his defection, it would seem that Ngapo, having been captured, decided to make the best of an unenviable position. In any case, he instantly became Tibet proper's first and leading party sympathizer.

With the main force of his army defeated and its commander a prisoner, the Dalai Lama and part of his government fled south to Yatung. Located near the tip of a triangle of land wedged between Sikkim and Bhutan, the town was an ideal spot from which to flee the country if that became necessary. The way was now clear for the PLA's march on Lhasa. However, still anxious to avoid making Tibet an international issue while wishing to consolidate its position there as soon as possible, the Peking government suggested negotiations. The defeated Lhasa government had little choice but to accept not only the Chinese offer but the conditions attached thereto.

The Dalai Lama's government, assuming that negotiations would be held in eastern Tibet, dispatched five high officials to Chamdo to assist Ngapo, whose "conversion" it did not yet suspect.[98] However, the party insisted on holding the talks in Peking, which was a definite psychological advantage for it, and on including several other groups in the negotiations. In addition to the five representatives sent by the Lhasa government, Tibet was represented by several high-ranking prisoners captured at Chamdo, Khambas representing the "Chamdo Liberation Front," a group from the Provisional People's Government that had been set up in Tibetan areas of Ch'inghai, and a delegation representing the Panchen Lama. In complete agreement as to what it wanted and with the military situation overwhelmingly in its favor, the Chinese side presented its disparate opposition with a Ten Point Draft Agreement.[99] According to the Dalai Lama, his delegation refused to accept the draft and argued at some length that Tibet was an independent state. The Chinese side then revised the draft to a Seventeen Point Agreement, which it presented to the Tibetan side as an ultimatum. Refusal to sign would mean violence, both to the persons of the delegates and in the form of military actions against Tibet.[100] While there is no independent corroboration of the Dalai Lama's story, parts of the Seventeen Point Agreement released by NCNA did read like an ultimatum. Such statements as this—"The Local Government of Tibet did not oppose imperialist deceptions and provocations but adopted an unpatriotic attitude towards the great socialist motherland. Under such conditions the Tibetan nationality and people were plunged into the depths of enslavement and suffering" [101]— would hardly have been agreed to by the representatives of the Tibetan government except under duress.

Briefly, the agreement proclaimed Tibet an integral part of China and charged the Lhasa government with welcoming the PLA's entrance into Tibet in order to consolidate the national defense. The Central People's Government would henceforth be in charge of Tibet's external affairs, and the Tibetan army would be integrated into the PLA. The Lhasa government agreed to accept the KMT-CCP candidate for Panchen Lama and to cease its support of the claimant it had previously sponsored. In return, Tibet would be given internal autonomy, its people's livelihood would be improved, and the existing political system would remain, as would the established status, functions, and powers of the Dalai Lama. Officials might remain in office provided that they did not engage in sabotage or resistance. The Central People's Government would not use compulsion to implement reforms, and the PLA promised to be fair in buying and selling.[102]

The agreement was signed on May 23, 1951, and released by NCNA four days later. By this step, the last important[103] minority area was brought under Chinese Communist control.

In sum, Chinese Communist minorities policy as it developed prior to liberation encompassed the equality of nationalities, the right to autonomy within a unified state, a united front with nationalities upper-class and religious personages who were willing to be cooperative, respect for nationality forms, the right to education in one's native language, and the development of a better standard of living for all.

This scheme used Soviet policy as a model, tempering it with the party's experiences in minorities work. Clauses that did not seem suitable, such as the theoretical right of secession, were quietly discarded as incompatible with the concrete situation in China. At the same time, the Chinese Communists were able to profit from knowledge of KMT mistakes in handling minorities' problems—for example, the enmity aroused among some minority groups by referring to them as "tribes." Indeed, Soviet and Nationalist Chinese policies toward ethnic minorities are on many points so antithetical that it is difficult to ascertain whether the Chinese Communists were reacting positively to the Soviet model or negatively to Nationalist practice. The issue of autonomy, vigorously championed by the Soviet and Chinese Communist parties, is one example of this. Another is the right of minorities to be educated in their own languages, which was generally opposed by the KMT and supported by Soviet and Chinese communists. The Soviet, specifically Stalinist, view on achieving a "drawing together" of nationalities by encouraging the development of their diverse cultures and languages was also adopted by the CCP, in contradistinction to the KMT's emphasis on assimilation.

However, despite this attractive-sounding, carefully developed, and eminently reasonable policy, the preceding account of the process by which minority areas were brought under Chinese Communist control shows that it was not the party's policy that brought it to a position of preeminence in minorities areas. Rather, it was a case of clear-cut military victories in Han areas, leaving minorities leaders isolated and with no choice other than negotiations, which might allow them to retain at least part of their former powers, or a fight to the end, which would almost certainly result in the loss of everything. The CCP, having only a small minority-group membership and seemingly genuinely afraid of "imperialist encroachments" in the border areas where most minority nationalities lived, was inclined to negotiate, as were many minority-group leaders and erstwhile KMT administrators in minority areas. Those who resisted the inevitable, such as Osman Bator and Tê Wang, or who were thoroughly unacceptable to the people because of corruption and/or past cruelties, were removed by force. But in general a strenuous effort was made to persuade the traditional elite to cooperate. It would seem probable that many who did choose to cooperate did not believe that the party's promises to them would be honored, but felt that behaving as if the promises would be kept was the best of several unattractive alternatives.

It now remained for the party to implement its policy statements in a manner that would win the loyalties of their intended constituency—or, as Mao Tse-tung might phrase it, to reconcile theory and practice.

5

The Early Years, 1949–1955

Communist victory over the KMT secured, party policymakers turned their thoughts toward postrevolutionary planning. Insofar as this concerned minority areas, planning was conditioned by a number of factors, foremost among which were:

1. a desire to adapt Soviet policy to the Chinese milieu while remaining within the bounds of Marxist-Leninist orthodoxy;
2. a perceived need to differentiate party policy from that of the KMT as much as possible;
3. awareness of the tenuous nature of their position in most minority areas;
4. a keenly felt lack of knowledge of conditions in many minority areas.

The presence of these factors seemed to militate against precipitous action and, as at Yenan, led to an interpretation of Marxism-Leninism that saw a gradual, unforced "growing together" of nationalities under socialism. The hard-line Marxist approach, that nationalism is merely a manifestation of bourgeois consciousness and Mao Tse-tung's extrapolation thereof, that all national struggle is in reality simply class struggle, were never actually discarded; their implications were conveniently ignored.

Legal and Administrative Changes

To ease this process of growing together, minorities were to be encouraged to develop their own spoken and written languages and to take pride in their history and cultures. Though the right to independence was not granted, minorities were given the right to autonomous government. In language strikingly similar to that used by the Soviet Union at a comparable stage in its formation, a *Jen-min jih-pao* editorial of October 2, 1951, declared that "At this point, any nationality movement which seeks to separate from the Chinese People's Republic (CPR) to become independent is reactionary since, objectively considered, it would undermine the interests of the various nationalities, and hence would work to the advantage of imperialism."

There were, then, limits to autonomy. However, no precise delineation of these limits was made at this time. The meaning of autonomy was to remain ambiguous until the promulgation of a General Program for the Implementation of Regional Autonomy in 1952.[1]

Under the rubric of the New Democracy, a united front of cooperation with "patriotic bourgeois nationalities upper strata," as with similar groups in Han areas, was proclaimed. Concessions made to members of the upper strata of minority nationalities were, however, more marked than those made to Han in comparable positions. The official rationalization for this preferential treatment was that minority nationalities had "special characteristics," among which were economic and political backwardness. The latter was believed to manifest itself in poorly developed class differentiation. Thus the party's theme of class struggle must be muted in minority areas in accordance with their level of development. Political education would have the inculcation of a spirit of patriotism and unity of nationalities as its main goal. Economically, an effort would be made to help the minorities catch up with the Han "big brother," and, culturally, minorities would be assisted in developing their respective languages, literatures, and folk arts.

Not surprisingly, political goals were deemed most important, and the promotion of unity and patriotism became the cornerstone of the party's minorities policy during these early years. The period of growing together was envisioned as a long one, with reforms being made gradually "in conformity with the wishes of the masses."

This moderate policy had the virtues of differentiating the party sharply from the KMT's blatant assimilationism and of minimizing the possibilities of resistance in areas in which party control was weak and its ignorance of local customs potentially dangerous. However, encouragement of minorities' "special characteristics" and tacit approval of their social structures might produce an effect the very opposite of that desired: the strengthening and perpetuation of minority separateness rather than its gradual erosion. While policy planners could not have been unaware of this possible contradiction in their thinking, the probability of its adverse consequences was played down. This seemingly unwarranted optimism perhaps stemmed from their Marxist faith that the desired unity was inevitable in the course of historical evolution. Through the ingenious escape clause "conditions not yet ripe," the party was able to bridge the gap between the theory that all national struggle is actually a matter of class struggle and the practice of a gradualist policy toward China's minorities.

The basic outline of this policy can be seen in those articles of the Common Program passed by the Chinese People's Political Consultative Conference (CPPCC) on September 29, 1949, relevant to minorities. Proclaiming the equality of all nationalities of the CPR both as to rights and to duties, it also reaffirmed the indivisibility of their territories from the ancestral land.[2] A system of regional autonomy was provided for in areas where national minorities were concentrated, with the level of the autonomous organs involved to depend on the population and size of a given region. Minorities were to be guaranteed a number of representatives on government bodies proportional to their percentage of the population in the area involved.[3]

Minorities' freedom to develop dialects and languages and to preserve and reform their customs, habits, and religious beliefs was also guaranteed, and the People's Government charged with the task of helping the minorities masses to "develop their outlook on politics, economics, culture and education." [4] The CPPCC also set up the Government Administration Council (GAC), forerunner of the State Council, which in turn created, among other bodies, a Nationalities Affairs Commission (NAC).

In nationalities work, as in other matters, government agencies received direction from, and interacted with, party organs. The party organization most closely concerned with minorities work was the United Front Work Department (UFWD) of the Party Central Committee. Originally set up in Yenan in 1944, the UFWD, before as well as after liberation, was responsible for shaping the broad outlines of policy in minority areas in accordance with the party line. It was also in charge of other aspects of united front work concerned with the implementation of the People's Democratic Dictatorship, which Mao had deemed appropriate for China in this transition period from New Democracy to socialism.[5] Li Wei-han, appointed head of the UFWD in 1944 at its founding, retained his post after 1949. United Front Work departments also existed as parts of the party apparatus on the provincial level. At lower levels where no UFWD existed, the Rural Work Department of the local party might fill the task of political guidance of minorities.[6]

On a central government level, broad guidelines from the UFWD were sent to the Nationalities Affairs Commission, which had responsibility for implementing them. Major pronouncements on minorities affairs were drawn up by the commission, then approved and promulgated by the GAC. The Nationalities Affairs Commission was then charged with implementing them. The commission also handled more routine business concerned with minorities affairs. Despite its subordination to the UFWD, the NAC, meeting every day and functioning much as would a regular ministry, had considerable powers. As defined by an organic law of February 22, 1952, these included:

1. execution of the nationalities affairs policies formulated by the CPPCC and enforcement of State Council regulations and decisions on nationalities affairs;
2. supervision and evaluation of the regional autonomy policy for minority nationalities;
3. development of political, economic, and cultural programs for minority nationalities;
4. strengthening of the unity of minority nationalities;
5. supervision of the study of the written and spoken languages of minority nationalities;
6. management of the minority institutes, compilation and translation work, and the training of minority nationalities cadres;
7. coordination with other departments of government in handling minorities affairs;
8. execution of State Council orders related to nationalities affairs;
9. processing of suggestions for the handling of minorities affairs.

The same law also outlined the form the NAC was to assume. It was to be composed of a general office and several departments, each dealing with the minorities of a single large geographical area, plus a counselor's office, translation office, publications committee, "other special committees," and the minority nationalities institutes.[7]

Another law passed at the same time provided for the establishment of Nationalities Affairs commissions on the provincial, special-administrative-district, and hsien levels in areas with substantial minority populations (see the chart).[8] Where the number of minority nationalities was not large and their problems "uncomplicated," they might be handled by the department of civil affairs of the relevant level, with a section office or designated official in charge.[9] Commissions are known to have been formed in most provinces and in the municipalities of Peking, Shanghai, and Tientsin.[10]

The original NAC at national level, formally constituted on October 19, 1949, had Li Wei-han (Han nationality) as director and Ulanfu (Mongol), Saifudin (Uighur), and Liu Ko-p'ing (Hui) as deputy di-

State Council

Nationalities Affairs Commission

Other Ministries and Commissions

- General Office (accounting, general administration)
- Translation Bureau
- Northeast Department (Mongols, Koreans, etc.)—"First Department"
- Northwest Department (Uighurs, Kazakhs, Hui, etc.)—"Second Department"
- Tibetan Department—"Third Department"
- Southwestern Department—"Fourth Department"
- East, Central-South Department—"Fifth Department"
- Political-Legal Department
- Cultural Department (health, education, entertainment)
- Finance Department
- Counselor's Office
- Publications Committee
- Nationalities Institutes

Autonomous Region NAC

Autonomous District, Municipal, or Special Administrative District NAC

Nationalities Affairs Bureau of County or Autonomous County

Provincial NAC

Autonomous District, Municipal, or Special Administrative District NAC

Nationalities Affairs Bureau of County or Autonomous County

Special Municipality NAC

Nationalities Affairs Bureau of County

Nationalities Affairs Personnel of Residents' Committees

rectors. The first three names will be familiar to the reader. As for Liu Ko-p'ing, he had joined the party in 1931, spent many years in KMT prisons, and served as a vice-principal of the East China Revolutionary Academy prior to 1949. Though little else is known of his background, his appointment to the sixty-three-member GAC in 1949 is indicative of his prestige. Among the twenty-two regular members of the NAC, nineteen were members of minority nationalities who had served the party prior to 1949 as military officers, members of party or government organs engaged in minorities' work, or leaders of liberation movements in their respective areas. Of the three Han, two were history professors who had been known for their liberal views, and one, Liu Ch'un, had been active in united front and minorities education work at Yenan. Like Li Wei-han, Liu also continued to serve on the UFWD, which, surprisingly, had no members of minority nationalities among its top leadership.

When the National People's Congress (NPC) was set up under the Constitution of 1954, another element was added to the formal structure of minorities work: the Nationalities Committee of the NPC. The committee, composed of all national minority delegates to the NPC, had no real powers, being confined to discussion and approval of measures previously decided upon elsewhere. Though its members wielded no powers by virtue of their participation on the committee, their selection as NPC members does provide some index of the party's assessment of their prestige in their own respective areas. Thus, while the committee itself is little more than a rubber stamp, its membership must be considered an important factor in minorities work.

Social Mobilization

Even before the formal structure of minorities administration work had been shaped, however, the party's actual work had begun. First on the agenda was the task of winning the trust of minority peoples. Cadres were instructed to "do good and make friends." [11] The motives behind this were not, of course, wholly altruistic in nature: mountains and other areas of difficult terrain have been the traditional refuge of those at odds with the authorities in China, whether minority groups withdrawing from conflict with Han or Han escaping from Han. The Chinese Communists themselves had been forced into such areas by the KMT's extermination campaigns, and now anti-Bolshevik groups had fled there. The cooperation of the local populace was vital to the success of any movement to wipe out such counterrevolutionaries, as the CCP with its oft-repeated slogan, "the army is the fish and the people the water," was painfully aware. The number of counterrevolutionary campaigns reported from minority areas in the early 1950's testifies to the importance of good relations with the local people.[12]

Good will is most efficiently won by good deeds, and the Communist plan shows both sensitivity and foresight—perhaps the result of many years' trial and error at Yenan. As an initial step, in the summer of 1950 two missions representing the People's Government were dispatched to the southwest and northwest. Lasting slightly over three months each, the missions served both fact-finding and propagandistic functions. Medical personnel and an entertainment corps were integral parts of the groups, whose tasks were defined as "...interviewing minority nationalities on behalf of the CPG and Chairman Mao, transmitting the deep concern of Chairman Mao and of the CPG for the minority nationalities, publicizing the nationalities policy of the Common Program and, when possible, gaining understanding of basic conditions and demands of the fraternal nationalities." [13]

As reported on by its chief, Shen Chün-ju, an official of the Supreme People's Procurocracy, the mission to the Northwest included 120 people, 60 of whom came from agencies of the GAC and the rest from the Peking Opera Corps. With P'eng Ssu-k'o (Pengsk, a Mongol), Sa K'ung-liao (Mongol), and Ma Yü-huai (Hui), all party members of some standing, serving as deputy chiefs, the group visited over thirty localities "in cooperation with the PLA."

Before beginning work in an area, the mission was briefed on the current situation there by local authorities and cadres. It also solicited their opinions on how best to proceed. A plan of action was formulated on this basis, and approval of the local authorities obtained before attempting to implement it. Generally speaking, work was carried out in three ways:

1. individual interviews (with leaders or representatives of various nationalities);
2. discussion forums (involving a small group, the size and composition —e.g., profession or status group—differing according to nationality and prevailing conditions);
3. mass meetings (large propaganda sessions ending in performances of Peking opera and/or cinema shows).

The mission interviewed over 300 individuals and convened 66 discussion forums with a total attendance of 4,080 representatives of various nationalities. Forty-five mass meetings were held with a total attendance of 280,000. The Peking Opera Corps performed 27 times to audiences totaling over 150,000, and 105 cinema shows were seen by more than 250,000 people. Shen calculated that 1 person in 80 had been contacted by the mission. Gifts were given after consultation with the local authorities as to the fitness of time and place of presentation. These included banners reading "All Nationalities of the Chinese People's Republic Keep United," said to have been inscribed by Chairman Mao personally, plus medical supplies, books, silk, cloth, tea, and sugar. In return, the minorities presented gifts to the mission and to Chairman Mao.

Members of the mission, on hearing of any instance of internationality dispute, would remind the disputees that it had "always" been the government's policy to persuade them to negotiate peacefully and to cooperate, and to avoid the imperialist-reactionary policy of divide and rule. Both this and the presentation of the banners described above are obvious attempts to implement the party's policy on promotion of unity among nationalities. In addition, they served to dissociate the party's policy from what many minorities people believed to have been the KMT's policy: the encouragement of dissension in order to strengthen its own control.

The mission reported that although it had received a warm welcome, the minorities remained suspicious, and vestiges of both Han and local nationalism could be discerned. The people they had interviewed seemed to have been generally pleased with the party's work so far, expressing particular satisfaction with its willingness to give minority groups their own representatives and to help them out economically in time of need. The mission's own assessment of party shortcomings, as Shen reports, focused on the lack of cadres at all levels and on the ideological level of such cadres as did exist.

Missions to the Southwest and Southeast operated in exactly the same manner.[14] These expeditions represented a complete reversal of the attitude noted by Pollard:[15] the Han had sought out the barbarians and wished to learn about them.

With the groundwork laid by these early expeditions, subsequent missions tended to be more specialized in nature and to concentrate on a more limited geographical area. A group headed by eminent anthropologist Fei Hsiao-t'ung spent more than six months living among the minorities of Kweichow, engaged in what seems to have been primarily research on the numbers and kinds of non-Han in the area. Fei's observations, published in 1951, are less interesting for their specific content than for the fact that he, as a trained anthropologist who had just undertaken a scientific study of the area, still apparently knew much less of its inhabitants than is detailed in a book published forty years earlier by a Western missionary who had been more interested in converting heathen souls than in ethnology.[16]

That Fei's group did not entirely neglect propaganda functions is illustrated in his account of a grievance meeting held with the Miao:

The Miao asked, "Who is responsible for this bloody history? Who has oppressed us? Who is our enemy?" Many answered that it was the Han who were the oppressors. Some [cadres or "plants"?] said dubiously, "But Chairman Mao is a Han. How is it that he helps us rather than oppresses us?" Discussion continued. Someone said: "The poor Han have suffered just like us."

Fei added:

Friend and foe had been recognized! Oppression and slaughter had stemmed from the greed of the landlord class, not from differences of language and dress. . . . but we Han were also partly responsible. Neither we nor our ancestors felt enough sympathy for our brother nationalities to firmly oppose our own rulers when they did these things.[17]

A medical mission to the Northwest headed by Dr. Hu Ch'uan-k'uei of Peking Union Medical College made a special point of cultivating the lamas of Ch'inghai province's renowned Kumbum monastery, since "they enjoy good prestige, politically and religiously, among the local populace." Hu reported that his group gave the lamas free medical treatment, and in turn the lamas

served as a medium of propaganda. For instance, when they got sick, the Tibetans had hitherto gone to the monasteries for cure by drawing lots, saying their beads, praying to God and following the oracle. Now the lamas of the monastery told the sick to go to the [medical] corps for treatment. During my stay at Kumbum, I was told by responsible lamas of the monastery that . . . 713 of their number had been cured or almost cured, and that they felt grateful to Chairman Mao, and were quite willing to contribute part of their land for agrarian reform.[18]

In that it had concretely demonstrable results while offending almost no one save a few local medicine men whom the party was generally careful to pension off, medical work was to prove one of the most popular aspects of the party's work in minority areas.[19] In a further attempt to amass knowledge, the countrywide census of 1953 asked each respondent to state his or her nationality.

Important as these efforts were to remedy the party's ignorance about minority areas in order to lay the groundwork for the introduction of socialism, the work of forming governments obviously could not wait upon their completion. Article Fourteen of the Common Program had called for the establishment of a system of military control in all liberated areas; local People's governments were to be formed composed of persons appointed by the CPG or by front-line military political organs. It was explained that, given these powers, military committees would be able to crush reactionaries by force while simultaneously protecting and inspiring the people and helping them to set up conferences of people's representatives and "organs of people's power of all degrees which . . . [would] gradually receive full powers." [20]

In practice, provincial-level governments were usually set up through direct negotiations with party authorities. Local-level People's Conferences were established under the supervision of the relevant military committee. The conferences, to include "people of all strata," were intended as a transition stage to allow some feeling of popular participation while a more permanent system was being constructed. Their functions were limited to debate, making proposals on adapting decisions of higher organs to their respective areas, and publicizing decisions of the government among the people. Resolutions passed by the conferences had the force of recommendations only. Eventually, when the situation became more stabilized and party-PLA control had been consolidated, conferences would be replaced by People's Congresses chosen through general elections.

From the party leadership's point of view, ideal choices for positions on these bodies would have been long-time CCP members of whatever nationality was indigenous to a given area. However, although the party had trained a fair-sized group of such people by the time of liberation, their number was not nearly equal to postliberation tasks. Moreover, they were confined to a relatively small proportion of China's minority groups, chiefly Mongols, Chuang, and Hui. Notably lacking were representatives of several Turkic minorities, of Tibetans from Tibet proper, and of most of the southwestern minorities. These were, of course, precisely those areas in which the party's pre-1949 work had been weakest.

Politically reliable members of minority nationalities were apt to be seriously overworked. For example, Sang-chi-yüeh-hsi, the young graduate of the Yenan Nationalities Institute mentioned in chapter IV, was simultaneously chairman of what are now known as Kan-tzu Tibetan Autonomous *Chou* and A-pa Tibetan Autonomous Chou. (A *chou* is the administrative level intermediate between hsien, or county, and province; usually translated "district.") He was a member of both the Sikang and Szechwan provincial people's governments, the SWMAC, the Standing Committee of the CPPCC's National Committee, and the Nationalities Affairs Commission.

There were, however, limits to the degree to which this supply of minorities experts who were also Red in politics could be stretched. Until a larger group of Communist experts on minorities could be trained, the party's attempt to consolidate its control of areas in which its knowledge of local customs was so scanty could be dangerous, perhaps even resulting in permanent damage to the party's image with the very people it had ostensibly come to help.

The CCP's policy of cooperation with "patriotic upper strata" may be seen as an effort to close this expertise gap: the traditional elite (including both traditional minorities leaders and KMT administrators who had not thoroughly discredited themselves with "the masses" in whose areas they served) was simply co-opted into the CPR governmental hierarchy on giving reasonable assurance of cooperation with Red elements. The latter were often embodied in the person of the PLA officer in the area. Naturally, party elements were not expected to remain permanently alien to their environments, but were given strict orders to familiarize themselves immediately with the ways of the areas to which they had been assigned.

As for the traditional elite, in return for recognition of their often very real authority, they served as guarantors of the population and tried to smooth relations between populace and party. As applied in this period, the policy of compromise was indeed probably the most efficient way to establish good relations with the masses and seems to have been accepted as such by all of the "top party persons in power." Obviously the political loyalties of this co-opted group were highly suspect, and they did not, with rare exceptions, become party members, serving instead at the level of the governmental hierarchy that corresponded with the party's assessment of their present prestige and potential future value.

The clear intent was to maintain the traditional symbols of power while gradually changing the content that they symbolized. The form of the focus of loyalty would remain constant while its essence was being altered. Another attempt at symbol manipulation was the granting of the Mongolian title "Bator" (hero), hitherto given to Mongol, Uighur, and Kazakh folk heroes by their own peoples, to heroes of labor.[21]

It was announced that all traditional leaders of the minorities who had "maintained close connections with the masses" and who were sincerely desirous of reforming themselves would be allowed to stay in office.[22] These criteria could be rather flexibly defined, depending on the party's perceptions of its needs in a given area. In Sinkiang a "United Democratic Government" was set up in December 1949 with Burhan, a Tatar who had been appointed under the KMT, continuing as governor. In his August 1950 report on the past five months' work, Burhan revealed that since there were "very few" Communist cadres in Sinkiang the majority of cadres at present were public servants of the old regime who had been held over.[23] Lung Yun, the governor of Yunnan during the Nationalist period, was made a member of the GAC, a vice-chairman of the National Defense Council, and a vice-chairman of the SWMAC. His half brother, Lu Han, was also made a vice-chairman of the SWMAC and head of the military and administrative committee for Yunnan as well. In Tibet, the preliberation governing elite had been kept on en masse in accordance with the terms of the 1951 agreement. In Kansu, Ma Hung-pin, brother of staunch anti-Communist warlord Ma Hung-k'uei, became a member of the NWMAC. Even in Inner Mongolia, where the party had a much larger number of trained, native cadres, it was, as seen in chapter IV, felt advisable to compromise with pro-Soviet as well as proindependence advocates and with those who favored joining the Mongolian People's Republic.

Of such politically doubtful material was the government apparatus engaged in minorities work formed. Obviously, this policy of compromise was never envisioned as permanent and was meant to be carried on only until the party's position had been consolidated and more politically reliable successors trained. As the party gained support, as local people gained expertise as cadres, and as outside cadres became familiar with the situation in minority areas, the party would have more room to maneuver against the will of the patriotic upper strata. At this point, members of the traditional elite would be forced either to go along with the party's policies or risk being discarded.

The Theory and Practice of Autonomy

Having prepared the way by substantially eliminating counterrevolutionary elements, persuading the traditional elite to compromise, and beginning work with the masses, the party began to give effect to its promise to establish self-governing areas. The General Program for the Implementation of Nationality Regional Autonomy of the Chinese People's Republic, which went into effect on August 9, 1952, classified these areas into three types:

1. areas in which the inhabitants belong to the same minority (e.g., a Miao Autonomous Chou might be set up in a predominantly Miao area);
2. areas in which the inhabitants belong to the same minority nationality with certain districts inhabited by a smaller number of people of a different nationality, these latter peoples having the right to autonomy in their own districts (e.g., a Yao Autonomous Hsien might exist under the jurisdiction of a Miao Autonomous Chou);
3. areas in which two or more minority groups form a significant proportion of the population. In this case, a multinational autonomous area might be set up. Where either group formed a cohesive bloc in part of this autonomous area, they would have the right to establish

an autonomous government in that part (e.g., a Yao Autonomous Hsien might exist under the jurisdiction of a Miao-Yao Autonomous Chou).

All autonomous areas were, it was reiterated, inalienable parts of the motherland, and all organs therein were to be formed in accordance with the principle of democratic centralism. While minorities were to be encouraged to develop their own languages and traditions, no special financial or military exemption provisions were made by the program.[24]

As to what autonomy might mean in practice, cadres were warned that there should be no mechanical application of methods that had been workable in Han areas to minority areas. An assessment of the special characteristics and concrete conditions of each individual minority area was to be made with an eye to ensuring social stability. It was also stressed that the policy of unity with all leaders, including religious leaders, who had ties with the masses was crucial to the attainment of social stability.

The key word in the formation of autonomous areas was "nationalization," defined as "national in form of autonomous organs, languages, and cadres." [25] In practice, implementation of the "national in form" provision chiefly involved calling Communist-style organizations by traditional names—that is, hsien in Inner Mongolia were to be called "banners" (*ch'i*) and chou were designated "leagues" (*meng*), in accordance with traditional practice. Some place names were also changed. For example, Wangyehmiao, a city whose Chinese name recalls the ancestral temple of a prince, was renamed Ulanhot, which means "Red City" in Mongolian.[26] Tihwa, Chinese name for the capital city of Sinkiang, was henceforth to be known as Urumchi, its Uighur name. A concerted effort was made to make use of minority languages and to train minorities cadres. It was with evident pride that NCNA would announce from time to time that the autonomous organs of X area had been "basically nationalized." [27]

This ideal, however, proved difficult to attain. Particularly in areas inhabited by traditionally warlike minorities, the tendency of Han cadres who were sent there was to exclude such peoples from participation in party and government affairs as much as possible. An angry editorial in *Kansu jih-pao* (Kansu daily) of October 1, 1949, noted that in Ho-cheng hsien, an area in which Hui were concentrated, there was not one single Hui cadre, and in fact the local People's Government had refused to allow Hui to enter the hsien capital. In neighboring Lin-hsia hsien, the government had arbitrarily decided that Han were to form two-thirds of the militia, although Hui were both more numerous and better soldiers. It was further revealed that in some unnamed areas Hui were being "arbitrarily" shot at and killed. This was not, the editorial warned, the way to win the trust of the masses or Hui converts to socialism.[28] Under such circumstances progress was slow, and there was probably more cooperation with the traditional elite than had originally been envisioned.

Grass roots work proceeded along much the same pattern of investigation and propaganda followed by organizing activities. Small work teams, typically composed of PLA men, who were often the sole representatives of the new government of China in a minority area, would go from hamlet to hamlet with the aim of winning the trust of the masses. Their task was not easy. One veteran cadre interviewed by a British correspondent in Szechwan recalled the hazards of lighting a campfire at night. Not only could the group's presence be detected by the smoke, but their silhouettes outlined by the flames provided snipers with a perfect target.[29] In nomadic areas, whole communities might decamp overnight, leaving startled cadres with no one to propagandize.[30]

Having surmounted these obstacles and survived long enough to make contact with their intended clientele, the typical procedure was for the work team to pay a call on the local headman. As the persons responsible for the fate of their communities vis-à-vis the outside world, headmen generally had had experience in dealing with outsiders as spokesmen for their respective groups. Often they could speak some Chinese when other members of their groups could not. Even if it had been possible for PLA men to communicate directly with "the masses," it would have done no good in many cases, for the common people considered such dealings beyond their comprehension. Thus, the dictates of ideology aside, the most efficient way to reach the masses was often through their headman.

If a headman was not disposed to cooperate, the work team was instructed not to force itself on him or her, but to move on until it found a person more amenable to the group's presence. The team would then ask what the problems of the area were and suggest solutions. For example, if drought were mentioned, they might describe and offer to help build a small irrigation project. If malaria was the issue, drugs might be supplied and a plan outlined for killing mosquitoes and draining swamps. The work team would also try to find out local customs from the headman so as to avoid offending local sensitivities. Such gaucheries as sitting to the right of a campfire when custom dictated the left, or preparing food in a manner considered unclean, could prove major setbacks to the party's good relations campaign.

Under a general theme of the "do good things movement" [31] the teams' slogan was "work together [with the minorities], eat together, live together." Daytimes were devoted to helping the people with such homely tasks as hauling water and cutting firewood. In the evenings, teams would occasionally put on entertainments, generally simple morality plays that linked what had been found out about the area's past history with the idea of class exploitation. For example, if the nationality's land had been stolen by Han, the play's villain might be an avaricious Han official who, it would be made clear, had been simultaneously oppressing the Han masses of the area. When one headman was impressed with the work the team was doing, it was hoped that he would tell another, who might then be persuaded to accept a team also. This was called the "point and area" system—building a point of trust and then expanding into the surrounding area.[32]

While dispensing free seed, tools, labor, and entertainment, team members were to learn the local language and propagandize party doctrine and party nationalities policy. Those who appeared especially receptive to the propaganda and who gave evidence of leadership qualities might be singled out for special treatment, some being sent to a PLA-run cadre school in the area. Having proved themselves there, these activists might then be sent on to a higher-level institution for more specialized political or technical training or both. Often people on the lowest rung of society were given special attention on the grounds that, being the most exploited members of their groups, they would be particularly receptive to the party's point of view. For example, when democratic reforms were carried out in Tibet, special notice was given to the presence of blacksmiths on local people's councils, blacksmiths representing a kind of pariah caste in Tibetan society.[33]

For the community as a whole, propagandizing was to lay the groundwork for a series of mass meetings that would culminate in democratic reforms. Where possible, agreement on reforms was to be reached by peaceful discussion at a meeting of the entire community conducted by the leader of the work team. People's Councils would be elected, theoretically with representatives from all strata of society. Meetings of the councils were to be scheduled at regular intervals to discuss the government's policies and to make suggestions as to adapting them to minority areas.[34] Meanwhile, the slower and more demanding task of creating a party organization could proceed.

The People's Councils as originally set up were, of course, never conceived of as more than first steps toward achieving genuinely peasant-, herdsman-, and worker-run organizations. The holder of the nominal first position was apt to be the traditional local headman or another traditional leader of some standing in the community. Typically, to maximize the prestige of the People's Council, as many traditional community leaders as could be persuaded to participate would be included in its membership. Party diatribes against the native officials (*t'u-ssu*) notwithstanding, they were still in existence in late 1951, and indeed were reported to have journeyed to a hsien city to offer congratulations on the newly formed People's Government.[35] Though he would generally occupy a position nominally secondary to a member of the dominant minority nationality of the area, the head of the PLA work team, nearly always a Han, was the real power in the council. The minority activists, on whom the party placed its hopes for the future, were naturally also included among its membership.

The party branch, when it was set up, would generally have the PLA work-team head as First Secretary and as many activists who had proved themselves as members. Here they would gain the experience necessary before they could take responsibility in their areas. Autonomous areas were set up beginning in 1951, their administrative status being determined by the relative proportions of the minorities to that of the areas involved. In what was apparently an attempt to remain flexible in terminology, it would be announced that an autonomous area had been established "with an administrative status equal to" a hsien, special district, or other unit.

Cadre Recruitment

Of course the scheme just outlined represents an ideal. In actuality, work team members faced many problems and frustrations. For one thing, conditions in minority areas were often incredibly primitive, even when measured by the standards of rural Han China. Malaria and various other diseases were real threats to life in the warmer areas; even when not fatal, they were often debilitating. In the case of the numerous minorities who lived in the mountains, unaccustomed cold weather and different diseases associated with the climate posed their own difficulties. In Tibet, high elevations produced not only extreme cold but thin air as well. Dizziness and lethargy were common reactions to the altitude. Those with weak hearts proved extremely susceptible to heart attack, and pregnant women were apt to miscarry.

As mentioned previously, frequently the minorities did not live in such areas of their own free choice, but had been forced there by Han who had usurped their land, sometimes many centuries before. Thus they were extremely suspicious of the newcomers. One work team member found a local saying: "As a rock does not make a pillow, a Han does not make a friend" (*shih pu-neng tang chen-t'ou han-jen pu-neng tso p'eng-yu*).[36]

Another, with orders to teach the Hani minority to read, was told by them that "reading is a Han custom only. If we read, our stomachs will ache, our crops will not grow, and our women will become barren." Having been refused permission to teach by all the local headmen, he tried a people-to-people approach, but found that the natives would simply say "I don't understand" in their own language and walk away.[37]

A third cadre, sent to an area inhabited by the Lisu nationality, took his first step in gaining the trust of the people by learning to chew the local tobacco, a mixture of grass, lime, tobacco, and sand that was to him utterly repulsive. He later found out that what had sealed their acceptance of him was the fact that he would sleep under the same quilt with them even though they were dirty and had lice.[38]

Given the sort of working conditions described above, it is hardly surprising that very few cadres were eager to work in minority areas,[39] and in fact the shortage of trained personnel in minorities areas has been a persistent complaint of party spokesmen.[40]

High priority was given to remedying the shortage of cadres. In 1949 Mao had stated that "without a large number of cadres recruited from the minority nationalities, we can never succeed in thoroughly solving the nationalities problem or in completely isolating the reactionaries of the nationalities." [41] Mass media took up the theme, explaining that: "It is natural that the members of any nationality will have respect for the cadres of their own nationality. Minority nationalities people . . . have often expressed the opinion that although Han cadres are very likable, they still cannot completely understand the situation and problems of the minorities." [42] It was stressed that minorities cadres were to serve as a "bridge" between party policies and their implementation in minority areas.

Future efforts illustrate the seriousness with which this task was viewed. A wide range of recruitment techniques was employed, from a search for activists at the grass roots level to the founding of a hierarchy of cadre training schools culminating in the Central Nationalities Institute in Peking. Methods were intended to be flexible in order to coordinate the needs of the party with the situation in a given area. For example, in Tibetan areas of Szechwan, underground party workers came in early 1949 ahead of the PLA to prepare the peasantry psychologically for invasion. After performing the usual deeds indicating good will and a desire to help, they began to organize young people who, when the PLA did arrive, served as a fifth column in its takeover by "arresting" KMT officials and setting up their "own" government. The PLA then established a cadre school to teach the young people basic Marxism-Leninism and organizational techniques.[43]

Underground agents also visited various monasteries and, after ascertaining who among its tenants were dissatisfied with the monastic regime, would hold forth the promise of a better life and offer to help them escape and gain entrance into cadre schools.[44] Many monks had, in accordance with Tibetan customs, been "donated" to the monastery as very young children or had entered it because it was virtually the only channel of social mobility in Tibetan society. It would therefore seem that there was a reasonable expectation of finding a fair percentage of discontented inhabitants.

When PLA units were ordered to march on Lhasa, these young trainees accompanied them, serving as interpreters and explaining the army's mission to the local populace en route. Some eventually joined the PLA themselves. They might also participate in one of the local-level governments that were set up or attend a higher-level cadre school or both.[45]

A more general pattern, however, was for recruitment to be done after the PLA entered an area. Minorities might be singled out as potential cadres through showing enthusiasm for the party message by "taking the lead in production." A young Yi girl who headed her commune's Women's Work Department attributed her rise to success to the fact that she had raised more cabbages than anyone else and hence had been asked to head a mutual-aid team. Only "later" did she "begin to take an interest in politics." [46]

In slaveowning areas, rather than make a frontal attack on the institution as such, the party began by quietly giving refuge to runaway slaves and providing them with food, clothing, and education. Word quickly spread, inducing other slaves to escape. Previously, though escapes had occasionally been attempted, there was literally nowhere to go. In Yi areas, slaves were tattooed by their masters to aid in recognition, and, even if the runaways succeeded in leaving Yi territory, they risked being killed by the people whose areas they entered. These peoples had themselves been the objects of slave raids and, recognizing the unique Yi style of clothing, would cheerfully do away with a potential enemy.[47]

The asylum offered by the PLA rapidly changed this situation. The successful escapees, who could be assumed to be among the more ambitious and daring of their groups, would then be given lessons in "advanced" production techniques to serve as an example to others and might receive cadre training. While this did not spare the party's image in the slaveowners' eyes, it did soften the emancipation process as well as eliminate the problems that would arise if the party had abruptly freed thousands of people who had never had the experience of caring for themselves.

Participation in mass movements, particularly in democratic and land reforms, was regarded as the acid test for potential cadres. Upon examination it is not difficult to see why: in taking an active role in the destruction of old patterns of government and production, and in the creation of new socialist-style organizations, the minority cadre symbolically stood with the party vis-à-vis his nationality's past way of life. The following vignettes are typical:

Tariftauriti, a Uighur not 34 years old, was the son of a house servant. He was 16 at the time of liberation in 1949, and followed with intense interest the peasants' movements in bringing charges against the landlords and demanding low rents. He joined the CCP during land reform in 1952, leading six families in his village in forming the first mutual-aid team and later the first agricultural cooperative. When Ucha Commune came into being in 1958 he became secretary of its Paotzuhungan Brigade Party Committee. He is also a representative to the Provincial People's Congress.[48]

Duthru, a Tibetan ex-slave, is now Party secretary and head of Red Flag hsiang in Gyantze. He has been chosen the hsien's outstanding worker for three years running. In the spring of 1960, when democratic reforms were first carried out in this area, he joined a working group of the People's Government, bravely carrying out the struggle against serf-owners and their agents. Later he led poor peasants in reclaiming land, boldly sowing where others had doubts. He took the initiative in organizing mutual aid teams, voluntarily teaching others farming techniques.[49]

Given the fact that cooperation with the upper strata was an oft-repeated part of party policy, and that the cadres could hardly serve as a bridge between party and minority group if they were required to separate themselves too sharply from their fellows, it is likely that the CCP took care to ensure the blunting of these public acts of renunciation.

Whatever the hardships attendant upon the performance of these deeds, reports from widely separated areas leave no doubt that activism was the main source of cadre recruitment. In a mixed Mongolian, Tibetan, and Kazakh area in Ch'inghai it was claimed that a majority of cadres had begun their careers as activists on mutual-aid teams (MAT's),[50] and the majority of nationalities cadres in Inner Mongolia were said to have been "either activists during mass movements or children of poor peasants and herdsmen." [51]

Cadre training classes were soon begun to instruct these promising activists in ideology, organization, and production techniques. Successful graduates of such local classes then became eligible for entrance into more specialized institutions that had been set up to give more advanced training. Inner Mongolia—which had the earliest Communist movement among the minority areas and had been the first large minority area to be liberated and first to attain the status of an autonomous region—led the way in this field, too. In 1946 an Inner Mongolia Military and Political College and an Inner Mongolia Autonomy College had been founded. The establishment of a People's Government in 1947 was quickly followed by the setting up of a wide variety of cadre training institutes, among which were the Inner Mongolia Cadre School, cooperative cadre training classes, animal pestilence training classes, and accountants' training classes. In 1950 a Workers and Peasants Short Term Middle School and Workers and Peasants Cultural Spare Time School were set up, with the avowed aim of "raising to a higher level the cultural standards of Mongol and Han cadres." By the end of 1951, a total of 485 cadres had been sent to pursue advanced studies in universities and schools outside Inner Mongolia. Over 25,000 cadres had been trained by that time.[52]

Though Inner Mongolia was often cited as the model to emulate, progress in other areas never quite caught up. In Sinkiang only two cadre training schools had been founded by 1955, one by the Sinkiang Provincial People's Government and the other by the CCP's Regional Sub-bureau, and only 10,000 cadres had been produced as of that date. Training classes in the various administrative districts had been opened only a few months before.[53]

In Tibet proper only one cadre school existed on the eve of the formation of a Preparatory Committee for the Tibet Autonomous Region in 1955. At that time its name was changed from "Cadre School of the Tibet Military District" to "Cadre School of the Tibet area," [54] perhaps to give an appearance of transfer from PLA to civilian control. No statistics on the numbers of cadres trained were released at this time. In a seemingly purposefully ambiguous phrase, it was simply announced that "a number" had been trained "in the past few years." [55]

While there are great advantages in training cadres in their native areas, including those of convenience, economy, and minimization of the risk of uprooting young zealots from their environment, local area training has disadvantages as well. Given the shortage of material resources and experienced, politically reliable teachers after 1949, it would have been virtually impossible to provide every minority area with a high-caliber cadre training school. There are also obvious benefits in exposing the trainees to others with similar political sympathies but totally different cultural backgrounds. Horizons might be broadened, tendencies toward narrow parochialism reduced, and the patriots' vision of all ethnic groups in China working together for the greater good of the nation be brought closer to realization.

For these reasons, it was decided to set up a Central Nationalities Institute in Peking and a network of large regional institutes at key points throughout China. The fact that plans for these began to be worked out early in 1950 may give some idea of the importance they assumed in party policymaking. Two directives, entitled "Tentative Measures for Fostering Minority Nationality Cadres" and "Tentative Measures for Founding the Central Nationalities Institute" were approved by the GAC on November 24, 1950. The former provided for the founding of a Central Nationalities Institute (CNI) plus branches in the Northwest, Southwest, and Central-South. Additional branch institutes might be established as they were deemed necessary. An institute was to be set up in Sinkiang on the basis of the existing Sinkiang Academy, which had been founded by Sheng Shih-ts'ai. The immediate goal of the institutes was to train within two to three years "an appropriate number" of cadres who had mastered both Han and a minority language. To this end, all civilian cadres of the special administrative district level and above and all military cadres above battalion grade who served in minority areas were to be sent to Peking or trained locally by rotation within the next two to three years.[56]

The Government Administration Council's directive on founding the CNI outlined the goals and curriculum of the new Central Institute. Briefly, it was to

1. train higher- and intermediate-level cadres for service in minority areas;
2. do systematic research in minorities' spoken and written languages, history, culture, and society;
3. compile and translate works on minority nationalities.

Both Han and non-Han were to be accepted as students. Two basic courses of study, one short-term and one long-term, were prescribed. The first, a four- to six-month political training course, was to be open to cadres at the special administrative district level and above and to "patriotic democratic personages" at the hsien level and above.

The long-term course, to last two to three years, would allow specialization in either politics or language. The political course, which aimed at the creation of a "revolutionary hard-core" group, would admit

1. those who had successfully completed the short-term course;
2. those who had participated in actual work and struggle for two or more years;
3. junior middle-school graduates or those of equivalent educational level.

A preparatory course of from six months to a year was set up to accommodate otherwise qualified applicants whose cultural level did not measure up to Institute standards.

Prerequisite for admission to the language course was a senior middle-school education or its equivalent. A language research department, administratively separate but in practice closely connected with the language teaching program, was also established.

In the interests of efficiency, those presently engaged in research on nationalities problems throughout the country were, if feasible, to be transferred to the CNI in Peking. This transfer was to result in the assignment of some of China's leading anthropologists, including Lin Yüeh-hua (author of *The Lolo of Liangshan*, a pioneering study of the Yi minority done in the 1930's) and Fei Hsiao-t'ung (author of *Peasant Life in China*, a field study of rural life in the Yangtze area; the study was a significant part of the rural reform work done during the republican era) to the CNI and to their subsequent preoccupation with minorities' research.

Primary and middle schools were to be set up attached to the Central Institute for the convenience of student, faculty, and staff children. The entire Institute network was initially to be directly supervised by the Nationalities Affairs Commission. After a period of unspecified length, it was to come under the supervision of the Ministry of Education, with the NAC retaining ultimate responsibility.[57]

Trade, Health, and Educational Policies

Although research on conditions in minority areas, the setting up of autonomous governments, and cadre training were immediate priorities in party work, other areas were not neglected. On February 5, 1951, the GAC promulgated its directive, "Some Decisions on Minority Nationality Affairs," which stipulated that special conferences devoted to trade, health, and education were to be convened in the latter half of 1951. Responsibility for the planning thereof was delegated to the ministries of Trade, Health, and Education, respectively, to be assisted in each case by the NAC.[58]

The All-China Minority Nationalities Trade Conference, held from August 17 through 31 of the same year, emphasized the contrast between past inequalities in the minorities' trade positions vis-à-vis the Han with present improvements: "some Mongols" were said to have been without salt for many years; the standard price for a single needle in Li areas of Hainan was a chicken. These practices were being changed. For example, whereas in 1947 the price of half a bolt of cloth was a ton of grain, a ton of grain would now purchase two bolts of the same cloth. Trade Minister Yeh Chi-chuang's report to the GAC noted that 750 business establishments, including state-operated sales offices, procurement stations, and processing factories, plus small mobile trading teams, had been set up in "most" minority areas and that there were now over 1,700 cadres engaged in trade with minorities. Yeh stressed that although this represented a great improvement over the past, it was still highly inadequate: the number of trade organs was far too small, they did not penetrate deeply enough into rural areas, and both capital and technical expertise were lacking.

He outlined a moderate policy for the future, emphasizing the need to adapt to local conditions:

1. State-operated trade organs should be established in minority areas in a more systematic fashion. The form of such organizations should be determined in accordance with individual areas and nationalities. Cooperatives should be encouraged only where public opinion was ready for them.
2. Since it would be a long time before state-operated trade organs could satisfy minority needs, particularly in areas where communications were poor, private merchants must be encouraged to work under the jurisdiction of such state organs as did exist. Traditional fairs should be rehabilitated and new ones established; state organs or mobile teams should be set up as part of these [this was undoubtedly an attempt to demonstrate by actual example the superiority of the state outlets over private merchants], while exercising strict supervision to ensure fair trade practices by all.
3. "Promising" minorities handicrafts should be encouraged.
4. Minorities trade cadres should be trained.
5. Badly needed items such as salt and tea should be supplied to minorities areas at low prices, even if this meant that state organs would operate at a loss. Consideration should be given to special needs of minorities in procuring items for supply to their areas.
6. The activities of trade organs should be closely coordinated with those of other state organs such as banking, agriculture, and communications.
7. Special trade-administration organs should be established in the departments of trade of various administrative levels to study trade with minority areas and give leadership to trade work.[59]

In addition to the benefits to the minority peoples involved, these measures would also, of course, result in tying their economies to that of Han China.

The All-China Minority Nationalities Health Conference, which met from August 23 through 30, followed a similar pattern of contrasting a dismal past with present improvements and ambitious plans for the future. Vice-Minister of Health Ho Cheng's report noted a serious decrease in population in minority areas, which he attributed to lack of knowledge of even the basic rules of sanitation. Ho did not attempt to explain why this ignorance, which presumably had remained constant for many centuries, should result in a recent decrease of population. Later analyses attributed it to a KMT policy of extermination. In any case, ninty-four health stations had been set up in Ch'inghai, Suiyuan, the Northwest, Southwest, and Inner Mongolia in order to reverse the population decrease. Already some results could be seen: the incidence of bubonic plague in Inner Mongolia had been "greatly reduced" and there had been success in the campagin against venereal disease in "certain areas" of the same province. In contrast to capitalistic medical practices, fees were decided in accordance with the patients' economic status, except for venereal disease treatment, which was free to all.

Future goals included the completion of a network of hsiang-level health organizations by 1952 and their coordination with mobile medical teams that would tour wide areas providing vaccinations and basic information on sanitation to outlying rural groups. Twenty more antimalaria clinics would be set up, four each in Sikang, Kansu, Ninghsia, Ch'inghai, and Inner Mongolia; existing stations in Sinkiang and Suiyuan would be expanded.

To solve the ever-present shortage of medical personnel, health cadres would be sent from Han to minority areas, and educated minority young people would be invited to study in medical colleges in Han areas. Since "educated" clearly implies a level of literacy in Chinese sufficient to profit from attendance at Han medical schools, said students would almost automatically be chosen from the assimilated upper class of a given minority. A plan for establishing medical training centers in minority areas was to be drawn up separately.[60]

Medical treatment was a relatively inexpensive way to demonstrate irrefutably the superiority of Han civilization and party beneficence, and insofar as such treatment could be provided, it served as an effective means of binding minority areas more closely to Han China.

The All-China Minority Nationalities Education Conference, held from September 20 through 28, stressed that the training of minorities cadres would be the foremost task in education policy. Minister of Education Ma Hsü-lun noted that so far six nationalities academies and one minority nationality institution of higher learning existed, and that eighty ordinary institutions had admitted minority students. The five cadre schools and eighteen cadre training classes now extant had a total enrollment of 4,400 students. Though being trained for service in minority areas, these students were not necessarily of minority nationalities themselves. Local-area cadre training classes were being set up all over the country.

As to minority education in general, Ma felt that it should systematically inculcate a spirit of patriotism that at present would center around the "Resist America, Aid Korea" campaign. Given the great disparity of educational levels among the various minorities, few other general statements were possible. For example, 92 percent of school-age Koreans already attended school as of 1951, whereas almost no one in many remote areas of Szechwan and Yunnan had had access to formal education at any level. Thus, the overall aim that every minority child should be given access to education would be implemented by widely differing means, depending on the area involved. Ma recommended "consolidation, development, regulation, and reformation" in accordance with the existing state of education among the minority nationalities.

Where a minority had its own language, that should serve as the medium of instruction, though the meeting is said to have voted unanimously to establish Chinese-language classes "in accordance with the needs of the nationalities concerned." Those minorities who did not possess a written language or whose written language was "imperfect" should be helped to develop and reform their languages. Teaching should utilize either Chinese-language texts or those texts customarily used by the nationality.[61]

Clearly, the intent was to teach everyone to read and write Chinese eventually, but to minimize the possibility of conflict with those minorities who had a well-developed language and literature in which they took pride. Introduction of a common curriculum and common language were naturally crucial elements in the integration of minority groups.

As in work team procedure, the experimental area technique was employed. In Sinkiang, Urumchi was chosen as the focal point of initial reforms. The "anticommunist antipeople" curriculum was abolished and orders issued that it was to be replaced with, among other things, party teachings on proletarian internationalism and the unity of the working classes of all nationalities. Classes were held for teachers, too, in order to "strengthen their ideology." Based on experience gained in the urban areas, work would gradually expand to suburbs, exurbs, and rural districts "in a planned and systematic manner." [62] In Tibet, Lhasa served a similar function, though due to the nature of the treaty signed with the Tibetan government and the party's more precarious position there, work was correspondingly slower. As of 1955, only one middle school and one primary school had been established. The bulk of teaching remained the prerogative of the monasteries and appears to have been little changed either in form or in content.

Other aspects of culture were not neglected. Mobile teams were set up to organize "culture clubs" in minority areas. These concentrated on bringing the story of the revolution, utilizing an impressive range of methods. Picture books, lantern slides, plays, films, storytellers, balladeers, and exhibitions on revolutionary themes were included. At first, the material was the same as that used in Han areas; later an effort would be made to dub in local languages and cast minorities in selected parts. However, since the presentations tended to have a high action content and to concentrate on illustrating a rather simple theme, it was pointed out that "there is no need to translate. The masses understand as soon as they hear." [63] The mobile teams tried to make their visits a festive occasion. Performers would offer to teach the minorities to dance the traditional north China *yang-ko* and to play drums and would in turn ask to be instructed in the nationality's dances and music.[64]

In line with the Common Program's promise to help minority nationalities preserve and develop their cultures, a Central Nationalities Song and Dance Troupe was founded in 1952. Consisting of nearly 200 performing members of a dozen nationalities, the troupe was to tour both within China and in foreign countries. It was also asked to collect and collate minorities music and dance forms.[65]

To carry out its avowed desire to encourage minorities to develop and use their own languages, the GAC set up a guidance committee for research in nationalities languages. The duties outlined at its inaugural meeting in October 1951 were directing and organizing research into the spoken and written languages of minority nationalities, assisting nationalities having no written language to create such, and helping those with an imperfect script to perfect one.[66]

A directive was issued, ordering that henceforth the characters used to designate minorities' names would employ the man radical; use of the dog radical was prohibited. The use of various derogatory epithets for nationalities was also banned. In general, minorities were to be known by the name they called themselves rather than the name by which the Han had known them. Thus, for example, the Lolo[67] came to be referred to as Yi, and Fan,[68] a generalized term meaning "barbarians," was replaced by specific ethnic group names. The term assimilation, *t'ung-hua*, which had been used by the KMT, became taboo. Propaganda emphasized that the party's aim was not assimilation of nationalities to the Han but the amalgamation, *jung-ho*, of all nationalities. Chiang Kai-shek's use of the term tribe, *pu-lo*, to designate certain ethnic groups was castigated as a malicious attempt to demean and degrade these groups.

Another directive decreed an end to place names that might be derogatory to minority nationalities, though cautioning that no such measures should be taken "without the fullest consultation with minority representatives." One NCNA release blamed the derogatory place names on "Manchu mandarins," undoubtedly an effort to show that other groups besides the Han could be guilty of ethnic discrimination. In a gesture further indicative of the party's mastery of symbolic techniques, PLA or CCP representatives made a holiday of the renaming date. Minorities were provided with picks with which to smash the old name tablets and gongs with which to ring in a new era of peace and friendship among nationalities. In this manner a "Bridge for Yi Suppression" was renamed "Liberation Bridge," and several Tibetan villages were redesignated in a similarly socialistic manner.[69]

Eager to assume the role of protector of minorities' cultures, the party also arranged a large celebration in honor of the seven hundred twenty-seventh anniversary of Genghis Khan's death. As part of the festivities, the Mongol leader's bones were reinterred in the mausoleum from which the KMT had taken them fifteen years earlier.[70] Five thousand "peasants and herdsmen from all parts of Inner Mongolia" heard Ulanfu express his opinion that the return of Genghis's bier to its former burial place "once again vividly illustrates the profound concern of the Chinese Communist Party and of Chairman Mao for the minority nationalities." He then urged his fellow Mongols to unite closely with the rest of the Chinese people so as to "construct together our great country." [71]

In a further effort to gain support from minorities and avoid a confrontation with their indigenous power structures, minorities were specifically exempted from numerous reforms imposed or bestowed upon the Han. Insofar as the early years of party rule are concerned, these exemptions concerned mainly land reform, the marriage law, and certain taxes.

Liu Shao-ch'i in his report to the second meeting of the CPPCC's National Committee in June 1950 noted that thus far land reform had been carried out only in the old liberated and relatively sinified Mongol and Korean areas of the northeast. Whereas it *might* be carried out in other minorities areas if the majority of the masses demanded it, this would have to be decided on the basis of work with the minorities and in accordance with their level of political awareness. Land reform in Han areas was to be completed by the end of 1952, but ". . . we should give the minority nationalities more time to consider and prepare for reform among themselves and we must not be impetuous. The draft agrarian reform we propose also stipulates that it should not apply to nationalities areas." [72]

Minorities were also exempted from the provisions of the marriage law, being unaffected by the raised minimum marriage age and its provisions concerning concubinage, the frugality of wedding ceremonies, and divorce.[73]

Taxes were lowered or rescinded for minorities on certain articles they held in high esteem. For example, in the autumn of 1950 the Finance Ministry exempted from the commodity tax snuff and cotton oil sold in Northwest minority areas. In December of the same year, the GAC announced that during the three major festivals of the Muslim religious calendar no butchery tax would be exacted on cattle slaughtered for Hui consumption. The commodity tax on tea marketed in border areas of southwestern Szechwan, Sinkiang, and Tibet was reduced from 25 percent to 5 percent, and wine brewed for home consumption by the Yao minority was made entirely tax-exempt.[74]

Self-examination and Future Plans

In 1952 Liu Ko-p'ing, vice-chairman of the NAC, summed up the results of the past three years with more than just a touch of pride. First and foremost, he said, results were already noticeable in the party's drive to radically improve minorities' living standards. Liu cited livestock increases and higher per-acre yields in selected areas of the northeast to bolster his claims.

Second, minorities had obtained new political and social rights. Up to the fall of 1952, 130 autonomous areas and over 200 coalition autonomous governments had been established. Discrimination on the basis of ethnic background had been made illegal, and its remnants were being erased.

Third, medical work had arrested the steady population decline among many minority nationalities. Over 50 health teams had been sent out to minorities areas of the Northwest, Southwest, Central-South, and Inner Mongolian administrative regions to give free medical treatment and, as of the beginning of 1952, 187 health clinics and centers had been set up in minority areas.

Fourth, education was fast being made available to minority children. More than 700,000 books and magazines had been published in the Mongolian, Tibetan, and Uighur languages. Radio broadcasts in their own languages and dubbed films had "opened new cultural vistas" and minorities' songs and dances were "charming the country," while prominent Han artists helped the minorities to develop their arts. Seventeen hundred people of 50 different nationalities had been given a grand tour of the socialist motherland, visiting Peking and other parts of China.[75]

By mid-1952, then, the party seems to have felt relatively satisfied with its accomplishments. Anti-Bolshevik groups in minority areas were no longer regarded as a serious threat, and a beginning had been made toward accumulating basic knowledge of minority groups. Forming a united front with relatively pliable members of the traditional minorities upper-strata had given the party an entrée into many of these societies from the top, and the policy of "doing good and making friends" was allowing an expansion of its influence at the basic level. The slow process of building party structures in minority areas had begun, and local people who were perceived as loyal were being groomed for positions of responsibility in these structures. People's Representative Conferences had been convened in most areas outside Tibet and the remote areas of Szechwan and Yunnan, and a framework for local area governments had been set up.

In order to assess the efficacy of its work before making any further moves, the party decided on a nationwide checkup. On August 18, 1952, the GAC ordered that a study of nationalities policy be made, and in the following month the Party Central Committee instructed relevant party committees at all levels to carry out a "penetrating and systematic checkup of the implementation of nationalities policy." Visiting groups, work groups, and "special persons" were dispatched to lower levels to supervise the investigation. These teams convened conferences of cadres to discuss their experiences in implementing nationalities policy. The investigatory personnel also "consulted the masses" to obtain their views on the party's work among them. The methods of criticism and self-criticism were then applied, experiences summed up, and a report prepared for forwarding to higher levels.

Results of the investigation were released the following October. Not surprisingly, they were said to prove the "complete correctness of the party's mission in connection with problems related to nationalities in the country and of the various nationalities." As is usual in such pronouncements, the really important message lay in what followed the word "but." In this case, it was that there had been "numerous mistakes," of which the most serious were deemed to be, first, the continued existence of pan-Hanism or remnants of it among "some cadres and people" and, second, haste and adventurism or mechanical application of the experiences of Han areas.

Though *systematic* pan-Hanism had been abolished under the provisions of the Common Program, vestiges of it were said to be hindering the growth of unity among nationalities. The continued existence of local nationalism was also mentioned. Since it was not dwelt upon, it was apparently not considered serious. Pan-Hanism was termed the principal danger to work, and authorities were called upon to develop a mass campaign to educate people on nationalities policy "in coordination with daily routine tasks in a stable and suitable manner." The experiences of the "support the army and love the people" campaign were to be consulted before planning this new campaign. Each year at a fixed date, mass meetings and fraternization gatherings should be held to bring people of all nationalities together. At the meetings, educative speeches should be made and self-criticism sessions held. Each side should stress its own defects and mistakes in problems connected with relationships between nationalities and should suggest suitable solutions to these problems. To increase conviviality, fraternization gatherings might be held on festival days. Party committees and governments were enjoined to experiment in selected localities with the scheme just outlined and to utilize the experiences gained therein before extending the system to the whole area under its jurisdiction.[76]

The investigation of minorities work also had uncovered instances of violations of law and discipline among basic level cadres, though these were evidently deemed less serious than pan-Hanism and haste and adventurism. In one rather spectacular revelation, the investigation team sent out by the Kwangsi provincial government discovered that a hsien branch of the People's Bank had been compelling the minorities of the area to turn over their silver ornaments. Such ornaments were an integral part of the nationalities' traditional costumes. The case is also interesting for what it reveals of the party's methods of action in mobilizing "support" for its reforms.

Allegedly trying to overfulfill the savings target set for his area, the manager of the hsien branch bank decreed that anyone refusing to exchange silver bracelets for savings certificates be labeled "unpatriotic." Since the theme of unity and patriotism constituted the main thrust of party propaganda in minority areas at this time, this charge was quite serious. The errant manager, moreover, mobilized all the tools of mass suasion for his campaign. He "encouraged activists to speak out and began a challenge campaign and voluntary declarations to see who could be induced to donate the most." He further called upon *hsiang*-level cadres to take the lead, demanding that they mobilize the people to inform on their ungenerous neighbors and that they organize primary school pupils to tell their mothers to convert their silver ornaments into savings certificates. At the same time, while publicly announcing that people would be compensated at the rate of 8,000 yuan per tael weight, he privately instructed cadres to compensate at only 2,400 yuan per tael weight, since the ornaments were generally made of an alloy that was only 30 percent silver.

Some cadres added to this already bad situation by physically forcing people to sell, by snatching ornaments from their bodies, or by branding anyone wearing jewelry as "feudalistic and backward." Occasionally people received no compensation at all.

The investigation team reported finding the masses in an agitated state and blaming party and government organs for the confiscations. Production had been adversely affected. No production conference could be convened in the hsien due to popular opposition, and one woman had even refused to weave cloth, fearing that she would receive only a savings certificate in return for her work. Not only the party and the People's Government were blamed, but Han in general. A T'ung cadre who was issuing the savings certificates reported being told that if he had been a Han he would have received his just deserts.

The solution of the problem could not have satisfied all parties. At a public meeting it was announced that jewelry that still bore the owners' names would be returned and that 6,000 yuan per tael—not the 8,000 originally promised—would be paid to those whose jewelry had already been melted down or who did not wish their ornaments back. The fact that individuals, not the party, were at fault was also emphasized. A minorities spokesman—who coincidentally happened to be a hsiang head—spoke out, saying that the state's offer was too generous; he did not wish it to incur such great losses. Since his jewelry's silver content was below 50-percent purity, he would take only 4,000 yuan per tael weight as compensation. The same man was then put in charge of "concrete remedial work." [77] Doubtless many felt they would have to follow his example of generosity or risk classification as unpatriotic and reactionary.

This one case aside, further revelations on the investigations of minorities work concern Kweichow province. The fact that the Kweichow investigation, and it alone, was given prominence in the national press seems to indicate that its problems were considered exemplary, and that the solutions it had worked out were worthy of emulation.

"Some Han cadres" in Kweichow had not given proper respect to minorities' customs and traditions. Minorities were told that they could not be considered progressive unless they adopted Han-style dress and spoke the Chinese language. In one district, female cadres had taken it upon themselves to cut the queues of two minorities women. Other cadres had prohibited minorities from holding traditional festivals or offering sacrifices thereat. In their zeal to eliminate superstition, cadres had disposed of crates of joss papers, pulled down Buddha images, destroyed temples, and felled "holy trees."

Marriage customs had also been interfered with. Several different minorities in Kweichow had a tradition of arranging marriages at a song and dance festival, after which their young people would pair off and make love. Cadres had announced that those participating in such rites could not expect to join the party or New Democratic Youth League. They also made no secret of the fact that they considered all who worshiped in mosques to be backward.

A second mistake committed by cadres was their disregard for special characteristics of the nationalities areas and their tendency to apply mechanically the work experiences of the Han areas. For example, during land reform cadres expropriated sacrificial land, "holy mountains," common grazing land, and areas that had been set aside for mating festivals. Even worse, in the redistribution, many minorities had been given either no land at all or less and poorer land than the Han.

A third sin attributed to Han cadres was their failure to foster cadres of minority nationalities; they were even accused of actively discriminating against them or usurping their positions. In one area visited by an investigation team, an armed Han cadre was quoted as telling the district's deputy head, a man of Yi nationality, "you have no power over me." In other areas, Han cadres became resentful when the party's policy of fostering minorities cadres meant that minority group members whose qualifications they considered inferior to their own received promotions and they did not.

The provincial party committee held a special meeting to deal with the results of the investigation, pointing out that these failures were due to the cadres' misunderstanding of the party's nationalities policy. The committee cautioned cadres not to prohibit or intervene, but rather to patiently convince people to "pay attention to austerity, commit no extravagance and avoid delays in production." It also pointed out that leadership personnel at all levels had failed to pay sufficient attention to nationalities work, had inadequately educated the cadres in their duties, and had not made an effort to rectify discrepancies in policy and practice within a short enough time.[78]

While cadres received a large share of the blame for deviations, being told that they had been insufficiently diligent in studying and applying Marxist-Leninist nationalities policy, an effort was made to avoid damaging their morale in the process of correcting these deviations. Party and government organs were told they must distinguish between cadres who made minor mistakes and those whose errors were more serious, and between cadres who on realizing their mistakes attempted to correct them and those who persisted in their mistakes. Actions restricting the Han cadres' activities or making them wary of taking responsibility should, the party committee cautioned, be avoided. In the future, quality not quantity should be the criterion for posting Han cadres to minority areas. Cadres who were chosen to go to minority areas would have to get rid of all vestiges of Han chauvinism, learn the languages of the area, and respect local customs and habits. Those already in minority areas should be given more intensive education. A series of short-term or rotational training courses was recommended, with cadres concentrating for ten days to two weeks on nationalities policy and on the summing up of experiences in nationalities work. Party committees in minority areas were required to set up these courses within a specified period of time, the exact length to be determined by higher levels. The comparatively rapid turnover of personnel in minorities areas, which had heretofore been common, must be ended: henceforth cadres, particularly "backbone" cadres, should expect their assignments to such areas to be more permanent. To make their tenure more palatable, improvements should be made in their political, economic, and cultural conditions. They should be "encouraged from all sides" and educated on the importance of attending to work with ease of mind.[79]

As is not unusual in such investigation campaigns, the examination was undertaken not only to rectify past mistakes but also with a view to determining the direction policy should take in future. The Third Enlarged Conference of the Nationalities Affairs Commission, held in June 1953, heard this aspect outlined by its chairman, Li Wei-han. Li noted that work in the past had been chiefly political, concentrating on inculcating a sense of patriotism and an attitude of trust in the new government. Although, in areas where the party's control was still tenuous, political work would continue to be the main focus, in other areas the general trend would be away from political work alone and toward a policy that balanced political work with economic and cultural construction. The improvement and development of production would be particularly emphasized. This new policy would necessitate further research and investigatory activities, providing "systematic, specialized solutions" to problems. The researchers were admonished to pay specific attention to areas with poor soil or impoverished inhabitants or both.[80]

The NAC conference also adopted two documents, a "Draft Basic Summarization of Experiences in the Promotion of Autonomy in National Minority Areas" and a "Draft Basic Summarization of Animal Husbandry Production in the Inner Mongolian Autonomous Region and in Certain Pastoral Areas in Suiyuan, Ch'inghai and Sinkiang." The former, after summarizing the results of the 1952 investigation of minorities work, emphasized again the need to take fully into account the special characteristics of the nationalities, to unite people of all strata around the People's governments, and to strive first and foremost for social stability. Not paying sufficient attention to minorities' special characteristics and mechanically applying experiences derived from Han areas had resulted in minority dissatisfaction, "leading to chaos in some areas." This was said to be not an isolated phenomenon of individual areas but a widespread occurrence. It was frankly stated that the establishment of autonomous areas had often heightened tensions between nationalities to a dangerous degree. Minorities frequently had expected that autonomy would mean complete separation from Han and were disappointed when the Han did not move away. For their part, Han were apprehensive about trouble from the minorities and began to think they should move away. In addition, smaller minorities worried that they would be discriminated against by larger minorities. This was decreed the result of too hasty establishment of autonomous areas. In the future, leadership organs should resolve such tensions during the preparatory stage for the autonomous regions. Particular attention should be paid to obtaining the cooperation of traditional minorities leaders. The need for gradual nationalization of autonomous areas was also stressed.

While those who wished to study Han Chinese should be given every opportunity to do so, there must be no compulsion "at the present moment." The Inner Mongolian Autonomous Region, Yenpien Korean, and Sikang Tibetan autonomous areas were held up as models in the use of national forms. In Sikang, for example, both administrative and financial organs had been adequately staffed with translation cadres and, within a year of the autonomous area's founding in 1952, all publications including official documents were being published bilingually.

Still, respect for national forms must not be carried to the point where customs that obstructed progress and development were preserved, or where such forms had already attracted the attention of the broad masses as calling for reform. This caveat, a reiteration of other guidelines for action in minority areas, was surely exactly what cadres had had in mind when they tried to restrict party membership to "progressives" who did not participate in their nationality's "decadent" mating ceremonies, and when they encouraged minorities' activists to forswear reimbursement for their confiscated jewelry.

It was frankly admitted that experience on the exercise of autonomous rights was lacking and that often such knowledge as was possessed had not been used. All who wished to were urged to offer suggestions.[81]

The results of this investigation were incorporated into the 1954 constitution. Whereas the Common Program of 1949 had been essentially a statement of intent with regard to minority areas, the constitution was more explicit, incorporating the experiences of the past years. The number and kind of autonomous areas classified in the Draft Basic Summarization of Experiences in the Promotion of Autonomy in National Minority Areas was reiterated, as was its warning that the experiences of Han areas should not be mechanically applied to the minority areas. The preamble promised that the state would pay full attention to the special features in the development of the various nationalities and that "... in all these matters the masses of peoples of various nationalities and their public leaders who are in close contact with the masses must be permitted to take their time to think [reforms] over and make their decisions in accordance with their own desires." The constitution also granted "limited powers to adapt the laws, regulations and decisions of higher authorities to the requirements of the particular nationality" with the stipulation that the central authorities must approve the regulations drawn up by local authorities.[82]

Liu Shao-ch'i's report on the draft constitution defended these special provisions at some length. Noting the vast differences in levels of development among the various nationalities, which made the special provisions necessary, he added that "It certainly cannot be assumed that all of the nationalities in the country can arrive at socialism at the same time and by the same means." [83] What these constitutional provisions meant in terms of actual power and practice varied according to the area and time period involved, as an examination of the chief minority regions will show.

Regional Progress

Over the next few years, work proceeded in accord with these guidelines. Activities followed a general assessment of conditions for that area. The Korean nationality district and agricultural areas of Inner Mongolia, both of which had a standard of living at least equal to that of neighboring Han areas[84] and a Communist movement of comparable age, carried out land reform at approximately the same time as Han areas.[85] The autonomous area structure of Inner Mongolia was formed as soon as it was liberated in 1947, and the Yenpien Korean Autonomous Area was set up in 1952. Though some problems of integration were posed by the fact that both Chinese Koreans and Inner Mongols could look across the border at a state governed by those of their own nationality, the Mongolian People's Republic had shown itself uninterested in irredentism, and the Democratic Republic of Korea was neither anxious nor in any position to push a claim to the Chinese Koreans. There was, in addition, a well-demarcated boundary between the two states. Moreover, local Communist movements in both Inner Mongolia and Yenpien were headed by native leaders clearly committed to Peking: Ulanfu and Chu Tê-hai.

Chuang areas, though liberated several years later, were not far behind Inner Mongolia and Korean areas in implementing reforms.[86] Land reform was carried out in 1951 and the West Kwangsi Chuang Autonomous Area established the following year. In this case also, the inhabitants' standard of living was comparable to that of neighboring Han, and their Communist movement had had a similar duration. Most Chuang had been assimilated to the point of thinking of themselves as Han and felt no ties with any foreign power.

Other areas were prodded ahead where progress was deemed possible. A regular party organization was set up in Pai areas only in 1947; though well assimilated to the Han way of life, the Pai, living in Yunnan, were far from the center of party activities and began preparation for democratic reforms only after the PLA arrived in the spring of 1950.[87]

The integration and socialization of Sinkiang, with its strong separatist tendencies, Moscow-oriented Communist movement, and distinct culture, posed much greater problems. Great distances, poor communications, local resistance, and a desire not to offend the Soviet Union all seem to have been involved in the slower pace of reforms. In the three northernmost districts, Ili, Tacheng, and Altai—strongholds of the former East Turkistan Republic and in close proximity to the Soviet Union—the local governments continued in separate existence under nominal party suzerainty and were not subordinated to the provincial government in Urumchi until the fall of 1950.[88]

Plans to instill a sense of Chinese patriotism in Uighurs and Kazakhs came athwart the demonstrably higher standard of living enjoyed by their kinsmen in the Soviet Union. They clearly would have preferred to link their economy with that of the Soviet Union rather than that of China. *Jenminpiao* (JMP) did not begin to replace local currency until November 1951,[89] much later than in other areas and a full six months later than in Inner Mongolia,[90] which was in itself an exceptional case.

In Sinkiang as a whole, democratic reforms were begun in 1952 and multinational hsiang created soon after. In urban and agricultural areas, elections to People's conferences began to be held only in 1953 and continued through 1954. Land reform was said to have been "basically completed" in these areas in 1953. In deference to Muslim feelings, land belonging to religious establishments was said to be untouched "except for certain plots already transferred to the peasants," and members of religious orders were given equal rights with the peasants in possession of land.[91]

In herding areas, including Sinkiang, Inner Mongolia, and Ch'inghai, a policy of "no struggle, no liquidation and no distinction of classes" was carried out. Reforms in pastoral areas centered on inducing the herdsmen to accept more efficient methods of production: scientific breeding techniques, inoculations against disease, and the like.[92] Cognizant of the mass animal slaughters that had characterized collectivization in the USSR two decades before, the party made efforts to reassure herdsmen that no such action would be taken without "adequate preparation and the consent of the masses." The party also promised to protect pasturelands from being appropriated for agricultural use, thus avoiding the KMT's major error in the herding areas.[93] Even so, elections could not be held in the three northern districts of Sinkiang until 1956, the official reason being that "conditions [there] were too unsettled." [94]

Another attempt at integration was the Production and Construction Corps, formed from the soldiers of the Han garrison who had defected to the CCP in the fall of 1949. Its avowed aim was to serve as an example to local peoples, both in agriculture and animal production.[95]

With the slogan "on one shoulder a rifle, on the other a hoe," the corpsmen were expected to increase production while guarding against counterrevolutionary movements and—as was admitted when Sino-Soviet friendship had begun to cool—defend the frontiers of the ancestral land.[96] The parallel with the military agricultural colonies of imperial China is obvious.

Both production and military functions were exercised from the beginning. Sinkiang's large uncultivated areas apparently responded well to Production and Construction Corps efforts, and large increases in grain, cotton, and animal production were reported, as well as the establishment of light, medium, and heavy industries. The corps also constructed four model farms, including irrigation works, and then turned them over, complete with tools, to peasants of Han, Hui, Uighur, Kazakh, Sibo, and Russian nationality. The corps also participated in road and railway building, which—just as native leaders had predicted when the KMT announced its intention to improve communications with China proper—opened the way for Han immigrants. During the period immediately preceding "voluntary" democratic reforms, the party transferred to the corps more than 10,000 party cadres and young urban intellectuals from outside Sinkiang to "help." [97]

Another KMT plan that Sinkiang leaders had resisted, the absorption of the East Turkistan Republic's army into regular Chinese forces, was accomplished by the CCP in 1950,[98] the corps' presence serving as a deterrent to any separatist plans this move may have called forth.

In fact, however, both democratic reforms and increases in production in Sinkiang during this period were overshadowed by the party's work in surveying and prospecting.[99] As late as the fall of 1948 only 3.6 percent of the province had been systematically surveyed; it was believed that the Soviet Union had done more extensive work during the period of its friendship with Sheng Shih-ts'ai, but results had been kept closely guarded.[100] All parties were agreed, however, that mineral deposits must be substantial. In line with the Sino-Soviet Treaty of 1950, the exploitation of Sinkiang's resources was initially carried out jointly with the Soviet Union. Though China probably profited from Soviet aid in the area, the joint exploitation provisions were clearly an affront to China's national pride and were removed after Stalin's death, following a visit by Khrushchev to Peking. The importance attached to Sinkiang by the party is reflected in the fact that despite extensive production and construction activities undertaken in Sinkiang, the province had no budget for the three years from 1950 through 1952. The large expenditures described above were financed from the central government treasury at a time when reconstruction of the wartorn economy of China proper and the Chinese commitment in Korea posed more pressing problems.

The founding of the Sinkiang Uighur Autonomous Region (SUAR) in September 1955 reflects the party's increased confidence in its position in Sinkiang. Wang En-mao, a Han and the PLA commander in the province since 1952, became First Party Secretary. Saifudin, the Moscow-trained Uighur who had been deputy governor since 1949, now became governor. He replaced Burhan, who had been retained as governor since his last-minute defection from the KMT. Burhan was demoted but not purged. Minority intellectuals such as Uighur writer Zia Samedi and Kazakh author Kazhykumar Shubdanov, often Moscow-educated but intensely aware of their own nationality's history and culture, filled many lower-level positions.[101]

Next to be reformed were the more remote areas of the Southwest. Here, despite the absence of an indigenous Communist movement, the party's desire to gain support was aided by the demonstrably superior Han standard of living. Some of the minorities in this area had a level of technology so low that they were unable to make cooking pots. Meals were prepared on three stones pushed together on top of a fire. Glass bottles were considered a great treasure. Such peoples could be vastly impressed with gifts entailing a relatively small capital expenditure; it was hoped they would then be more apt to accept cadres' suggestions that to travel the socialist road under the party's direction would bring them, too, the benefits of Han civilization. In addition, no other power was seriously competing for these peoples' allegiances. Though many of the nationality groups were divided by an artificial border separating China from the states of Southeast Asia, none of these states was a match for China, nor did any exercise more than nominal control over the areas near its borders.

On the other hand, the primitive life styles of the inhabitants made it difficult for them to grasp even the most simplified concepts of communism. It was at first assumed that groups classified as being in the stage of "primitive communism" would be relatively easy to lead toward socialism: their lands, or at least part of them, had been held in common and they had not developed an attachment to private property. Unfortunately, while there was indeed little problem in convincing these people to share, it proved virtually impossible to link their generosity with the drive to increase production. Such people had always lived for the present, had no concept of long-term hedonism, and, having generally been provided for in their hour of need by one of their more affluent fellows, refused to be convinced that there was any use in working harder. Given pigs to breed, they killed all of them and held a feast; given a month's supply of grain, they ate all they could and fed the rest to their animals. The idea of work points proved particularly difficult to get across. The Chingpo minority, for example, had an extremely low opinion of those who kept tallies on what one person did for another, feeling that this was evidence of a "bad heart." One elderly man expressed his—and the party's—dilemma succinctly: "It's all nonsense. Life isn't like that. I was a child, then a man, and now I am old and weak. That's life and we are all the same. I don't agree with these work points. One day I feel like working, another day I want to have a drink or sleep. In a lifetime everyone does about the same. So I say share and share alike, and never mind what a man does on this or that day." [102]

In addition, such minorities may have felt that what they would have to sacrifice in order to attain the Han Chinese living standards was too great to make the effort worthwhile.

Though the presence of many relatively small minority groups lessened the possibility of organized resistance to the party, it also increased the difficulties of dealing with the area as a whole. Cadres would have to be trained in dozens of different languages and acquaint themselves with widely varying customs. A bewildering complexity of social organizations existed in which one minority group might control another and in turn be controlled by a third. Among one group, the Yi, slave society had become so highly stratified that it was possible for slaves to own slaves. A variety of superstitions abounded; not least among cadres' problems was the Wa minority's belief that their crops would not grow unless fertilized each year with a fresh Han head.

The small work-team method backed up by the military potential of the PLA proved the most effective way to reach such peoples, although it was risky to the cadres involved. Teams were coordinated by organizations known as Production and Cultural Stations located on the hsiang level [103] and were under the supervision of the Nationalities Affairs Commission in the hsien capital. The origin of these stations was said to be a similar device used earlier by the USSR in dealing with its Eskimo population. In addition to assigning teams, the stations were in charge of trade work—supervising local markets, setting up stores for the distribution of state-supplied goods, and sending out mobile trading groups. They also set up and coordinated medical services, schools, technical training classes, and in general were responsible for day-to-day work in their areas. Until a more regularized government organization could be set up, the Production and Cultural Stations constituted local government.[104]

More orthodox government organizations could not be set up for a long while in many areas. To speed the process, an exception was made to the general rule that democratic reforms should precede the founding of an autonomous area. Even in the case of the relatively advanced Tai, the founding of the Hsi-shuang-pan-na Tai Autonomous Chou preceded by a full year the carrying out of democratic reforms in 1956.[105]

Analysis of a group's readiness to carry out reforms was relatively so-
phisticated. For example, the Yi of some areas were judged to have
entered feudal society by the time of liberation; they were expected to
carry out democratic reforms several years earlier than Yi whose society
was based on slavery.[106] Among the latter, the drive to abolish slavery
began only in late 1956, followed by democratic reforms the next
year.[107] Still, a leading slaveowner became hsiang head and a delegate
to the National People's Congress.[108]

A similar policy of differentiating between two groups within the
same nationality was followed with regard to Tibetans. Though the
treaty signed with the government of the Dalai Lama in 1951 did not
specify the area to be regarded as Tibet, the party informally treated the
area west of the Chin-sha River as being under the nominal jurisdiction
of the Tibetan administrative area. This informal arrangement was
formalized when the KMT-created province of Sikang was abolished in
1955. The land east of the Chin-sha became part of Szechwan and that
to its west, of Tibet.[109] Preparations for the establishment of autonomous units in the eastern sector began much earlier than in the west,
with democratic reforms beginning in Tibetan areas of Sikang, Szechwan, and Ch'inghai in 1954.[110]

Tibet's reputation as a land of mystery notwithstanding, it is here
that our knowledge of Chinese Communist efforts at integration and
reform is most complete. This is not, of course, a result of party publicity, but an indirect result of revelations made in the wake of the Tibetan
revolt and during the course of the Cultural Revolution. With its relative isolation from China, unique culture, geographical proximity to
India, and desire for independence, Tibet provided the CCP with its
severest problems in national integration. Both administrative changes
and changes in the infrastructure of Tibet began almost immediately
after the PLA arrived in Lhasa, though, in deference to clauses in the
1951 agreement that provided for maintenance of the administrative
status quo, the former were kept muted.

A program of road building was the most noticeable initial undertaking, with Tibetan peasants being hired to help at what constituted a
high wage for the area. The first route connected Sikang with Lhasa. A
second, begun only a few months after the first, connected the Tibetan
capital with Ch'inghai, and a third, passing through land claimed by
India, connected Lhasa with Sinkiang. Though not extensively built up
until several years later, the roads did make traffic between Lhasa and
other parts of China significantly easier. Several spurs, varying in quality
and degree of usability, soon linked other important Tibetan cities with
the larger trunklines.[111]

By 1952, telegraphic and postal communications had been instituted with China proper.[112] A Tibetan language radio program was being broadcast from Chungking,[113] and a newsletter, the Lhasa Daily, was being published in separate Chinese and Tibetan editions.[114] It later became a full-fledged newspaper. Branches of the Bank of China were set up in Lhasa and Shigatse. A gradual reorientation of trade from India to China began. Possibly as a result of promises made to Khamba traders such as the Pangda brothers in return for their cooperation during liberation, a certain amount of leeway remained in trade relations. As late as 1958, luxury items that had all but disappeared from Chinese markets were available in Tibet. Swiss watches and expensive cameras and fountain pens were reportedly available in Lhasa at prices considerably below those in Hong Kong.[115]

A primary school, said to be the result of six months' joint planning by the PLA, Lhasa residents, and the Local Government of Tibet, opened its doors in 1952. The pupils' first act was to send a telegram of thanks to Mao Tse-tung for his beneficence.[116] Branches of mass organizations, including the Cultural Society of Patriotic Youths and the Lhasa Association of Patriotic Women, were instituted, also generally acknowledging the assistance of the PLA. Though names of Chinese advisers appear frequently on the name lists of various organizations, they were, of course, predominantly staffed by Tibetans. In accordance with the provisions of the united front, there was heavy reliance on the so-called upper strata. For example, Madame Ngapo Ngawang Jigme, wife of the defector, was head of the Lhasa ladies' organization,[117] and family members of the Dalai and Panchen lamas figured prominently on many committees and mass organizations. Cadres were being trained at a PLA-run school in Lhasa, and in February 1952 it was announced that Tibetan troops were being integrated with the PLA.

In its attitude toward the government of Tibet, the party again demonstrated expertise at using fissures within a group to its own advantage. As has been seen, Tibetan society was highly factionalized, a major source of friction being that between the secular nobility and the church hierarchy. Within each group cleavages also existed: the noble families sought to gain ascendancy over one another, and each monastery jealously guarded its own prerogatives. Geographical cleavages were added to this, with the Khambas of Chamdo and Goloks of Ch'inghai distrusting the citizens of Lhasa and in turn being distrusted by them.

The nobles, seeking to increase their power over the church, both as a group and as individuals, might have been sympathetic to the party's desire to set up a purely secular government, and some at least allowed themselves to be associated with such efforts. The Dalai Lama and his advisers clearly wished to expand on the previous reincarnation's work in centralizing power in Lhasa and in carrying out various reforms. Attempts made prior to the PLA's arrival had fallen short of completion due to resistance from vested interests.[118] For the Panchen Lama, co-operation with the Chinese meant an opportunity to return to his traditional place in Shigatse. Khamba merchants were placated with promises of trading privileges.

The Panchen Lama was duly returned to Tibet after being treated to a grand tour of China. Press releases from his various stops stressed his humble gratitude for the hospitality shown him.[119] Accounts of his triumphal entry into Shigatse described the city as gay with *red* flowers and banners, and noted that many youths in the crowd wore pictures of Mao on their breasts. Banners in Chinese and Tibetan were festooned across the parade route, proclaiming the unity of the Dalai and Panchen lamas in their joint efforts to build a new Tibet. The communiqué modestly added that political workers of the PLA had participated in the preparatory work for the event.[120]

Chinese policy was to treat the government of Tibet as if it were composed of three subdivisions: the government of the Dalai Lama centered in Lhasa, that of the Panchen Lama centered in Shigatse, and a purely secular government centered in Chamdo. This arrangement, which could be seen in the composition of the Tibetan delegates to the conference that drew up the 1951 agreement between Tibet and China, was later formalized when a preparatory committee for the Tibet Autonomous Region was set up in 1955. Tibetan areas of Ch'inghai, the Tibetan province of Amdo, were dealt with through the regular Ch'inghai provincial administration. The Lhasa government, which maintained, with some justification, that is spoke for all Tibetans, fumed quietly but could do nothing. The term *divide and rule* is somewhat misleading in this context, since the Chinese did not divide so much as use existing divisions to further their own ends. By enlisting all available factions in a government, the party not only maximized its chances to play one side off against another, but also was able to cast itself in the role of peacemaker.

Meanwhile, the Lhasa government found other problems more pressing. Bound under the terms of the 1951 agreement to supply the PLA with food, the Lhasa government found it difficult to meet the army's requisition orders. The Dalai Lama's outspoken prime minister, Lukangwa, pointed out that the army's appropriation of local food supplies was inconsistent with its statements that it had come to help Tibet, that this confiscation and its road building projects were causing a severe inflation, and that soldiers' burning bones[121] in the city of Lhasa was offensive to Tibetan religious beliefs.[122] The Chinese then insisted on his dismissal. There were no personal reprisals. In fact, Lukangwa was escorted to the Indian border and was apparently allowed to take much of his wealth with him. Since the shortcomings listed by Lukangwa were publicly admitted by the Chinese,[123] the prime minister's outspokenness would not seem to have been the primary reason for his dismissal. Rather it would appear that his ouster allowed the Chinese more direct access to the hitherto sacrosanct presence of the Dalai Lama. Further evidence indicating an effort to remove the aura of mysticism surrounding the Dalai Lama can be seen in his announcement in 1953 that henceforth he would be accessible to all subjects.[124] Hitherto the custom had been that commoners could not even look upon his person.

By 1955, with road and telegraphic links to China proper functioning, trade increasingly oriented toward China, army units integrated into the PLA, and preliminary, if rather limited, indoctrination work being done via schools, newspapers, radio, and cadre training, the formation of the Preparatory Committee for the Tibet Autonomous Region was announced. Its composition reflected the party's previous policy. Of a total of fifty-one delegates, fifteen were from the government of the Dalai Lama at Lhasa, ten from the Panchen Lama's government at Shigatse, ten from the Chamdo People's Liberation Committee, eleven representing the larger monasteries, religious sects, and mass organizations, and five from Chinese personnel stationed in Tibet. The Dalai Lama was named chairman. In conformity with the pattern seen elsewhere, General Chang Kuo-hua, the real power on the committee, did not hold first place on it, but shared a position as deputy chairman with the Panchen Lama. Chief collaborator Ngapo Ngawang Jigme was named secretary general. Tibet, however, deviated from the pattern seen in most other minority areas in that the establishment of a preparatory committee was not correlated with the completion or imminent undertaking of democratic reforms. In fact, an important part of the Dalai Lama's speech at the inaugural meeting of the preparatory committee was specifically aimed at quieting fears on this score:

Recently some news from nearby provinces and cities where reforms are being carried out or prepared through peaceful and consultative methods have reached Tibet and aroused suspicion and worry among some people here. Simultaneously, some people with ulterior motives state that reforms will be introduced in this area following the establishment of the Preparatory Committee for the Tibet Autonomous Region. This is vicious rumor mongering and incitement. . . . Chairman Mao has often told us that we should carry out reforms slowly and with patience. . . . What we should consider first is how to unite ourselves and make active efforts to carry out the work of the Preparatory Committee . . . and by continuously promoting the work of Tibet we can carry out reforms from the upper level downwards by means of peaceful consultations at the appropriate time.[125]

Tibet, then, represents the extreme end of the spectrum as far as the implementation of reforms is concerned.

In sum, the first five years of minorities work in the CPR were characterized by moderation and flexibility. Efforts were made to profit from the experiences of the USSR and of the KMT. Roads, telegraphs, newspapers, and radio stations were constructed to link the infrastructure of minorities areas with that of Han China. In order to remove outstanding grievances between Han and non-Han, minorities were given legal equality, and derogatory place names and proper names for minorities were replaced with more dignified titles. The policy of "doing good and making friends" allowed the party to gain the trust of minorities peoples while obtaining a basic knowledge of their areas that would facilitate future moves to bring about social change. Modest efforts were made to improve the economic position of minorities peoples, but generally speaking these were attempted only when they could be achieved without coming into conflict with the overriding goal of attaining solidarity with minorities peoples—that is, by introducing new cultivation techniques where they were not forbidden by religious beliefs and superstitions, or by making available certain desired commodities that had been in short supply. A concomitant result was to tie the economy of such areas with that of Han China.

A wide range of policies was followed in various areas, differing according to the party's assessment of conditions in a given area. This assessment would frequently result in different policies being pursued toward two groups in the same nationality: for example, land reform might be carried out among agricultural but not pastoral Mongols. Selective health, educational, and cultural programs were undertaken. A system of political units ensuring minority representation was devised on an experimental basis, then revised and codified. The main thrust of political work, however, concentrated on instilling a consciousness of being Chinese in minority peoples and on helping them to feel a sense of participation in a multinational Chinese state. Mao Tse-tung, portrayed as the leader of all nationalities, was to personify this new unity. Subsidized distribution of radios and magazines with a nationwide circulation laid the groundwork for the development of a common culture. Minorities activists and cadres were carefully trained and the more promising recruited into the party. Party structures were created in those areas where they had not existed; party organizations that had existed in minorities areas prior to liberation were expanded and strengthened. The establishment of People's governments, though typically containing a number of the personages who had constituted the traditional elite, set up an alternative form of government and left the traditional structures to wither away. National party and government organs portrayed themselves as patrons of all nationalities' cultures. Though there were unmistakable overtones of the "Han man's burden," every effort was made to publicize the idea that each nationality had not only something to learn from the others but something to contribute as well. Unlike preceding Chinese governments, the CCP had sought the minorities out.

6

The Radical Experiment and Its Background, 1956-1958

The policies pursued during the early years of the Chinese People's Republic might have been undertaken by any strong liberal government trying to achieve integration with the least possible friction, and in general they proved quite successful. Resistance was localized or passive and was not a cause of serious embarrassment for the government. In many areas, ideology seemed to be held in abeyance, both in actions taken toward minorities and in the attitudes expected of them. Acquiescence toward the presence of the Han and the broad principles of socialism rather than wholehearted enthusiasm for either was deemed sufficient. As late as 1956 it was stated that this would continue to be the case, at least for the forseeable future.

Gradualism Continued

In June of 1956, Nationalities Affairs Commission Chairman Ulanfu delivered a major speech to the National People's Congress. Entitled "Success in Nationalities Work and Questions of Policy," it dwelt at length on the achievements attained by the party's policies in minorities areas during the past years. These achievements were said to prove the correctness of the party's policies. Ulanfu stated that while reforms could be carried out externally and by order from above, they would prove superficial and cause resentment. Truly meaningful change would occur only if minorities genuinely desired reforms and were able to implement these reforms themselves. Liu Shao-ch'i's earlier statement was reiterated: that because different nationalities had vastly different economic and social levels, no one timetable of reforms could possibly apply to all.

With respect to the position of members of the minorities' upper strata during reforms, Ulanfu promised that their political position would not be changed, that posts in the new governments would be found for them, and that their standard of living would not be reduced. The People's Government would even pardon those elements who had opposed democratic reforms if they would repent and no longer oppose reform. Those who had worked on consultative bodies prior to the reforms would be permitted to continue their duties; those who had initially refused to cooperate but who had changed their minds would be assigned to proper posts.[1] Ulanfu's choice of the phrase "no longer oppose reforms" as the criterion for acceptance into People's governments is indicative of the low level of commitment expected from minorities and of the efforts made to woo them.

Although policies continued in accordance with the earlier flexible, experimental approach, an attempt was also begun to classify and systematize past experiences in order to prepare for the absorption of minority areas on a more regular basis. In January 1956, the State Council moved to formalize the autonomous area system. The nationalities democratic coalition governments, which had been set up in earlier years to ensure minorities participation and to protect their rights in areas where they had been abused, were abolished with the proviso that they become either autonomous areas or regular administrative units of the CPR, as the relative proportions of the population and "desires of the masses" seemed to demand. In the case of those areas that reverted to regular administrative status, Chou En-lai explained that while coalition governments had been necessary during the early days of the CPR, their raison d'être had disappeared. The principle of equality of nationalities was now thoroughly established, appropriate numbers of minorities' representatives had been provided at all levels of government, and the rights of all nationalities were safeguarded by the constitution. Where the concrete situation seemed appropriate, autonomous areas were to be set up at the provincial, prefectural, and county levels. Autonomous areas equal in status to a province would be known as autonomous regions (*tzu-chih ch'ü*), those equivalent to a prefecture as autonomous chou (*tzu-chih chou*), and those on the county level as autonomous hsien (*tzu-chih hsien*). Autonomous hsiang (*tzu-chih hsiang*) might also be set up at the administrative village level.

Where personnel turnovers or reductions were required, a "good job" was to be made of arrangements for those displaced and explanations made to the populace affected. To prevent rash and hasty actions, the timetable for these changes should be decided in accordance with the concrete conditions of the areas involved, but work was to be completed by the end of 1956 at the latest.[2] These moves toward systematization appear to reflect the party's increased confidence in its position in minorities areas and the better-organized administrative structures it had developed there.

In July of the same year the Nationalities Committee of the National People's Congress met in plenary session to discuss a new, long-term program of regional autonomy. As explained by Hsieh Fu-min, a vice-chairman of the committee, the need for a new outline had been prompted by problems that had emerged in setting up autonomous areas in the last few years. The draft plan he presented was intended as an outline to provide the autonomous areas with a basic reference work in their efforts to formulate regulations on local self-government; it was to enable autonomous areas to administer their internal affairs in accordance with the constitution, take special characteristics into account, and carry out the socialist transformation and construction smoothly.[3] Despite these extravagant claims, the document itself contains little that is new. It seems to have been drawn up to provide autonomous areas that might be founded in future with a ready-made administrative blueprint and to state more emphatically than had heretofore been the case that, although autonomous areas would have plenty of time to prepare, they must expect to carry out socialist reforms eventually.

Research and Classification

Undoubtedly closely connected with this warning that socialist reforms would have to be carried out eventually was the announcement two days later that a massive, long-term social history project on the minority nationalities was being undertaken. The study was to take four to seven years to complete and would include eight separate areas: Szechwan, Yunnan, the Northwest, Kweichow-Hunan, the "Tibetan region," Kwangsi-Kwangtung, Inner Mongolia, and the Northeast. Each would have its own team. A total of two hundred people would staff the eight teams, including historians and anthropologists of the China Academy of Sciences, professors and students from the Central Nationalities Institute and other universities in Peking and elsewhere. Experts on music, art, and literature were also included. The roster of names contained four scholars of international repute: Fei Hsiao-t'ung, Lin Yüeh-hua, Hsia Kang-hung, and Weng Tu-chien. All teams would make use of cameras, tape recorders, and motion picture equipment.[4]

The NCNA communiqué noted that on completion of the study, "the social and economic structure, the social classes and the customs and traditions of the major national minorities of China will be clearly understood. This will serve as a guide in future nationalities work and will also provide concrete and rich data for writing the history of various nationalities of China and the ancient history of mankind since the days of the primitive commune." [5]

Though the investigation is presented as primarily a scholarly undertaking, the timing of its announcement—that is, immediately after the draft on regional autonomy, with its stress on social reform, and the NCNA communiqué's admission that the knowledge gained in the investigation would serve as a guide in future nationalities work—leaves little doubt that a major purpose of the study would be to provide information necessary for the further implementation of socialist reforms.

In mid-August 1956, *Jen-min jih-pao* published a series of articles co-authored by Fei Hsiao-t'ung and Lin Yüeh-hua that summarized the preliminary work.[6] The better to assess their readiness to proceed with reforms, minorities were to be classified in accord with their level of social advancement. The categories of classification were set by Marx's analysis of societies based upon the relationships of production therein: primitive, slave, feudal, bourgeois-capitalist, socialist, and communist, arranged in ascending order. The initial task of the classifiers was simply to amass sufficient information on minority groups so that they could be fitted into this scheme of analysis.

Classified as in the stage of primitive society, characterized by dependence on hunting for a living, very simple tools, no fixed abode, communal ownership of land, work done in teams, equal distribution of crops, and no major divisions of labor, were the Olunchun of Northeast China, Kawa or Wa of Yunnan, Li of Hainan, and Kaoshan of Taiwan. Listed as belonging to the category of slavery society were the Yi of certain areas in Yunnan and Szechwan and the Chingpo of the same area. Feudal society, a much larger category, was divided into three subclasses. In one subclass, represented by the Tai of Yunnan, feudalism had been built onto the ruins of a past communal society, of which strong overtones still existed. The feudal aristocracy were believed to have emerged from the position of the local headmen, who had gradually institutionalized their informal position of leadership within a community and made it hereditary. In order to support their newly attained dignity, the hereditary headmen changed the traditional rule of equal distribution of land among members of a commune into equal distribution of financial obligations toward themselves. By this process, they were transformed into feudal lords.

A second subclass, said to be exemplified by the Uighurs of Sinkiang, entailed limited personal freedom for serfs, the requirement that serfs render free service to the landlord, and the landlord's allocation of land to serfs in return for a high percentage of the crop yield.

A third subclass, in which Tibet was included, was characterized by unity of state and religion, which, the authors noted, produces a strong socioeconomic basis for the society. Another characteristic of this type of society, according to the Fei-Lin analysis, is the obligation of peasants and herdsmen to render taxes and free service to the state, religious institutions, and feudal lords.

Fei and Lin, scholars in spite of their adoption of Marxist terminology, warned that "the social nature of minorities is complex" and not subject to facile generalization, that "hastiness and rush in classification must be avoided," and that "repeated investigation of materials" would be necessary. The tentative nature of data presently available was stressed and restressed.

The flexibility of their approach is also evident in that even nationality names were not accepted as fixed. Fei and Lin's work shows an attempt to come to grips with the problem of what exactly constitutes a nationality within the Marxist-Leninist framework. Prior to the elections of 1954, as part of the constitution's guarantee of suitable representation for minorities, voters were asked to state their nationality. Several hundred names were duly reported. Nationalities workers, mindful of the promises made to minorities, were doubtless appalled at the idea of helping several hundred groups to develop several hundred separate written languages, training cadres in these languages, setting up individual autonomous areas, and finding niches for a satisfactory number of their residents in government offices and on representative bodies. Fei and Lin were emphatic in their statement that a self-reported name of a nationality cannot automatically be assumed to confirm the existence of that nationality group.

As to what should serve as criteria for the existence of a nationality, the authors were less clear. Paying due respect to the elements of nationalism enumerated by Stalin in his essay "The National Question and Leninism"—common language, territory, economic ties, and psychological factors—the authors proceed to discuss their relevance to the investigative materials unearthed so far.

A language "common to a certain extent" does, they agreed, exist in the tribes and clans studied. But this does not imply that all the people in a certain tribe or clan must fully understand the speech of all the other people. There may be marked differences even within a single tribe or clan. The dialects of the Miao nationality, for example, vary considerably. These differences might indicate that people who originally spoke the same language came, through geographical separation of one group from another, to adopt certain features that would be unintelligible to the other group. On the other hand, it might also indicate that different groups who originally spoke different languages had gradually been coalescing into a single group with a common language that retained certain regional peculiarities. A case in point here was the Yunnan group which Han refer to collectively as Chingpo. Some of these people speak a language commonly referred to as Chingpo, while others speak a tongue called Tsaiwa. Both languages belong to the Tibeto-Burmese linguistic group, but Chingpo is classified under the Tibetan branch and Tsaiwa under the Burmese branch. Clearly these are differences between languages and not between dialects of the same language. But Chingpo and Tsaiwa speakers possess a similar social structure and economic relations. This could be one nationality evolving into two or two into one; in either case, classification would be difficult.

With regard to common territory, because of migratory and refugee movements, the area inhabited by a group might not be continuous, although its people retained common social ties and ideas. Examples given were the Hui and Miao, both of whom are found in widely scattered areas. Thus, territorial discontinuity does not rule out common nationality.

Application of the criterion of common economic ties was blurred by the presence of Han traders in many minorities areas. Living in market towns, they would often control the collection and distribution of goods in these areas, perhaps also owning a major portion of the land in the vicinity. Through this commanding position they in effect welded several groups with different language, customs, and religion into a single economic structure. Nonetheless, the groups could not be considered to have lost their separate characteristics through participation in this economic structure.

The criterion of common psychological traits, because of its abstract nature, was most difficult to deal with. The authors, struggling with a definition of the term, said that they felt a common psychological state could be referred to as a "national characteristic," but that there were "grave difficulties" in pinpointing it.

Since, according to Marxist doctrine, nations are characteristic of the bourgeois-capitalist stage of society, and since China's minorities had not evolved this far, there was the additional difficulty of identifying groups still in a formative period.

The authors stressed the impossibility of a simple measurement of nationality, the tentative nature of their data, and the fact that research must center on the concrete analysis of concrete problems. Clearly anxious to avoid conclusions—for reasons that probably reflected a desire to forestall charges of ideological unorthodoxy as much as a desire for careful scholarship—Fei and Lin were at pains to point out that their study was not an attempt to decide on behalf of a given group whether they were in fact one or several nationalities. On the contrary, their work was "merely a study of the evolution of various human communities," a bringing together of data and analyses to help those peoples who had reported themselves under so many groupings to decide "in consultation" what nationality they actually belonged to.

Unsatisfactory as it is, this represents the most detailed explication made under the CPR of what constitutes a nationality. While a genuine desire to classify minorities in accordance with scientific criteria was doubtless involved, Fei and Lin's tentative words on the subject also opened the way for an essentially political definition of nationality in which groups or, in party terminology, "the masses," having been given a set of facts prepared by party and government sources, may hold "peaceful consultations" and opt for the conclusions inherent in the data with which they have been provided.

The exact enumeration of minorities remained in flux for many years. In 1950 Fei Hsiao-t'ung had stated that China had "possibly more than one hundred nationality groups"; [7] this figure was reiterated by Liu Ko-p'ing in 1952.[8] Only a few days later, the party's theoretical journal *Hsüeh-hsi* (Study) struck a more hesitant note, saying that "so far as we know" there were only sixty minority nationalities.[9] A year later, *Ti-li chih-shih* (Geographical knowledge) declared that there were "about forty." [10] The 1956 edition of *Shih-shih shou-ts'e* (Current affairs handbook) listed forty-five,[11] and the 1957 edition of *Jen-min shou-ts'e* (People's handbook), forty-six.[12] By the time the 1959 edition appeared, five more had been added, totaling fifty-one.[13] The 1963 edition listed two more,[14] and the figure fifty-three remained stable through the 1965 issue.[15] This was the last issue published, presumably because of the Cultural Revolution, but other sources add a fifty-fourth.[16]

Generally speaking, those groups added later have been small groups living in remote areas—for instance, the Lopa and Menpa of Tibet— and those deleted have been considered either so assimilated, by the Han or by other groups, or so small as not to warrant a distinct status— for example, the Kelao and Ketou. Other names were eliminated when it was decided that they constituted branches of other minorities. The all-but-completely assimilated Manchus are officially considered a separate nationality, with their population listed as 2.43 million in 1965. Since the assimilation of the Manchus was a point of pride under the

KMT government, the CCP decision to give them a separate status was presumably taken for political reasons. Similarly, the highly assimilated Chuang and Pai might have been subsumed under the Han population save for a desire to avoid accusations that the party was consciously advocating a policy of assimilation.

Interestingly, while Russians (*O-lo-ssu*) have always been considered a minority, the Vietnamese have not been listed as such since 1954. The descendants of intermarriage between Han soldiers and Kweichow minorities were not declared to be a separate nationality, although they were unrecognizable as Han by Han arriving in Kweichow in the twentieth century.[17] By contrast, the Tunghsiang of Kansu, the offspring of Mongol soldiers intermarried with Han, Hui, and Tibetans,[18] were accorded separate status, possibly because the anomaly of their Islamic faith and Mongolian language did not allow easy inclusion into any other group.

The large (600,000) T'u-chia nationality was not "discovered" until 1956, the official explanation being that the T'u-chia had had to hide their national characteristics before liberation because of fear of repression.[19]

An announced investigation into the nationality status of the Tanchia (Tanka), a boat-dwelling people of south China, must have opted for a negative decision, since the group was not subsequently listed as a nationality. The Hoklo, another boat-dwelling people, are also not considered a minority. Linguistic and cultural subdivisions of the Han are not classified as minorities. Those groups now known as Cantonese and Hakka are descendants of Han Chinese who moved southward during the course of history. Their speech preserves archaic elements that have been discarded by present-day mandarin speakers. Thus, neither is classified as a minority nationality, nor should it be expected that they would be so designated. Other names are occasionally mentioned as nationalities in the Chinese Communist press, but since they do not appear in official listings, they must be presumed to be branches of nationalities that have been erroneously identified as separate groups. The Hsü-min of Fuchow and Amoy, mentioned in *Min-tsu yen-chiu* in 1958, are a case in point (see appendix).[20]

While Soviet ethnographers assigned to help the Chinese in classification work have openly disagreed with some of their hosts' decisions,[21] it would seem that since no single criterion for differentiating one nationality from another can be advanced, and since the accepted criteria occasionally conflict, some ambiguity must remain. If a decision on nationality status must be made, it might in several cases be made either for or against with equal validity.

Self-examination and Criticism

While classification work was considered the prime prerequisite for devising plans for reform, the party was understandably loath to wait for complete results. A second countrywide investigation of minorities work was undertaken in 1956, following a pattern similar to the first. Ulanfu summarized preliminary findings as:

1. insufficient attention to training minorities cadres for, and promoting them to, leadership positions. The party committees of some autonomous chou and hsien had not taken on any additional minority members for several years;
2. restrictions on minorities' rights to manage their own business and financial affairs in some autonomous areas;
3. lack of vigorous and practical support for devising and promoting written languages for minorities;
4. usurpation of minorities' cadres work by Han cadres.[22]

The existence of these defects notwithstanding, Ulanfu opined, much progress had surely been made, enabling "bold new strides" to be taken soon on the path to socialism.

This optimistic attitude was echoed in the Yunnan Party Committee's report on its investigation of minorities' work. A communiqué dated June 6, 1956, declared that a "new stage" had begun, manifest in "new demands" among the peoples of various nationalities. However, the ideology of the leadership had lagged behind the demands of the new situation. Their attitude was one of complacency over past achievements and of unwillingness to lead the minority peoples onward toward socialist development.[23]

It was unlikely that the masses were demanding socialist reforms, however. On the contrary, party ideologues had apparently become convinced that in most areas the preliminary work of consolidation had been achieved and that it was time to push onward to a new stage on the road to socialism. There now remained the problem of convincing a less-than-enthusiastic bureaucracy that the masses would respond positively to these changes.

The "new era" for minorities was to be made concrete in two ways: first, by a speed-up in the pace of socialist reforms in nationalities areas, and second, by the inclusion of minorities in the Hundred Flowers and antirightist campaigns. With regard to socialist reforms, an article published by *Hsüeh-hsi* in 1956 quoted Mao as saying: "Some people say that among the minority nationalities cooperativization cannot be carried out. This is incorrect. We have already come upon many cooperatives run by people of Mongol, Hui, Uighur, Miao and Chuang nationalities, and they have registered very good achievements. These refute the mistaken viewpoint of those who adopt an attitude of looking down on the minority nationalities." [24]

This was quickly transformed into a rapid increase in collectivization in minority areas. Whereas in July 1955 only 8.6 percent of the households in the West Kwangsi Chuang Autonomous Area (population 70 percent Chuang) had joined lower-level cooperatives and a target of 70 percent participation was set for the end of 1957,[25] in September 1956, 86 percent of the population had joined higher-level agricultural producers cooperatives (APC's).[26]

In July 1955, 52.5 percent of the agricultural population of the Yenpien Korean Autonomous Area (approximately 75 percent ethnically Korean) and over 40 percent of the Mongol agricultural households in Inner Mongolia had joined APC's; [27] in mid-1956 it was announced that "over 70 to 90 percent" of both nationalities were participating in APC's.[28] In Sinkiang, where the total non-Han population was over 85 percent, only 5.3 percent of the total number of agricultural households had joined lower-level APC's by September 1955. In June 1956 it was announced that by the end of that year "basic realization of cooperativization" (usually indicating a figure from 65 to 75 percent, but conveniently ambiguous in a specific case) would be realized in Sinkiang, the West Hunan Miao Autonomous Chou, the Hainan Li-Miao Autonomous Chou, and nationalities agricultural areas of Kansu, including Tibetan areas that were outside Tibet proper.[29]

Lower-level APC's came to minorities areas of Kweichow in the spring of 1956; by the end of that year, higher-level APC's had become "widespread." [30] In Tai areas of Yunnan, mutual aid teams were formed in 1956. Land reforms had been carried out there only the year before.[31] The more backward ethnic groups of Yunnan began democratic reforms in 1956, with Yi and Chingpo beginning to emancipate their slaves as well.[32] No land reforms were undertaken in Tibet proper.

The pace of reform in herding areas was also increased. The earliest reported instance of a herdsmen's cooperative, Inner Mongolia's *Ulan Aotu* (Red Star) co-op, was set up on a trial basis in 1954; [33] by the end of 1957, 24 percent of the IMAR's herdsmen—virtually all of whom are of minority nationality—were reported to have joined.[34] In Sinkiang, the speed-up in pastoral reform chiefly involved mutual-aid teams. By mid 1956, 40 percent of the SUAR's herdsmen were said to have joined, as opposed to 72.7 percent in Inner Mongolia.[35]

The speed-up in collectivization in minority areas dated from 1956, more than six months after Mao's July 31, 1955, order for an increase in the pace of collectivization in Han areas. Moreover, since most minorities areas started from levels of socialist reform far behind the Han, the percentage of minority families entering collectives stayed well below levels for Han China.[36] Collectivization in minority areas aimed at preventing minorities from falling further behind the Han on the path to socialism; it did not attempt to make them catch up. The same areas considered "advanced" in 1949—that is, on a level of development similar to the Han, usually achieved through living in close proximity to the Han, and with an indigenous Communist movement of some size—continued to carry out reforms at a level comparable to that of Han areas. The chief nationalities involved were the Chuang, Koreans, and agricultural Mongols.

Hui—though on an economic level comparable to the Han, but still, as a whole, fiercely independent and, partly because of their religious beliefs, not as receptive to communism—remained below these "advanced" nationalities in their levels of socialist achievement. Still further behind were the herding areas of Mongolia and Sinkiang and Tibetan areas outside Tibet. All of these had been much less influenced by Han culture over the course of history, all lacked a strong indigenous Communist movement, and all were somewhat removed from central government control because of geography and climate.

The still more remote areas of the Southwest, where conditions might truly be described as primitive, lagged yet further behind. Even their movement into the stage of mutual-aid teams while areas were forming cooperatives must be described as cautious. Last came Tibet proper, where not even land reforms were attempted at this time. As ever, it was protected by its geographical inaccessibility and internally well-integrated culture. As of early 1956, it still had no native party members.[37]

In other words, the differences between Han and non-Han areas in 1949 continued to influence the pace of these areas' integration into the CPR eight years later. Differences had not been removed, they had simply been raised to a higher level, socialistically speaking.

Minorities leaders' and intellectuals' opinions were solicited as a routine part of the 1956 investigation of minorities work. They were further encouraged to speak out by the rhetoric of the Hundred Flowers campaign, in which China's intellectuals, artists, and managerial personnel were urged to express their views frankly on the shortcomings of the CCP and its policies. Mao's presumption in launching this campaign appears to have been that allowing freer expression of opinions would release pent-up pressures against party and government and, by bringing these mistakes to light, permit the speedy correction of these mistakes. In the process, the unity of all Chinese under the socialist state would be strengthened.[38]

As reprinted in subsequent attacks on rightist "local nationalists," minorities spokesmen proved adept at using the party's statements against it. They were alleged to have argued that the system of unified purchase and sale of grain to the state was a violation of nationality customs, and that because of minorities' "special characteristics" co-operativization was unsuitable for them. The presence of Han cadres in minority areas was said to be counter to the party's principle of national-ization of autonomous organs. The conviction that the party was giving class education to nationalities cadres in order to divide and dissolve nationalities ideologically was expressed. A persistent complaint was that the Han were seeking, by means both devious and overt, to assimilate the minorities.[39] The policy of regional autonomy was termed "as useful as ears on a basket" (*lung-tzu ti erh-tuo*),[40] and nationalities cadres were termed "traitors to their nationality" or "jackals serving the Han." [41]

Separatist movements were reported among the Uighurs, who wished to set up an independent Uighurstan, Kazakhs wishing to unite with their fellow Kazakhs across the Sino-Soviet border, and Hui who wished to set up an Islamic state. A less radical form of separatism simply demanded that all Han leave minority areas, arguing that this was im-plicit in the party's promises to "nationalize" minority areas and to allow minorities to be "masters in their own houses." Some advocated that the unitary state be replaced by a federal system; others asked only for larger administrative areas and more positions for minorities therein. A common complaint was that minority areas were being exploited by Han. An interrelated and persistently voiced grievance was that autono-mous areas lacked control over their own finances. Yet another com-mon irritant was succinctly expressed by *Nan-fang jih-pao* (Southern daily): "Many rights in theory, few in practice" (*ming-tuo shih-shao*).[42]

Many Hui refused to accept the "advice" of party personnel, claiming that their only valid political mentors were the *Ahron*, or prayer leaders. Others refused to serve in the PLA on grounds that their "special characteristics" forbade participation in any war save a holy war.

Minorities cadres who considered themselves dedicated socialists also had their complaints. Han cadres, they felt, tended to be arrogant and overbearing. They were unwilling to learn minorities languages, loath to observe local etiquette when it did not suit their convenience, and in general exuded an air of what the party had called Great Han chauvin-ism. And, last but not least, the regulation of autonomous area finances had not been suitably worked out.[43]

Rectification and Reassessment

The decision to include minorities in the antirightist campaign was taken by NAC-sponsored forum on nationalities work held in Ch'ing-tao during the summer of 1957.[44] This was some weeks after the reversal of the Hundred Flowers policy in Han areas, which began in early June. Not surprisingly, the principal content of the campaign in minority areas was declared to be the struggle against local nationalism. This decision having been made, the mass media dutifully followed along with wordy denunciations of local nationalism and righteous indignation at the ingratitude of a "small group" of minorities malcontents and those who had been misled by them. No longer would parochialism be overlooked in the effort to eliminate pan-Hanism. Forums on local nationalism were to be held and problems dealt with immediately. Since local nationalists employed remnants of ill will among nationalities left over from the past in order to undermine the unification of the ancestral land, they jeopardized the socialist cause. Thus local nationalism was equated with antisocialism, whether or not the local nationalist was actually against social reform. These "bad elements" must be "dragged out" by the masses and criticized. Punishments would range from imprisonment and reform through labor to demotion.

Considering the provocations with which it was confronted, the party's response was surprisingly mild. Beneath a torrent of criticism of local nationalism, there can be discerned a real effort to avoid destroying the fragile structure the party had put together with such difficulty in minority areas. Party Secretary General Teng Hsiao-p'ing in his report on the rectification campaign stressed that criticism of local nationalist tendencies must not be made too hastily and should have the support of the majority of party personnel and nonparty activists of minority nationalities.[45] When one excepts the majority of minorities' party members and activists from criticism in the campaign, the wording of Teng's speech seems to indicate that the traditional elite which had been co-opted into the CPR government would bear the brunt of the campaign. The speed-up in collectivization that preceded the Hundred Flowers period had, where feasible, placed minorities activists and new party members of minority nationalities in charge of cooperatives and mutual-aid teams, thus undercutting the position of the traditional elite. No longer considered as indispensable as they had seemed in 1949, held responsible for many problems that had arisen in the course of collectivization, and doubtless disgruntled enough to have voiced dissatisfaction during the period of blooming and contending, they were logical targets for the *cheng-feng* movement.

Any suspicions that this meant the end of cooperation with the traditional elite were quickly dispelled, however. Wang Feng, then a vice-chairman of the Nationalities Committee of the NPC and a deputy director of the UFWD, emphasized that the party would continue its united front policy and unite with all who could be united with. While admitting that "quite a number of persons in the upper strata of the nationalities" objected to socialism, he stated that their problems were still to be regarded as within the ranks of the people.[46]

Criticism of minorities was to be carried out by minorities, while Han cadres were told to concentrate on rooting out Great Han chauvinism. This tactic was, of course, designed to avoid the appearance of a confrontation between nationalities. In minority areas where democratic reforms had not yet been completed (i.e., Tibet) or where democratic reforms had been carried out but where the socialist transformation of the means of production was not yet complete (most of the Yunnan minority areas and the more "backward" nationalities of the North), the struggle against rightists was not to be waged among the general public, though socialist education might be conducted "within certain segments and in an appropriate manner." [47] Whether those convicted of harboring local nationalist sentiments were to undergo thought reform and reform through labor would have to be determined on a voluntary basis and in accord with their physical condition "and other factors." [48] The responsibility for such decisions was given to the local party organizations in minority areas.[49]

The severity of the campaign thus varied considerably from area to area. Hardest hit seems to have been Sinkiang, where local nationalism had been strong before 1949 and continued to be so. Zia Samedi, well-known Uighur writer, head of the autonomous region's Department of Culture and chairman of its Writers' Union, Ibragim Turdi, a Uighur and head of Sinkiang's Department of Internal Affairs, Abduraim Saidi, Uighur mayor of Urumchi, Abduraim Arsa, a Kazakh and head of the Ili Kazakh Autonomous Chou, and Kazhkumar Shabdanov, a prestigious Kazakh writer, were among those sentenced to reform through labor.[50]

Many were also purged in Hui areas, including numerous "progressive personages" on the autonomous chou level in Kansu, Honan, and Shantung, as well as traditional leaders who had been absorbed into the government structure of these provinces after 1949. Among those most prominently mentioned were Hsieh Hsi-san, Pai Ching-chang, "the P'an family," and Ting Tzu-cheng of Honan[51] and the chairman and vice-chairman of the national-level Chinese Association for the Promotion of Hui People's Culture, Ma Sung-t'ing and Ma Chen-wu.[52] An interesting sidelight to the accusations made against the Hui—and the Hui only—is that they were in sympathy with Chiang Kai-shek's desire to retake the mainland. In the case of Hui leaders in Shantung who were purged, this support was said to have taken the form of active collusion.[53] Reports issued from time to time by the Taiwan government claim the active support of groups in Shantung,[54] making the CCP claim seem at least plausible.

The minority areas of Hainan, relatively primitive compared to Sinkiang and the Muslim areas and more insulated from the disruptive effects of mainland mass movements, received a directive to bloom and contend only after the rectification campaign had begun on the mainland.[55] The antirightist campaign in the Li-Miao Autonomous Chou thus took on a rather peculiar tone in which the party and government, told to carry out rectification, could find no spokesman for the rightist case. An article in *Min-tsu t'uan-chieh* entitled "Is There Nothing to Oppose?" sought to resolve this dilemma by criticizing as local nationalism the unprogressive nature of Li cadres. This was said to be evident in such attitudes as considering the written language created for them under party auspices a nuisance, preferring to live in their traditional thatched huts rather than build tile-roofed houses, and tending to blame all shortcomings and mistakes on Han cadres.[56] In fact, however, only one Li cadre, on the hsien level, was accused of localism. The rest of those labeled "localists" or "rightists" were Han, of whom the majority had "inferior class backgrounds" or bad personal relations with their superiors. Smaller in number but more prominent were members of the former Hainan guerrilla units who had held effective power in the area for a long time and were declared localists because they regarded the island as their "independent kingdom." [57] This method of declaring Han administrators in minority areas to be localists in that they resisted interference with "their" territories appears again in the case of Sun Tien-ts'ai, member of the Kansu party's standing committee and a deputy governor of the province. He was accused of opposing the transfer into his "kingdom" of Hui cadres from other provinces.[58]

The most prominent person purged in Yunnan was Lung Yun, the ex-warlord who had remained a high-ranking member of the provincial government. Lung was accused of conspiring with fellow Yi in order to further a base plot calling for Yunnan for the Yunnanese and also of criticizing the alliance with the Soviet Union.[59] In keeping with the party's desire to avoid disrupting minority areas in which the socialist transformation had not yet taken place, the *cheng feng* campaign was not waged among the general public in Yunnan.

In Tibet, which had not yet undergone democratic reforms, the chief news in 1957–1958 concerned the withdrawal of a number of Han cadres and the promulgation of a policy of no democratic reforms in Tibet for at least six years. This last had been promised by Mao Tse-tung himself, as part of the chairman's celebrated essay "On the Correct Handling of Contradictions among the People." [60] Mao had added that even after the expiration of this six-year period, reforms would be undertaken only at the behest of the masses. No mass criticisms and no purges were carried out.[61] An NCNA communiqué merely noted that the Party

Work Committee in Tibet had "taken steps" to give local cadres and members of patriotic and mass organizations a course in socialist education.[62]

In considering the campaign as a whole, one is struck by the party's attempt to answer the charges of its critics on minorities policy and even, in some cases, to correct policy in accord with criticism. The three main instances thereof were:

1. demands for larger and more numerous autonomous areas;
2. charges that Han were exploiting minority areas, and that so-called autonomous areas were powerless to stop the process;
3. allegations of Han chauvinism.

While denouncing demands for larger and more numerous autonomous areas as local nationalism, the party soon brought to fruition plans to create two new provincial-level autonomous areas, the Kwangsi Chuang and Ninghsia Hui autonomous regions, both inaugurated in 1958. The debates on whether (in the case of Kwangsi) to set up an autonomous region at all and on what areas should be included therein (in both Kwangsi and Ninghsia) were carried out with surprising frankness and reveal that the party was willing to antagonize significant numbers of Han to set up these areas.

In Kwangsi, the problem involved turning an entire province into an autonomous region for the sake of a Chuang minority of approximately 33 percent. Moreover, over 70 percent of the Chuang lived in an already existing autonomous chou in the west of the province, and most preferred to think of themselves as Han in any case.[63] At a meeting of the provincial assembly Chou En-lai, peppered with questions on the validity of such an action, tended to stress the necessity for Han to atone for their past ill treatment of the Chuang. He hoped that those who could not or would not accept this "theory of repayment of a debt" (*huan-ch'ing*) would be happier with the phraseology "tendering an apology" (*p'ei pu-shih*). The minorities must have concrete examples to show that Han were anxious to cooperate with them. Chou added that such a move was not unprecedented, as the inclusion of Suiyuan, with its assimilated Mongol minority, into the IMAR illustrated.[64]

In the case of the Ninghsia Hui Autonomous Region, the area for it was to be carved out of Kansu Province. The revelations of the Hundred Flowers period showed that holy wars continued to exist,[65] albeit on a small scale, after 1949, and relations between Hui and Han were extremely strained in some areas. In order to undercut the "slanders" of "reactionary instigators using religion as a cloak to stir up anti-Han feelings," these areas were, where geographically feasible, to be included in the new autonomous regions.[66]

With regard to charges that Han were exploiting minority areas, the party cited several instances where gifts of seed, grain, tools, and medicine had been made to needy peoples and pointed out that Sinkiang's entire budget had been underwritten by the central government for three years.[67] A campaign was launched to teach minorities that they and the Han were complementary: the Han, with their superior technology but overcrowded areas, merely sought a fair exchange of this technology for some products of the underpopulated and technologically backward minority areas.[68]

In addition, in June 1958, the State Council announced new regulations on finances for autonomous areas. Receipts from seven taxes (commodity, commodity circulation, business, income, agriculture, animal husbandry, and salt) formerly shared between central and local governments would henceforth be retained by the autonomous chou and hsien. Though localization of financial arrangements was a general power introduced at this time and not confined to minority groups, still ordinary administrative districts and hsien would continue to render a share of these taxes to the central government. As for remaining taxes (for example, on public utilities, livestock trading, local enterprises, vehicles, amusement, and so on) a fixed amount ought to be paid to higher authorities, this amount to be determined in accordance with local conditions. Any revenue remaining after payment of this fixed amount would not be taken by the state and would be retained by the local governments. The central government promised that the amount to be paid to higher levels would not be changed for five years. In case of a deficit on the local level, autonomous governments could request a subsidy, to be adjusted each year in accordance with the area's needs. Emergency subsidies could be requested in addition to this regular subsidy in time of natural calamity. New enterprises could, when approved by the central government, be financed by it under a special subsidy. The central government also promised to budget a higher expenditure level for autonomous chou and hsien—7 to 8 percent for the former and 4 to 5 percent for the latter. Autonomous areas were also given the power to reduce or exempt certain state taxes in accordance with local conditions and the special characteristics of nationalities.[69] The new measures, allowing autonomous areas greater flexibility and encouraging productivity and the development of local industry, were designed to reduce minorities' fears that they were being exploited by the Han.

As for allegations of Han chauvinism and the arrogance of Han cadres, the party countered with numerous examples of local nationalism and high-handed behavior on the part of minorities' cadres. One man, for example, was said to have gone to a hospital and, though not seriously ill, insisted that because he was a cadre of minority nationality, he had a superior claim to medical attention. Those ahead of him in line, even those sicker than he, should wait. A student riding a bus was alleged to have refused to pay for his ticket, feeling that his nationality entitled him to a free ride. Some minorities cadres would insist that Han cadres study their respective languages while refusing to study Han themselves. Others, who were able to speak Han, refused to do so and insisted on bringing interpreters with them everywhere.

The media allowed that these were particular rather than general situations. Still, they illustrated a more widespread ideology that included a one-sided emphasis on minorities' "special characteristics"; this was the very antithesis of the constitution's guarantee of equality. The party took great pains to point out that it was not saying that nationalities' special characteristics would be ignored in the future, it was simply that the revolutionary interest of the whole would have to be considered before that of any of its component parts.[70] Meanwhile, Great Han chauvinism would continue to be opposed as well.

The party also took care to reply to charges that it had gone back on its promises to "nationalize" minority areas. Nationalization had indeed been defined as the application of nationality methods, the use of nationality languages, and the appointment of nationality cadres in autonomous areas, but the party pointed out that it had never promised that *only* minority cadres would be appointed. The goal was and always had been not nationalization for its own sake, but nationalization in order to realize the leadership of the working class in the worker-peasant alliance. Nationalization was simply the means to this end: a method of harnessing minorities' political activism and enthusiasm for the communization of China. The nationalization of the organs of autonomous government would have to be subject to this greater good of the state and, at least at present, experience proved that it was necessary to maintain a number of Han cadres in minority areas to help in the administration thereof.[71] "Formalization," or rigid adherence to the idea of nationalization of autonomous area personnel, was to be rejected.[72] Still, party spokesmen made clear, efforts would be made to train minorities cadres.

Minorities continued to be given exemptions in certain areas such as the drive to reduce ostentatious funerals, the provisons of the divorce law, and the birth control campaign.[73] The party's concessions on these points cannot, however, be counted as a victory of the forces of ethnic diversity against the process of socialist integration. The antirightist campaign was used in many areas to speed collectivization. In Inner Mongolia, for example, "some people who thought of pulling out of [mutual-aid] teams and cooperatives" were persuaded to change their minds after being informed of the link between resisting cooperativization and holding bourgeois rightist sentiments. It was reported that, having learned about this link, "many herdsmen are offering to join the teams and cooperatives, and many mutual-aid teams want to reorganize themselves as co-ops." [74]

Similarly, no liberalization of policy is implied in the party's vehement denial that it desired assimilation. The problem was simply defined out of existence. Assimilation, *t'ung-hua*, was said to connote forcible suppression of nationality characteristics and to be the method employed by imperialist-bourgeois governments like the KMT. In socialist states, as the construction of industry increases, a common proletarian culture will gradually emerge and the similarities (*kung-t'ung hsing*) among peoples will become greater and greater as the differences become smaller. With the advent of Communist society, all differences will be amalgamated (*jung-ho*) in a common whole. This was a necessary, unavoidable law of historical development that was independent of one's subjective will. Only the subjectivist nationality viewpoint of the bourgeoisie and other exploitative classes was opposed to this historical materialist nationality viewpoint of the proletariat. Only such bourgeois exploiters or those duped by their spokesmen believed that a nationality was an already fixed form, unchanging throughout eternity.[75]

Closer attention was paid to the content of books and magazines circulating in minority languages, with some apparently shocking discoveries. In some areas, the proportion of "foreign materials" was found to constitute from 50 to 70 percent of all reading matter in circulation. Moreover, minorities tended to stress their own cultures and ignore "advanced" Han culture.

Some anthologists committed the heresy of putting "foreign poets" to the front of their works while relegating Mao Tse-tung and Chu Te to the back. Others appeared to deliberately avoid using Chinese terminology, preferring a Russian or English loan word, or would go to great lengths to translate a new concept into their own languages rather than borrow the Chinese term. It was alleged that often they would even reject Han terms that the local populace had already learned to use.[76]

These discoveries sent a clear message to party and government personnel: minorities often did not consider Han culture superior to their own. This was not only true for such groups as the Koreans, whose technological level was comparable to that of the Han, but occurred even where a given nationality's technology was obviously inferior to that of the Han Chinese. In seeking to understand this attitude on the part of minorities, the Chinese might have reflected on their own ninteenth-century efforts to adopt Western technology while leaving their own culture unchanged—"Western learning for practical use, Chinese learning for the essence," as the slogan of the day went.[77]

These slights to Han pride aside, some translations horrified socialist sensitivities as well. Capital (building), for example, was rendered as "the palace in Peking" and the CPG as "the imperial house." The Chinese civil war that brought the CCP to power was described as a "war between kingdoms," [78] thus implicitly denying the apocalyptic nature of what the CCP tended to see as a titanic struggle between the forces of good and evil. Henceforward, Han terms were to be employed in translating new concepts, and the mass media in minority areas would be more closely supervised.

The local nationalism manifested by minorities cadres was deemed due to their generally upper-class background,[79] thereby casting doubt on the credibility of earlier party claims of relying on activists among the poor and lower middle peasants. Educational institutions serving minorities were ordered to replace emphasis on patriotism with stress on the theory of class struggle.[80] Hereafter, the mistakes of minority cadres would not so readily be condoned.[81] The composition of the student bodies at minorities institutes also changed somewhat, the trend being toward admitting those of more humble class backgrounds. This did not mean that the children of "upper strata" were excluded; for example, the multitudinous offspring of Tibetan collaborator Ngapo Ngawang Jigme continued to gain admission to the Central Nationalities Institute as they came of age.[82]

Thus, while the events of the latter half of 1957 and early 1958 reaffirmed the party's desire to obtain complete integration, it was still envisioned as a long-term, gradual process. The antirightist campaign had given integration a gentle push, but no more than this. Relatively few minorities personages were purged; the concepts of nationalization, support for minorities' special characteristics, and the training of nationalities cadres continued. Rather than constituting a radical new phase in minorities policy, the *cheng feng* represented merely a logical continuation of past policy. The minorities had been included in the political events of Han China to a greater degree than before, but continued to be treated as special cases. The sins that had to be corrected in the campaign were deemed to be the result of a misunderstanding of the party's policy by both Han and non-Han and were not to be attributed to faults in the policy itself. The antirightist campaign, for all its sound and fury, amounted to no more than a gentle, cleansing rain.

The Great Leap Forward

Such gains as the minorities may have made in their desire to maintain separate identities were short-lived. A growing mood of impatience with China's progress was becoming manifest, ultimately to result in the Great Leap Forward. During the early years of its rule over minority areas the party, to ease the process of integration, had worked out a number of compromises with various nationality groups—on levels of cooperativization, timing of cooperativization, cooperation with the traditional upper strata, respect for "special characteristics," and encouragement of local languages. In the Great Leap Forward's plans to increase production, simplify administration, eliminate bureaucratism, and achieve pure communism, this congeries of compromises seemed to represent so many more examples of obstacles to success. Clearly such an ambitious program required unity. Diversity being the antithesis of unity, ethnic diversity came to be regarded as a hindrance to the achievement of the Great Leap's goals.

The party's desire to launch a vigorous move ahead in minority areas was also doubtless encouraged by the feeling that much progress had been made in training minority cadres and party members. In November 1957, *Min-tsu t'uan-chieh* proudly announced that China now had the core of a minority nationality party leadership group: 400,000 Communist party members, 400,000 cadres at or above the hsiang level, and 600,000 members of the Communist Youth League.[83] The party's desire to rely on these newly trained activists was reinforced by the feeling that many of the difficulties that had arisen during cooperativization in minority areas were due to the resistance of members of the traditional minorities elite. While cooperation with this upper stratum had been desirable until a group with more acceptable class backgrounds could be trained, the new elite was now, it was felt, ready to take over. The traditional elite was thought to have fulfilled its historical mission and, indeed, to be hindering further progress.

Justifiable as the party's pride in its accomplishments was, it tended to ignore the fact that progress had been uneven. The Mongols, who had had the best-developed Communist movement prior to liberation, also had a higher percentage of CCP members than any other minority. Three percent of the Mongols in Inner Mongolia were party members, as opposed to 2.3 percent of the population of Inner Mongolia as a whole.[84] The Chuang had a party membership of only 1.2 percent,[85] and the very first Tibetans from Tibet proper to be admitted to the party, a group of seven, had been initiated on July 1, 1956.[86] The Mongols' lead over other nationalities is further indicated by statistics on numbers of cadres. One and seven-tenths percent of the minority nationality population of the IMAR were cadres, whereas Han cadres were only 0.9 percent of the total Han population of China. With the exception of Kirin province, where 1.3 percent of the minority population (chiefly Mongols and Koreans) were cadres, minority nationalities cadres were always underrepresented in relation to the total minority population of the area.[87]

The Mongols' advanced position is also evident on examining party leadership in the autonomous regions. On the eve of the Great Leap, four out of five party secretaries and deputies in the IMAR were Mongols. At the time, the Han population of Inner Mongolia was estimated to have outnumbered the Mongol population by a ratio of approximately seven to one. In the Ninghsia Hui Autonomous Region, where the population was about 35 percent Hui, three out of six secretaries and deputy secretaries were Hui. In the Kwangsi Chuang Autonomous Region, where Chuang made up about a third of the total population, two out of six secretaries and deputies were Chuang. In the Sinkiang Uighur Autonomous Region, where the Han population was probably no more than 10 percent of the total and the Uighur population about 75 percent, there was only one Uighur deputy secretary out of a total of six secretaries and deputies. The others were all Han. In Tibet, where the population is virtually all Tibetan, there were no Tibetan secretaries or deputies.[88]

A perceived need to erase these disparities of economic and social advancement among the minorities was clearly one factor in the application of the Great Leap Forward to minorities areas. Another factor was the feeling that certain minority group members were deliberately impeding progress. Claims of the Hundred Flowers period, such as that minorities could not undertake socialist reforms because it would be against their special characteristics to do so, were especially irritating to many party people. It seemed that minorities had been using a concept devised to ease the transitional period in order to delay reforms indefinitely. Henceforward, claims to be inherently "different" or special in any sense would be regarded with utmost skepticism.

The drive for unity was not, of course, new in itself. But whereas previous policy seemed formed around a concept of unity within diversity, allowing a degree of ethnic and cultural plurality, the Leap aimed at unity through uniformity.

One of the first perceived barriers to unity was linguistic, and it is surely no accident that shortly after the announced beginnings of the Great Leap a "new high tide of enthusiasm for learning Han" was found to exist.[89] It was explained that since the Han were the main nationality both numerically and in terms of culture, to study Han did not mean assimilation but merely a desire to advance one's own nationality and all China by erasing the linguistic hindrance to learning advanced ways.[90] Even if one did not work in areas where there were Han, he or she would surely wish to know the language in order to study the Han elder brother's advanced experiences. Moreover, translation was both expensive and time-consuming; it would surely be more efficient if everybody could read the basic works of this advanced culture in their original form. Spare-time schools were established in order to fill linguistic and other gaps, and eager peasants of all nationalities were reported to be studying late into the night while working to produce more during the day, heedless of such basic needs as sleep.[91]

The attack on linguistic barriers to unity was accompanied by increasingly acerbic attacks on minorities' special characteristics. A few months earlier, propaganda had criticized those who tended to stress nationalities' special characteristics one-sidedly over the common characteristics of the whole, but as the Leap gathered momentum, the sector of valid special characteristics tended to diminish and the characteristics that the party felt properly belonged to Chinese of whatever nationality increased proportionately. The rationale behind this leveling process was, as expressed by Kweichow First Party Secretary Chou Lin, that "the fewer [the] differences among peoples, the faster development can be." [92] Dissension was fraught with danger, since protestors were apt to be labeled rightists or counterrevolutionaries.

In their zeal to increase production, the minority masses were said to have discarded decadent customs. Ironically, as short a time ago as the investigation of minorities work of 1956, the party had vigorously defended their right to these customs. Tibetan women in Kansu were said to have realized that the weight of their elaborate headdresses slowed down work in the fields and agreed to discard them. Then, too, the style used up a great deal of cloth that could be employed in more utilitarian ways. Others were reported to have ceased to wear the decorative sashes that had been the most conspicuous part of their national dress. The enormous amount of time spent in making these could now be devoted to field work, and the erstwhile wearers would be able to bend over unencumbered. The money saved would be used to buy wheelbarrows.[93]

Numerous festival days were abolished in the name of increasing production, and the ritual slaughter of animals was prohibited for the same reason. A thousand-year-old custom that Tai women did not work in the fields was reported "smashed." [94] Lamas and other religious figures who had not traditionally engaged in productive labor were reported to have taken up the theme and joined the happy throng on the way to the fields.[95] The exemption from burial and funeral laws was only a few months old when the press announced a cemetery relocation in Ch'ing-hai minority areas. The relocation, carried out so that 532 *mou* would be freed for cultivation, was reportedly a success despite the misgivings of "a few people." [96]

The Hui, whose eating habits constituted an important part of their religion, and who had been provided with special restaurants and ritual baths in many areas, were now reported eager to join multinational communes in whose mess halls they would be treated just like everyone else. A drive to encourage intermarriage, of which the Hui had been the chief opponents, was begun. A letter to the editor of *Chung-kuo ch-ing-nien* (Chinese youth), official publication of the Young Communist League, asked, "Is marriage between Hui and Han young people permissible?" It was answered in the affirmative. In fact, the editor pointed out, since Lenin had said that socialism meant the merging of all nationalities into one, intermarriage was indicative of a heightened socialist consciousness. Hui opposition, it was admitted, did exist, but the editor attributed it to outdated views and a failure to understand that happy marriages depended on common political aims and true love.[97] In Sinkiang, where a supplement to the national marriage law had been in force exempting minorities from the law's provisions on minimum age of marriage, divorce, and monogamy, it was revealed that the masses had "spontaneously" come to realize the dangers of early marriage and were demanding monogamy and legal sanction for divorce.[98]

The study of nationalities history and social conditions, once deemed so essential to the success of socialism in minority areas, came to an abrupt halt when it was decided that the scholars who had been taking part in it were guilty of "so-called bourgeois scientific objectivism." [99] This mistaken attitude manifested itself in a desire to "do research for the sake of doing research" instead of to increase production. Where dictionaries of a few hundred basic characters would suffice to communicate with minorities peoples, these researchers insisted that only by compiling works of tens of thousands of characters could communication be carried out properly. They had exaggerated the backwardness and special characteristics of minorities and ignored both the progress they had made and the numerous characteristics that all nationalities had in common.[100]

Fei Hsiao-t'ung was among those required to confess his errors on this score. He and others confessed inter alia to an attitude of "making thick the old and slighting the present" (*hou-ku po-chin*), which had caused them to gloss over the class struggle[101]—a glossing over which, it will be remembered, the party had seemed wholeheartedly to favor until 1957. In line with the Leap's slogan "more, better, faster, and cheaper," the minorities social history project, which had been envisioned as a four-to-seven-year undertaking, was given a year in which to be completed. Instead of the complete compendium of China's minorities originally planned, a simplified history and simplified gazetteer would be published.[102]

The idea of class struggle was introduced, thereby endangering the position of the traditional elite who had been co-opted into the CPR's organizational structure and who had profited by the party's decision that class structure in minority areas was not well developed. As in Han areas, the past attitude of reverence toward folk heroes and famous people of the past was now declared reactionary and counterrevolutionary. Much was made of Genghis Khan's brutality, in sharp contrast to the attitude that had led the party only a few years previously to hold a large celebration in honor of the Mongol leader.[103]

The leveling process of the Great Leap extended even to such apparently innocuous areas as entertainment. Minorities song and dance troupes began to sing revolutionary songs in the Han language and to adopt Han dance forms; it was asserted that the art forms of a nationality, like other nationality forms, were not permanent or unchangeable. They must continuously develop and change in accordance with the nationality's own development. In the "high tide of neighborliness" brought about by the Great Leap Forward, each nationality would unavoidably absorb the progressive and good things from "the more advanced nationality," and this absorption included art forms as well.[104]

The drive to attain a unity of purpose through the unity of external characteristics had been undertaken in the name of increasing production, and it was inevitably in the economic sphere that the main impact of the Great Leap was felt. Industry in minority areas was said to have gone "from nought to have" (*tzu-wu tao-yu*) in a few short months, thereby belying the party's previous claims to progress in such matters. Communes were formed in nearly all minority areas outside Tibet in the same few days in August 1958, regardless of the prior level of socialist reforms. Chuang and Korean higher-level agricultural producers' cooperatives, the lower-level co-ops and mutual-aid teams of herding areas, and primitive southwestern areas, which had only recently carried out democratic reforms, were transformed, literally overnight, into communes.[105] Minorities' cadres, newly trained in accordance with the party's post–Hundred Flowers policy of relying on the poorer classes, suddenly found themselves in positions of responsibility in the new units. It was announced that not only areas where conditions were comparatively good could form communes; so, "very definitely," could areas where conditions were most backward and difficult. The crucial factor that would allow these areas to bridge the gaps in their socialist development was, it was made plain, the help of the Han big brother.[106]

The better to obtain this help, mixed nationality communes were formed. Whereas previously the inclusion of more than one nationality in socialist cooperative units had been done cautiously and only where prospects seemed promising, the planners of the Leap, with their conviction that nationalities relations had entered a new era and their passion for large-scale organization, proudly announced the formation of multinational communes. Mess halls would also have mixed nationality dining.

Multinational units were to be formed, and not only in areas where nationalities had traditionally lived side by side. Where nationalities lived in discrete units, multinationalism was to be helped along by moving immigrants in. The State Council's announcement on October 14, 1958, that youth would be given a new role in building socialism resulted in large numbers of urban, educated Han youth being sent down (*hsia fang*) to minority areas, particularly to Ch'inghai, Kansu, Ninghsia, Sinkiang, and Inner Mongolia.[107] There they were expected to bring enlightenment to the natives while helping to develop the local economy. A contemporary woodcut showed costumed herdsmen (whose national dress presumably had not yet been judged to interfere with production) enthusiastically greeting participants[108] in this sinified version of "Go West, young man."

A large number of factories was planned, with the aim of encouraging self-sufficiency in areas that had begun to seem rather too dependent on state aid, and an ambitious project for transforming land once thought suitable only for grazing purposes into agricultural land was announced. As in purely Han areas, backyard blast furnaces and new agricultural techniques such as deep planting and close planting were employed. By November of 1958 it was announced that 145 communes had been set up in minorities areas, including 315,000 nationalities peasant households, or 77 percent of the total.[109]

As in Han areas, the deficiencies of the Great Leap began to be apparent very quickly. The December 1958 issue of *Min-tsu t'uan-chieh* reprinted an editorial from the *Inner Mongolia Daily* of November 5 that admitted that the socialist education movement had been "progressing slowly." A need to discuss, "especially to discuss communism," was stressed, and it was explained that for the present the so-called half supply system—that is, from each according to his labor rather than the pure communist system of from each according to his labor, to each according to his need—would be in force. Resistance to the communes was frankly acknowledged, with minorities capitalists held responsible.[110]

Other articles in the same issue alluded to "difficulties and unfavorable conditions" connected with the *hsia fang* movement,[111] the mess halls,[112] and the difficulties of trying to convince minority groups who, until a short time before, had been told that their class structures were not well developed, that they should be carrying out class struggle.[113]

By March of 1959, *Min-tsu t'uan-chieh* noted that despite the great accomplishments of the communes, problems existed in "a few areas," which were enumerated as:

1. mess halls
2. steel manufacture
3. labor
4. ideology
5. production
6. livelihood
7. administration
8. distribution
9. leadership work
10. nationality relations.[114]

Many of these problems were very similar to those occurring in Han areas. There was, however, one crucial difference between the impact of the Leap in minority areas and that in Han areas: the Great Leap Forward in minority areas was perceived as having been imposed from outside in an attempt to erase native culture and ways of life. The party's actions were clearly at variance with previous pronouncements that reforms would not be carried out except according to the desires of the minority masses themselves, and by them themselves. Introducing class struggle where the party had only recently declared that class tensions were not serious proved a mistake as well; the decision to move beyond the traditional ruling classes had apparently been made too quickly. The party was also perceived as having abandoned the role it had originally set itself as protector of minorities' cultures. The gap between past promises and Leap performance had, the Party admitted, caused it to "lose the trust of the masses in some areas" and production had "suffered disruption." [115]

Resentment against the party and government took many forms, ranging from passive resistance to grumbling and small-scale sabotage to rebellion. The revolt in Tibet is, of course, the most extreme example. It may seem paradoxical that Tibet, exempt from class struggle, the antirightist campaign, and the Great Leap Forward, and in which traditional customs and the position of the traditional elite had been little changed, should cause the party its major embarrassment in minorities policy. On further reflection, however, the paradox is more apparent than real.

Though the party had promised to allow Tibetan society to remain virtually intact in the near future and had, at least according to its own perception, tried very hard to keep this promise, party presence in Tibet could hardly avoid disrupting the traditional society. The need for laborers on roadbuilding projects disrupted the local economy and conflicted with serfs' duties to their masters. Even a modest cadre training effort provided an alternate channel of social mobility to the monastic career that had constituted the only indigenous method. The existence of serfdom deeply offended the socialist conscience and came into direct conflict with cadre training programs. Only a few months after Mao's speech promising no reforms in Tibet for at least six years, the area's party Work Committee ordered the abolition of corvée for its Tibetan cadres. While there is no evidence that the local committee shed any tears at having to rescind the Chairman's orders halting reforms, its action seems to have been forced by the conduct of a landlord who had beaten his serf, a cadre, who had refused to perform his traditional corvée duties. Knowing that no serf who opted for cadre training would be safe from his master's wrath if this type of action went unpunished, and that such an atmosphere would hardly be conducive to the training of social activists, the Work Committee "persuaded" the Tibetan government to exempt cadres from services to their masters.[116] Conversely, of course, this exemption would increase the attractiveness of a cadre career to the Tibetan masses, and it is quite possible that the assault was stage-managed by the party Work Committee with this end in mind.

Minor incidents such as the desecration of temples by unruly soldiers, the burning of animal bones by Han personnel—which ran counter to Lamaist beliefs—and the installation of radio facilities on consecrated peaks added to the Tibetans' grievances.[117] The intermarriage of Han PLA men with Tibetan women may have disturbed the Tibetan male-female ratio.[118] Whether or not such things were consciously planned by the party, they had exacerbated Sino-Tibetan relations to the point where small-scale rebellion was endemic. The introduction of reform in any one sector of the well-integrated Tibetan society seemed to disrupt normal functioning in its other areas. Party demands were given outward assent by the traditional administrative structure, which then apparently worked in private to avoid compliance. Resistance movements went unchecked by the local government and were perhaps even supported by it. The Tibetan government also could, and allegedly did, pardon or give absurdly light sentences to such saboteurs and snipers as could be apprehended by the Han. An uneasy stalemate developed, in which the Chinese, ruling through the indigenous power structure, could do little without the willing help of the government, which was rarely forthcoming, and the government was not strong enough to rid itself of the Chinese presence.

Reaction to the rhetoric of the Great Leap Forward proved the destabilizing element in this precarious equilibrium. Though Mao himself had promised that reforms would be undertaken in Tibet proper only at the behest of the masses, the official media had made Tibetans uncomfortably aware of reports of "mass" enthusiasm for reforming decadent customs emanating from other parts of China during the Great Leap Forward. They were also keenly aware of the discrepancy between officially alleged reports of mass enthusiasm for reform and reports of mass distaste by Tibetans who had personally experienced the introduction of reforms in Tibetan areas outside Tibet proper. These had caused revolts in the Tibetan areas of Szechwan in 1956 and in similar areas of Kansu and Ch'inghai in 1958.[119] Though the rebellions were suppressed, a significant number of refugees, particularly Khambas from east of the Chin-sha, made their way to Lhasa. There they became a center of resistance to the Chinese and a fertile source of rumors. Being from that segment of society most dissatisfied with life under the CCP, their reports were distinctly unflattering to the party and made the task of accommodation between the local government of Tibet and that of the CPR infinitely more difficult.[120]

The proximate cause of the Tibetan revolt occurred when the PLA employed a somewhat irregular procedure in inviting the Dalai Lama to attend a theatrical performance. The rumor spread that he was to be kidnapped and that sweeping reforms would then be inaugurated.[121] The rebellion aimed at forestalling this alleged Chinese plot.[122]

It has been suggested that the Chinese themselves planned the uprising, in order to allow them to discard the inhibiting agreements they had made with the local government of Tibet. The Chinese allege that the revolt was planned by members of the local government who had entered into a conspiracy with Indian and U.S. imperialists to sever Tibet's connection with China. On careful consideration, this writer believes that neither explanation is correct. The evident embarrassment of the Chinese government, the fact that it was deemed necessary to move additional troops into Tibet *after* the revolt began, and the lack of a concrete plan for Tibet's future until several weeks after the revolt began, all indicate that the Chinese were taken by surprise.

That the Tibetans were planning some sort of military action is apparent from the amount and kinds of weapons they were able to raise against the Chinese. Almost certainly they were helped by sympathetic Indians and Americans, with the knowledge of at least certain elements in their governments. However, the haphazard way in which the Tibetans carried on the revolt and the poor showing their army made hardly betoken a well-planned international conspiracy. It would seem more likely that the Tibetan anti-Chinese faction heard the rumors that their God-king was to be abducted and, though realizing that their preparations for an uprising at some future date were still inadequate, decided on an act of desperation. George Ginsburgs and Michael Mathos, in an excellent study of the revolt, conclude that it occurred essentially accidentally and that active participants constituted a minority of the population.[123] Sympathy for the rebels was, however, widespread.

The Dalai Lama, who knew nothing of the revolt until it actually began, fled to India on the suggestion of his advisers. Many thousands of Tibetans, representing all economic levels of society, followed him into exile. The Chinese, being told by Ngapo Ngawang Jigme that the lama had been forcibly abducted, railed out against the abductors. Letters written by the Dalai Lama stating that he had left Tibet of his own free will were said by Ngapo to bear evidence of having been translated from English to Tibet, thus strengthening the international-conspiracy theory of rebellion.

In any case, the rebellion was quelled with relative ease. Two weeks after fighting began, NCNA announced that it had ceased "except in a few remote places." Military control commissions were set up in the major cities except for Shigatse, seat of the Panchen Lama's government, where no fighting seems to have taken place. The Chinese made it clear that they considered the 1951 treaty abrogated, as well as Mao's promise of no reforms in Tibet for at least six years. A State Council directive of March 28, 1959, ordered the dissolution of the Local Government of Tibet. Henceforward the Preparatory Committee for the Tibet Autonomous Region would exercise its functions.[124] The preparatory committee had to be reconstituted, since eighteen of its forty-eight Tibetan regular members proved to have actively participated in the revolt.[125] The new committee had the Panchen Lama as acting chairman in the absence of the Dalai Lama. Though it was becoming increasingly clear that the Dalai Lama had not been abducted, it must have seemed preferable to keep up, at least temporarily, the fiction that he had been. The possibility thus remained that the God-king could be persuaded to return and lend his legitimizing presence to the committee. Pebala Choliehnamje, a leading figure in the Lamaist hierarchy, and Ngapo Ngawang Jigme were named vice-chairman and secretary-general, respectively. Both they and the majority of the sixteen Tibetan regular members of the reconstituted committee were nobles, showing that the revolt, though it had destroyed the moratorium on reforms in Tibet, had not ended the party's policy of cooperation with the upper strata. Clearly, this was done through necessity: too little educative work had been done among ordinary Tibetans to permit their participation in the higher levels of government.[126]

With the necessity of working through the 1951 agreement at an end, a much more ambitious propaganda and training program was begun. A plan for the implementation of democratic reforms and the socialist transformation was announced, and in August one hundred Tibetan graduates of the Central Nationalities Institute in Peking were returned to Tibet to help.[127] Democratic reforms were defined as land redistribution and the "three anti's": antirebellion, anticorvée, and antireliance on personalities (*jen-shen yi-fu*).[128]

Even the completion of democratic reforms would, of course, leave Tibet far behind the level of socialism achieved in other minority areas, not to mention that of Han China. But the important point is that Tibet had formerly been treated as a special case: as a result of the revolt it could now be regarded as were the other minority areas. The net effect of the revolt was to facilitate the integration of Tibet into the regular administrative system of China. Whether this would enable closer integration in the psychological sense would depend on the efficacy of the party's social mobilization program.

While the end result of the revolt may have been to allow closer integration of Tibet with China, it is doubtful that the party would have purposely chosen this particular method to obtain such an end. The bulk of the estimated 60,000 Tibetan refugees has now relocated in northern India and Nepal, ideally situated to cause trouble for China. Its members have heaped reams of invective on CCP rule, charging the Chinese with, among other things, genocide through sterilization, assimilation through enforced intermarriage, desecration of religious beliefs, and outright seizure of food and other resources.[129] The popularly accepted divine ruler, once suspected by the Chinese of maintaining contacts with imperialist powers, can now do so openly. India, no friend of the CPR since the two countries' border dispute, permits the publication from its territory of at least one journal detailing Chinese abuses in Tibet,[130] and it is not difficult to imagine other, more active "imperialist plots" which might be worked out with the émigré community.[131] While the refugees' stories very likely exaggerate and distort Chinese actions, at the very least they severely embarrass the CPR propaganda about its progress toward a well-integrated, nonexploitative Communist state.

Whereas *fear* of drastic reforms had caused the revolt in Tibet, the disturbances in Sinkiang were a direct result of the Great Leap's pressure on minorities to adopt radically new institutions and social patterns. Militant opposition to the reforms occurred in several areas in 1958 and 1959, but the resistance was apparently uncoordinated and was put down without great difficulty.[132] Later, as the rift between China and the Soviet Union widened, Sinkiang critics expressing their dislike of drastic reforms found sympathy and encouragement from their neighbors to the north, where Khrushchev had openly declared his contempt for the Great Leap Forward. The economic difficulties occasioned by the Great

Leap caused further distaste for Chinese rule among Sinkiang minorities, a situation compounded by the obvious disparities between living standards on the Chinese side of the border and the Soviet side. The frontier, fondly referred to by the official press as "Friendship Border," had not been closely patrolled, and it was common, for example, for Kazakh herdsmen to graze their flocks on one side or the other in disregard of it.

As Sinkiang minorities became increasingly dissatisfied with the situation in China, an exodus to the Soviet side began. The Chinese charged that this exodus was being aided by the Soviet Union. Soviet consular officials in Sinkiang reportedly issued thousands of passports to Uighurs and Kazakhs. Many more persons emigrated illegally, often taking their herds with them. Though the Chinese are said to have attempted to close the border, an estimated 70,000 refugees had crossed into Soviet Kazakhstan by 1963.[133] The exodus was facilitated by a revolt of unknown proportions which broke out in 1962. Mentioning it for the first time in December 1964, Chou En-lai said only that "under the instigation and direct direction of external forces, a group of the most reactionary protagonists of local nationalism staged a traitorous counterrevolutionary rebellion in Ining [capital of the Ili Kazakh Autonomous Chou, excapital of both the East Turkistan States, and approximately 70 miles from the Soviet border] and incited and organized the flight to foreign territory of a large number of people near the frontier," and that these "subversive and traitorous activities" had been "resolutely crushed" by people of all nationalities.[134] Most of the refugees appear to have been resettled in Kazakhstan.

No doubt also as a result of the revolt, several minority personages of note who had been undergoing reform through labor in China appeared in the Soviet Union, where they have ever since been employing their mastery of the vernacular in denouncing the Chinese to their erstwhile compatriots in Sinkiang, and to the world at large. The comparison is invariably made with the better life in the Soviet Union, where nationalities cultures thrive and material goods are readily available.[135]

While the credence given specific charges must be tempered by the fact that the speakers are guests of the Soviet Union, two points consistently made are, first, that the Chinese aim at rapid assimilation by all means including force, and, second, that the communes caused extreme economic and social hardship to Sinkiang's minorities. Both specific and general accusations are remarkably similar to those made by Tibetan refugees, save that the Sinkiang refugees have not charged the Han with attempting genocide through sterilization. Both groups have alleged that there were forced intermarriages, that Han personnel in their areas received extra rations, and that their cultures were systematically suppressed. In Sinkiang, as in Tibet, a hostile émigré community was created on the soil of an increasingly hostile neighbor, and China's minorities policy was denounced as forcibly assimilative.

Less spectacular uprisings were reported in Hui [136] and Yi areas.[137] A campaign was begun to root out the reactionary Hui mullahs and the evil family-branch system in Liangshan.

In sum, the reforms occasioned by the Great Leap Forward tended to be regarded as assimilative in aim[138] by many minority peoples and aroused intense reaction among them. Economic scarcities that followed the initiation of the Leap resulted in competition for limited resources, which increased ill will among ethnic groups. Ironically, the great effort to erase differences among nationalities resulted in heightening minorities' awareness of these differences and seemed to induce a stubborn desire to retain them. In this sense, the Great Leap slowed down the process of integration.

However, the effect of the Great Leap on integration was not wholly negative. Some of the more distinctive minority customs were effectively destroyed and never resuscitated. Unwilling though some minorities may have been to study Chinese, the result was to facilitate communication between them and the great majority of their countrymen. The changes they were encouraged to make in animal husbandry and agricultural techniques were apparently not very successful in raising productivity, but may have encouraged a spirit of innovation and a willingness to throw off the fetters of tradition. After the Great Leap Forward it became more possible to speak of *a* policy toward minorities rather than a broad goal—that is, integration through the gradual introduction of socialism—with very different manifestations in policy for different areas. A wide variety of economic arrangements used by minorities had been replaced by communes. Many of the goals of the Great Leap Forward with regard to minorities could never be implemented; other Great Leap policies with regard to them had to be undone. But the minority areas never fully returned to their pre-Leap situation.

Still, these gains were at best modest in size in comparison to the economic hardship and widespread resentment of party and government which the Leap had engendered among minorities. If the Leap had been a failure in Han areas, it was a fiasco in minority areas. An increasingly vocal segment of party leaders came to favor modifications in its policies.

7

Reaction and Resurgence, 1958 –1965

The winter of 1958–59 was a difficult one for the party and for China. Drought, flood, and the more ill-advised policies of the Great Leap Forward had reduced the economy to a precarious state. In addition, there were problems of foreign policy. The frontier areas where most minority peoples live seemed increasingly vulnerable after a border dispute with India and the cooling of relations with the Soviet Union. The latter had been partially caused by Soviet reaction to the Great Leap Forward.

Corrective Measures

Though there was broad agreement that something would have to be done to cope with the situation, what particular course of action to pursue became the subject of bitter controversy in top party echelons. The deterioration of the economy that followed the initiation of the Great Leap encouraged those relatively conservative party members who had opposed, or who had had reservations about, the Leap to become more outspoken. This group, led, it was later alleged, by Liu Shao-ch'i, favored measures that amounted to a return of the economic, social, and foreign policies of the mid-1950's, including a rapprochement with the Soviet Union. They were opposed by more radically inclined groups, who took Mao Tse-tung as their leader and saw continuation of the Great Leap Forward as the best and most appropriately Marxist-Leninist was to extricate China from its present difficulties.

The Wuhan Plenum of December 1958 provided an index of the comparative strength of the two groups at that time. It was at this meeting that Mao Tse-tung relinquished the chairmanship of the People's Government, ostensibly so that he could devote more time to his theoretical writings. However, though the significance of it was not fully appreciated in the West at the time, the writings of Mao published in the official press after the Wuhan Plenum tended to be from his earlier years, and they emphasized moderation and planning rather than speed and enthusiasm. Chinese mass media took up these themes, and retrenchment became the order of the day. The shifts in policy heralded by the publication of these writings concerned minorities in both general and specific ways.

A February 1959 *Jen-min jih-pao* editorial entitled "Take the Whole Country as a Chessboard"[1] provided the new policy with a slogan. Like grand masters, those in charge of economic planning would calculate each decision with careful consideration as to how this might affect future moves. Painstaking coordination of all sectors would replace haphazard calls for more, better, faster, and cheaper. As good chess players, too, the planners would concentrate their attack at strong points, the more quickly to win the struggle against poverty and imperialism. The unspoken inference was that minority areas, clearly among the weakest sectors in Chinese industry, would be among the first pawns sacrificed, and indeed this was the case.

The lead article in *Min-tsu t'uan-chieh* in July 1959 contained a lengthy rationalization of the application of this chessboard policy to minority nationalities' areas. Its author, Saifudin, stressed the magnanimous proportions of state aid to minorities in the past and promised that the government would continue to help out. However, because of "changed circumstances," some "items of investment would be reallocated, causing a temporary postponement of the degree of progress." Meanwhile, a short-term lag in production and transportation difficulties had caused shortages of some agricultural products in minority areas. Saifudin conceded that this temporary situation had produced "definite negative feelings among those whose understanding [of the chessboard policy] was deficient." However, he felt that ideological education could overcome these misapprehensions. In the long run the chessboard policy would actually benefit the nationalities, because after the state took important areas and important items and set them to rights, it would have greater strength to devote to minorities areas.[2]

While the economics of this policy may have been impeccable, the reference to dealing with *important* areas and items first and then taking up minority areas' problems demonstrates either lack of sensitivity or a calculated slight on the author's part. Surely those who had harbored "negative feelings" about the chessboard scheme in the first instance must have felt that Saifudin's article constituted confirmation of their fears that minorities were considered second-class citizens.

Though those among the nationalities who hoped for extensive state aid in their immediate economic difficulties were disappointed, the policies introduced after December 1958 did much to alleviate the economic and social pressure on minorities. The first and foremost task in minorities areas was considered to be reestablishment of rapport between party and nationalities. This harmony achieved, production was expected to increase apace. The Great Leap Forward in minorities areas had been, it was felt, counterproductive in terms of more than economic statistics: it had exacerbated nationality differences and created a substantial credibility gap between party and minorities. The desire to reestablish nationality harmony and recoup production losses resulted in policies characterized by a scaling-down of both rhetoric and goals. A case in point was Ulanfu's December 1958 speech outlining Inner Mongolia's tasks for the coming year. With regard to nationalities he mentioned only "mastery of certain specific questions . . . particularly unity among the nationalities and the development of animal husbandry." [3]

In contrast to the Great Leap Forward's desire to achieve unity through uniformity, the policies introduced after December 1958 seemed to envision unity in diversity. Whereas the Leap had sought to hasten the emergence of a common proletarian culture by rapidly erasing differences among nationalities, immediate post-Leap policies were characterized by the conviction that "slower is faster."

The feeling that the Great Leap had disrupted such unity of nationalities as the party's earlier gradualist policy had been able to establish and had actually heightened the perception of nationality differences appeared most prominently in discussions of cultural work. An article in the Yunnan Daily in December 1958 noted that during the Leap "class struggle was quite sharp" and opined that "exclusive emphasis on the class question, mechanical application of the methods used in other parts of China, neglect of nationality characteristics and neglect of historical nationality barriers will all lead to disputes among the nationalities themselves." [4] To reestablish unity, the "exclusive emphasis on class struggle" was to cease and, as the title of a February 1959 article in *Min-tsu t'uan-chieh* put it, "The Reform of Nationalities Habits and Customs Should Be Done According to the Free Will of the Masses." [5]

The upper echelons of the party seem to have been genuinely surprised at the amount of minorities' resistance to Leap policies and quickly realized the source of the misleading information on which they had been acting. Lower-level cadres and officials, anxious to stress the progress made in their areas and avoid charges of local nationalism, declared that the nationalities they worked with had arrived at a stage of receptivity to these reforms which the people had not in fact reached. Since "inadequate attention had been paid to mobilizing the masses" for reforms, the masses perceived those reforms as having been forced upon them. Such acts made a "bad impression" on them. In addition, zealous cadres insisted on changing customs that had marginal or no relevance to increasing production and reported exaggeratedly high production figures to prove the efficacy of their efforts. Acting on these exaggerated statistics, those in charge of economic planning were misled into allocating a harvest that did not actually exist and into raising production quotas, which in turn further oppressed the masses.[6]

Soon becoming aware of the discrepancy between report and reality, the party took immediate steps to rectify the situation. Nationalities Affairs Commission Vice-Chairman Yang Ching-jen, himself a Hui, published an article entitled "Ideas on Strengthening Planning Work for Minority Nationalities," chiding cadres for not reporting on actual conditions. Since party committees had many other jobs to perform, he warned, they could not constantly repair to lower levels to find out for themselves the conditions there, nor could they check the veracity of everything that had been reported. Hereafter, reports were to be based on actual field observation rather than abstract theorizing. Investigators were forewarned that they must report failures as well as successes. Local circumstances were to be taken into account before a general policy was applied.[7]

Detailed investigation and careful report writing require that time and energy be devoted to the process, and "bourgeois scientific objectivism" was again sanctioned, in fact though not in name. And despite Yang's reminder that higher levels would continue to exercise decision-making powers, his injunction that local circumstances were to be taken into account allowed the return of a certain flexibility at lower levels.

There was considerable feeling that many of the excesses of the Great Leap Forward had been caused by newly trained cadres who were not equal to the demands placed on them. Unfortunately, lamented a writer in *Kwang-ming jih-pao*, "at present there are still very few Communist hard-core elements who are capable of political leadership among the minority nationalities." [8] In light of this realization, the position of the traditional elite was reassessed. An editorial in *Jen-min jih-pao* entitled "People of Nationalities Upper Strata See a Bright Future" [9] promised them just that. A propaganda campaign was carried out to explain to the masses that "certain shortcomings and defects" had been due to cadres overinterpreting the party's directives, to remnants of Great Han chauvinism among some cadres, and to their improper understanding of the party's nationalities policy. Since it is possible that at least some members of that mystic entity, the broad masses, did tend to see their oppression in personal terms—that is, as perpetrated by an unpleasant or excessively ambitious cadre—it is conceivable that a purge of such persons would convince the masses that the local cadre and not his superiors had been at fault. Removing such persons would, it was hoped, help to close the party's credibility gap. At any rate, the masses would find it satisfying to be rid of the "culprit." A relatively severe "cadres to the ranks" campaign was carried out to make sure that cadres would not again allow themselves to become so estranged from the mass mood. Other cadres were given short training courses to raise their political consciousness.

The problems of the herding areas, where the large majority of residents were of minority nationality, were considered most serious, and attempts to deal with their grievances quickly appeared. Specifically, these grievances involved the introduction of class struggle into pastoral communities which had had the impression they were exempt from class struggle, the sudden collectivization of animals, the conversion of pasture areas into agricultural land, and the influx of untrained, unacclimatized, and generally unwilling urban Han to the areas.

The beginnings of a new policy were heralded by Ulanfu in a March 1959 article for *Red Flag*, entitled "Quickly Develop the Livestock Industry." Stressing the great gains achieved in animal production through cautious reforms and adequate compensation in a way which invited comparison with the policies of the Great Leap, Ulanfu also emphasized the importance of undertaking careful investigation of an area's special characteristics before plans to implement policy were decided upon. In light of this, he continued, the policy of "emphasize agriculture and slight herding" (*chung-nung ch'ing-mu*) was wrong. It demonstrated both isolation from reality and separation from the mass line. While a purely pastoral economy would necessarily be weak, the development of a diversified economy should, he felt, support animal husbandry, not undermine it.[10]

Ulanfu's efforts to assuage the herdsmen's feelings had been relatively subtle; others' were increasingly less so. Losses of animals were admitted, though generally blamed on inclement weather or the sabotage of a small number of unreformed herd owners. The continued existence of this small number notwithstanding, class struggle in the herding areas was quickly "completed," and it was announced that "the improper large-scale cultivation of grassy plains in livestock areas for grain crops" must be avoided.[11] Stories on the glories of the communes and the satisfactions of throwing off decadent customs were replaced with discussions on better breeding techniques. An eight-point program for improving animal production was promulgated; it stressed the importance of such basic elements as water, fodder, and pasture. Particularly in the cooperativization of Sinkiang, it was said, "we must pay attention to going a bit slowly and relaxing a bit." [12]

As to the movement to send surplus population from Han urban centers to cultivate lands traditionally associated with minority groups, "people from advanced areas" were warned against affecting stylish clothes and manners and were advised that they would be happier in their new homes if they learned local languages and customs. Some youth solved the difficult problems of adjustment in their own way, by taking advantage of temporarily chaotic conditions to flee back to the urban areas whence they had come. Without ration cards and hence not legally employable, they were forced to rely on relatives and friends or resort to petty theft. That a large number preferred to do so rather than return to the border areas is indicative of the conditions they had had to endure there.[13]

The high tide of the minority masses' enthusiasm to learn Han seemed to have ebbed as quickly as it had risen, being replaced with a campaign to study each other's languages. The spare-time schools disappeared from mention in mass media, possibly victims of a directive that peasants be guaranteed eight hours of sleep a night.

Other retreats from the Great Leap Forward's emphasis on uniformity followed. As in Han areas, the communes were ordered decentralized, mess halls reorganized, and private plots returned, albeit in a restricted manner. The decentralization of communal power, down to the brigade level at this time[14] and later to the team level, allowed a relaxation of tensions that had arisen when two or more nationality groups with widely different customs and economic levels had been forced together. An article discussing the application of communes to minority areas announced that while the general rule had been and would remain that a commune's jurisdiction would equal that of a hsiang, exceptions could be made. Where the territory of a hsiang was comparatively large, as was often the case in minority areas, which tend to be sparsely populated, that hsiang could be divided into several communes managed jointly by the hsiang. Villages included in a commune where conditions were not yet "mature" could be managed as small-scale cooperatives under the leadership of a commune.[15]

In most minority areas communes were, as in Han areas, disbanded in fact but not in name. However, some nationalities' communes, including those of the Tai, Yi, Lisu, and some Tibetans, were disbanded in name as well.[16] As befits unpleasant news of any sort, the decisions were announced without fanfare: an article extolling the particular minority's achievements since 1949 would simply add that despite its poor background, the minority had even "tried" (*shih-pan*) communes. The unspoken inference was, of course, that the trial had been judged a failure.

In those communes which were not disbanded and in which nationality integration had taken place at the brigade and team level, members of one nationality who had been invited into the collective of another to give technical assistance were to be guaranteed the income level they had enjoyed in their original area. Thus, it was announced that Koreans resident in a commune in Inner Mongolia had had their grain ration increased by 50 percent.[17]

Mess hall reorganization, which included provision for many smaller dining units at team level, allowed special tastes and customs to be taken into account. If a nationality's food preference included a certain kind of vegetable, they were encouraged to grow it on special plots designated for mess hall use. Hui would no longer be obliged to dine with pork eaters, Mongols were to be allowed buckwheat, and Koreans given the variety of rice they favored.[18]

The muting of the rhetoric of the Great Leap Forward and emphasis on reforms continued throughout the summer of 1959. In August the CCP held the Eighth Plenum of its Eighth Central Committee in Lushan, a resort area in Kiangsi. A communiqué issued during the conference admitted that the agricultural statistics reported for 1958 had been "overassessed" and that plans for national development had been "readjusted" in line with a new set of statistics. Careful planning and thrift were urged, as they had been for the past nine months, to cope with economic difficulties.[19] But the most interesting part of the Lushan Plenum did not become public knowledge until many years later. Defense Minister P'eng Tê-huai, an advocate of the conservative group that opposed the policies of the Great Leap Forward, openly took Mao to task for the haste and fanaticism thereof. The results were not to P'eng's personal benefit. He was censured by the meeting and relieved of his position. A campaign to "surmount any rightist-inclined sentiment" was begun, and there was a revival of the exhortative language of the Great Leap.[20]

At the close of the plenum, an NCNA release reported that "national minority people throughout China have greeted the communiqué and resolution of the party with pledges to step up production." [21] The September issue of *Min-tsu t'uan-chieh* duly condemned rightist tendencies and cited the assertion that the Great Leap Forward was suitable for Han only as one example of such tendencies. Readers were assured that the communes "by their excellent nature" would enable all difficulties to be overcome.[22] Han language study was again emphasized,[23] and the spare-time schools were revived.[24]

The Little Leap

In February 1960, *Min-tsu t'uan-chieh* began a campaign to study the works of Chairman Mao, and the bulk of the March issue was devoted to outlining which among his many pronouncements to implement whole-heartedly. Partially in response to domestic critics but patently directed at the Soviet Union, Mao's wisdom was extravagantly praised, and he was called the era's leading Marxist-Leninist theoretician. With regard to minorities, Mao's plan for liberation and development of minorities areas was called "part of a systematic solution for the whole of China." Several references to the evils of modern revisionism served to warn those who criticized the party's minorities policy on grounds that it deviated from that of the Soviet Union.[25] Plans were announced to substitute the romanized *pin-yin* alphabet for Cyrillic in writing the minority languages of Sinkiang, since "the previous script" (unnamed) had shortcomings, and "the more the shortcomings, the more the language is unsuitable for . . . the needs of the continuing Great Leap Forward in socialist construction." [26] The chief shortcoming of Cyrillic, also unnamed, seems to have been that its use provided a bond between Sinkiang minorities and their counterparts in the USSR. The use of *pin-yin* would not only standardize the writing system in Sinkiang to conform to those of most of Chinese minorities, it would also make communications between Turkic minorities who lived on opposite sides of the Sino-Soviet border more difficult.

A more favorable attitude toward reform in general was again evident, and religious figures were described as pleased with their decision to take up productive labor. The lamas of the large Kumbum Monastery in Ch'inghai were praised for having achieved "basic self-sufficiency in food," while those of the T'ien-chu Tibetan Autonomous Hsien in nearby Kansu were working in a plastics factory. In Labrang, also in Kansu, lamas were receiving thought reform to aid them in over-coming rightist tendencies.[27]

However, the revived Great Leap Forward was a pale version of its former self. The new rectification campaign was directed against rightist tendencies rather than rightists, and the actions taken as a result were correspondingly milder. Repeated announcements that the situation was really very good [28] and numerous "conclusive refutations" of rightist slanders have a suspiciously defensive tone. Then, too, it would have been surprising if those who had been convinced by the propaganda that accompanied the start of the first Great Leap Forward could have responded with the same innocent enthusiasm to the second. In short, the rhetoric of the "little Leap" reminds one of the lady who protested too much.

After its March 1960 issue, *Min-tsu t'uan-chieh* temporarily stopped publication for the first time in its four-year history. Whether the reasons for the cessation were political or the result of a countrywide paper shortage is unknown. *Min-tsu yen-chiu,* its more scholarly counterpart, also failed to appear. Articles on minorities in other Chinese publications at this time were characterized by extreme caution and a dearth of solid information. A piece entitled "Great Victory of the Party's Nationalities Policy in Ch'inghai" which appeared in *Red Flag* in May 1960 attributed that province's successes to people's communes but, compared with the language in common use in 1958, the praise is faint indeed. "Rapid advances" were said to have been achieved since the founding of the communes, but the only statistical comparisons made were with 1949. These advances were held to prove the correctness of the party's— not Mao Tse-tung's—nationalities policy. Ch'inghai's nationalities were said to have planned to do their utmost under the leadership of the party and Chairman Mao to modernize their province, but it was a 1949 statement of Liu Shao-ch'i's on the virtues of regional autonomy that was cited as the best way to do this.[29]

In April 1961, *Min-tsu t'uan-chieh* reappeared. Whereas the March 1960 issue had been numbered 30, the April 1961 issue was listed as number 35, indicating that four issues had been published in the interim, but with restricted circulation.[30] That the circulation must have been very limited is shown by the effort made to review the events of the past year, as if trying to catch its readers up on what they had missed. While such a recapitulation would have been entirely normal in a January or December issue, it is out of place in an April one, if not for the reasons given.

Min-tsu t'uan-chieh took on a new format as well. A note explained that it had absorbed *Min-tsu yen-chiu* and would henceforth combine the duties of both publications. The magazine would, it was added, continue to "... promote Marxism-Leninism and the thought of Mao Tse-tung on the theory of the nationalities question and the Party's nationalities policy, promulgate the proletarian view on nationalities, criticize revisionism, bourgeois nationalism and bourgeois nationalist studies, promulgate our Party's solution to the nationalities question and the accomplishments of its nationalities work, reflecting the three great red banners of the general line, the Great Leap Forward, and the people's communes." [31]

Unity in Diversity

While the three great red banners floated aloft, a good deal of deviation from the rigid orthodoxy they symbolized was tolerated at ground level. These deviations differed both qualitatively and quantitatively from those of the first half of 1959. Whereas the reforms introduced prior to the Lushan Plenum were essentially attempts to patch up problem areas that emerged from the Great Leap Forward, the revisions introduced in 1961 gave the impression of being parts of a well-integrated plan. They were more extensive in scope than the 1959 reforms, and a greater attempt was made to justify them theoretically. Mao Tse-tung had apparently withdrawn from active participation in party and government affairs, either voluntarily or under pressure.

The slogans current in minority areas at this time were similar in essence to those in Han areas, but with significant additions. As in China proper, policy was to be adapted to local conditions and in a manner suitable to time and place (*yin-ti chih-yi, yin-shih chih-yi*). The concrete situation must first be taken into account (*chiu-t'i ti shih-shih ch'iu-shih*), research done, and consultations held with the masses. The hundred flowers were told to bloom again, signifying a greater toleration of differing opinions. Policy changes specific to minorities were:

1. The re-recognition of the existence of their "special characteristics," above and apart from devices used by reactionaries to hide from the propertyless the fact that their true best interests lay with the propertyless of other nationalities. In line with this, concessions were made in languages, art forms, religion, and historiography.[32]
2. A reward system to encourage study of the theory and practice of the party's nationalities policy.[33]
3. Emphasis on the solution of the nationalities question being a long term process.[34]

Significantly, the only important article not specifically concerned with minorities affairs to appear in *Min-tsu t'uan-chieh* from April 1961 until October 1962 was Liu Shao-ch'i's speech celebrating the fortieth anniversary of the CCP. Admitting that temporary difficulties had been caused by "not a few shortcomings" as well as natural disasters, Liu cautioned that relying on emotion and "subjective phenomena" must be avoided. He advocated "learning from the advanced experience of the Soviet Union and other countries." Both suggestions damned the Great Leap Forward by implication, though Liu gave favorable mention to the three red banners and to Chairman Mao's thought.[35]

Economically, policies were similar to those in Han areas, aiming at increasing production by allowing the "toiling masses" to enjoy more of the fruits of their labors. The basic unit of the communes was further decentralized, to the level of production team. The *san-pao yi-chiang*, a system of fixed targets for output, workdays, and costs with a part of the extra output as reward, the *ssu-ku-ting*, or fixed use of manpower, land, farm tools, and draft animals, and other incentive plans were instituted. Private plots that had not been given back earlier were returned, as were some personal possessions that had been seized during the Great Leap by cadres who had "misunderstood" the party's policy. With economic conditions as bad as they were, however, it is unlikely that full compensation could have been made. Domestic sideline occupations were fostered, and fairs and bazaars at which locally produced products could be exchanged were again permitted.[36] Thus, the private market was encouraged to take some of the strain off the state distribution system.

In herding areas, which are virtually synonymous with minority nationalities areas, the same goals obtained, but there an even greater degree of flexibility was permitted. The compelling reason for cooperativization was, it was explained, the *inefficiency* of scattered individual herdsmen—not, let it be noted, Marxism-Leninism or the thoughts of Mao. But while collectivization must be the principle, there might be several ways of implementing it. Even within a given cooperative there could be different ways of handling a problem, and it would not be necessary to stress only one way.[37]

Reorganized herding communes paid compensation for shares of animals. Also, on grounds that "herdsmen's materials of production are the same as their livelihood," herdsmen could be allowed to own some animals—the equivalent of the return of private plots in agricultural areas. A secretary of the Inner Mongolia Party Committee's secretariat pointed out that herdsmen used animals for meat, milk, production, transportation, and labor. With a rare sentimentality, he added that "some of these animals [were] especially dear to the herdsmen, and some had been given to them as gifts." These they should be allowed to keep, as long as the percentage of privately held animals did not exceed 10 percent of the collective's total animals. A suggested assortment was one or two saddle horses, one or two cattle as shares, a camel or donkey, one to four milk cows, and ten to twenty cattle. The importance of exercising special care in herding collectives was reemphasized, since "the economic management level of the cadres in herding areas [was] quite low" and there were "definite difficulties in the leadership of collective production." This and the particular nature of animal husbandry meant that it was "very easy to meet with losses." [38]

Precisely one year later, a reporter interviewing "responsible personages" in Inner Mongolia wrote that that area's successes had been due to "gradual steady reforms," including "no purges, no division of property, no class distinctions," "mutual benefit of herdsmen and owners," "uniting with all those forces which can be united," and "peaceful methods."

As a final insult to the Great Leap Forward, communes received no mention whatsoever.[39]

A truce was apparently declared with the nomads as well. Though it was stated that great advances had been made in nomadic herding, cadres were admonished to remember that nomadic herding was still an important style of production that made definite contributions to the state's economy.[40]

Another important "mistaken ideological tendency," that of "emphasize agriculture, slight herding," was to be corrected. It was explained that when Mao had said that the national economy should take agriculture as its basis, he had meant agriculture as opposed to industry, and not agriculture at the expense of herding. In a sense, herding was the agriculture of the pasturelands.[41] An article entitled "Several Questions Regarding the Directive on Pasturelands People's Communes' Developing Agriculture as the Basis of Economic Development," which appeared in *Ti-li* (Geography) in early 1961, became the subject of repeated criticism. Its authors, a research team from the soil evaluation department of Lanchow University, had declared that the pasturelands were suitable for crop raising.[42] Those who disagreed said that not only was the pastureland not suitable for agriculture, but neither was the requisite manpower available for it. Development of the pasturelands for agriculture would entail capital investment, which would cause a contradiction with agriculture. Moreover, the country would be deprived of needed meat, milk, milk products, fertilizer, work animals, and leather. The mistakes of these policies would be "bound to be reflected in nationality relations." This had been proved by ten years' experience with the pasturelands. To improve nationalities solidarity and the economy as well, it was imperative that the slogan "take agriculture as the basis of the economy" be interpreted in the pasturelands as giving priority to animal husbandry. The contention that animal raising was part of agriculture was supported with references to Marx and to a 1934 statement of Mao Tse-tung.[43] In sum, it was concluded, "all other matters must be subordinated to increasing our herds" (*ch'ian-wu wan-wu tseng-chia sheng-ch'u shih ti yi-t'iao*).[44] In keeping with a policy that emphasized economic growth, accomplishments tended to be measured in terms of per capita income. That of Mongolian herdsmen, for example, was said to have risen 83 percent since 1958.[45]

In Tibet, the ambitious plans announced late in 1959 for "speedy realization" of the socialist transformation were quickly repudiated. On April 2, 1961, Lhasa Radio stated that Tibet was still at the stage of democratic revolution, and that, moreover, the socialist transformation would not be carried out nor agricultural and livestock breeders' cooperatives established for the next five years, "so that efforts can be concentrated on completing the democratic reform movement and on leading the Tibetan broad masses to further develop production and practice economy." The decision to defer further socialist reforms was intended to "create a solid foundation for carrying out the socialist revolution in Tibet in the future. Furthermore, it will undoubtedly create a direct impetus to the development of agricultural production and animal husbandry in Tibet." [46]

Two days later, on April 4, Lhasa Radio quoted Party Work Committee First Secretary Chang Ching-wu as saying that current policy was to "consolidate" the democratic revolution. The postponement of the socialist revolution would "allow the creation of favorable conditions" for carrying out the socialist transformation in the future.[47] Even regulations governing the redistribution of goods confiscated from rebels seemed designed to make minimal changes in the status quo. The rebels' cattle and goods were to be given to poor herdsmen "in their own tribes." Rebels' dependents were to receive their fair share, and the party pledged to persuade this group to undertake "experiments" in mutual aid and cooperation, which would gradually be popularized in "qualified" areas.[48] This decision to postpone further reforms had clearly been taken as a result of continued resistance by Tibetans. Party control was well established in only a handful of Tibetan cities. In other areas, it was admitted, "certain phases" of the democratic reforms had not been carried out properly, the superiority of mutual-aid teams had not been made clear, and the masses' understanding of socialism still left much to be desired.

The tendency to speak more frankly of what had happened during the Great Leap Forward revealed that even regional autonomy, the cornerstone of the party's minorities policy since 1921, had been attacked. It was now vigorously defended. Wang Feng, a vice-chairman of the Nationalities Affairs Commission and deputy director of the United Front Work Department, declared that the idea that regional autonomy was outmoded (*kuo-shih*) after a country had entered the period of socialist construction was "incorrect and against Party policy." So was the idea that since the broad masses had already taken on a basic socialist orientation (*fan-shen*)[49] regional autonomy must be unnecessary. On the contrary, regional autonomy should be more fully developed and perfected. It should certainly not be destroyed or abolished. He cited Mao Tse-tung in contending that a people's (n.b., not *min-tsu* but *jen-min*) most fundamental right was that of managing their own affairs. Those cadres who had been saying during the past two or three years that the nationalities question had been solved and that no attention need be paid to minorities as such were not only mistaken, but placed themselves in opposition to the leadership of the party and of

Chairman Mao as well. From now on, autonomous area peoples' congresses and nationalities affairs meetings should be held according to schedule. The organs of autonomy ought to have translation facilities and should use nationalities' languages except when putting out documents for national-level use. Han cadres must not neglect their language studies.

Wang also rebutted attacks on the united front with nationalities upper strata. He quoted Mao as saying in early 1950 that "those who are capable of managing affairs must be given the opportunity to do so" in this difficult period. They ought to be treated with respect and jobs found for them suitable to their authority. They should also be helped to reform, using the method of "gentle winds and light rains" (*ho-feng hsi-yü*).[50]

These themes of defense of the autonomous area system and united front policies were echoed by NAC vice-chairman Liu Ch'un in his outline of nationalities policy for 1962,[51] and by historian and Nationalities Committee member Lü Chien-jen in the spring. Lü argued that because of the traditional influence and functions performed by the upper strata of minority nationalities, the party's policy of cooperation with upper-class democratic personages had made possible the stabilization of the social order, increased nationalities solidarity, socialist improvement, and the development of the economy and culture. This proved, he said, that a policy of moderation (*huan-ho*) and peaceful negotiations could achieve the best results and also reduce resistance and religious and nationality tensions. Far from harming the basic interests of the proletariat, it would achieve the greatest benefits for them. In carrying out reforms, the cooperation of the upper strata should first be obtained, and the masses mobilized for reform afterward. This policy of cooperation had not only been necessary in the period of socialist reforms, it would continue to be so during the period of socialist construction.

Thus, Lü urged that the masses be persuaded of the necessity of working with the upper classes. It was most important to choose "comparatively compromising methods" and not carry out a struggle between one side and another.[52] Since the main reason Lü had advanced for cooperating with the upper strata was the influence they had over the masses, it would seem that the author was in reality trying to persuade not the masses but a segment of the party to cooperate with the traditional upper strata.

As 1961 drew to a close, regional and local area meetings were called to sum up the results of research studies and to discuss special problems relevant to minorities work. Liu Ch'un reported that party members and cadres had made good progress in their understanding of the party's nationalities policy and that the organs of autonomy in many minority areas had been made "healthy and abundant" (*chien-ch'uan ho ch'ung-shih*). The harvest in minorities areas in 1961 had been slightly better than in 1960. Liu also made clear that the gradualist policies of 1961 would be continued in 1962, a "crucial" year in the readjustment of the national economy.[53]

In early 1962 several members of the traditional elite who had been purged were rehabilitated. Two of the most prominent were Lung Yun[54] and Hui leader Ma Sung-t'ing.[55] Cooperation with minorities religious leaders was accompanied by a greater toleration of religion in general. This was rationalized by a scholar and Nationalities Committee member, Chang Chih-yi, as necessary while the preconditions for the gradual disappearance of religion were being created.[56] Other writers supported Chang's position, noting that religious and nationality questions were often closely connected and that thus there should be no discounting of the party's policy on freedom of religion.[57]

Similarly conciliatory statements were made at a month-long meeting on nationalities work held in Peking during April and May. Said to be of "great significance," the meeting was attended "in person" by Liu Shao-ch'i, Chou En-lai, Chu Tê, and Teng Hsiao-p'ing, with major speeches given by First Secretary of the Peking Party Committee P'eng Chen, UFWD head Li Wei-han, and NAC Chairman Ulanfu. The correctness of the policies of regional autonomy, the united front, religious tolerance, respect for nationalities' special characteristics, and the long-term nature of any solution to the nationalities question were agreed upon, and the need for research was recognized. The discrepancy between existing numbers of nationalities cadres and the number needed was taken note of. Han cadres must help train nationalities cadres and the two groups must cooperate for the good of the people[58] rather than resenting each other's presence and status. The emphasis on learning from the advanced experience of the Han was transformed into a campaign whereby all nationalities learned from each other, complete with down-to-earth homilies. For examples, commune members in Yenpien were said to have noticed that the type of plow used by Han made deep furrows in the soil but damaged the ground, while the plow favored by Koreans made only a superficial cut in the earth and did no damage to the soil. Commune members reportedly talked over the problem and decided to combine the best features of the two. They eventually came up with a design that permitted deep plowing without damage to the soil, and they named it the "unity plow." [59] The moral, though left unstated, was obvious: mutual cooperation had resulted in mutual benefit, and another difference among nationalities had disappeared.

In Yenpien, also, the autonomous chou government instituted an annual "Publicize Nationalities Solidarity Month." Each September, mass meetings would be held to publicize the party's nationalities policy and to provide a forum for the airing of grievances. Awards would be presented to winners of "Model of Nationalities Solidarity" competitions in the chou, and also on the hsien, commune, and production team levels, and in factories and schools.[60] The cadres who encouraged this unity were those who spoke both Han and minority languages fluently, whatever their own nationality, and who "combined the party's policy with the concrete situation." They listened to the people and led the masses not through commandism but by their own virtuous example.[61] Though good party members would surely be horrified by approval from such quarters, Confucius would have wholeheartedly agreed with this idea of leadership by example.

In the fall of 1961 a campaign to train more minorities cadres was begun.[62] In line with their new linguistic and research responsibilities, cadres and student cadres were to be given more time to learn. Kwangsi Nationalities Institute, for example, announced that it had "strictly restricted" the number of required political meetings in the interests of upgrading academic standards.[63] The nationalities social history project was revived, interested parties being told that "the style of work of research and investigation according to the facts is an excellent tradition of our party and the basic method of Marxism-Leninism." In sharp contrast to the Great Leap Forward's condemnation of the initial study as overresearched and mired in excessive detail, it was stated that the work of several years ago had had "definite accomplishments but [was] only a beginning . . . this is a duty which must be completed." [64] Earlier investigation work had disclosed that different minorities' levels of development were uneven, which explained why the nationalities social history investigation would have to be "firmly carried on for a long time. It is necessary for nationalities work and for scientific research." Now that the party "had issued a great call . . . Those comrades engaged in the minorities social history project investigation ought to enthusiastically respond to the Party's call, thoroughly study Comrade Mao's works and his important directives on investigation and research, combining it with examination and summarization of the experience of the last few years' work." [65] A large, elaborate Palace of Nationalities was opened in Peking, with some of the materials from the investigation on view in its exhibition room.[66]

The science of historiography in general had a renaissance, with various provinces organizing conferences to discuss problems in minorities history. Within very broad Marxist-Leninist guidelines—that is, that history can be divided into stages characterized by the preeminence of a particular economic class and that class struggle is the motivating force of the historical process—a good deal of ideological leeway was permitted. Disagreement among the participants was polite. Both the tacit assumption that more than one point of view was worthy of representation and the absence of polemics on which point of view was most accurate contrast sharply with the situation during the Great Leap Forward.[67] Though somewhere within the text was always a gentle reminder that the historian's research proved that there had always been the closest relations between X minority and the ancestral land, the dedication to scholarship is evident.

The party's admission that research into the past was important encouraged overt pride in the past accomplishments of one's nationality. At the suggestion of UFWD Chairman Li Wei-han, Ulanfu, as chairman of the NAC and First Party Secretary of the IMAR, invited a group of historians, authors, and artists to visit Inner Mongolia. After tours, banquets, and meetings, the group returned to Peking, having "broadened their vision and collected valuable historical and creative materials." All agreed that those who worked on China's minorities should actually visit those areas, and they hastened to celebrate Inner Mongolia's charms in their poetry, music, and painting.[68]

Nationalities heroes were also resuscitated, the most outstanding example being Genghis Khan. In honor of his eight-hundredth birthday, a commemorative conference was held and his achievements—the unification of the Mongol clans, the alleged unification of China, and the compilation of the *yasa* code—given due credit.[69] The transformation of Genghis from bloodthirsty monster and tool of local nationalism to progressive personage had taken four years. In another instance, Koxinga was hailed as a great hero who had liberated Taiwan's Han and Kaoshan from the oppression of the Dutch—a rather limited view of that gentleman's accomplishments—and was therefore "the steadfast friend of all China's nationalities." [70]

Respect for a nationality's past accomplishments included a positive attitude toward its language. Though examples can be found on the development of many different minorities languages, a disproportionate number of articles concern Mongolian. In a typical instance, the KMT's alleged attempt to drive a language out of use was cited as if to prove that the party's course must ipso facto be encouragement of the language. Pre-Great Leap Forward regulations calling for the establishment of translation bureaus in relevant party and government organs were taken note of, as was the need for bilingual personnel at stores, hospitals, and post offices. In Mongolia, cadres were required to study Mongolian, and an award system was set up to honor outstanding units and individuals on all levels from autonomous region down to commune level. Much was made of the fact that eight newspapers and magazines were published regularly in the Mongolian language and that there were Mongolian radio broadcasts and books as well. While the "correct" policy was felt to be equal fluency in Mongolian and Han, one must "proceed from reality." For example, a better knowledge of Han was expected of Mongolian cadres and students than that demanded from ordinary persons, but in herding areas (that is, those which had been most isolated from Han influence) one must not expect even their knowledge of Han to be "too high or acquired too quickly." Educational methods should concentrate first on teaching Mongol cadres and students their own written language, which, it was anticipated, would give them "a suitable basis" for the later study of Han.[71] Presumably the masses were to be treated still more leniently.

On the important question of the absorption of a new vocabulary, a renewed flexibility was evident. Whereas policy in 1958 had been conditioned by a categorical directive that new words were to be absorbed from Han, in 1962 it was possible to state that Mongolian was an ancient language with a well-developed vocabulary and internal grammatical structure; therefore Mongolian should not be expected to take in new expressions without regard for its special characteristics. Three rules for creating new vocabulary were given. It must:

1. utilize the existing vocabulary and grammatical structure;
2. be created in accordance with the linguistic practice, political struggle, and production struggle of the masses;
3. be introduced while keeping in mind the dictum "from the masses to the masses."

Adherence to these guidelines was considered absolutely necessary, since "the haphazard creation of a new language [is] not helpful to mass study and use . . . the Mongolian language not only should not be weakened, it should be fully developed." [72]

In a further effort to integrate minorities into the Han-Chinese Communist system with minimal friction, minorities who expressed willingness to participate in the institutional framework set up by the party received special consideration relative to that accorded to Han Chinese. Care was taken to publicize these cases. In one example, a certain Yi of poor peasant ancestry began his association with the party in a base area as a "little devil," a term of affection used in the base areas to refer to young persons who helped the party cause by performing messenger service and other such tasks.[73] Later, having entered school, he had great difficulties but was helped and encouraged by Han comrades and teachers. Though his record should have prevented him from entering flight training—he ranked 114, and the rules stipulated that only the top 30 students were eligible—the party directed that he be admitted nonetheless. In the end, he conquered all obstacles and became a "five good fighter, ready to defend the ancestral land against all obstacles." [74] The reaction of his helpful Han comrades who ranked from 31 to 113 is not recorded, but may be imagined. The policy of granting individuals from potentially troublesome areas special preference in the imperial examination competitions in order to facilitate acceptance of central government rule was a feature of pre-1911 China, though the imperial system, unlike that of the CCP, had control rather than integration as its goal.

A "remember bitterness" campaign to contrast harsh conditions prior to liberation with the freedom and dignity enjoyed by all nationalities in New China was begun as well. It was, of course, designed to convince minorities that no matter what their present economic circumstances, conditions had been much worse before the CCP took over. For example, a Manchu elementary school teacher recalled that before 1949 she had always written "Han" in the "nationality" box of her annual registration form because of the discrimination and oppression that prevailed in those days. Now, because of the party's enlightened policies, she proudly entered the character "Manchu." [75] A Korean lady toured Yenpien schools, contrasting for the pupils life under the Japanese and Chiang Kai-shek with conditions now and speaking of her great love for the party.[76] A Tibetan entertainer reminisced about his life as an itinerant dancer and singer. He had had to perform twenty to thirty times a day for a mouthful of food. Although he owned nothing, the feudal headman levied taxes nonetheless. After liberation, he was "discovered" by members of the Central Nationalities Song and Dance Troupe and invited to join the group. Now, thanks to the party and its encouragement of Tibetan art forms, he was well fed, had congenial companions, and played to appreciative audiences.[77]

The Tenth Plenum and Socialist Education

As mirrored in the official press, the emphasis on economic retrenchment and gradualist policies reached its height in September 1962 with statements like, "All other matters must be subordinate to increasing our herds." [78] In that same month the party, buoyed by reports of the first good harvest in three years, held its Tenth Plenum in Peking. The meeting marked the return of Mao Tse-tung to active participation in party and government affairs, a hardening of the Chinese attitude toward the Soviet Union (still referred to simply as "the modern revisionists"), and a warning that "revisionist ideology" existed within the CCP as well. As a signal that the conservative group's strength had waned, the communiqué stated that the Lushan Plenum had "smashed the revisionism of right wing opportunists" and protected the party line and party unity. Otherwise moderate in tone, the communiqué noted that the national economy was improving despite natural disasters, shortcomings, and mistakes in work over the past few years. The transition from capitalism to communism was expected to take several decades, during which time class struggle was expected to continue. Meanwhile, production should be strengthened in accordance with suitable time, place, and materials available. The masses must help to solve present difficulties through hard work and frugal living. Cadres were chided for not having "welcomed the masses." [79]

A commentary meant for nationalities workers contained the usual enjoinder to carry out the spirit of the Tenth Plenum and reiterated its emphasis on strengthening the collective economy.[80] However, with the exception of increasingly vindictive references to the nameless modern revisionists who were accused, inter alia, of having slandered the three red banners and of fomenting dissension among China's nationalities[81] (this being the time of the revolt in Sinkiang), very few changes in previous policy are discernible. The formula for strengthening the collective economy was said to be proceeding gradually step by step, adapting to local conditions, and making technological improvements. Though cadres were reminded that spontaneous tendencies toward capitalism would exist throughout the period of transition into communism, and that this would result in a struggle between two roads which would be reflected in nationalities problems,[82] the reminder was a gentle one and cannot be considered a theme in the writings of this period. In the months following the Tenth Plenum, class struggle was in fact nearly absent from articles about or directed toward minorities. In view of China's difficulties with Sinkiang dissidents, who were encouraged both by the Soviet Union and by the fact that supply lines for PLA units fighting with India stretched across a generally hostile Tibet, the decision to emphasize nationalities unity over class struggle seemed expedient. The "glorious patriotic movement" launched at this time was, however, less than wholly ideational in content: minorities were reminded that the state had aided them in their time of need; now they should reciprocate by selling more than their established quota to the state.[83] While the state would continue to aid minority areas when necessary, "some" had become too accustomed to relying on it and could not see beyond the needs of their own commune and nationality to those of state construction, disaster areas, and urban dwellers.[84] Minorities must be made to realize that selling their produce to the state was the glorious duty of all nationalities,[85] and that their first duty was to collective, not private, interests. In this connection, an elderly lady was praised for having gone voluntarily to protect the commune's sheep one bitterly cold night.[86]

In line with the Tenth Plenum's advice on welcoming the masses, a limited socialist education campaign began in December 1962, apparently on an experimental basis.[87] In addition, there was an increased emphasis on social mobilization. Lenin was quoted (though with the caveat that "there are differences in the concrete situation in our country") as saying that revolution could not be made by the vanguard alone.[88] The socialist message must be spread to all, that they might understand their glorious duty. Lest this sound too radical, however, it was explicitly stated that the best way to bring the socialist message to minorities was in their own languages. To do this, skilled linguists would have to be trained to "massify" translations and correct their present woeful inaccuracies.[89] One way advocated for inducing minorities to sell more to the state was first to supply the fraternal nationalities with the necessities of production and daily life, consonant with their special characteristics. Among their "special needs" were listed rugs, lacework, and ceremonial hats (*li-mao*).[90] The party's support for minorities culture was reiterated, and an article detailing its help in repairing a temple in Inner Mongolia quoted the lines to a local folksong praising Genghis Khan.[91]

In short, the six months following the Tenth Plenum resulted in minorities being called upon to dissociate themselves from ties with the Soviet Union and its nationalities policy and to involve themselves in a mass mobilization movement to love the state and sell more to it. The nationalities question was still considered to be a long-term problem; in the interim, nationalities' special characteristics would remain and must be catered to. Increased production was encouraged, but by means of careful planning and with agriculture or herding as its basis.

April 1963 saw an increase in radical propaganda directed at minorities. *Min-tsu t'uan-chieh* introduced its readers to Lei Feng and exhorted minorities to respond to Chairman Mao's call by emulating Lei Feng and his proletarian class viewpoint.[92] Minorities were reported enthusiastically affirming their devotion to the Chairman by taking Lei as their model.[93] In May there appeared a report summarizing the experiences of a socialist education campaign in rural Yunnan.[94] The publication of this summary coincided with the promulgation at the national level of what has been called the first major policy directive on implementation of the socialist education campaign, the "Draft Resolution of the Central Committee on Some Problems in Current Rural Work," or "First Ten Points." The leitmotif of the directive was class struggle, aiming at both masses and basic level cadres. Both were felt to have developed unhealthy tendencies, including hoarding, speculating, and cheating on work points. Some cadres were alleged to feel themselves superior to the masses, when in reality service to the masses was their whole raison d'être. Through propaganda recounting the revolutionary struggles of the past and education on the lessons contained therein, spontaneous tendencies toward capitalism and other sins against socialism could be overcome and the collective economy strengthened. This would provide a basis for the mobilization of poor and lower middle peasants. An integral part of setting the socialist economy to rights was the so-called "Four Cleans": clean up account books, granaries, properties, and work points. Cadres were told that they should join the labor force instead of separating themselves from production.[95]

The Yunnan report contrasts sharply with the relative sophistication of the First Ten Points. Since the P'englung and Chingpo inhabitants of this region are among the most backward of China's minorities, the results of this campaign are not necessarily typical of the experiences of socialist education in other minority areas. Still, the unspecific title given the report ("In Nationalities Where Differentiation Is Unclear, Progress Systematically with Class Education and Socialist Education") and the fact that it received nationwide circulation indicate that its contents were considered generalizable in some sense. Many party officials had in fact stated that class differentiation was unclear in all of China's minorities.

In any case, education in socialism in this area began from a very low level. Participants discussed the meaning of exploitation, how it had come about, and how it could be abolished. The group's early answers cast doubt upon the effectiveness of party propaganda in the area in the past. Some participants felt that poverty and hunger depended on one's horoscope, others that it was caused by the dominant nationality (the Tai) as a whole. Eventually, as in all good propaganda stories, the group leader managed to elicit correct conclusions. Private ownership was the root of all exploitation, and the Tai and Han masses had been exploited by their overlords too. As there is only one egg under a chicken, there is only one road, the socialist road, and all must take it. The report ended with the masses, having been apprised that class differences existed, heading happily down the collective road. They were still blissfully unaware of the four cleans, poor and lower middle peasants' associations, and the intricacies of class struggle.[96]

Other news on and for minorities at this time revealed few discontinuities with the gradualist policies of the past, concerning such matters as the latest episode of the Sino-Soviet dispute,[97] an explication of the party's policy of religious freedom (allowing true worship by eliminating exploitative practices),[98] the achievements of the revived nationalities social history project,[99] and the virtues of increasing production gradually in accordance with local conditions and reality.[100]

In July of 1963 there was a further escalation of radical propaganda. Minorities were introduced to a new hero, Nahsi party member Ho Chen-ku, who exemplified all the traits now officially considered virtuous. Ho always placed the common good first and would work after hours, refusing to accept extra work points. He believed cadres should be one with the masses and refused to put on airs. He was killed defending the commune's property. During a fight with a thief in the communal supply shed, a lamp was knocked over and the shed began to burn. Ho, though mortally wounded, fought the flames until his dying breath.[101] A commentary quoted Han dynasty historian Ssu-ma Ch'ien and, incidentally, Mao Tse-tung, as saying that everyone must die, it is how one dies that is important.[102]

Lest cadres receive the impression that one's redness could only be proved in unusual circumstances like these, a model for behavior under everyday conditions was also presented. The Chuang protagonist of a story entitled "Cadres: Common Laborers" was begged by commune members to accept work points for his administrative duties and to rest once in a while. He refused, declaring that he was a son of the working people. If he did not work, he would be forgetting his origins. To him, the party was his parents (compare this with the Confucian concept of officials as "father and mother" of the people) and cadres were the servants of the people (*ch'in-wu yüan*, the same phrase alleged to have been used by Nahsi hero Ho).[103]

In August the campaign to increase class awareness was begun in earnest. A *Min-tsu t'uan-chieh* editorial explained that class awareness was the basic component of the socialist education campaign then unfolding all over China. However, the editorial elaborated, special conditions existed. Most minorities lived in border areas where imperialism, reactionary regimes, and modern revisionists could plot with reactionary elements among the minority nationalities to destroy the unity of the ancestral land by stirring up nationality emotions and fomenting trouble in nationality relations. How then, it asked, could the masses' socialist consciousness be raised while avoiding encouragement of these reactionary elements? The answer was felt to be a "remember bitterness" campaign, which, it was said, had been successful in various test areas.[104] As always, the printed response was immediate, and the mass media were flooded with stories of evil landlords of one's own nationality,[105] starvation as a way of life before the arrival of the PLA,[106] and the like. Confining tales of class conflict to the bad old days before liberation may well have raised minorities' class consciousness while avoiding exacerbation of nationalities' tensions, but relegating such tales of woe to the pre-1949 period probably did little to arouse the masses' activism against cadres with unhealthy tendencies and members of the still-influential traditional minorities elite, which had been co-opted into the government after 1949.

The passage of a directive entitled "Some Concrete Policy Formulations of the Central Committee of the CCP in the Rural Socialist Education Movement" in September seems to have resulted in no changes at all in minorities policy. Also known as the "Later Ten Points," the directive set forth concrete forms for the implementation of the aims of the First Ten Points, including the formation of work teams to carry out socialist education in selected areas. The work teams were also expected to rid basic-level party units, mass organizations, and commune and brigade-committee memberships of corrupt and ideologically backward elements. Increased emphasis was placed on cadres' performing actual physical labor.[107]

In sharp contrast to the spirit of the Later Ten Points, news from minority areas this fall tended to dwell on the fifth or tenth anniversaries being celebrated by various autonomous areas. It was the custom to state that the area's minority group cadres had greatly increased over the years and to note proudly what percentage of them were "separated from production"—that is, had reached positions where physical labor was no longer required of them.[108] Progress was measured in terms of material improvements since the party had arrived in the area: an article concerning one Miao area, for instance, contrasted the miserable conditions of the past with the fact that today people had "stylish" clothing and each family had several bed quilts, chickens, and ducks. Mao's name was mentioned only once, and then in parallel with that of the party.[109] Technical expertise was still much admired, as exemplified in a story praising the dedication of two agricultural specialists who had spent the better part of a year studying cultivation methods for a certain type of mushroom found only in Inner Mongolia. The author wished the specialists success in their continuing efforts, so that the whole country might some day be able to enjoy this delicacy.[110]

In December another nationalities hero emerged, with updated revolutionary virtues. Clearly a blueprint for the ideal cadre in nationalities areas, Wu Hsing-ch'un, though a Han, was called by the people of southeast Kweichow "a true son of the Miao and T'ung." After spending the entire day in physical labor, Wu studied Miao and T'ung, including various dialects thereof, in the evening. He shunned praise, saying that whatever he did was easier than making the Long March. Finding that collectivization had not been fully understood by the masses and hsiang officials, Wu corrected their misapprehensions. He also taught the peasants to keep records, trained an ox to do the plowing, and created an experimental plot to demonstrate the efficacy of new agricultural techniques. Though this was backbreaking work, Wu forgot his aches and pains when he saw that the masses were learning. He helped to train minority cadres, was always humble, and organized mutual-aid teams, cooperatives, and communes in his area at the appropriate times. So far, there was nothing really new in Wu's biography. A subtle change was introduced only at the end of his story, when it was stated that after the three lean years (1959–1961), people had gone all out to increase production and "the numbing influence of peaceful ideology was felt" (*ho-p'ing ma-pi ssu-hsiang*). Wu, who had ardently studied the works of Chairman Mao, instructed the masses on the necessity of class struggle and helped them to overcome their mistakes. A lengthy excerpt from his diary gave all credit for these accomplishments to Chairman Mao.[111]

As the campaign to study Wu Hsing-ch'un unfolded in the first half of 1964, other ideas representing the radicals' point of view were introduced via his experiences in minority areas. Through tales of Wu's foiling plots by die-hard class enemies, cadres in minority areas were told that they must "seize class struggle." If reforms were not progressively implemented, the old feudal capitalist class would make a comeback, and it would be useless to speak of increases in production. Mao's dictum that the nationalities problem was in actuality a problem of class, all but ignored in recent years, was reintroduced,[112] as was his belief that "if the masses seek to move ahead and we do not do so, this is right opportunism." Wu was also reported to have always "managed things according to principle" (*an yuan-ts'e pan-shih*), in distinct contrast to the 1961 model cadre,[113] who always consulted with the masses before applying policy, and who was careful to adapt policy to time and place. Moreover, unlike the 1961 model, Wu Hsing-ch'un was an enthusiastic and vocal proponent of Mao study.[114] Whereas his earlier counterpart had formulated policy by intuitively combining party directives with the masses' opinions and his own knowledge of local conditions, Wu found his guide to policy in the words of Chairman Mao. He had, it was stated, truly "taken root, flowered, and borne fruit" (*cha-ken k'ai-hua chieh-kuo*) in his area.[115]

In April, minorities were told that they must "compare, study, catch up, and help"; like the rest of the country, they were urged to emulate the poor but intrepid members of the Tachai brigade.[116] A marked shift in story content took place, with the material satisfactions derived from accumulating bed quilts and poultry after liberation replaced by the spiritual satisfactions of serving the masses in an area unreachable by car,[117] or of carrying a diarrheic child two days through the rain on one's back to reach a hospital.[118]

The theme of the necessity of class struggle in minority areas, presented metaphorically in stories about Wu Hsing-ch'un, was made explicit in a *Red Flag* article by UFWD deputy director Liu Ch'un. However, though agreeing that the term "nationality" really meant the peasants, herdsmen, serfs, and slaves of such a group—that is, that the majority of a nationality group was poor and exploited—Liu continued to defend the United Front. If the minorities' upper strata continued to take the anti-imperialist, patriotic, socialist road and worked hard to reform themselves by reading Marx, Lenin, and the thoughts of Mao Tse-tung, unity should be sought with them in the struggle against imperialism and modern revisionism. Contradictions with the nationalities' upper strata were contradictions within the people. Thus, the upper strata and nationalities' special characteristics, if not exaggerated, could continue to be tolerated.[119] In short, Liu envisioned class struggle in minority areas as a relatively mild educative process that would not fundamentally change policies already in force therein.

During the latter half of 1964, references to "class enemies" increased, and it was this "small handful" rather than, as had been the case in 1961–62, "natural disasters and shortcomings in our work," who were held responsible for deficiencies in the collective economy. A salient exception was P'eng Chen's speech at the fifteenth anniversary of the CPR, which continued to place blame on shortcomings in party work. Though his report contained nothing specifically relating to minority nationalities, it was reprinted in full as the lead article in the October issue of *Min-tsu t'uan-chieh.*[120] This exception aside, the emphasis on propaganda in the closing months of 1964 was on educating the masses in the Marxist class theory so that they would be able to recognize reactionary slanders promulgated by the small handful of class enemies for what they were. This did not involve "dragging out" the offenders to expose their crimes.[121] There was no evidence that the small handful in a given area were thought to have any links with the small handful in any other area, or that they had protectors in party or government leadership positions.

While class enemies received verbal abuse, the rural masses and their art and literature became the focus of increased solicitude. The Ministry of Culture and Nationalities Affairs Commission agreed jointly to sponsor an All China Minority Nationalities Masses Spare-Time Literature and Art Exhibition, which opened in Peking in late November 1964.[122] According to *Jen-min jih-pao*, its aim was to help develop a working masses' literature and art with true revolutionary spirit. Lest this be seen as an attempt to force all artistic activity into a single mold, it was stated that "nationalities art cannot be alike and must not be alike." Still, budding artists were warned that "minorities culture also has its dregs, reflecting slaveowners, serfholders, landlords, and bourgeoisie. These seek to destroy nationalities unity and split up the ancestral land." [123] In effect, then, minorities had been given carte blanche to adorn their pictures of Chairman Mao or of the happy life on the communes with stripes or curlicues, whichever their tradition held in more esteem. Genghis Khan and the wise king of Tibet who had first established relations with the Han slipped quietly from mention, having been demoted from progressives to the ranks of ghosts and monsters. The exhibition was also seen as evidence that the gap between those who worked with their hands and those who worked with their minds could be closed. Revolutionary peasant artists, it was hoped, would be both red and expert.

Amid the many references to the sharpening of class struggle and revolutionization of proletarian art and literature, Ulanfu's speech at the closing of the exhibition contained one jarring note. Calling the art shown at the exhibition the embodiment of Chairman Mao's teachings on literature and art and a progressive step in the revolutionization, *nationalization* (emphasis mine), and massification of the country's literature and art [124] was a distinct departure from the formula in current use. In addition, the term "nationalization" (*min-tsu hua*) had been socialistically unacceptable ever since it had been declared overused during the Hundred Flowers campaign.

Further evidence of increased attention to mass literature and art was manifest in the wide publicity given to the so-called Ulanmuchi troupes. Though reportedly founded in 1957, groups began to be publicized only in the closing days of 1964. The term Ulanmuchi (*wu-lan-mu-chi*) is the Chinese transliteration of a Mongolian term meaning "red branch," which had been used to designate mobile culture teams in Inner Mongolia.[125] Its ten founders were said to have been inspired by reading Mao Tse-tung's thoughts on literature and art and to have immediately vowed to "actively serve the herdsmen, the socialist revolution, and socialist construction by forming a mobile literature and art troupe." Mass media praised the group, seven years after its founding, for portraying the actual life of the herdsmen it served, and also because its performances combined nationalities' special characteristics with socialist content. Participants were both red and expert, and the membership of the troupe was kept small enough so that everyone could engage in all kinds of propaganda work. When not propagandizing, the team members would help the masses in their daily work.[126] The group was reminiscent of the work teams of an earlier, less bureaucratized period of nationalities policy, and became the model for a countrywide movement. Leading performers in a wide variety of art forms, PLA cultural workers, and "others" were sent to bring a new revolutionary repertoire to the masses in remote rural areas.[127]

Against this background of escalating class struggle and leveling cultural differences, Chou En-lai's December 1964 outline of future minorities work seemed surprisingly moderate. He advocated continued consolidation and development of the united front and promised a bright future to patriotic minorities upper strata who were in favor of socialist reforms. Thus united, all could march ahead to carry out the most important task: completion of the democratic and socialist revolutions.[128]

Despite this relatively mild prognosis, 1965 saw a steady rise in revolutionary propaganda. The salient characteristic of 1965's model cadre, unveiled in February, was his discovery that the nationality struggle was fundamentally a question of class struggle. Prior to this revelation he had looked at his nationality as "a dear, great family" and a complete entity; he had not noticed its class divisions. Significant also was the fact that he was a soldier. According to an excerpt from the hero's diary, he had made his ideological breakthrough in 1960, while heeding Lin Piao's call to *correctly* study Chairman Mao's works.[129]

In March the half-work half-study schools were re-revived, being termed "the fundamental road to education in minority areas." Descriptions of the schools were strikingly similar to those of the minorities institute in Yenan, with students raising crops and making their own bricks.[130] An interesting change was that while previously propaganda had differentiated between the masses and the class enemy, stories of the half-work half-study schools described conflicts between the poor and lower middle peasants on the one hand and rich peasants on the other.[131] Like the campaign to promote spare-time artistic endeavors and the Ulanmuchi performers, the half-work half-study schools were designed to reduce differences between intellectuals and laborers and to develop political consciousness in rural areas. Both themes had, of course, been part of the Great Leap Forward.

A follow-up story on the Ulanmuchi spirit in the summer of 1965 noted that the first troupe had been founded not, as previously stated, in 1957, but in 1958 "as part of the Great Leap Forward." [132] Though earlier stories had not been specific on the teams' propaganda work, a mid-1965 account declared that Ulanmuchi troupes helped the people to study Mao's works, "especially the three constantly read articles." [133] Like the work teams of years gone by, they practiced the "three togethers" (live together, work together, eat together),[134] and at least part of the Ulanmuchi teams were revealed to be composed of youths recently "sent down" to minority areas.[135]

Like the rest of the country, minorities spent the middle third of 1965 hearing about the Tachai brigade,[136] supporting their revolutionary brethren in Vietnam,[137] and achieving great successes by applying the policy of one divides into two.[138] In accordance with Maoist interpretations of the dialectic, the "one divides into two" slogan generally means a harder class line has been adopted: a synthesis has divided into thesis and antithesis, and there is a contradiction, or struggle, between the two. However, the application of the "one divides into two" slogan to minorities areas in mid-1965 did not seem to be accompanied by a harder class line. This may have been because the movement was thwarted by those who would later be called reactionary capitalist roaders. An equally plausible explanation is that the sloganeering constituted preparatory work for the much harder class line that emerged in the late fall.

The long-delayed inauguration of the Tibetan Autonomous Region (TAR) filled the headlines in early September, as did the tenth anniversary of the Sinkiang Uighur Autonomous Region in the latter part of that month. No great radical content was apparent in the reports of either event. At the former,[139] it was revealed that most areas in Tibet had not yet formed mutual-aid teams, and no plans for the formation of cooperatives were mentioned. The united front was to be "consolidated and developed," and upper strata personages were promised the usual bright future so long as they remained patriotic and progressive. Ngapo Ngawang Jigme was named chairman of the autonomous region, living proof that reformed members of the upper strata could remain prestigious, and PLA Commander Chang Kuo-hua, head of the Tibet Military Region since early 1952, became First Party Secretary. The designation "Work Committee" of the CCP was dropped, indicating that Tibet was now considered to have a full-fledged Communist party.

Ngapo's appointment, accompanied by denunciations of the Dalai Lama, implied the abandonment of earlier hopes that the Dalai Lama would return to Tibet voluntarily. Indeed, as early as 1962, the Chinese seemed to have accepted his absence as permanent. Apparently the Panchen Lama, who had served as acting chairman of the preparatory committee for the TAR during the Dalai Lama's "absence," had proved an unacceptable substitute. In the announcement of the Panchen Lama's dismissal, Tibetan activists were said to have denounced "the planned and organized activities of the reactionary clique of serfowners represented by Panchen Erdeni." [140] It would seem peculiar that the heretofore compliant Panchen Lama should begin resisting party plans for Tibet at this late date, and indeed the communiqué merely said that he had represented the serfowners. Still, the Panchen Lama had been a relatively young man when the CCP returned him to Tibet, and his perceptions of its presence there may have crystallized only gradually. There were rumors that his dismissal followed the Panchen Lama's refusal to denounce the Dalai Lama publicly. What is particularly interesting, however, is the fact that a secular figure had replaced a religious one as head of the Tibetan government. It may be that the real reason behind the dismissal of the Panchen Lama was the party's desire to secularize the Tibetan administration now that the area was achieving formal parity in the CPR provincial system. A minor revolt followed the dismissal, but it was easily put down.[141] The fact that this change was accepted with relative equanimity by the Tibetans may indicate a victory for party efforts toward secularization. On the other hand, it might also be argued that most Tibetans continued to regard the Dalai Lama as their ruler and considered the identity of whatever puppet the CCP tried to substitute as irrelevant.

In Sinkiang, tenth anniversary speeches stressed the increases in production achieved through the cooperation of people of all nationalities; they did not stress ideology. The Soviet Union was condemned for its subversive plots to undermine the unity of nationalities. Han First Party Secretary Wang En-mao's speech mentioned the need to consider class background as well as nationality origin as criteria for recruitment into the party, but added that Sinkiang had many characteristics that were different from those of Han areas. Therefore, in carrying out work in the autonomous area, it was necessary to first investigate the concrete situation and then integrate the thought of Mao Tse-tung with it.[142]

In October 1965 revolutionary propaganda was escalated anew. Whereas, before, the socialist education campaign had been carried out in a way that exposed many minorities to the rhetoric of the campaign without demanding as much participation in the matters of Mao study, class struggle, and administrative reordering as was expected in Han areas, these activities now seemed to be its sole emphasis. A *Min-tsu t'uan-chieh* editorial, refuting the slanders of "some comrades" who felt that Mao study would be useless to minorities because their cultural level was too low and might even interfere with production, indicates that an important opposition group must have been defeated at this time. The comrades were warned that they must not underestimate the ability of the masses to study and apply the works of Chairman Mao, and anecdotal material was introduced to prove that not only was Mao study not detrimental to production, it was actually a stimulus thereto.[143]

One thing Mao study was said to have stimulated was collective manure production. Lin Sheng-nan, a Korean production team leader, reported that studying "On Contradictions" had enabled him to discover that the principal contradiction in insufficient manure production was that there were problems in the relationship between the individual and the collective. After further study he was able to discern the principal aspect of this contradiction: that there were problems in the method of receiving manure and in paying for the manure received.

Having thus isolated the contradictions, Lin was able to solve his collective's manure production problems.[144]

Class education now replaced all other news from minority areas. Among other manifestations of this increased attention to socialist consciousness, the section of *Min-tsu t'uan-chieh* heretofore devoted to summarizing the results of nationalities research and historiography disappeared, being supplanted by a section entitled "Class Brothers' Toil and Tears." The symbolism was clear: research, which had bourgeois overtones, had been replaced by tales of class struggle, which were more properly proletarian. Still, it should be noted that while tales of the upsurge in revolutionary consciousness were legion, it was often only the formula according to which events were presented that had changed rather than the actual content of stories. In a typical instance, whereas a 1962 story was entitled "New Motor Road in Inner Mongolia," [145] a similar story four years later was headlined "Tibet's Latest Bridge Demonstrates the Might of the Thought of Mao Tse-tung." [146]

Shortly thereafter, an incident occurred that seemed to portend more than symbolic changes. In November 1965 the Ch'inghai Provincial People's Congress met, dismissing Vice-Governor Shirob Jaltso and appointing a hitherto unknown person in his stead. Like Shirob, the newcomer, Tsai Chieh, was a Tibetan. The provincial media described him as a thirty-six-year-old carpenter who had suffered tremendously at the hands of reactionary landowners and had been separated from his family for eighteen years. After liberation, the party and government had helped reunite the family and guided Tsai Chieh to transform himself from an illiterate into a politically aware proletarian fighter. Prior to his election, he had served as deputy director of a party school in the Yushu Tibetan Autonomous Chou.[147] Shirob was an elderly Living Buddha who had spent much of his earlier life in Peking studying Buddhist scriptures at monasteries which imperial and republican government patronage had helped to maintain. He had served as vice-governor of Ch'inghai since 1949.[148] Although the media gave no reasons for Shirob Jaltso's dismissal, there was obvious significance in the fact that a young worker trained and educated by the party was replacing this venerable, aristocratic, religious personage.

From November on, there were infrequent reports of "four cleans" work teams in minority areas[149] and of minorities complaining of mistreatment by cadres of low ideological outlook.[150] Hsien secretaries seemed to be absorbing much of the blame for lower-level cadres' mistakes. Again, this sequence followed the pattern of events in Han areas, save that it lacked the intensity.

In sum, the socialist education campaign in minority areas appears to have followed the same stages at the same time as the campaign in Han areas, but to have demanded less in terms of minorities' participation. Even taking into account the accusations of radicals that the campaign had been subverted in Han areas, the socialist education campaign appears to have been mitigated still further in minority areas.[151] Administrators tended to defend the continuation of the united front and due allowance for minorities' special characteristics as absolutely necessary at this stage of history. Perhaps remembering the disruptions caused by rapid change during the Great Leap Forward, they tended to avoid sharp reversals in policy or severe criticism of cadres, fearing that the resulting instability would reopen nationalities schisms and disrupt production. Wang En-mao's statement that the thought of Mao Tse-tung should be integrated with the concrete situation is probably the clearest expression of this point of view. Naturally, the administrators' solicitude over production statistics and the maintenance of order in their areas was often tinged with a desire to keep their own positions secure and their personal organizations intact.

8

The Cultural Revolution, 1966–1969

In November 1965, Shanghai Party Committee member Yao Wenyuan launched an attack on historian Wu Han, who was also the vice-mayor of Peking. Thus began a new, more virulent campaign to revolutionize culture, erase references to and vestiges of the decadent past, and criticize those who opposed such radical ideas. The campaign to study the works of Mao intensified in proportion. At first concerned mainly with the cultural sphere, by June 1966 this revolution had resulted in the purge of leading figures in the Peking Party Committee. In August the Central Committee held its Eleventh Plenum, and the Great Proletarian Cultural Revolution was born.

The Cultural Revolution—a misleading title in that much more than culture was involved—became a conflict over the ideology by which China should be governed and a personal power struggle as well. Following the chairman's orders to "Bombard the Headquarters," Maoist radicals took the offensive against Liuist conservatives, intending to cleanse the party and government of "rotten elements," even if party and government had to be destroyed in the process. A "Cultural Revolution Group" based in Peking was to supervise this task, aided by revolutionary representatives from the army, cadres, and mass organizations. A three-way alliance of these groups was to "seize power" from decadent bureaucrats at all levels and to form so-called Revolutionary Committees at these levels. The purity of their composition would be judged by the Cultural Revolution Group. The revolutionary committees would combine party and governmental duties until both could be reconstructed on a more acceptably Maoist basis. PLA chief of staff Lin Piao was named Mao Tse-tung's successor, and the army's prestige rose concomitantly. Mao's wife, Chiang Ch'ing, emerged as the guiding spirit of cultural reform as well as the leader of the most radical group of Maoists. Revolutionary youth were mobilized into the Red Guards, who also became closely associated with Chiang Ch'ing. The Guards were charged with destroying the Four Olds (old ideas, culture, customs, and habits) and encouraged to travel to "exchange revolutionary experiences." Both duties were assumed with alacrity.

The events of August 1966 were immediately reflected in minorities areas. Mass rallies of "people of all nationalities" in Urumchi, Huhehot, Yin-ch'uan, Nanning, and Lhasa were reported enthusiastically greeting the Central Committee's Decision on the Great Proletarian Cultural Revolution, and Red Guard groups were duly formed. Precisely as in Han areas, headquarters began to be bombarded by activists whose zeal unfortunately did not make them authorities on the redness of the occupants of these headquarters. Administrators anxious to save themselves organized other Red Guard groups who would defend them, with both sides claiming to be true Maoists. The groups also bombarded each other's headquarters or simply fought each other where the time and terrain seemed suitable. Chaos of varying degrees ensued, which administrators hesitated to put down openly lest they be thought counterrevolutionaries trying to thwart Mao's plans. A "seizure of power" might be carried out by conservatives pretending to be radicals, and not all radical groups were equally radical. All professed to be Maoists. Thus, the Cultural Revolution Group often found it extremely difficult to decide which organizations to legitimize. Many high officials made self-confessions, and some were summoned to Peking for further examination.

Two special features distinguished the early stages of the Cultural Revolution in minority areas from that in Han areas. First, the attack on the Four Olds was more far-reaching, because of the party's previous leniency in regard to retention of old customs, ideas, culture, and habits. Second, the Red Guards and other activist groups, despite the idealistic principles on which they had been formed, contained a small but determined group of Han who had been sent to minority areas against their will. Some used the enjoinder to exchange revolutionary experiences as an excuse to return to their urban homes. The groups they joined or formed were loyal to whomever seemed less likely to send them away again or, in the case of those who could not easily leave the areas to which they had been assigned, to whatever official seemed most likely to arrange their transfer. Many embattled officials were not above appealing to such sentiments. Such groups, feeling that their entire future hung in the balance, fought fiercely. One Shanghai youth interviewed in Hong Kong said that he and his friends had vowed that even death would be preferable to returning to Inner Mongolia.[1] Minorities who harbored "local nationalist sentiments" were only too happy to see the young people leave; those minority group members whose primary concern was status advancement saw an exodus of Han cadres as increasing their chances of promotion. In this mixture of motives the terms "Maoism" and "Liuism" often had only tenuous relevance, thus making the Cultural Revolution Group's task even harder.

The relative candor with which opinions on minorities policy were expressed at this time provides one index of the party's success in dealing with the nationalities problem to date. For this reason, it is worth examining the events of the Great Proletarian Cultural Revolution in detail.

On a national level, the united front was bitterly attacked. This was a logical extension of the emphasis on class struggle. If nationalities problems are in reality class problems and class struggle must be carried out to solve the nationalities problem, then it follows that there can be no solution while a united front of all classes composing the nationality is maintained.

Those who bore the brunt of the radicals' attack, however, were not members of the traditional nationalities upper strata who had retained their prestige as a result of the united front policy, but party members associated with united front work and, of course, chief scapegoat Liu Shao-ch'i. In this sense, party membership actually rendered its holders more vulnerable to attack than membership in the traditional elite cooperating with the party would have made them. The explanation for this may lie in the reasoning that while those remnants of the old society were simply doing what historical necessity expected of them— that is, trying to salvage their old positions insofar as possible—the Communist "new men" had actually sold out the interests of the revolution. The traitor within was more to be feared than the enemy without. In rectifying this situation, the CCP's structure for dealing with minority nationalities as a group separate from the Han population was destroyed, and most of the elite group staffing it purged as well.

With the clarity of hindsight one can see a portent of later attacks in the removal of Li Wei-han as UFWD director in 1965, on grounds of capitulationism in united front work.[2] He was replaced by Hsü Ping, his longtime deputy director, and for a short while all appeared to be functioning well. It was, after all, not the united front itself which had been attacked but the allegedly capitulationist activities of one member, albeit the director thereof. Still, Li had been in charge of united front work since 1944 and would have been ineffectual indeed had he failed to choose subordinates of like views, or at least to indoctrinate new recruits in these views.

With the coming of the Cultural Revolution a year later, the entire united front came under attack as a screen behind which Liu Shao-ch'i and his agents pursued their allegedly capitulationist schemes.[3] It is worthy of note that the most vehement denunciations of the united front and of previous nationalities policy came from two sources: first, Shanghai, and second, the so-called Red Army Corps of the K'angta Commune of the Central Nationalities Institute. That Shanghai, the stronghold of radicalism during the Cultural Revolution, should put forth such views is not surprising. There is also an obvious explanation for the radicalism of the Nationalities Institute students. Carefully chosen for their socialist activism and leadership potential, the students' upward mobility had been limited by the party's alliance with the traditional upper strata. The Cultural Revolution's call to attack entrenched power-holders was therefore advisable for personal as well as ideological reasons. For those students who came from upper strata families, denunciation was, of course, expedient as well. Genuine social cleavages and intergroup tensions doubtless also underlay many of the denunciations.

Specifically, Liu Shao-ch'i and his "black gang" were accused of perpetrating the false notion that there could be a "socialist united front." Liu's words at a national conference on united front work in 1953 were quoted in support of this scandal: he had alleged that uniting with the upper strata of nationalities not only prevented rebellion but caused the old elite to "bow to and serve socialism. This saves a lot of trouble." [4] The united front was also held responsible for the Tibetan revolt, specifically in the person of Party General Secretary Teng Hsiao-p'ing. In 1952 Teng was said to have arranged for passage to India for a prime minister of the local government of Tibet after the prime minister had outspokenly disagreed with party policy in his country.[5] The ex–prime minister later played an important part in planning the 1959 revolt. Teng's reasoning had been that incarceration of the prime minister would seriously affect united front work. He was also alleged to have used this reasoning to protect a Han PLA commander whose relations with the Local Government of Tibet had been particularly cordial. The commander joined the rebels in 1959 and was subsequently decorated by Chiang Kai-shek. Teng had in addition, it was said, proposed to recruit upper strata lamas as party members and agreed with "Chang XX's" (Chang Kuo-hua or Chang Ching-wu's) desire to set up only patriotic-education classes and not class-education classes in 1957, arguing in both cases that united front work would be adversely affected otherwise.[6]

Attacks extended beyond the united front to other aspects of the party's nationalities policy. Liu Shao-ch'i's 1948 essay "On Nationalism and Internationalism," once mandatory reading for cadres in minorities areas, was now castigated for stating that "National problems are *linked with* class problems." [7] Presumably a true Maoist would have written that national problems *were* class problems.

A 1937 statement of Liu's, supporting self-determination for all China's nationalities and promising them party help in organizing their own autonomous governments, was purported to prove his opposition to national unification and advocacy of nationality separatism. His warning that without a promise of autonomy "the minority nationalities might be utilized by the Japanese bandits and hoodwinked into opposing China and the Han people" was similarly interpreted as splittism.[8] Approval of regional autonomy such as that promised in the 1954 constitution was denounced as "obliterating the essence of proletarian dictatorship," [9] and caution in instituting land redistribution and reforms of customs, and in handling emergencies in minority areas, was termed "suppression of minority nationalities' revolutionary demands for emancipation and liberation." [10] "Peaceful reform" was, of course, interpreted as obliteration of class struggle.[11]

A draft party constitution circulated in the name of the Shanghai masses in 1968 stated, inter alia, that

The old party constitution stresses only the special characteristics of the nationalities and the conducting of social reforms according to their own wishes, but not the party's leadership and the socialist revolution. It says "the development of many national minorities has been restricted" and "the party must make a special effort to improve the position of the various national minorities." By emphasizing nationalism to the exclusion of patriotism and internationalism, it in reality creates national schism. The broad revolutionary masses maintain that the following directive from Chairman Mao should be stressed in the new party constitution of the Ninth Congress: "National struggle is in the final analysis a question of class struggle." The unity of all nationalities on the basis of the thought of Chairman Mao Tse-tung and on the socialist road should be stressed.[12]

With regard to the united front, the Shanghai *Wen-hui pao* of September 6, 1968, stated that "the party absolutely cannot and will not share leadership . . ." [13]

The perpetrators of these crimes were duly attacked. Hsü Ping was charged with following in Li Wei-han's path and "surrendering to the bourgeoisie and upper strata of national minority and religious groups ... and forming cliques for private ends." [14] Liu Ch'un, a deputy director of the UFWD and concurrently vice-chairman of the NAC and president of the Central Nationalities Institute, was accused of "completely controlling the business of the NAC" while collaborating in Liu Shao-ch'i's plots.[15] Wang Feng, another long-term member of the UFWD who was also an important figure on the NAC and First Party Secretary of the Kansu Committee, and who had been outspoken in his defense of the united front,[16] was removed from all his positions on grounds he had abetted the schemes of China's Khrushchev.[17]

The theory of minorities' special characteristics was again attacked, as it had been during the Great Leap Forward, as part of these schemes. In effect, radicals called for all special privileges to be abolished and for members of minority nationalities to be treated exactly as were Han— that is, for complete assimilation. Like the attacks on established power-holders, this demand reflected mixed motives. For reasons of personal self-interest, many Han resented the special treatment accorded to members of minority nationalities. From a more idealistic standpoint, they saw special treatment of minorities as a barrier that set the nationalities apart from the rest of Chinese society and prevented them from participating in it on a completely equal basis. Their attacks extended beyond central party and government organs to those whose chief bases of power were at the provincial and autonomous chou levels. As at national level, the timing and intensity of these attacks closely paralleled similar events in Han areas.

Inner Mongolia

In the IMAR, the municipal party committee of the capital city, Huhehot, was purged in early August, ostensibly because of its members' "national splittist" and "capitalist" activities.[18] Red Guard groups were reported in action a few weeks later, demanding that old habits and customs be discarded and that Inner Mongolians "take up the iron broom of revolution to sweep away the dust of the old society." [19] From the many factions formed, two main groups coalesced, the Inner Mongolia East Shines Red United Revolutionary Rebels, abbreviated as the United Rebels, and the Third Headquarters of the Revolutionary Rebels of Huhehot, abbreviated as the Huhehot Third Headquarters. Purges began to be reported from various parts of the autonomous region, with the persons purged frequently accused of "inciting discord between the Mongol and the Han peoples," "overemphasizing the problem of national minority affairs," and "hampering nationalities solidarity." [20] In September the acting mayor of Huhehot was "dragged out by the masses" for "frenziedly promoting revisionism and nationality splittism." He was said to have forced the masses to study Mongolian in order to divert their attention from the works of Chairman Mao, and to have told them that so long as they raised hogs properly, he could not care less whether they read the works of Chairman Mao.[21] Mongols were said to be resisting attacks on their decadent customs, and party and government organizations apparently ceased to function. Radio Huhehot stopped broadcasting local news and began to relay Radio Peking's domestic service.

From the early fall of 1966 until mid-March of 1967, Inner Mongolia virtually disappeared from mention in Chinese mass media. What was lacking in official data was supplanted by rumor and Red Guard newspapers, the two not being mutually exclusive. NAC Chairman Ulanfu, who held a monopoly of the autonomous region's top positions (e.g., Party First Secretary, governor, commander, and political commissar of the Inner Mongolia Military District, president of the Inner Mongolia University) and who, as an alternate member of the Politburo, was China's highest-ranking member of a minority nationality, made his last public appearance at the October First National Day rally in Peking. In January 1967 a Peking wall newspaper accused Ulanfu of backing anti-Maoists in a speech calling for "Mongolia for the Mongols." The paper also told of a pitched battle in the offices of the Inner Mongolia Daily between Maoists and anti-Maoists, the latter supported by PLA troops armed with rockets, artillery, and machine guns.[22]

As in other areas of China, the army moved in early in 1967 to quell disorder, a stage which radicals later referred to as "the February adverse current." A Peking Red Guard newspaper which appeared at this time reported that Inner Mongolia had been cut off from the outside world for the past several months and that "a small group of addled eggs" led by Liu Ch'ang, a deputy political commissar of the military district, had established a "fascist dictatorship" which was terrorizing and suppressing revolutionary left-wing elements. Revolutionary rebels from Peking, Shanghai, and elsewhere were reported en route to Inner Mongolia to help their besieged comrades.[23]

In early March, Radio Huhehot resumed broadcasting of locally originated material. The Inner Mongolia Military District Command announced it had convened an "urgent meeting" to mobilize all forces for the successful completion of spring farming, in order to combat the class enemies' sabotage. Its deputy commander, "relaying the spirit of instructions from Lin Piao" emphasized that production must be put on a practical basis.[24]

A few weeks later, the Huhehot Municipal Revolutionary Committee was formed, its three-way alliance distinctly top-heavy with military men, including the leader of the "addled eggs" whom Red Guards had accused of heading a fascist dictatorship.[25] Further reports in March noted that "with the active support of PLA officers and men" production was proceeding smoothly.[26] Fascist or not, the army seemed to have restored order.

On April 13, however, the party central committee in Peking handed down a "Decision on the Handling of the Inner Mongolia Question," [27] which criticized the military for its suppression of leftists. This was clearly a response to shifting power relationships in Peking: a week before the Inner Mongolia decision the radical Maoists, led by Chiang Ch'ing, had succeeded in issuing a directive limiting the army's power to intervene and telling commanders to give more support to revolutionaries. Nonetheless, the decision also approved the membership of a preparatory committee for Inner Mongolia's revolutionary committee, which was predominantly military in its upper echelons. The radicals were not appreciably discouraged by this, and it was later admitted that "national splittists, capitalist roaders, and those with extreme leftist ideas" had forced the autonomous region to the brink of civil war at this time. Railroad and highway transport and telegraph and telephone communications were repeatedly disrupted, and production suffered.[28]

In August, Ulanfu began to be publicly condemned by name. One of the more interesting accusations against him was that in December 1965 he had held a top secret meeting to plan a counterrevolutionary coup on the twentieth anniversary of the founding of the IMAR (May 1, 1967). He was also alleged to have slighted the role of Mao Tse-tung by advocating integrating the chairman's thoughts with the reality of Inner Mongolia.[29] In addition, Ulanfu was said to have opposed class struggle by "arbitrarily quoting" Mao as having written that "the heart of the nationalities problem is unity as well as the development of production." [30]

In August, also, disruptions reached a peak, and in September the military district's powers to curb radicals were expanded. Again this was in response to shifting power relationships in Peking, where two leading radicals had been purged and Chiang Ch'ing induced to accept a more conservative course. In Inner Mongolia, a late September public trial sentenced two "counterrevolutionaries" to death and imprisoned many others. An acceptable level of stability was apparently achieved, and on November 1, the IMAR Revolutionary Committee was formally inaugurated, with the military maintaining prominence. With just one exception, Wang Tsai-t'ien, all the Mongols associated with Ulanfu were purged with him, including K'uei Pi, Chi Ya-t'ai, and

Wang To. The revolutionary committee contained no Mongols among its top leaders, and there were apparently only two Mongols on the committee as a whole, Wang Tsai-t'ien and a newcomer, Paojihletai.[31]

Two weeks after the committee's inauguration, Chairman T'eng Hai-ch'ing issued a "stern warning" to saboteurs and called upon all nationalities to work together in bringing about peace. Mass organizations and individuals were forbidden to exchange revolutionary experiences in frontier (predominantly Mongol) areas, and no one was to interfere with or obstruct the PLA and local security departments in fulfilling their normal duties. Such persons or groups as well as saboteurs and speculators would be strictly dealt with, he warned.[32]

The revolutionary committee, having admitted that "the great victory may be lost again," [33] began a mass campaign to denounce Ulanfu. He was said to have distorted the role of the party in relation to the Mongolian people's revolution in the 1930's and 1940's; to have eulogized Genghis Khan; to have placed undue emphasis on the study of the Mongolian language and cultural heritage in order to divert people's attention from the study of Mao's works; and to have believed himself superior to Mao to the extent of wishing to replace the study of the thoughts of Chairman Mao with the study of the thoughts of Ulanfu. He was also said to have plotted to reunite Inner and Outer Mongolia as an independent kingdom with himself as ruler.[34] A group of Mongols, pleading for reversal of his verdict, allegedly argued that "if Ulanfu is finished, we Mongols are also finished," [35] and reports of groups seeking to reinstate him continued to be heard for several years thereafter.[36] Interestingly, however, there are no reports of organized Mongol participation in the events of the Cultural Revolution. Their physical resistance seems to have been limited to ad hoc attempts to defend their property, persons, and customs from the attacks of zealots. Most reports of fighting emanated from Huhehot or other large cities where Mongols are a small and generally well-assimilated minority of the population.

In sum, the protected position given the Mongolian language and culture by previous party policy constituted one of the principal bases of radical attacks during the Cultural Revolution. While reports indicated the continued existence of ethnic group sentiments, these sentiments were apparently not strong enough to cause the formation of a Mongol group willing to fight for the retention of this protected position, or for greater Mongol representation in leadership positions. The party must be credited with having made progress in its efforts at integration, for this relative passivity would have been unthinkable twenty years before. However, the victory was only partial: the Cultural Revolution in Inner Mongolia centered around urban areas where ethnic ties were weakest and was carefully limited in the frontier pasturelands where they were strongest. This is not, of course, to argue that nationality identities necessarily become blunted by urban living. Indeed, ethnic animosities of minor import in relatively isolated and sparsely populated areas may become exacerbated by the proximity of urban living. This does not seem to have been the case in Inner Mongolia. Mongols are a small fraction of the population of the major urban areas, and most of them do in fact seem to have been well assimilated.

Sinkiang

In Sinkiang, unlike Inner Mongolia, the party eleventh plenum did not result in immediate revolutionary activity. This began a month later when, in mid-September, some four hundred Red Guards arrived in Urumchi to exchange revolutionary experiences and destroy the Four Olds. Peking wall posters soon began to complain that the plenum's decision on the Great Proletarian Cultural Revolution was not being carried out in Sinkiang and that nationalist, religious, and counterrevolutionary elements were actively opposing it.[37]

First Party Secretary Wang En-mao was either less reluctant or less subtle than Ulanfu in employing force to keep disorder within bounds, and, predictably, numerous Red Guard and wall newspapers accused him of suppressing the revolution. A group known as the Sinkiang Red Second Headquarters emerged as the leading radical organization. Its periodicals claimed that Chou En-lai had certified the group's revolutionary credentials.[38] Within Sinkiang, it was supported by the 7335 unit of the PLA, thought to have been sent into the SUAR by radical leaders in Peking. The Red First Headquarters, considered the conservative organization, was supported by the so-called August First Field Army.[39] Wang En-mao was the favorite target of radical leftist groups, who alleged that he backed their conservative rivals.[40]

The first major clash between the two groups occurred in Shih-ho-tzu on January 26, 1967, with the leftists admitting they had suffered a bloody defeat. Their publications held Wang responsible,[41] and demanded revenge for what became known as the January 26 incident. Wang was in Peking at the time, presumably arguing for the authority to suppress violence. The Shih-ho-tzu clash, with one hundred persons reported dead and another five hundred injured, may have proved his point: on January 28, the central committee's military commission, mentioning Sinkiang by name, authorized border area military regions to postpone the Cultural Revolution "for the time being." [42] Two weeks later, regulations issued jointly by the central committee, its military commission, and the State Council (but, significantly, not the Cultural

Revolution Group) ordered the Production and Construction Corps in Sinkiang to carry out its Cultural Revolution under military control. To facilitate war preparations, members of the Production and Construction Corps were barred from participating in the "four bigs" (big airing, big blossoming, big debate, and big character posters). Severe restrictions were placed on power seizures, and anyone possessing stolen arms or ammunition was to be arrested as a counterrevolutionary.[43] Peking Red Guard posters later reported that on January 25 the central committee had authorized the indefinite suspension of the Cultural Revolution in Sinkiang as a whole.[44]

His mission apparently a success, Wang En-mao returned to Urumchi. However, his victory had been achieved during the countrywide "adverse current" of conservatism. In April, radicals were encouraged by the ascendance of Chiang Ch'ing's faction in Peking, and fighting began anew. Disruptions continued to center around Shih-ho-tzu, a "new town" composed chiefly of members of the Sinkiang Production and Construction Corps, and the Tu-shan-tzu oil fields; rebels referred to Shih-ho-tzu in particular as an "old den of the [conservative] August First Field Army" and described in gory detail the fate of rebels there.[45] Calls for persons who had previously been sent down (*hsia fang*) to Sinkiang to return there, where they were needed, indicate that runaways were also posing serious problems.[46]

Radical publications reported that the seriousness of events in Sinkiang had prompted Chou En-lai to take a personal interest in the situation,[47] thus lending credibility to a Moscow Radio broadcast stating that the Urumchi-Lanchow railway, Sinkiang's chief link with the rest of China, had been cut.[48] After a series of clashes between PLA unit 7335 and August First–backed groups in November 1967,[49] Wang was again reported back in Peking. Leftist publications claimed he had been "dragged back" and that they had been assured by members of the Central Cultural Revolution Group that his political demise was imminent.[50] Still, Wang's social standing remained high enough to allow him to attend a reception held by Mao on December 31.[51] While in Peking, Wang reportedly argued that the disruptions of the Cultural Revolution would encourage rebellion and lead to war with the Soviet Union; there were repeated rumors that he had threatened to seize China's nuclear installation at Lop Nor if his demands were not complied with.[52]

Wang disappeared from sight for several months after his visit to Peking, though attacks on him continued. In addition to suppressing the Cultural Revolution, Wang was also charged with revisionism in nationalities policy. Since he is a Han, Wang could hardly be accused of the same degree of local nationalism as Ulanfu, but he was said to

have pandered to counterrevolutionary nationalist interests and therefore to be guilty by association.[53] Two other officials, Imonov, Uighur
vice-chairman of the regional people's congress, and Burhan, a Tatar
and ex-governor of Sinkiang, were denounced as "local nationalists,
national splittists and traitors who link up with foreign countries from
within." [54]

Despite Wang's alleged special treatment of minorities, there are no
reports of his being defended by his minority constituents. In fact,
information on Sinkiang minorities' reactions to the Cultural Revolution
in general is sparse. A native of Ining, interviewed in 1972, said that he
had heard of, though was not himself a witness to, savage fighting between separatist Uighur nationalists and the PLA in 1967. He believed
the proximate cause of the revolt was the suppression of Islam during
earlier phases of the Cultural Revolution. The uprising ended in 1968
when its leader, Meejit (phonetic), was captured by the PLA and
shot.[55] This may have been the same revolt referred to by Reuters in
January 1969; an unconfirmed report told of fighting between 4,000
Uighurs and the PLA at Kuldja (an alternate name for Ining). Uighur
language broadcasts from the Soviet Union offered refuge to the rebels.[56]
In April 1968, a group affiliated with the Red Second Headquarters ran-
sacked the home of Uighur governor Saifudin, but Chou En-lai issued
an immediate directive forbidding such conduct in the future. Everything taken was to be returned "immediately and completely"; failure
to comply would be interpreted as "going to the opposite side" (that is,
the group would be reclassified as anti-Maoist).[57] During this time, too,
there was an increase in efforts to send rusticated youth who had returned to such places as Shanghai back to Sinkiang; refusal to go back
would also be taken as evidence of an anti-Maoist stance.[58]

Wang En-mao appeared at May Day celebrations in Peking, thus
casting doubt on rumors he had fallen from power. He also attended
other official functions in the capital during June and August. What
was transpiring in Sinkiang during this time, however, remains unclear,
since Urumchi Radio relied wholly on relays of Peking home service
from February 3 through August 30.

On September 5 a revolutionary committee was finally formed. Sinkiang and Tibet were the last provincial level areas to form revolutionary committees and, unlike the other provinces, did so without benefit
of prior preparatory committees. The chairman was not Wang En-mao
but Lung Shu-chin, a military man and newcomer to Sinkiang. He was
said to be a protégé of Lin Piao,[59] and he was indeed a member of
Lin's Fourth Field Army.[60] Lung assumed Wang En-mao's position as
commander of the Sinkiang Military District as well. Wang, who had
been associated with the First Field Army,[61] was demoted to the level

of a vice-chairman of the revolutionary committee. Saifudin was also named a vice-chairman, as was one Zia (Tzu-ya) of unknown background but, judging from his name, a Uighur.[62]

The SUAR revolutionary committee's second plenum in December of 1968 criticized an unnamed "promoter of the adverse February current," almost certainly Wang En-mao, as "actively promoting Liu Shao-ch'i's counterrevolutionary line in the course of the socialist revolution and socialist construction and in the fields of culture, nationality relations, religion, and the united front." [63] Wang's position thus declined further.

While nationalities affairs formed an important focus of criticism during the course of the Cultural Revolution in Sinkiang, radicals seemed more concerned with the attitudes of the "top persons in power" toward the conduct of nationalities policy rather than being concerned with the nationalities themselves. Reports of factional fighting were almost exclusively concerned with groups of Han, and there apparently was no repetition of the 1962 mass exodus of minorities toward the Soviet Union.

Tibet

A rally was held in Lhasa in mid-August to celebrate the Eleventh Plenum's decision, and on August 25 Red Guards invaded the Jokhang, Lhasa's central temple, and destroyed its images.[64] Chou En-lai ordered an end to such acts, but the Guards apparently were permitted to destroy other vestiges of the feudal society. In September NCNA reported that the prayer flags that formerly flew from Lhasa roofs had all been replaced by the five-star national flag, and that walls and household shrines now contained images of Chairman Mao in lieu of "superstitious" pictures.[65]

The ethnic and geographical origins of these Red Guards are unclear. A contingent of "revolutionary teachers and students" of the Tibetan Nationalities Institute at Hsienyang, Shensi, entered Tibet in early September, and a group from Peking's Third Red Guard Headquarters was also in Lhasa at that time. However, several other groups were reportedly waiting in nearby provinces, suggesting that some contingents considered permission necessary before entering Tibet.[66] This may indicate that the Guard groups from Peking and Hsienyang were composed of Tibetan students. In October Chou En-lai explicitly forbade Han students to exchange revolutionary experiences in Tibet but the Guards, charging that the TAR party committee was attempting to circumvent the Cultural Revolution, seem to have entered nonetheless.[67] Thereafter, the ethnic composition of the groups was predominantly Han. Reports concerning the Cultural Revolution in Tibet include Tibetan names only rarely; one source estimated their direct participation at approximately 1 percent of the total population.[68]

In November, with an estimated 1,300 nonlocal Red Guards in Tibet, the State Council repeated its order banning the exchange of revolutionary experiences in the TAR. However, the Guards appealed to the Cultural Revolution Small Group in Peking and apparently received permission to stay. This angered many persons in the Tibet committee, which had already given the Red Guards a farewell celebration.[69]

The differences between the party leadership in Tibet and the more radical members of the Cultural Revolution Small Group in Peking were reflected in differences among Red Guard organizations. Factionalism centered around clashes between the Lhasa Revolutionary Rebel General Headquarters (Rebel Headquarters) and the Great Alliance Rebel General Command Post of the TAR Proletarian Rebel Revolutionaries (Great Alliance), with the former the more radical of the two. The Great Alliance was accused by Rebel Headquarters of having been founded by First Party Secretary Chang Kuo-hua to protect his position, and it is a matter of record that while Chang Kuo-hua was being attacked by the Rebel Headquarters as "rotten" and the "emperor of Tibet," the Great Alliance said only that despite his "shortcomings," he need not be overthrown.[70]

Two main issues seemed to separate one Han faction from another. First was the degree to which they thought radical social and economic policies ought to be applied to Tibet, and how this reflected on the ideological orthodoxy of the present leadership. Second, and perhaps more important, was the matter of the status positions of the various Han groups in Tibet. In contrast to the situation in many other areas when people were sent down to the countryside, most Han sent to Tibet held skilled or semiskilled positions. Some of these jobs, however, including truck driving, factory work, and the bottom echelons of the PLA, involved fairly low prestige and difficut working conditions. Many Han who occupied these jobs were exceedingly dissatisfied with their situation. They wanted either to be returned to their homes or to advance in the status hierarchy, and they bitterly resented what they referred to as "the entrenched powerholders." [71]

In January, with the arrival of Red Guards from Peking to help members of the more radical Rebel Headquarters, attacks on Chang Kuo-hua mounted. At the end of the month, the Rebel Headquarters triumphantly announced that it had seized power,[72] but at this crucial juncture their chief target, Chang Kuo-hua, was transferred to Szechwan, and it was not he but his erstwhile subordinates who suppressed the Rebel Headquarters during the February adverse current. The military, apparently receiving orders from Jen Jung, who had been deputy commissar of the Tibet Military Region under Chang, stepped hard on "anarchist thinking," and the *Lhasa Daily* spoke of "disorders" caused by enemies of the Cultural Revolution who were deceiving the masses with false rumors.[73] This pattern of suppressing rebel activities on grounds that they were playing into the hands of imperialists and class enemies has a familiar ring, having been used by Wang En-mao in Sinkiang and by T'eng Hai-ch'ing in Inner Mongolia. Of course, the Rebel Headquarters' promises to institute radical changes in Tibetan society did indeed alarm the Tibetan masses, as the "entrenched power-holders" had been quick to point out.

In April the rebels were again encouraged from Peking, and new fighting broke out. A report from New Delhi that Tibetan collaborators had been publicly denounced in Lhasa[74] was indirectly confirmed by reports in several Red Guard newspapers that Chou En-lai had ordered a cessation of attacks on Ngapo Ngawang Jigme, because Ngapo had "gained much merit" by denouncing the Panchen Lama.[75] The flow of refugees into India, Nepal, Sikkim, and Bhutan increased at this time, as did reports of sabotage by Tibetan guerrilla groups.[76] With Han occupied fighting other Han, supply depots and ammunition caches could be raided by Tibetan guerrillas with less fear of reprisal. If the raid were carried out cleverly enough, one faction might even blame another.

In September, the line in Peking having moderated again, the central committee ordered the Rebel Headquarters and the Great Alliance to resolve their differences, turn in their weapons, and return to work.[77] Members of the Rebel Headquarters must have felt they were unlikely to achieve a fair compromise under Jen Jung, who had moved against them only a few months before, and factionalism continued. The following June an anguished Jen Jung appealed for an end to civil war and the restoration of communications and transportation. Relaying instructions from Chou En-lai, Ch'en Po-ta, and K'ang Sheng, Jen warned that factional infighting reduced attention to national defense and cautioned against border incidents. Indian, Soviet, and American reconnaissance patrols had been detected along the borders, and "traitors and bandits" within Tibet were "itching for action" there.[78]

In September 1968 a revolutionary committee was finally inaugurated, apparently by fiat from Peking and, as in Sinkiang, whose revolutionary committee was installed the same day, without even the formality of a preparatory committee. Tseng Yung-ya was named chairman of the committee. Like Lung Shu-chin in Sinkiang, Tseng was a member of the Fourth Field Army[79] and was said to be closely associated with Lin Piao.[80] He seems to have entered Tibet at the time of the Sino-Indian border war in 1962, and he held the post of deputy commander of the

Tibet Military Region prior to the Cultural Revolution. At some point after Chang Kuo-hua's transfer to Szechwan, Tseng was apparently named acting commander of the TMR.[81]

Tseng was clearly more acceptable to radicals than Jen Jung.[82] However, Jen was named first vice-chairman of the revolutionary committee. The two appointments may well have been designed by Peking as a compromise meant to appease both major factions in the TAR, neither of whose leaders seem to have been included in any position on the committee. The eleven other vice-chairmen included four Tibetans: the perennial Ngapo Ngwang Jigme plus Thubten Nima, Tsering Lamu, and Pa Sang.[83]

Neither the apparent leadership compromise designed in Peking nor repeated orders to end factionalism resulted in a cessation of hostilities. In February 1969 Lhasa Radio formally repudiated Wang Ch'i-mei and Chou Jen-shan, both members of the Secretariat of the TAR party committee until 1966 and favorite targets of the left.[84] This did not mean that the central government had decided in favor of the leftist faction, however, since representatives of both groups were reportedly in Peking for "study classes" to improve their attitudes toward unity. By the time the Ninth Party Congress was held in mid-April, Tibet still had not formed many of its subregional revolutionary committees, presumably a reflection of this factionalism.[85]

This strife within the Han Chinese elite did not preclude social reform within the TAR. Communes began to be introduced in the Lhasa area in June 1966 as an experiment, with Liu Shao-ch'i and other safely discredited exleaders later held responsible for the long postponement of collectivization.[86] During the latter days of 1968 it was reported that busts of Chairman Mao had replaced images of the Buddha in Lhasa household shrines.[87] Still, it should be noted that these two reports, and virtually all others on the Cultural Revolution in Tibet, concern Lhasa or the strategic communications lines therewith. Strict discipline was apparently maintained on the borders, and, despite Jen Jung's warning, there are no confirmed reports of factional fighting in the frontier areas. Tibetans might better be said to have taken advantage of the Cultural Revolution for their own ends than to have participated therein.

Kwangsi

Red Guards were active in the Kwangsi Chuang Autonomous Region from August of 1966 onward, and on January 23, 1967, a group known as the Kwangsi Revolutionary Rebellion Army announced it had seized power from the autonomous region's party committee and occupied the Nationalities Printing House in Nanning. A celebration rally the following day was attended by 40,000 people.[88] However, this seizure did not receive legitimization from Peking, and the local PLA command ousted the rebels and urged Kwangsi residents to the "frontline" of spring farming where they were to make revolution "thriftily" and without lowering grain production.

A multiplicity of Red Guard factions crystallized into two major groupings, the radical "April 22" organization, which had taken part in the January seizure, and the more moderate Kwangsi Proletarian Revolutionaries Combined General Headquarters, generally referred to as simply "Combined Headquarters." The April 22 group held First Party Secretary Wei Kuo-ch'ing responsible for suppressing rebellion in Kwangsi and denounced him vigorously and often, with no discernible signs of success. In November the central committee, its Military Commission and Cultural Revolution Group, and the State Council jointly issued a "Decision Concerning the Question of Kwangsi," which confirmed Wei in power. Though admitting that Wei had committed some errors, it considered that his attitude was "generally good." The text of the decision made explicit Mao's approval of Wei and named a preparatory committee for the KCAR Revolutionary Committee, with Wei as chairman. It also reminded the people of Kwangsi that their province was on the front line of aiding Vietnam and urged both Red Guard factions to unite with the PLA in resisting sabotage by the United States and Taiwan.[89]

During the spring and summer of 1968 there was a radical resurgence in Peking and, despite the unequivocal nature of his backing a few months before, Wei was repeatedly attacked by April 22 groups. Their tabloids noted with satisfaction that a preliminary list of revolutionary committee members submitted by Wei to Peking had been turned down because it totally excluded members of their faction. He was also accused of responsibility for several massacres, with the rebels repeatedly appealing to authorities in Canton and Peking for help.[90] Foci of the fighting were Wuchow, Kweilin, and Nanning, Kwangsi's principal cities, with railway workers and local military units most often accused of opposing the young rebels. Hundreds of corpses were thrown into the West River, eventually to drift into Hong Kong. The death toll for the spring offensive alone was estimated at over 100,000.[91] Alleging that napalm, incendiary bombs, and torture were being employed against them, many of the April 22 adherents fled to Canton.[92]

Meanwhile, Wei presided at a mammoth spring rally in Nanning at which he and other preparatory committee members praised the excellent situation in Kwangsi, based on its revolutionary great alliance.[93] However, according to an April 22 tabloid, just six weeks after this rally Mao, K'ang Sheng, Ch'en Po-ta, and other leaders of the Cultural Revolution Group were criticizing Wei and asking him to examine whether he had made any mistakes in supporting the left—albeit in the context of ensuring smooth railway transportation and the transmission of supplies to Vietnam.[94] A few days later, the party central committee, Military Affairs Commission, and Cultural Revolution Group jointly dispatched a telegram marked "specially urgent" to Kwangsi revolutionary factions, warning against "looting our country's support Vietnam supplies and arms and equipment of the PLA." It was frankly admitted that trains had been attacked and tracks destroyed, and that supplies to Vietnam, foreign trade, and "part of the living of people in Kwangsi, Kweichow and Yunnan" had been "badly affected." [95] The contents of this directive were repeated several times during the summer,[96] showing that it was not being followed. Meanwhile, April 22 groups continued to claim that they were being brutally suppressed.[97]

Neither criticism by central government leaders nor his suppression of local radicals seem to have shaken Wei Kuo-ch'ing's position. In late June, only a few weeks after the alleged criticism of Wei took place, and during a period of radical preeminence, Mao explicitly sought Wei out at a banquet and arranged to have their picture taken together.[98]

In August, Mao's gift of mangoes to a worker-peasant propaganda team signaled a rise in the power of moderates. News of factionalism in Kwangsi abruptly ceased. The angry recriminations of April 22 were replaced by bland claims of harmonious revolutionary alliance from provincial authorities. On August 25, Nanning Radio carried a dispatch entitled "Excellent Revolutionary Situation in Kwangsi," [99] and, on August 27, just as worker-peasant propaganda teams were entering Peking universities to reeducate the students,[100] the KCAR Revolutionary Committee was formally established, with Wei as its chairman. At least one other Chuang was among the leading members of the revolutionary committee. However, the "revolutionary leading cadres" whose absence led to the rejection of Wei's original membership list were not among the fifteen names listed in the NCNA report hailing the formation of the new committee.[101]

One should note that although Wei is a Chuang, the charges against him nowhere concern his nationality or accuse him of pandering to ethnic interests. In fact, apart from the abortive seizure of the Nationalities Publishing House in January of 1967, the existence of minorities in Kwangsi at all is only discernible via a standard formula in which people of all nationalities praise Mao Tse-tung and condemn Liu Shao-ch'i. Fortunately for Wei, most Chuang were all but assimilated long before 1949, and he was not obliged to take a strong stand for or against their customs and language. For all the Maoists' vaunted concern with rural areas, there is virtually no mention of Cultural Revolution events in mountainous western Kwangsi where the less-assimilated Chuang and T'ung live. It is conceivable that, as speculated by Tillman Durdin, Wei's truly remarkable penchant for survival under repeated leftist attacks may be due to Peking's desire to avoid offending the Chuang.[102] But, if so, it was probably a subsidiary factor, less important than Wei's ability to restore order to an important communications network and to keep supplies flowing to Vietnam. There has also been speculation that Wei's durability is due to Mao's personal fondness and respect for him.

Ninghsia

Though Soviet and Indian sources reported the destruction of mosques and mistreatment of Hui, more reliable information on the Cultural Revolution in Ninghsia is sparse. Having no foreign border,[103] it produced few refugees, and its newspapers, Red Guard and otherwise, did not reach the outside world. Ninghsia's radio station, difficult to monitor under the best of circumstances, began thirteen months of relaying Radio Peking in January 1967. When, in February 1968, Radio Yin-ch'uan again began to broadcast locally originated material, a preparatory committee had just been set up, and the "numerous fierce struggles of the proletarian revolutionaries and broad revolutionary masses during the past year or so" were hailed.[104]

It was later disclosed that during the spring of 1967 a group called the Mao Tse-tung Thought Red Guard Revolutionary Fighters had launched an attack against First Party Secretary Yang Ching-jen and the province's leading deputy secretary, Ma Yü-huai, both of Hui nationality. In May, agents of the "evil" Yang-Ma group allegedly closed down an exhibition in praise of the Cultural Revolution being sponsored by revolutionaries. The closing of the exhibition led Red Guards to begin a two-month struggle against Yang and Ma, which "enabled many of the deceived masses to awake to the vivid facts and exposed Yang and Ma as counterrevolutionaries." [105]

In April of 1968 Ninghsia's revolutionary committee was formally inaugurated, with K'ang Chien-min, a former deputy political commissar of the Lanchow Military Region as its chairman. Two of the committee's four vice-chairmen were also military men, with one Hui who had been a vice-chairman of the regional people's council from 1958 to 1960, and one person of unknown background. Yang and Ma, both of whom had been vice-chairmen of the Nationalities Affairs Commission as well as leading figures in the province, were named as China's Khrushchev in Ninghsia and his chief agent, respectively.[106] No criticisms of

Yang and Ma's policy toward Hui were made, though available information from Ninghsia is so sparse that one cannot simply conclude that such allegations did not exist.

Yunnan

In Yunnan, which has a large minorities population, a Radio Kunming broadcast announcing the suicide of First Party Secretary Yen Hung-yen charged him with, among other things, undue concern for living standards in minority areas. Yen was said to have investigated conditions in an unnamed autonomous hsien and reported that the inhabitants "want to wash their feet and hands; they want to be clean. They need shoes, houses and furniture." The broadcast called this "revisionist poison" and "an attempt to restore capitalism in the border areas," [107] apparently because Yen's solution to the need for creature comforts involved disbandment of minorities' collectives. An NCNA release of May 5, 1968, mentions the visit of "a certain person from higher levels," probably Yen, to the Tulung Valley of southwest Yunnan after "the bad years of 1959–1961" and his capitalist conclusion that private ownership there would have to last a long time. This area suddenly became the focus of much attention. *Jen-min jih-pao* devoted a full page to the progress of the Cultural Revolution in Tulung, where "investigations" had shown that seventeen years after liberation "some chieftains and slaveowners were still riding roughshod over the Tulung peasants." [108]

Szechwan

Southwest China Party Bureau First Secretary Li Ching-ch'uan was accused of extensive distortions of Mao's nationalities policy in Szechwan; charges against him were similar in essence to those made against Yen Hung-yen in Yunnan. Interestingly, the most comprehensive critique of Li came from T'ien Pao (*Sang-chi-yüeh-hsi*), the Szechwan-born Tibetan who had risen to become a full member of the Politburo. Among other crimes noted by T'ien Pao was Li's pardon of all imprisoned rebels in the A-pa Tibetan Autonomous Chou in 1956. This amnesty allegedly allowed the uprising there to continue for several more years and caused "great difficulty." T'ien Pao also accused Li of refusing to do anything the minorities upper strata would not agree with and of showing undue solicitude for the living standards of the upper strata and rebels. Li allegedly advocated placing slave- and serfowners on governing bodies, including the party central committee, and in fact over 80 percent of Szechwan's minorities upper strata were members of governing bodies of various sorts. All eleven Szechwan minority delegates to the First NPC were said to have been from the upper strata; not a single representative of working-class background attended.

In 1959, on the pretext that it might "create side effects," Li had refused to transmit a letter from Mao to minority areas. Later, when obliged to do so, he appended the commentary, "People should treat Chairman Mao's instructions from an objective point of view." He was said to have regarded establishing communes in minority areas as akin to allowing babies to play with fire. Failing to set up communes at all in some areas, he was pleased to disband in 1961 many of those in areas where they had been set up. During the following year he ruled that upper strata persons should be compensated for property taken from them, even that which had been confiscated as a result of their participation in rebellion.[109] In early 1968 the discredited Li was replaced by Chang Kuo-hua, whose record as First Party Secretary in Tibet was not dissimilar to Li's.

Subprovincial Units

During the Cultural Revolution some minorities in the Hainan Li-Miao Autonomous Chou had been deceived by class enemies' propaganda that all members of the same clan and surname were one big family.[110] Discord had arisen, including resistance to destruction of the "four olds" and to the idea of class struggle. The party committee was said to have moved vigorously against the sabotage activities of these misguided persons. After dragging out a number of "deeply hidden class enemies," they destroyed old ideas, established atheism, and "fundamentally guaranteed unity among nationalities and strengthened the dictatorship of the proletariat in minority nationality areas." [111] The inauguration of the autonomous chou's revolutionary committee in April 1968 was accompanied by denunciations of the revisionist poison spread by China's Khrushchev and his agents concerning the nationality problem.[112] When hsien committees began to be set up, it became clear that, in addition to tolerating superstitious religious practices and mitigating class struggle, local authorities had allowed "various forms of individual farming and capitalist practices." [113]

In the Yenpien Korean Autonomous Chou, First Party Secretary Chu Tê-hai, a Korean, was denounced as China's Khrushchev representative, a national splittist, local nationalist, and would-be monarch of an independent kingdom. He was also charged with deviously employing the theory of nationality special characteristics to cloak his splittist activities.[114]

The Revolution Assessed

The events of the Great Proletarian Cultural Revolution in minority areas closely followed those in Han areas, both in time and in intensity. On a national level, the United Front Work Department and the Nationalities Affairs Commission, respectively chief party and government organs responsible for minorities work, were purged of leading members. Given the shifting power relationships in Peking and uncertainty over the correct ideological course, it is doubtful that any but the most routine matters connected with minorities work could be carried out.

On a provincial level, of the first party secretaries of the five autonomous regions prior to the Cultural Revolution only one, Wei Kuo-ch'ing of Kwangsi, remained in his post at the end, and one, Chang Kuo-hua of Tibet, had been transferred in good standing. Military men were appointed heads of revolutionary committees in four of the five autonomous regions—again the exception is Kwangsi, and again the pattern follows that set by Han China. In two autonomous regions, Ninghsia and Inner Mongolia, military leaders had replaced civilians in the top administrative posts.

Beyond these general features, the new leaders represented no one clear ideological or institutional affiliation. In view of recent concern with field armies, it may be relevant to point out that two of the new leaders of autonomous regions were members of Lin Piao's Fourth Field Army, replacing first party secretaries who had been affiliated with the Second Field Army (Tibet) and the First Field Army (Sinkiang). However, Chang Kuo-hua's new position in Szechwan could hardly be considered a demotion, and the new leader of the IMAR, T'eng Hai-ch'ing, was a member of the Third Field Army. Though Wei Kuo-ch'ing's duties had been largely nonmilitary since 1954, he too had been associated with the Third Field Army.[115]

The need to maintain border defense in potentially volatile minority areas must also be considered a factor in the survivability of leaders in autonomous regions. In at least three of the five autonomous regions, Sinkiang, Inner Mongolia, and Tibet, radical groups accused powerholders of using nationality differences to reinforce their own positions through arguing that instability in nationalities areas played into the hands of the imperialists beyond China's borders. Despite its alleged links to Liu Shao-ch'i, to waving the red flag in order to oppose the red flag, and to base self-interest, this argument seems to have carried a good deal of weight in Peking. It may well have been instrumental in the political survival of Chang Kuo-hua and his successor Jen Jung. Wei Kuo-ch'ing and, at least temporarily, Wang En-mao seem also to have profited by the necessity to maintain border defense. On the other hand

Ulanfu, commanding a vitally important long border with the MPR, did not survive. And Wang En-mao's success was short-lived.

It is perhaps significant that three of the very small number of prominent minority party members to survive, Saifudin, Wei Kuo-ch'ing, and T'ien Pao, had no connections with united front work. Linkages with the united front entailed cooperation with upper strata personages and a tolerant attitude toward at least some of minorities' customs and traditions. These charges weighed heavily in attacks against Ulanfu and Wang En-mao, and they were also made against the first party secretaries of Yunnan and Szechwan, Yen Hung-yen and Li Ching-ch'uan. However, Chang Kuo-hua, whose tenure in Tibet necessitated a high degree of toleration of minorities traditions as well as cooperation with the upper strata, did survive.

The political situation in a given province at a given moment is an additional factor to be considered. Wei Kuo-ch'ing, for example, was shriven of his sins only after factionalism in Kwangsi had disrupted railway transport to the extent of causing serious shortages of supplies in the southwest and in China's shipment of war materiel to Vietnam. A desire to retain some minority group representation in highly visible positions may also have been a consideration. Saifudin, the only prominent Uighur Communist in the Sinkiang Uighur Autonomous Region, had in addition been particularly vigorous in his denunciations of both Uighur nationalism and Soviet revisionism.[116] His continuation of these activities during this nadir in Sino-Soviet relations must have seemed advisable. T'ien Pao, a man of proven talents and the only prominent CCP member to have arisen in eastern Tibet, and Ngapo Ngawang Jigme, one of the few successful collaborators the party had been able to produce in Tibet proper, where there had been no prominent native CCP members, had similar symbolic value.

In short, survivability in minorities areas during the Cultural Revolution seems to have been conditioned by a number of factors, none of which was crucial in itself. The ability to maintain border defense and communications lines where others might not be able to was important. So, it would seem, was the lack of connections with the united front. Not having been involved with the economic retreat from the Great Leap Forward was distinctly advantageous. Possessing unique characteristics, such as being the only well-known member of a minority group in that group's autonomous area, also seems to have helped. Having an affiliation with Lin Piao was probably a positive factor in certain cases. The final hurdle came in being able to bring these advantages to bear at precisely the right moment during the shifting power relationships in both Peking and one's own area. At this point, one's persuasive powers, native shrewdness, and simple good luck became important as well.

An examination of the charges made during the Cultural Revolution shows that they had at least partial validity. The radicals' contention that previous minorities policy had created nationality schism was overdrawn: nationality schism under the CPR had been simply a continuation of historic internationality tensions that were exacerbated by the party's more thorough methods of dealing with minorities. It is undeniable, however, that the united front apparatus contributed to the perpetuation of nationalities as separate entities and in this sense did, as the radicals charged, stand in the way of nationalities unity. It would have been plausible to argue that, although united front arrangements might have been necessary while the party was consolidating its control over minority areas, the need for them had passed by the time of the Great Leap Forward, and those who insisted they must remain were simply trying to protect their own vested interests. However, to contend, as the radicals did, that Liu Shao-ch'i had been consistently distorting the party's true minorities policy since 1937 and had succeeded in incorporating these "anti-Marxist-Leninist-thoughts-of-Mao" views into the constitution is clearly untenable and, to say the least, portrays Mao as a very poor leader indeed.

The charge that those in power in the UFWD had surrendered to the minorities upper strata and formed cliques with them for private ends is more plausible. While the plots that UFWD members are said to have perpetrated in collusion with minorities' upper strata are hardly likely to have been as well planned or as far-reaching as some radicals contended, it is true that in establishing the apparatus of minorities work the party in effect created an organization with a vested interest in the perpetuation of minority separateness in order to perpetuate its own power. The necessity for a certain amount of cooperation with or, as the radicals would say, "capitulation to" the minorities upper strata was built into the concept of the united front, and it is not unlikely that this cooperation became the basis for a certain amount of what could be construed as factionalism or clique-ism. Party officials and the traditional upper strata co-opted into government positions shared responsibility for administration, and this common interest would tend naturally toward the establishment of some degree of rapport in some cases.

The closely related charge that policymaking for minority areas was usurped by a group of entrenched powerholders also has a good deal of validity. There was indeed substantial continuity in the party and government personnel engaged in minorities work. An examination of the Nationalities Committee of the National People's Congress, for instance, shows that forty-three out of eighty-four members elected in 1965 had also been members in 1955, a holdover of better than 50 percent.[117] Taking into consideration the fact that many members of the original body were local patriarchs of advanced age whose absence from the 1965 committee was a result of natural death rather than purge, the continuity becomes even more striking.

While there had been substantial continuity in the government personnel engaged in minorities affairs, there had been virtually no change at all in the party elite engaged in minorities work. Li Wei-han had been head of the Party Central Committee's United Front Work Department since 1944. He had been assisted by Hsü Ping since 1949. In 1952 the Nationalities Affairs Commission had a chairman and five vice-chairmen who were party members. Thirteen years later, five of the six still held these or other high positions in minorities work, and the sixth, Liu Ko-p'ing, had been demoted only a few years before.

Of the first party secretaries of the five autonomous regions in 1966, Ulanfu had held his position in Inner Mongolia since 1947 and Wang En-mao his in Sinkiang since 1952. Wei Kuo-ch'ing had been governor of Kwangsi since the founding of an autonomous region there in 1958; three years later he took on the post of First Party Secretary as well, when the original incumbent was transferred to a similar position in Honan. Chang Kuo-hua, who became First Party Secretary in the Tibet Autonomous Region when it was founded in 1965, had been in Tibet since 1951. Yang Ch'ing-jen, who had held important positions in minorities work since the Yenan period, had become first secretary of the Ninghsia party committee in 1960, replacing Liu Ko-p'ing, the purged member of the Nationalities Affairs Commission who had been accused of being a rightist.[118]

A by-product of this extreme stability in the elite group engaged in minorities work is the fact that those minorities activists trained by the party since liberation had languished in lower-level positions. Of twenty-three vignettes on successful minorities activists published by the Chinese Communist press, none held a party office higher than the hsien level or a government post higher than the chou level. Five had been named delegates to provincial or autonomous area peoples congresses, positions of little consequence. Upward mobility in Han areas after the early 1950's had been limited as well, though this probably did not assuage the ambitions of many minorities activists.

With regard to charges against individuals, the radicals tended to perceive errors of judgment as premeditated crimes. Thus Teng Hsiao-p'ing's desire to avoid bloodshed in Tibet by allowing its dissident prime minister to leave the country unmolested was seen as complicity in the revolt that occurred seven years later. As for Ulanfu, charges that he was a secret nationalist who planned to detach Inner Mongolia from the CPR and join it with the Mongolian People's Republic under his leadership and the protection of the Soviet Union are patently absurd. A member of the CCP since his early youth and so unnationalistic that he did not speak Mongolian, Ulanfu had not taken advantage of his numerous chances to join with the Soviet Union and Mongolian People's Republic when CCP power in his area was so weak that he could have done so with impunity. His protection of the Mongolian language and culture are more likely to have been designed to attract conservative citizens of the Mongolian People's Republic away from their increasingly russified government and back toward China.[119] This was magnified into a plot to promote "national splittism."

On the other hand, however farfetched the charges made by extreme radicals, the Cultural Revolution Group itself carried its attacks on the old society and on entrenched powerholders in minority areas only so far. When nationality schism threatened national unity and defense, compromise was ordered. The Cultural Revolution Group, generally with Chou En-lai as spokesman, intervened repeatedly to see that "exchange of revolutionary experiences" did not disrupt border areas and made repeated calls for the unity of nationalities.

Moreover, there seems to have been some effort to include minority group members on revolutionary committees. When the Preparatory Committee for the Ch'inghai Revolutionary Committee was announced in mid-June 1967, it contained no ethnic minority representation.[120] A few weeks later, simultaneous dispatches from Peking and Sining began to praise the revolutionary deeds of one Ta Lo, a Tibetan said to have been a poor herdsman prior to liberation. Through the party's help, he received veterinary training and later rose to become deputy secretary of the veterinary college associated with Ch'inghai University. It was made clear that his solid revolutionary nature had not been recognized before, because he had been falsely accused by entrenched powerholders. Now, however, the truth had come out.[121] When the Ch'inghai Revolutionary Committee was formed in August, Ta Lo's name was included, as a ranking vice-chairman.[122] The fact that Ch'inghai's population is approximately one-half non-Han, when taken with the circumstances of Ta Lo's sudden rise to eminence, makes it plausible to speculate that the omission of minority names from the preparatory committee was noted belatedly in Peking, and Ta Lo's name included to ensure minority representation.

The experiences of the Tulung Valley excepted, reports on the Cultural Revolution in minority areas concerned large urban centers or important communication links, and not the rural areas where ethnically cohesive minority populations tend to be found. It is unlikely that the Cultural Revolution affected rural minority groups more profoundly than an occasional Mao study session led by a mobile PLA group or heard on the radio, and perhaps an increase in the previous level of collectivization. There is at least one piece of evidence to indicate that the main reaction to incessant praise of Mao was boredom and withdrawal: a group of Yao who had moved across the border into Thailand during the food shortages of the early 1960's told a visiting anthropologist that they had ceased to listen to Chinese radio broadcasts in 1966 and now preferred the lighter fare dispensed by Australian stations.[123]

The argument may be made that reporting from the Cultural Revolution period had an urban bias and that therefore a content analysis of the Chinese media during this period would underestimate the extent of rural and, by extension, minority problems. However, a careful day-by-day study of one province, Ch'inghai, indicates that the various aspects of the Cultural Revolution were not introduced into the rural, minority areas until well after the more extreme manifestations of whatever reform was being introduced had moderated. Whereas Red Guard movements against the "four olds" and mass class struggle were well developed in the Sining area by August 1966,[124] not until late May of 1967 did the provincial radio station call for extending the class struggle to "those comparatively remote chou and hsien" [125] where most of the province's minorities live. The move to extend the Cultural Revolution into outlying areas preceded the public announcement of the formation of a preparatory committee for the provincial revolutionary committee by a scant three weeks.[126] If this caution characterized the situation in Ch'inghai, which has no foreign border and does not occupy a particularly important position within China, either economically or strategically, it would seem reasonable to assume that a similar, if not greater, degree of caution was exercised in bringing the revolution to minority areas of provinces like Sinkiang, Inner Mongolia, Tibet, Kwangsi, and Yunnan, which are considered vital to China's defense against external attack.

Caution was also evident when some of the reforms that had been demanded by Cultural Revolution radicals began to be introduced into minority areas. In contrast to the wholesale communization of August 1958, collectivization proceeded slowly. For example, communes in Tibet were introduced first on an experimental basis in the area around Lhasa and only gradually extended outward. As of June 1970, only 34 percent of Tibetan villages had communes.[127] In August 1971, 60 percent of Tibet's hsien were said to have communes, although not all of the 60 percent had been completely communized. The average Tibetan commune contained about one thousand people, the approximate size of a production team elsewhere.[128] Moreover, agricultural taxes continued to be collected on an individual, not a collective, basis.[129] The smaller size and unusual taxation method of these communes indicate that attention to minorities' "special characteristics" continued to exist in fact if not in name. That this recognition of differences continued to exist was noticeable again when universities began to reopen in late 1970. National minorities constituted separate categories for admission, with a certain number of places often being reserved for them.[130]

While it is obvious from the above account that the desire of the more radical group in the Cultural Revolution to ignore all nationality differences was not achieved, it seems equally certain that the Cultural Revolution resulted in minorities' losing power and cohesiveness as minority groups. Events after 1968 tended to bear out this impression and portended a policy that, although slower-paced than the radicals might have wished, was also less gradualistic than the conservatives desired.

The decline of the Red Guards in the fall of 1968 was accompanied by a major effort to *hsia fang* members of disbanded youth organizations to border areas, particularly in Sinkiang and Inner Mongolia. This, of course, further diluted the percentage of minorities in these areas. Clashes with the Soviet Union along the Ussuri River and on the border of Sinkiang in 1969, along with intensified Soviet propaganda aimed at Chinese minorities, served to enhance the desirability of settling Han in the border areas, and the movement was expanded. Production and Construction Corps of Han settlers, modeled on the Corps founded in Sinkiang in 1949, were set up on the border areas of Inner Mongolia, Heilungkiang and in Tibet. Additional troops were moved into border areas and efforts made to tighten control. One such effort involved the removal of three leagues from Inner Mongolia and their incorporation into Heilungkiang, Kirin, Liaoning, and Kansu. This resulted in a loss of one-third of the IMAR's territory. In addition, the Inner Mongolia Military Region was downgraded to a military district subordinate to the Peking Military Region.[131] While the redistricting was probably undertaken to facilitate resistance to the Soviet Union in case of war, and made sense in terms of existing communications links as well, it also resulted in the division of the Alashan Mongols from the Mongols of the more eastern areas. Whereas previously the IMAR had approximated the area of Inner Mongolia under the Ch'ing, it now resembled the area promised the Mongols by Chiang Kai-shek. The CCP's promise to unite all Mongols had not proved permanent. That no major conflagration resulted from this redistricting may be taken to indicate the party's success in reducing Mongolian nationalism.

The new party constitution promulgated in April 1969 mentioned minorities only once, noting that the party must lead all China's nationalities in carrying out class struggle and the struggle for production and scientific experimentation, and in consolidating and strengthening the proletarian dictatorship.[132] A list of the party's Ninth Central Committee released soon after the promulgation of the constitution did not indicate the nationality of the members, though at least 5 of the 170 full members—a minimum of 2.9 percent—and 4 of the 109 alternates —a minimum of 3.7 percent—can be definitely identified as minority group members.[133] Whether by design or accident, the 5 full members represent the major nationalities of China's five autonomous regions: Liu Ko-p'ing, Hui; Paojihletai, Mongol; Saifudin, Uighur; T'ien Pao (Sang-chi-yüeh-hsi), Tibetan; and Wei Kuo-ch'ing, Chuang. Their presence was not necessarily due to their holding offices in those particular autonomous regions. Liu Ko-p'ing was chairman of the Shansi Revolutionary Committee, not that of the NHAR, and T'ien Pao was at that time a vice-chairman of the Szechwan, not the Tibetan, Revolutionary Committee.[134]

A draft state constitution promulgated at the end of 1970 confirmed the existence of autonomous areas by noting their inalienability, but reduced their rights. Though granting the use of minority languages, it made no mention of retaining customs and habits, as had the 1954 constitution, and the latter's clause forbidding discrimination on account of nationality was omitted.[135] While the draft constitution did not, of course, have any legal force, its provisions on the use of minority languages did in fact describe the practice at that time: that is, the use of minority languages was allowed, not encouraged as the 1954 constitution had suggested. Pre-Cultural Revolution propaganda that stressed the party's concern with translating texts and Marxist-Leninist-Maoist classics into minority languages had disappeared. By contrast, Radio Kunming mentioned a new method of teaching Yunnan minorities the Han characters necessary to read the works of Mao,[136] and *Jen-min jih-pao* urged relevant comrades to "quickly overcome all the obstacles which prevent the national minorities from reading the works of Chairman Mao in Chinese." [137] In Sinkiang, however, it was apparently sufficient to use the Uighur and Kazakh scripts based on *pinyin*.[138] Naturally, this would at least serve to differentiate its users from their fellows across the border, whose written language is based on Cyrillic.

While Soviet propaganda continued to allege that the Cultural Revolution was, among other things, a Maoist plot to exterminate the minorities, implying that members of minority groups were being given a choice between assimilation and physical annihilation,[139] indications were that the separate treatment of minorities that so annoyed Han radicals persisted. Minority names, identified as such, appeared on lists of newly formed party committees in rough proportion to the population strength of a minority in a given region. At least 9 minority group members were among the 158 persons appointed first or second secretaries, secretaries or deputy secretaries of provincial level party committees.[140] This represents a minimum minority group presence of 5.7 percent, closely approximating the actual proportion of ethnic minorities in the population as a whole. Whether they were present as spokespersons for their nationalities or as assimilated individuals remained unclear. Several old standbys, such as Tibetans Ngapo Ngawang Jigme and Living Buddha Ngawang Jaltso,[141] remained in official positions of various sorts. Clearly they could not be counted among the assimilated. But minority newcomers to these committees, such as Pa Sang in Tibet, Ta Lo in Ch'inghai, and Paojihletai in Inner Mongolia, are far more likely to have been selected because they represented the party's point of view to people of their nationality than because they represented their nationality's point of view to the party. Most seem to have distinguished themselves in mass mobilization campaigns and production drives. Though Uighurs and Tibetans were underrepresented in proportion to their share of the population, this hardly constituted a change from the pre–Cultural Revolution situation. The purge of Mongols in Inner Mongolia actually had the effect of reducing their past overrepresentation.

In addition, there soon appeared hints that the United Front Work Department and the Nationalities Affairs Commission might be revived. In May 1970 NCNA reported that the funeral of educator Ma Hsü-lun was attended by "leading members of the UFWD,"[142] and Tan Tung, a vice-chairman of the NAC who was attacked during the Cultural Revolution, was identified as a member of a group of "leading comrades and representatives of the revolutionary masses in various departments of the State Council" at May Day[143] and National Day[144] rallies in the same year. NCNA confirmed that nationalities middle schools were still in existence,[145] and at least some Hui festivals continued to be celebrated.[146]

Still, radical Cultural Revolution goals on nationalities policy were partially achieved. Minorities rights were reduced, their economies brought further into line with that of Han China, and the ethnic cohesiveness of their areas further diluted. It may be objected that these changes were general goals of minorities policy in China and therefore not specifically linked with the radicalism of the Cultural Revolution. But the essential differences between radicals and moderates were not on end goals, but on timing. Moderates would probably have agreed with most statements the radicals made on minorities policy during the Cultural Revolution, but would have objected that conditions were not yet ripe for implementing these policies. Thus it was the rapidity with which changes were to be made which set radicals apart from moderates during the Cultural Revolution. The situation that emerged, though falling far short of radicals' desires and Soviet accusations, seemed conducive to the further integration of minorities into both Han and Communist society—a case of Lenin's "two steps forward and one step backward."

9

After the Cultural Revolution, 1970–1975

Though the Cultural Revolution resulted in neither genocide nor assimilation, as its more extreme critics had alleged, minorities were a low-key presence in the CPR in the years immediately following the revolution. Their existence was barely acknowledged by the 1969 party constitution and, though there was a marked increase in references to minority nationalities in the latter half of 1969, this seemed prompted by a perceived need for the unity of all Chinese against the Soviet Union in the wake of the border incidents that year, rather than by a change in attitudes toward minority groups. In this drive for unity, minorities were treated as Han by any other name; *Jen-min jih-pao*, for example, recounted a meeting in Sinkiang in which "A Kazakh herdsman said, 'Do not let them take a blade of grass or a shrub'" of China's sacred soil.[1] The theme of friendly relations between army and minorities was also stressed, as in an NCNA release that stated "The Tibetan people love the PLA and helped [a] unit [stationed there] overcome all kinds of difficulties."[2] Where problems existed, collective Mao study was considered the key to their solution, as well as the sine qua non of increasing production in minority areas.[3] On the rare occasions in which special characteristics were mentioned at all, it was in the context of denouncing the fact that Liu Shao-ch'i had encouraged the continued existence of these characteristics.[4]

With regard to the general attitude expected of minorities, a story printed by *Jen-min jih-pao* in February 1970 is revealing. Aunty Jenchin, an elderly Mongol who had been a beggar prior to liberation, was sent to Peking for medical treatment. While en route to the hospital, she had had Chairman Mao's residence pointed out to her. On her release, she refused to take a car but instead "doggedly walked" the seven or eight *li* to Mao's home. There she sat down, gazing at the gates and, chanting in Chinese, repeatedly wished Chairman Mao a long, long life.[5] Interestingly, an NCNA English translation of this article that appeared two days later neglected to mention that Aunty Jenchin had spoken her good wishes in Chinese.[6]

As for other communications media, radio broadcasts in minorities languages were severely restricted. The Kwangsi regional service did not include programming in Chuang, and Huhehot Radio's Mongolian language service was limited to translation and rebroadcast of items from Peking Radio and the NCNA file. The result was a scarcity of items explicitly about ethnic groups and their members.

Leadership Changes

In mid-1971, closely coinciding with the purge of Lin Piao and many members of his Fourth Field Army faction, a change in nationalities policy began, which eventually encompassed encouragement of the use of minorities languages, a more positive view of minorities special characteristics, including religion, and a drive to recruit more minority group members into party and government institutions. Changes in leadership preceded the changes in policy, with three of the five autonomous regions receiving new heads. Institutionally, the changes appeared marginally to favor members of the Second Field Army and to downgrade the positions of several members of Lin Piao's Fourth Field Army.

In Inner Mongolia during the spring of 1971, Yu T'ai-chung, a Second Field Army veteran, became First Party Secretary and chairman of the revolutionary committee,[7] replacing T'eng Hai-ch'ing, whose affiliations had been with the Third Field Army.[8] At the same time in Tibet, Tseng Yung-ya, a Fourth Field Army person who was revolutionary committee chairman and commander of the Tibet Military Region, was transferred to a less prestigious position in the Shenyang Military Region. Jen Jung, who succeeded him as revolutionary committee chairman, was also named acting first secretary of the TAR's party committee when it was formed during the summer of 1971. Though Jen's affiliations, like those of his predecessor, had been with the Fourth Field Army, he had been repeatedly criticized during the Cultural Revolution for his conservatism.[9] Moreover, he succeeded only to Tseng's position of civilian leadership; the post of commander of the Tibet Military District vacated by Tseng's transfer was given to Ch'en Ming-yi,[10] a veteran Second Field Army commander.[11] This bifurcation of the powers held by Tseng, when taken with the initially temporary status as party first secretary given to Jen, may well have been aimed at restricting his actions.

Several months later in Sinkiang, Lung Shu-chin, also associated with the Fourth Field Army, relinquished his posts as revolutionary committee chairman and first party secretary to Saifudin, thus putting a civilian and a Uighur in charge of the Sinkiang Uighur Autonomous Region for the first time. Command of the Sinkiang Military Region was given to Yang Yung, also of the Second Field Army.[12]

In Ninghsia, revolutionary committee chairman K'ang Chien-min retained his post and became first party secretary as well; [13] Wei Kuo-ch'ing followed the same pattern in Kwangsi.[14] K'ang's ties had been with the First Field Army[15] and Wei, though he had been a civilian for the past several years, had been closely associated with the Third Field Army.[16] Leadership changes in the autonomous regions thus tended to confirm Mao's claim of having "mixed in some sand" [17] in an effort to reduce the power of Lin and his Fourth Field Army, which had become so disproportionate during the Cultural Revolution.

Policy Changes

Though the precise linkages between changes in leadership and changes in political decision-making cannot be clearly documented, the personnel changes made in minorities areas during the latter half of 1971 and in 1972 were accompanied by evidence of distinct changes in policy toward minority groups. In Tibet, a vigorous purge that had been taking place during the spring of 1971 to eliminate those accused of "sabotaging the unity of nationalities and using religious superstitions in a vain attempt to restore the feudal serf system" [18] was brought to an abrupt end. In mid-June, *Peking Review* headlined an article entitled "Tibetan Cadres Maturing," praising the great strides being made by the Tibetan people. The article noted that four Tibetans had attended the Ninth Party Congress in Peking, and that one of them had been elected an alternate member of the party central committee. Biographies of the new committee member and of several other outstanding Tibetan cadres were included.[19] A few months later, the same magazine ran an article explaining how agricultural experimentation was enabling the Tibetan people to grow and process the particular type of tea they favor.[20] This was as near to an acknowledgment of the right to existence of nationalities special characteristics as had appeared in the past several years.

During 1972 the trend toward moderation continued, with the party undertaking repairs toward monasteries and other historic buildings and easing restrictions on Tibetan religious practices and cultural activity. In July, Lhasa Radio began referring to the party's policy of "four basic freedoms": freedom to practice religion, to trade, to lend money at interest, and to keep servants. Shortly thereafter, a series of mass meetings was held in several areas of Tibet, with higher-level cadres telling the people to be "neither unduly excited nor to show any abnormality if the Dalai Lama chose to return to Tibet, influenced by the victories of Mao Tse-tung." [21] The abrupt change in policy was rationalized by explaining that past repressions had been the fault of anti-Mao revisionists.

Rumors began to circulate that the Chinese were negotiating with the Dalai Lama regarding the exact circumstances under which be might be persuaded to return to Tibet, and indeed the Tibetan leader publicly stated during a trip to Britain, "I have developed respect for my former enemies. In my autobiography I comment on Chairman Mao. I like him and admire him very much." [22] A short while later, in Geneva, the Dalai Lama praised the Chinese for some of their recent modifications of policy in Tibet and said he was hopeful that he might return to his country soon. [23]

The exile-published *Tibetan Review* seemed to be preparing the Tibetan refugee community for the possibility of this startling change with editorials such as this, explaining:

The exiled Tibetan public and the educated youth in particular are progressively coming to realize the actual concepts of modern politics as a changing phenomena [sic] and of the fact that support can be gained from quarters whose interest[s] mutually coincide with that of Tibet. . . . The only possible ground where two or three interests can mutually coincide is the strategic importance of the Central Asian piedmont for the countries that surround Tibet . . . the current complexity . . . introduces a new dimension to the Question of Tibet. [24]

Since the negotiations were secret, the positions of the respective sides can only be guessed at. However, judging from concessions the Chinese made in the religious sphere, it appears likely that they would have been willing to accept the Dalai Lama back in his capacity as a religious leader. It is also likely that they wished to limit his influence in the political sphere to the sanctioning of policies previously decided upon elsewhere. The Chinese combined conciliatory gestures with pressure, inducing India to agree that Tibetans should no longer be called refugees, thus rendering them ineligible for United Nations aid.[25] This was an attempt to force Tibetans to choose between Indian nationality in India, Chinese nationality in Tibet, or a stateless and almost certainly scattered existence in whatever countries would be willing to accept groups of them. The Tibetan refugee group was doubtless also aware of the fact that the American Central Intelligence Agency had lost interest in subsidizing them.[26]

For the Dalai Lama's part, he had repeatedly called for a free, internationally controlled plebiscite to decide whether the people of Tibet wanted to live under Chinese rule.[27] However, he must have realized that the Chinese side would never agree to the holding of such an election unless certain that the results would be favorable to them. Given, then, his acceptance of the inevitability of a Chinese presence in Tibet, there are no indications that the Dalai Lama would have been unalterably opposed to a reduction of his political power: his public pronouncements seemed to indicate that he is more concerned with the spiritual than the temporal aspects of his position. But he surely hoped to induce the Chinese to give the concept of regional autonomy for Tibet more actual content, including putting Tibetans in positions of real political and administrative power, protecting and preserving the Tibetan language and culture, and allowing freedom of movement into and out of Tibet.[28] It was on this basis that negotiations probably took place.

Though Tibet was the most noticeable example of the switch toward a more moderate policy toward minorities, it was not an isolated case. Other changes were evident in the content of mass media. In May 1971 Radio Peking inaugurated broadcasts in Uighur and Kazakh, and on October 1 the Kwangsi regional service resumed the Chuang language broadcasting that had been interrupted several years before. A few weeks later Hulunpeierh and Chelimu (Jerim) Leagues, which had been detached from the IMAR in 1969 and placed under Heilungkiang and Kirin, respectively, began local broadcasting in Mongolian.

On November 1, JMJP began a drive to recruit more cadres of minority ethnic groups into leadership positions. An article entitled "Help Minorities Cadres with Their Study of Marxism-Leninism and Mao Tse-tung's Thought" noted that the proverbial "small number" of such cadres had been discouraged because of their low cultural level and suggested a solution for such problems. The party committee of the Tu-an Yao Autonomous Hsien, recognizing the difficulties that reading and studying party directives could pose for aspiring minorities cadres, had organized these comrades for remedial work. The cadres involved had thus had their ideological consciousness raised, were more confident of themselves, and were now in a better position to lead and serve their areas. It was clear that the Tu-an party committee's example was meant to be followed.[29]

Kwang-ming jih-pao quickly echoed the sentiments expressed by *Jen-min jih-pao*. In an article concerning Yunnan, it pointed out that the efforts of the Nuchiang Lisu Autonomous Chou's party committee had resulted in a doubling of minorities cadres since 1965, and that many of these persons had assumed the first and second positions in leadership squads at different levels.[30]

At the same time, it became respectable to refer to minorities' special characteristics again. An NCNA release, also from November of 1971, noted that Ch'inghai factories had been organized to supply goods suited to the "special needs" of the province's ethnic groups. A sizable list of examples was given; besides felt boots, Tibetan-style knives, cooking utensils, and other staples, it included such nonessentials as ceremonial caps, sashes, and ornaments. Factory personnel were described as paying close attention to retaining the traditional nationality characteristics of their products. Leading cadres and technicians would visit the grasslands regularly to solicit the herdsmen's views of their products. Where it was not convenient for herdsmen to come to state stores, trading agencies in many places would arrange to send goods by yak or camel direct to the herdsmen's tents.[31]

Other minorities areas made similar arrangements. Kwangsi reported that department stores in its Lunglin Multinational Autonomous Hsien had set up special counters to sell brocades and printed headdresses to Chuang, calico and jade to Miao, and beads to Kelao. The embroidery needles, silk thread, and lace needed to create the elaborate and expensive traditional minorities costumes were also on sale. Arrangements had been made to have small local factories manufacture the types of farm tools minorities preferred and to produce shotguns and ammunition so that they could hunt in their accustomed manner. As in Ch'inghai, the personnel of commerce departments were expected to make on-site investigations to determine what goods the minorities desired and how their departments could improve service.[32]

In nationalities areas of Yunnan and in a Mongol banner that had been transferred from the IMAR to Kirin, trade fairs, once considered revisionist, were reported revived. The special commodities now available for minorities could be bought and sold there, with state trading agencies actively participating in the exchange process. In addition, both gatherings showed a revival of interest in minorities art forms. The Yunnan trade fair featured a program of Pai songs and dances as well as exhibitions of Chinese boxing and fencing.[33] In Kirin, fair-goers were entertained by Ulanmuchi troupes as well as Chinese films.[34]

In January of 1972 the Central Nationalities Institute reopened, with a class of 700. Forty-six of the 54 officially recognized minorities were represented, as well as Han youth who had been sent down to nationalities areas.[35] By October enrollment had risen to 1,100 and included 48 nationalities.[36] Students were being trained as cadres, teachers, translators, and literary and art workers. The faculty included representatives of more than 20 nationality groups, and teachers reportedly spoke their native languages in class.[37]

A Western tour group which visited the institute soon after its opening found that approximately 20 percent of the student body were Han and that 60 to 65 percent were from southwestern ethnic groups, mostly Chuang. They were told that a majority of the students were workers, peasants, and soldiers, and that selection had been based on voluntary application followed by culling first at the local level and subsequently by the revolutionary committee of the Nationalities Institute. Academic standards were apparently more flexibly applied than political standards: one student the tour group met had had only three years of elementary school before being admitted to the institute. Translation work occupied an important place in the curriculum, and students wore traditional costumes to class, though they changed to Chinese garb while outside of school to avoid being stared at in the streets of Peking. It may be that the practice of wearing traditional costumes to class reflects the fact that the institute has become a focal point for foreign tour groups. Thus certain aspects of its appearance may not accurately represent the party's minorities policy.

The time-consuming admissions process and widely differing academic levels of the students noted by the tour group may account for the CNI's relatively small enrollment. Teachers had formerly represented 27 different nationalities, and at several times in the 1950's and early 1960's enrollment had been reported at from 2,300 to 3,000,[38] more than twice the number in attendance in 1972.

In early 1972 also, the Tibetan Nationalities Institute reopened in Hsienyang, Shensi.[39] A large majority of the students were reportedly illiterate and had to be taught Tibetan as well as Chinese.[40] A similar situation prevailed at the Yunnan Nationalities Institute when it reopened a few months later.[41]

Clearly, the institutes could attempt to remedy the academic deficiencies of only a small number of persons, and it was soon evident that a major effort had begun to raise educational standards in minorities areas themselves. An article in *KMJP* praised the efforts being made by Yunnan's Lichiang Nahsi Autonomous Hsien to revise teaching materials for use in minority areas and to adopt flexible forms of school operation that would make it possible for minorities children to attend school.[42] Similar efforts to adapt education to minorities life styles were reported from Ch'inghai province.[43] The dispatches do not reveal what the language of instruction was, but the emphasis on having Han teachers study the language of the areas to which they were posted indicated that the minority language was used at least in the lower grades or until the pupils had mastered enough Chinese for lessons to be conducted in Mandarin. Promising minorities students were sent out of their immediate areas for further training, it being noted that graduates who had returned to their production brigades were often asked to serve as accountants, teachers, work point recorders, and barefoot doctors (paramedics).[44] There was a special effort made to train minorities as teachers to serve in their native places, with various areas noting that the numbers of minorities teachers had increased by large percentages within the preceding few years.

While efforts were undoubtedly being made to teach minorities Chinese, there was also greater toleration, and even encouragement, of minorities' own languages. *Peking Review* proudly announced that in 1972 and 1973 the Inner Mongolian Autonomous Region had published more than five million copies of books in Mongolian, equal to the total number of Mongolian language books published in the five years preceding the Cultural Revolution. When one recalls that one of the charges brought against Ulanfu was that he had overemphasized the Mongolian language, the magnitude of the policy changes made after 1971 becomes apparent. *Peking Review* went on to claim that before liberation the Mongolian written language had been on the verge of extinction, and the article credited the party with having rescued it from almost certain annihilation. A Mongolian Language Research Institute was revealed to be in existence, government organs and state enterprises were required to use both Mongolian and Han as working languages, and all radio broadcasts were said to be bilingual. The masses were encouraged to write books in Mongolian and, thanks to state subsidies, the prices of Mongolian language books were lower than those of the same books printed in Chinese.[45]

In Tibet, Doje Tsaidan, head of the region's Bureau of Culture and Education, was quoted as saying that new socialist Tibet offered "bright prospects for the development of the Tibetan language." A modern printing house was set up in 1972, explicitly to publish Tibetan books. In addition to providing translations of the Marxist classics, the enterprise also turned out traditional works, including almanacs and catalogues of indigenous medicinal herbs. Doje, himself a Tibetan, pointed out that, because of the party's enlightened educational policy, literacy had increased greatly, as indicated by the fact that circulation of the Tibetan edition of the *Tibet Daily* had risen from 2,000 in 1956 to

25,000 in 1974. A large number of original theatrical works had been composed in Tibetan, and Han actors in Tibet had learned to speak Tibetan and to sing Tibetan songs. The 1964 edition of the Han-Tibetan dictionary was being revised, and more Tibetan typewriters were being manufactured.[46]

In Sinkiang, where a new effort at introducing *p'in-yin* script had begun in 1971, publicity centered on the advances being made in teaching people to use it. The script reform was described at the time of its introduction as "an intensive revolution involving an acute struggle between the two classes and line," though all that could be said after two years of such struggle was that "fairly good results have been achieved." [47] New script or old, the language being encouraged was indisputably non-Han. Judging from repeated mention of study classes and workshops in the new script, efforts to popularize it continued at a high level, and some months later it was reported that circulation of the new script edition of the Kazakh language *Ining Daily* had exceeded that of the old script edition.[48] In addition, over seven million books had been published in minority languages in the SUAR during the first half of 1974.[49]

With regard to other aspects of minorities culture, 1972 saw a return to the "national in form, socialist in content" dictum of many years before. In the spring Urumchi Radio announced that literary and art workers in Ili had launched a mass movement for creativity. Through paying attention to the characteristics of the area and its peoples, they were emphasizing the development of national forms in order to make literature and art serve socialism better.[50] It even became possible to adapt revolutionary model operas, *Jen-min jih-pao* publicly inviting cultural workers to transplant (*yi-chih*) the operas and express their ideas through nationalities art forms.[51] By two years later, troupes in Sinkiang had reportedly adapted such operas as "The Red Lantern," "On the Docks," and "White-Haired Girl," using the languages and folk songs of Uighur, Kazakh, Kirghiz, and Sibo nationalities.[52] Similar efforts were reported from Yunnan.[53] This increased attention to national forms may not have always involved attaching socialist content; it was claimed that spare-time cultural workers in a Kazakh area were traveling from tent to tent collecting indigenous folk songs.[54] It is, of course, entirely possible that the songs, once collected, were changed to give them a more ideologically orthodox content.

In June 1972, the index for *Peking Review* began to list minorities as a separate category for the first time since the Cultural Revolution began.[55] Hitherto, news about minorities had been categorized under more general topics, such as a 1969 entry under the heading "Living Study and Application of Chairman Mao's Works": "Mao Tse-tung

Thought Lights Up the Hearts of the People of All China's Nationalities." [56]

Steps were also taken at this time to expand health care services in minority areas. A medical team from Peking was reported working in the Tai and Lahu areas of Yunnan during the spring of 1972, with its doctors and nurses learning the local languages in order to better serve the people.[57] Medical groups from eight different provinces and municipalities were revealed to be active in Tibet.[58] One team, stationed in the desolate Ari area for a full year, had had to cope not only with language difficulties but with numbingly cold temperatures, dizziness, and nausea brought on by the area's high altitudes and the necessity of learning how to ride yaks. In addition to performing conventional medical tasks under these difficult conditions, the doctors ran classes to train minorities people as barefoot doctors.[59]

There was also a new emphasis on training minorities for technical jobs. Chuang, Yao, Miao, and other ethnic minorities were reportedly being taught to run railway trains in the Kwangsi Chuang Autonomous Region,[60] and in Sinkiang, classes were held to instruct Uighurs and Kazakhs in the operation and maintenance of farm machinery.[61] In Tibet it was announced that the Menpa, one of the TAR's small ethnic groups, were being trained as work point recorders, health workers, movie projectionists, and electrical workers.[62]

With improved training came increased opportunities for promotion. During the summer of 1972, Mao's statement that without a large number of cadres of minority nationalities it would be impossible to solve the nationalities problem began to be quoted again.[63] There was no mention of his other major statement on the nationalities problem, that it was merely a manifestation of class struggle. The latter had, of course, held sway during the Cultural Revolution, to the complete exclusion of the former. In the Kangsu mining area of Sinkiang, it was announced that 70 percent of the mine's new cadres were members of minority ethnic groups, with about half of them in leading posts in the party and revolutionary committee.[64] In Kwangsi the Pama Yao Autonomous Hsien's party committee proudly announced that 86 percent of its leading cadres at hsien, commune, and production brigade level were minority group members. Eighty-one percent had been trained in the past few years, chiefly as a result of study classes that had been held for minorities since 1971.[65] In K'anglo hsien in Kansu, 54.3 percent of the newly promoted cadres in the hsien were Hui or Tunghsiang.[66] In Langkatzu, in the Shannan area of Tibet, Tibetan cadres were now almost nine-tenths of the cadres at hsien, commune, and township level.[67]

Since the minority population of Pama was reportedly 84 percent of the total, that of K'anglo "about half," and virtually all of the inhabitants of Langkatzu were Tibetans, it would seem that the aim of the new drive was to have the percentage of minorities cadres approximate the percentage of minorities in the population of the area as a whole. While this is tantamount to the "nationalization" policy that had been advocated nearly two decades before, the discredited term was not used. Rather, it was explained that minorities cadres, "being familiar with local conditions, were better at forming ties with the masses" [68] and that this helped "rally" the minorities for the socialist revolution and the consolidation of the dictatorship of the proletariat.[69] These factors were also used to justify the rehabilitation of minorities cadres who had been purged during the Cultural Revolution.[70] Efforts to train new minorities cadres and to rehabilitate old ones were justified on the basis of increased production figures. Anecdotes of the efforts of newly appointed minorities cadres were typically followed by claims of higher crop yields[71] or overfulfillment of state plans.[72] It is difficult to escape the inference that increasing the number of minority group members in responsible positions had led to increased production. Similar sorts of reasoning had, however, been denounced as revisionist heresy only a few years before.

The Tenth Party Congress

In fact, the Tenth Party Congress, which met during the summer of 1973, rehabilitated some of the high-ranking party people who had been criticized for their handling of minorities policy. Most prominent among them were Ulanfu, Li Ching-ch'uan, and Teng Hsiao-p'ing. Because of the nature of his position, Ulanfu had, of course, been more directly concerned with nationalities policy than either Teng or Li. However, while Teng moved back into a position of importance in decision-making almost immediately (if temporarily), this does not seem to be true of Li and Ulanfu. Though both were appointed full members of the Tenth Central Committee, their duties, if any, are unclear. Both have remained in Peking rather than returning to Szechwan or the IMAR, respectively, and they appear frequently in ceremonial capacities.[73] In this sense they resemble another perennial figure in CPR nationalities policy, Ngapo Ngawang Jigme. Not obviously in Tibet since the onset of the Cultural Revolution, Ngapo, too, appears frequently in ceremonial capacities in Peking. He was, for example, ranked fourth, after Chou En-lai, Chiang Ch'ing, and Li Hsien-nien, in a delegation welcoming the Prime Minister of Trinidad-Tobago to Peking[74] and fifth in a similar delegation greeting the Congolese president.[75] He is also featured prominently in television broadcasts of such state occasions as the National Day celebrations. Ngapo is, of course, a tangible symbol of the party's willingness to cooperate with those of differing class and ethnic backgrounds who are willing to cooperate with it. The presence of Ngapo, Ulanfu, and Li in Peking rather than in their former provinces may indicate the more conservative post-Lin leadership's desire not to anger leftists. While all three have high social status, they have been separated from their political power bases and are hence presumably divorced from the decision-making processes in those areas.

The Tenth Party Congress, like its predecessor, did not indicate the nationalities of its delegates, the official communiqué mentioning only that "a certain percentage" of national minority representatives was present.[76] However, at least 7, or a minimum of 3.6 percent, of the 195 full members and 6, or 4.8 percent, of the 124 alternate members elected to the Tenth Central Committee can be positively identified as minority group members. These figures compare favorably with the minimum percentages of 2.9 percent and 3.7 percent[77] for full and alternate members of the Ninth Central Committee. The persons thus honored with membership on the Tenth Central Committee represent an interesting mix of backgrounds and nationalities. Wei Kuo-ch'ing, Saifudin, T'ien Pao, and Ulanfu can be classified as "old revolutionaries" of Chuang, Uighur, Tibetan, and Mongolian nationalities, respectively. Ismail Aymat, a Uighur, Pa Sang, a Tibetan, and Paojihletai, a Mongol, were described as having been tempered in the struggles of the Cultural Revolution. Pa Sang, reportedly a slave in preliberation days, had been sent to school by the party. Active in the democratic reform movement, she had been chairman of a hsien women's federation and a deputy hsien head at the time of the Cultural Revolution.[78] Paojihletai, member of a commune which had been designated "the Tachai of the grasslands," had dared to repudiate old customs and the "Liu Shao-ch'i-Ulanfu line" in order to grow grain in what had been regarded as pasturelands. Her efforts in leading the commune in grain production were rewarded when she became a vice-chairman of the IMAR Revolutionary Committee and later a deputy chairman of the autonomous region's party committee.[79]

Similar themes characterize the careers of the few alternate Central Committee members for which data are available. The career of Ta Lo, a Ch'inghai Tibetan, was described in chapter VIII, and Chilin Wantan was a militia hero in Yunnan;[80] judging from his name, he is also a Tibetan. The backgrounds of these newcomers seem to epitomize the advice on nationalities given in the party constitution passed by the Tenth Central Committee: "The party must . . . lead the people of all nationalities of our country in carrying on the three great revolutionary movements of class struggle, the struggle for production, and scientific experiment." [81] Beyond this very general advice, however, the new party constitution was silent on the party's duties toward minorities.

No obvious efforts were made to justify the return of those who had been so vilified during the Cultural Revolution or to explain the changes in minorities policy that had taken place in the past two years. During the campaign to criticize Lin Piao and Confucius following the Tenth Party Congress, minorities were informed that Lin had sabotaged the party's policy on nationalities, thereby splitting the unity of the ancestral land,[82] and that he had held minorities in low esteem. One article alleged that Lin "twaddled that when the people of Mongol nationality meet each other, they know only how to ask 'How is livestock?' This is a blatant slander of the Mongol people!" [83] Speculation on minorities' receptivity to such explanations is intriguing but, unfortunately, inconclusive.

Three other aspects of minorities policy since Lin Piao's fall deserve mention: a major push for economic development in Tibet, further escalation in the propaganda war with the Soviet Union over minorities policy, and the greatly increased *hsia fang*, or rustication, movement to minorities areas.

Developments in Tibet

Despite their early promise, the negotiations between the Dalai Lama and the Chinese government seem to have broken down in 1973, causing immediate repercussions in Tibet. The official media, which had presented a rather moderate view of the Dalai Lama during the period of negotiations, now began to attack him fiercely. NCNA sponsored a mobile exhibition on life in Tibet before the democratic reforms, replete with examples of the Dalai Lama's alleged cruelty. Revolutionary art depicted the erstwhile head of government with a butcher knife in one hand and prayer beads in the other; among the exhibits was a rosary made of the cranial bones of 108 persons, said to have been used by the Dalai Lama.[84] Denunciation meetings were held in connection with the exhibition, with emancipated slaves declaring that they would never tolerate restoration.[85] The repudiation of the Dalai Lama was accompanied by a major effort to develop Tibet and integrate it more thoroughly with China proper. A large-scale scientific survey of the Ch'inghai-Tibet plateau was initiated in 1973 to accomplish the diverse needs of development. More than 30 teams composed of members from the Chinese Academy of Sciences and most of China's leading universities were assigned to study such topics as the optimal growing range for winter wheat, the causes of degeneration of domesticated animals at high altitudes, the potential for expanding irrigation facilities, and the location of mineral reserves. The survey was further expanded in 1974.[86]

The often delayed drive to communize Tibet picked up fresh momentum, with communes reportedly set up in more than 90 percent of the TAR's townships by the end of 1974.[87] No effort was spared to ensure the communes' success. Agricultural specialists and party members skilled in mass mobilization were sent in during the winter and a mass drive begun to ready everything for spring planting.[88] PLA units and the Tibet Production and Construction Corps were enlisted in transporting manure to the fields and in constructing irrigation works. Tractors, pumps, chemical fertilizer, insecticides, and special seed grain were rushed in from other parts of China, it being announced that the volume of freight entering Tibet in 1973 was just under 50 percent higher than that of 1965, and that the amount of goods shipped in for agricultural use had increased by 100 percent.[89] Local factories were also reported working at top speed to serve the needs of agricultural development. Peking Radio emphasized that this was but one more manifestation of the central government's generosity to Tibet, pointing out that from 1960 to mid-1974 state outlays for agricultural and industrial development, health care, pensions, and relief in the TAR had amounted to three times the total taxes paid by the people of the region.[90] Study tours of Tachai were organized so that Tibetans could see for themselves how poor natural conditions could be altered.[91] In November of 1974 Ch'en Yung-kuei, the hero of Tachai and now a Politburo member, made a highly unusual week-long visit to Tibet to investigate the situation and transmit "important instructions with regard to work in [the] region." [92]

Though enthusiastic claims were made for the great successes being achieved in planting not only grain but vegetables, apples, pears, and even peaches in Tibet's forbidding climate,[93] there were also indications that all was not as well as might have been expected. TAR First Party Secretary Jen Jung spoke of work falling very short of the demands of the party central committee,[94] and an editorial in the *Tibet Daily* opined that blame for the fact that some localities had not increased agriculture and livestock production should not be placed on the masses but on difficult production conditions.[95] It is, of course, just such difficult production conditions that the spirit of Tachai was said to have overcome, which perhaps explains the reason for Ch'en's visit to Tibet. In the opinion of some persons familiar with agricultural conditions in Tibet, it is possible to obtain the kind of results the party claims only in a very few well-protected valleys. The acreage involved is rather small, with the large expenditures necessary to provide the equipment mentioned above being made as a matter of political faith and a hortatory device, rather than actually to change China's food situation by any significant amount.[96]

There was also an effort made to expand the educational system current in the rest of China to Tibet. In mid-1974 a total of 389 teachers was selected from half a dozen provinces, municipalities, and departments under the State Council and sent to Tibet. The transfer, the first of its kind to be publicly announced, differed from the typical rustication movement in that most of the teachers appeared to be CCP or CYL members with many years' teaching experience, and all had been chosen after a rather involved screening process. Prior to their departure, they had received an orientation course. Most were assigned to eight middle schools in the TAR; some would be involved in setting up a teacher's college in Lhasa. All the transferred educators were expected to train Tibetans as teachers.[97] In 1973 and 1974, also, approximately a thousand Tibetans were sent to universities in China proper to study, a move said to be unprecedented in Tibetan history.[98]

While this increase in collectivization, transfer of material and personnel into Tibet, and the setting up of a teachers' college, all seem to point to a tightening of party control in the TAR, other liberal aspects of policy remained in force, including the increased publication of Tibetan language books, respect for minorities special characteristics,[99] and efforts to train local people for leadership positions.[100] Moreover, at an educational work meeting held in the closing days of 1974, First Party Secretary Jen Jung stated explicitly that schools should be run according to local conditions.[101]

Relations with the Soviet Union

The years following the demise of Lin Piao also saw a major effort to refute the charges of the Soviet Union with regard to China's nationalities policy. Since Lin had been declared a pro-Soviet schemer, it became convenient as well to associate Lin's mistaken policies with those of the Soviet Union.

Chinese propaganda on the subject of minorities has involved a two-pronged attack, First, the Chinese media have sought to destroy the Soviet Union's self-proclaimed image as a state in which all nationalities are treated equally. Thus, Chinese broadcasts have portrayed the USSR as a Russian-dominated colonialist regime oppressing such areas as the Ukraine and Central Asia,[102] and *Peking Review* regularly denounces Soviet nationalities policy as "another fig leaf for forcible Russification." [103] As proof, Lenin's statement that there must be no compulsory official language in the Soviet Union is juxtaposed with a quote from Brezhnev to the effect that every citizen should master Russian and that the Russian language should be taught even in preschool child care institutions.[104] The Soviet leadership is also accused of having moved large numbers of non-Russian peoples from their traditional homelands in order to disperse them among Russians.[105]

Second, Chinese propaganda has attempted to show that similar charges of oppression made by the Soviet Union against China have been untrue.[106] China's historical control over disputed areas is stridently asserted. At a 1974 criticism rally in Urumchi, organized by personnel of the Sinkiang Cultural Relics Museum, 15,000 participants saw archaeological finds "proving" that Chinese influence in Sinkiang had existed since antiquity.[107] A similar multinational meeting was held in Turfan, where a series of ancient tombs had been excavated "proving that Sinkiang has been an inseparable part of the motherland [for 2,000 years]." Lest those reading the report of the meeting miss the point, the correspondent added that "In plotting to sabotage the unity of nationalities and split the unity of China, reactionaries at home and abroad can only be daydreaming and embarking on a wild goose chase." [108]

Much time is also spent in trying to disprove the charge that China's ill-treatment of her nationalities has alienated their loyalties. When a Soviet helicopter was captured in Sinkiang in March of 1974, the Chinese press was at pains to point out that it was captured by members of various nationalities standing together to defend their country. The commander of a militia platoon in the hsien where the helicopter was captured, himself a minority group member, was brought to Peking to participate in anti-Soviet rallies; the Chinese media also took special note of his presence at National Day celebrations in the capital.[109] In his speeches, the commander was careful to repeat that the Soviet vehicle "was surrounded immediately by the militia and masses of various nationalities . . . the militiamen and people of various nationalities in China are not to be bullied." [110] Similar reports detail the devotion of Mongols, Tungans, and other nationalities to defend the country's borders and develop its frontiers.[111]

Effect of the Hsia fang Movement

From Mao's 1968 directive that it was very necessary for educated young people to go to the countryside to receive reeducation by poor and lower middle peasants to the beginning of 1975, an estimated 10 million young people were sent to rural areas.[112] One to 2 million more youths were expected to join them each year. There are, as usual, many difficulties involved in interpreting these statistics. A significant amount of double counting may have occurred, as discontented youth left the rural areas to return to the cities, were picked up, and were sent back to the country. Moreover, despite frequent official pronouncements that these rusticated young people are to stay in the countryside forever, it is obvious that a number of legal routes out of the countryside exist: being chosen for university entrance, being recruited by an urban factory, and joining the PLA are several paths that have been used with varying rates of success. In addition, there are many different kinds of rustication, which have affected the countryside involved very differently. For some urban youth, rustication may involve settling on a suburban commune within easy bussing distance of their parents and friends and the amenities of their former life styles. Their problems, and their impact on the areas to which they have been sent, will be far different from those young people who have been sent to remote areas involving total separation from their past way of life, and perhaps an adjustment to a greatly changed climate and diet.

No statistics exist on how many of these rusticated young people have been sent to minority areas. The CPR's general reticence on the subject of numbers is probably reinforced in this instance by considerations of border defense and the desire to avoid charges that it is attempting to assimilate its ethnic minorities by swamping them with Han colonists. Despite our lack of specific knowledge on how many youths have been sent to minority areas, the numbers are undoubtedly large. In 1974 alone, 21,000 middle school graduates settled in Yunnan's rural, predominantly minority, areas;[113] in Kweichow the figure exceeded 38,000.[114] The Sinkiang Uighur Autonomous Region reported that 200,000 educated young people had settled in its rural areas during the previous six years.[115] Many of the young Sinkiang settlers were absorbed into the Production and Construction Corps;[116] the same appears to have been true of the Production and Construction Corps established in Inner Mongolia and Tibet.[117]

While at first glance it would seem that such a large influx of Han to minority areas would almost automatically result in drastic changes in minorities life styles, such does not appear to have been the case. In fact, the government has apparently made careful plans to keep the mixing of nationalities to a minimum. Insofar as can be ascertained, the young people have not been absorbed into minority collectives but have been placed in separate units composed almost exclusively of members of their peer group. Kiangsu, for example, was said to have conducted an overall examination of its resettlement program in 1970 and, on the basis of opinions of both poor and lower middle peasants and educated youth, decided to set up small collective farms with separate accounting systems for educated young people.[118] The Kwangsi Chuang Autonomous

Region was also said to be proceeding on the principle of settlement in teams.[119]

This impression that educated young people existed apart from the minorities in whose areas they had settled is reinforced by the lack of reference to members of minority nationalities in accounts of the young people. A typical case is contained in a lengthy *Jen-min jih-pao* article entitled "A Settlement on Chingpo Mountain." The educated young man who is the focus of the story arrived in a production brigade in the Tehung Tai-Chingpo Autonomous Chou in 1969. The story of his sojourn there makes only the briefest of references to the existence of a Chingpo nationality; the young man's trials center about his relations with his parents when he declines an invitation to become a worker in Kunming and later refuses to accept his commune's nomination for a place in the university. The story ends with his younger brother deciding to join him on Chingpo Mountain, with the full support of their surviving parent.[120]

Similarly, a young man sent to Jahoda (Chao-wu-ta) League, a Mongol area transferred from the IMAR to Liaoning in 1969, writes of the conflict between bourgeois and proletarian definitions of love. A member of the "Educated Youth Learn from Lei Feng" production team, the name virtually confirming its nonindigenous membership, he did not mention minorities at all.[121]

Interview data also support the contention that rusticated youth have been kept separate from minorities. A Cantonese doctor who had practiced in the Yunnan-Burma border areas from 1959 through 1973 reported that young people were sent to state farms in the area rather than to native villages. Those like himself, whose work of necessity took them into native villages, found that the authorities had given up pushing too hard for conformity. The party had instructed him to conduct his medical work in alliance with indigenous witch doctors, and everywhere in the villages there remained rotting buffalo and pig heads hanging about—the traditional protection against disease.[122]

A certain amount of mixing of nationalities probably does take place. As a case in point, at a rally of the CYL held in Lhasa in 1974, a young woman from Peking said that she had learned to plow together with several other women who were daughters of liberated slaves.[123] But this seems to be the exception rather than the norm. While a continuation of the present large influx of Han youth to minority areas must certainly affect traditional life styles in those areas, the effect up to the present has been minimal.

Whatever the future implications of the *hsia fang* movement, and despite a tightening of some aspects of party control over Tibet, the more liberal policies set down at the time of Lin Piao's demise have in general continued, with special emphasis being placed on the need to implement the 1973 party constitution's enjoinder on tempering minorities cadres in the three revolutionary movements. Though many reports have been issued claiming success in this venture, hard data on countrywide results are lacking. Typically, a report will concern statistics on the increased party membership in a single hsien, with that hsien being chosen more because it has been unusually successful than because it can be considered representative. The nearest to a countrywide figure that has been made public thus far is contained in a mid-1973 NCNA release stating that over 143,000 members of minority nationalities had been admitted to the party in the five autonomous regions plus Yunnan.[124] This would represent an increment of more than 35 percent over the last reported figure for nationalities membership in the CCP, 400,000 as cited by *Min-tsu t'uan-chieh* in 1957.[125]

The 143,000 figure may be accepted only as a very rough approximation. In addition to being rather too rounded for statistical accuracy, it excludes important minority areas in Ch'inghai and Kweichow and those Mongol banners which were transferred from the IMAR. In addition, it is not clear that all of these are new admissions to the party; the effort to rehabilitate those who had "made mistakes" during the Cultural Revolution may have resulted in a number of readmissions. Moreover, party membership seems to have been unevenly distributed, with particular efforts being made to recruit individuals from the smaller nationalities. Fifty of China's 2,700 Tulung were said to have joined the party, as well as "dozens" of the 600-odd Ho-chih.[126] There were compelling ideological reasons for wishing to give special treatment to peoples like the Tulung, where alleged exclusion from the benefits of socialist society formed one of the chief minorities policy scandals during the Cultural Revolution.[127] But they and other smaller ethnic groups such as the Ho-chih and Menpa are also among China's more primitive groups. To enroll so many new party members among them within so short a time seems to imply that a lower level of ideology and leadership skills is expected of them than is required of other party members. This may make it difficult for them to play the role in society normally expected of party members. Hence, their presence in the ranks of the CCP is more indicative of future hopes held for them rather than of their levels of achievement at present.

There is ample evidence that this second-class status within the party is not confined to smaller and less-advanced nationalities. An article in *Kuang-ming jih-pao* intriguingly entitled "Teach Han Cadres to Learn Modestly from Cadres of Minority Nationalities," is illustrative. The story concerns a hsien in Sinkiang inhabited by members of the Kazakh, Uighur, Sibo, Han, and Hui nationalities.

Although the cultural standard of K'o-ma-erh-han, the deputy secretary of the hsien party committee, is rather low, still in studying the works of Marx and Lenin and the writings of Chairman Mao, he delves diligently into study and asks questions on what he does not understand of people . . . he is making very good progress. His spirit of study has deeply educated the Han nationality cadres among the leading members of the hsien party committee.[128]

In other words, what the Han cadres were learning was K'o-ma-erh-han's spirit of humbly seeking guidance from his cultural superiors. Whether other minorities cadres are content with such a modest role remains to be seen, but the situation is strikingly similar to that which prompted minorities to complain of "many rights in theory, few in practice" [129] nearly two decades before.

The Fourth National People's Congress

The changes that occurred in minorities policy after the fall of Lin Piao continued to be evident in the deliberations of the Fourth National People's Congress in January of 1975. The official communiqué and other congress documents included the phrase "people of all nationalities" so often as to seem ostentatiously redundant, and affirmations of the great unity of all China's nationalities were almost as numerous. Though percentages were given for the number of women, and for workers, peasants, and soldiers attending the congress, it was simply stated that "There were deputies from our 54 minority nationalities." [130] At least four of the twenty-three persons chosen as permanent chairmen of the presidium are members of ethnic minorities: Wei Kuo-ch'ing, Saifudin, Ulanfu, and Ngapo Ngawang Jigme, ranked, respectively, 7, 8, 17, and 18 in the congress's communiqué.[131] The same four were elected vice-chairmen of the NPC's Standing Committee.[132] The new constitution adopted by the NPC reaffirms the equality of all nationalities and gives minorities freedom to use their own spoken and written languages and to exercise autonomous government. The preamble recognizes the need for consolidation of the unity of all nationalities and for the development of a revolutionary united front.

Though shorter in its discussion of minorities rights than the 1954 constitution it replaces, the 1975 document as a whole is a fraction of the length of its predecessor. The reduction in articles relevant to minorities may have been motivated by a desire for brevity of expression rather than intended to reduce minorities rights. Much will depend on how the newer, shorter version is interpreted. For example, article 77 of the 1954 constitution says:

Citizens of all nationalities have the right to use their own spoken and written languages in court proceedings. The people's courts are required to provide interpreters for any party unacquainted with the spoken or written language commonly used in the locality. In an area entirely or largely inhabited by a minority or where a number of nationalities live together, hearings in the people's courts are conducted in the language commonly used in the locality and judgements, notices, and all other documents of the people's courts are promulgated in that language.[133]

The comparable article, number 4, in the 1975 constitution states simply:

All the nationalities have the freedom to use their own spoken and written languages.[134]

This change may indicate the belief of the framers of the 1975 constitution that the rights given by the earlier version, being new, had to be spelled out in some detail. However, twenty-one years later, these rights had become accepted as a matter of course, and such an enumeration was no longer necessary. On the other hand, removing the specific guidelines interpreting minorities' freedom to use their own languages might also be construed as a move toward a more assimilationist form of linguistic policy. While present practice militates toward acceptance of the former argument—that it is no longer necessary for linguistic rights to be enumerated in detail—the new constitution undoubtedly allows for changes toward a more restricted use of minorities languages.

Similarly, whereas article 68 of the 1954 constitution guarantees each nationality appropriate representation in its area's governmental organs, and present practice makes scrupulous efforts to observe this, the 1975 constitution nowhere mentions such a guarantee. Thus, it may well be argued in the future that proportional representation for minorities is unnecessary, since ethnic differences will have been reduced to the point of irrelevancy. In the meantime, however, the newly elected presidium of the Fourth National People's Congress includes 13 among its 218 members, or almost precisely 6 percent, who can definitely be identified as of minority nationality. Since many minority group members have Han-style names, this percentage may well be higher. However, the Nationalities Affairs Commission does not seem to have been revived.

While it is impossible to predict future policy, it should be noted that the present constitution far more closely resembles its 1954 predecessor than it does the draft constitution being circulated in 1968. On the other hand, should the present power struggle, in which former Minister of Public Security Hua Kuo-feng has displaced Teng Hsiao-ping, result in a shift to more assimilationist policies, the new constitution will present few barriers.

Not surprisingly, minorities were said to be exceedingly happy with the new constitution. Provincial radio broadcasts from widely scattered areas of China reported uniformly joyous responses from Chuang, Daguors, Koreans, Mongols,[135] and Kazakhs.[136] Their comments are perhaps more indicative of how the party leadership hoped the nationalities would respond to the Fourth NPC than of how the nationalities actually felt. A typical reaction was:

A Uighur fighter said with feeling: "Representatives of all the minority nationalities attended the congress. Our Uighurs' representatives discussed the major affairs of state and decided on the constitution together with the representatives of all nationalities. This fully embodies the political situation in which the laboring people of all nationalities are the masters of the country. The new constitution adopted by the congress made particular stipulations on the rights of the minority nationalities. This fully shows that the socialist motherland led by the CCP headed by Chairman Mao truly embodies the equality and unity of the people of all nationalities. No enemy can destroy this steel-like unity." [137]

The Postrevolution Period Assessed

It is necessary to avoid overstating the significance of the changes in policy toward minorities that have taken place since Lin Piao's demise. Representatives of minority groups were not totally excluded from positions of power during Lin Piao's period of ascendance, nor was the pressure toward assimilation total or unremitting. Judging from evidence presented above, there was an extremist faction that would have enforced these stringent standards, insisting, for example, on total destruction of the "four olds," including historic temples, and on removing all vestiges of compromise with minorities' unique characteristics. However, since policymaking during the zenith of Lin's power did not implement this policy, one must conclude either that such extreme views were not entirely typical of Lin's thinking, or that Lin and his group had had their actions constrained by a more moderate group.

Moreover, though many of the changes in attitudes toward minorities since Lin's demise have been startlingly abrupt, these changes do not add up to a uniformly pluralistic policy. The emphasis on learning Chinese continues, and one cannot escape the feeling that recent encouragement of nationalities languages is being done with a view toward publicizing the party line more thoroughly. For example, the only reported use thus far of the recently founded [138] Kannan Tibetan Autonomous Chou Nationalities School has been to provide translators, so that the campaign to criticize Lin Piao and Confucius can be brought to non-

Han-speaking minorities in rural areas.[139] The transplanting of revolutionary model operas would fall into the same category.

Despite the attention drawn to the recent encouragement of minorities wearing their traditional dress, the actual use of these costumes appears to be limited to holidays, other occasions when the photographer or foreign guests are present, or in situations where, as in the case of Kazakh boots and sheepskin garments, they are unequivocally better suited to the climate than standard socialist cotton garments.

This is not to argue that the changes made since mid-1971 have been negligible. However, one must doubt that there are fundamental differences in aim between leftists and moderates. Both groups appear firmly convinced of the inevitability as well as the desirability of eventual assimilation. The shifts in policy since Lin Piao's downfall may be seen to represent differences in tactics rather than strategy, with the leftist group wishing to make haste and the more moderate group arguing in essence that haste makes waste; that the shortest distance between two points may not always be a straight line.

One also should not underestimate the degree to which the present moderate policy may be a response to external influences rather than solely to internal ideological considerations. The Soviet Union's charges of genocide and assimilation have led to a major Chinese propaganda effort to refute these accusations.[140] Many of the CPR's press releases on the encouragement of minority languages and on the degree to which ethnic minorities participate in leadership groups sound remarkably similar to Soviet descriptions of the happy life led by its own minority population, which were aimed at Chinese minority areas during the Cultural Revolution; it is entirely possible that some of the Chinese decisions to change aspects of minorities policy were influenced by a desire to disprove the Soviet charges.

10

Minorities Policy: An Overview

Policy toward minority nationalities under the Chinese People's Republic has been motivated by a desire to integrate the life patterns and institutions of these groups with those of China, both Han and Communist. Treatment of what is referred to as "the nationalities problem" has hinged on Mao Tse-tung's dictum that the nationalities problem is in essence a problem of class. According to this analysis, nationality and ethnic distinctions will disappear when class differences disappear, and a homogeneous proletarian culture will come into being. Policymaking has thus been conditioned by the dominant party group's assessment of the class situation in China at any given time.

Initially, the leadership considered that a transitional, or democratic, stage of revolution would have to be completed before China could progress to socialist revolution and finally enter a period of true communism. During the transitional period, those of differing political background could join in a united front against the major enemy of this period, imperialism. Minority groups were considered part of this united front, with the distinction that since they were in general more backward than other components, it was anticipated that they would remain in the transitional period for a longer time. In this interim stage, the administrative skills of a "patriotic upper strata" drawn from the traditional minorities elite could be tolerated while a successor generation of properly proletarian background was trained.

Since nationality characteristics could not be expected to fade out of existence until class differences had ended, and since this could not be expected to happen during the period of democratic revolution, nationality characteristics could also be tolerated, at least for a time. Administratively, a system of autonomous areas was borrowed from the practice of the Soviet Union, to allow the concrete manifestation of these nationality characteristics. It was hoped that allowing the relatively free expression of ethnic characteristics would lead to a gradual diminution of nationality tensions and result in more harmonious relations among ethnic groups. As trust among ethnic groups increased, the close connection between ethnic group forms and political loyalties would weaken, creating the basis for the emergence of a more homogeneous culture. Thus, paradoxically, the first step toward eliminating nationality characteristics was to allow them to continue unrepressed.

Language, forms, and a fair proportion of the administrators of an autonomous region were to come from the nationality whose name the region bore. Ambiguity on how many minority group characteristics should be tolerated, and for how long, has always existed. This ambiguity is in large part due to Karl Marx's own ambiguity on the degree to which proletarian culture was to be homogeneous and on the time it would take to achieve the state of pure communism. In general, although the party has always insisted that integration—that is, the achievement of a common proletarian culture—would be based on a blending of all nationalities' characteristics, it is Han characteristics which are expected to be adopted by the minorities. Indeed, given the overwhelming proportion of Han to the total population and their preeminent economic and technological position therein, it would be unrealistic to expect otherwise. Thus, statements on the eventual emergence of a homogeneous culture are tantamount to predictions of assimilation. However, owing to its unflattering connotations and its association with the KMT, the term for assimilation, *t'ung-hua*, is never used; the euphemism *jung-ho* is employed in its stead. Strictly speaking, the latter term means a melting together or amalgamation. It may be loosely translated as integration. Though integration is considered to be inevitable in the course of history, the party has employed various methods to speed the process. General features of China's minorities policy since 1949 have included:

1. abolition of legal distinctions among nationality groups and prohibition of discriminatory treatment;
2. development of the country's infrastructure to encompass minority

areas. Railroads, airline services, telegraph and postal systems have been expanded to facilitate physical interchange between minority and Han areas, and to link the economies thereof;

3. orientation of propaganda and education to create a sense of patriotism and encourage the transfer of allegiance from ethnic groups to the Chinese Communist party and Chinese state;

4. development of minorities' spoken and written languages to facilitate the reception of this propaganda and education, so that the party's message is received through the medium of the ethnic group's own vernacular. Languages have been standardized on the basis of the *p'in-yin* alphabet developed under party sponsorship, with the stipulation that new terms be borrowed from Han Chinese. In view of the introduction of many political and technological terms into minority areas where such concepts simply did not exist before, these additions are likely to have been substantial;

5. development of magazines, films, and radio broadcasts with nationwide circulation, to encourage the beginnings of a uniform common culture;

6. encouragement of historiography to
   (a) emphasize the historic and friendly relations between Han Chinese and minority peoples;
   (b) downplay minorities' connections with other countries, and their periods of relative independence;

7. use of the theory of class struggle to explain such nationality antagonisms as do exist. Discriminatory treatment of minorities in the past is interpreted not as a conflict between Han and minority, but between the exploitative Han upper class colluding with the exploitative upper class of minority groups to maintain their own privileged positions vis-à-vis the working classes of both nationalities. In view of upper-class minority group members' participation in the Chinese imperial and republican systems, this explanation would have a ring of truth;

8. attempts made to convince minorities that their economic advantage lies in participation in the Han Chinese/socialist state;

9. encouragement of minorities' participation in the Chinese state through the development of a multinational party, bureaucracy, army, schools, mass organizations, factories, and so on. Special privileges are often granted to minority group members to enhance the attractiveness of participation.

These methods were, like the system of autonomous areas, borrowed from Soviet practice. However, the union republics of the USSR are technically able to secede, while the constitution of the CPR makes autonomous areas inalienable parts of China. In addition, on a central government level, China has no equivalent to the Soviet of Nationalities. The Soviet Union has also, with notable exceptions during parts of

Stalin's rule, allowed greater use of nationality languages and other cultural forms. While present Soviet policy seems to accept the continued existence of an essentially pluralist form of integration in which the Russian language and socialist economy are common token, Chinese policymakers seem committed to a much more assimilative course. In part, this reflects the existential situation of the two countries: China's minorities constitute a far smaller percentage of her population than is the case in the Soviet Union, and fewer of them are the technological equals of the dominant group. While borrowing the forms of Soviet minorities policy and, during the transitional period which ended in 1957, seeming to envisage a pluralistic form of integration that resembled the Soviet *sblizhenie*, or drawing together of peoples, minorities policy under the CCP has been closer to that of the KMT in its goal of assimilation. With fewer limitations on its power than the Chinese Nationalists, and able to profit from the latter's mistakes, the party was able to launch a more comprehensive attack on minorities problems and to make its authority felt at the grass roots level. Greater attention paid to proselytizing minorities and more careful supervision of the activities of individual cadres have also been important factors in the integrative successes achieved by the CCP.

Both KMT and CCP policy differ from pre-1911 policy, which amounted to a loose form of pluralistic integration aiming at control rather than assimilation. The Chinese imperial government's apparatus for dealing with minorities, like that of the KMT and unlike that of the CCP, generally did not extend below the hsien (county) level, if that far. In the transitional period before 1957, however, the party demanded only a vague commitment of loyalty to the party center and to the principles of socialism it embodied. This was roughly comparable to the similar commitment, demanded by imperial policy, to the emperor and to the Confucian principles which he embodied. The parallel with imperial policy is limited, however, in that the CCP's plans even during this transitional period involved a belief in the importance of converting all to its philosophy, an active program for recruitment of minority group members on all levels of society including the most basic, and the expectation of the eventual emergence of a homogeneous egalitarian community.

Integration has involved a dual process of sinification and modernization, with the two often inextricably intertwined. In general, only knowledge of the motivation behind a decision will indicate which process called it forth. For example, standardization and unification are basic ingredients of the modernization process. Han Chinese, in a variety of dialects, being the language of 94 percent of the population of the CPR, it is clearly more practical to adopt it as the lingua franca of the country rather than Thai, Uighur, or Tibetan, the respective literary achievements of those groups notwithstanding. On the other hand, the decision to adopt Han Chinese as the standard form of communication is inevitably a step toward sinification as well.

In addition, no matter on how idealistic a basis a decision is reached, there always exists the possibility that the group whose way of life is affected by it will perceive the decision as motivated by a base desire to assimilate, or that they will not perceive the benefits of modernization in the same favorable light as the decision-makers. The advisability of a decision is not always as obvious as the example given above of adoption of Han Chinese as a lingua franca. The party or its individual representatives have at times been proven incorrect, opening a credibility gap. For instance, in certain minority areas the traditional slash-and-burn technique was shown to be a more suitable form of cultivation than so-called advanced techniques introduced by Han cadres over native opposition. Here the motivation behind introducing the new technique was almost certainly that of raising the area's material prosperity. However, it was interpreted as an effort to force adoption of Han ways. In a more ambiguous case, northern Han cadres' attempts to teach wheat cultivation to rice-eating minorities was perceived as forcing an assimilative change in diet rather than, as alleged by the cadres, opening up a potentially lucrative cash crop to the minorities.

Each effort at integration was apt to be cancelled out by an equal but opposite disintegration and reaction. For example, the abrupt removal of legal discrimination created tensions with the continued existence of marked social discrimination, which could not be easily removed. Minorities cadres who were told they were equal to Han cadres, but who could not perform the same functions because they lacked skills possessed by the Han, became resentful and skeptical of party propaganda. Improvements in the transportation and communications network could exacerbate tensions heretofore muted by geographical distance. Bringing Peking near when Peking's intentions were not perceived as friendly was potentially dangerous. Propaganda and education have been shown to be useful only within certain limits, after which continued exhortations to love the ancestral land or commit to memory its leader's sacred writings may produce apathy, boredom, or even antagonism toward the intended objects of veneration.

The development of written languages may encourage ethnic separatism rather than amalgamation, and the newly literate may prefer to explore their own group's culture rather than receive the socialist message. Stalin's formula "national in form, socialist in content" has its shortcomings in that national culture will inevitably shape content: translations of magazines and dubbing of films produced by Han and originally intended for Han audiences may strike minorities as irrelevant, dull, or simply incomprehensible. These efforts might well slow rather than hasten the development of a common culture.

Encouragement of historiography may reinforce pride in a nationality's cultural achievements and induce a nostalgic recall of the days of less rigid control by the Chinese state, rather than encouraging nationalities' solidarity. The theory of class struggle may be at variance with recollections, either mythical or actual, of historical events. For example, an uprising that party propagandists interpret as a conflict between peasants and exploiters may be remembered in terms of a minority group hero who gained fame by resisting the Han. Or, the party's insistence that tension between nationalities results from pre-1949 collusion between the upper classes of minority group and Han vis-à-vis the toiling masses of both may point up the fact that the party has also encouraged cooperation with the minorities' "upper strata," thereby revealing an essential similarity to the past governments it castigates.

Attempts to encourage minorities' participation in party and government organizations and in new professions produced strains in traditional societies as new paths of social mobility were made available. These strains were often blamed on the party's intrusion. Giving special consideration to minorities in education or promotion in recognition of cultural deficiencies engendered resentment among Han who were passed over despite equal or superior qualifications.

The better economic conditions promised by the party did not always materialize. Tibetan complaints that the quality of material life has declined since 1950 have been persistent, and Saifudin's explication of the "Whole Country a Chessboard" policy in 1959 made it clear that minorities, being the weakest points on the board, were considered expendable in time of crisis. Moreover, during the Cultural Revolution minorities were told that economic incentives were the forbidden fruit of the Liuist snake, meant to entice the faithful from pure socialist austerity onto the capitalist road.

With each measure intended to hasten integration having its respective advantages and disadvantages, it was inevitable that differences of opinion should arise on which measures should be favored, to what degree, and at what time they should be employed. In the years immediately following liberation, there was broad agreement that the pace of integration would have to be slow, and that it would be expedited by the system of autonomous areas, promises of economic benefit, encouragement of the use of minority languages, and development of native cadres, while cooperating with the traditional upper strata and muting class struggle.

By 1957 an influential group of party leaders including Mao Tse-tung had decided that the preparatory stage of integration had ended (Tibet being an exception) and that a new phase, entailing closer adherence to Han-Chinese Communist patterns, could begin. They were opposed by a more conservative group taking Liu Shao-ch'i as its leader. Radicals and conservatives did not express differences on ultimate goals, but only on the speed and means by which these goals could best be implemented. In general, the Maoists tended to favor ideational appeals to integration and a faster pace to the achievement thereof, while the Liuists emphasized the material benefits of integration and the advantages of a slower pace. Though China had never adhered rigidly to Soviet minorities practices, the Maoist group was more willing to deviate from the Soviet model. Red Guard allegations to the contrary, these differences were not evident before 1957.

The reasons why the Maoist group chose to move ahead on integration at this time are unknown. They were doubtless encouraged by the growth in numbers of party trained minorities activists and buoyed by a seeming world trend in favor of socialism, symbolized by technological advances made by the Soviet Union. It is also possible that accusations against party policy made by minority-group members during the Hundred Flowers period convinced the more radical group that further cooperation with the traditional upper strata and continuation of the gradualist approach would simply strengthen a set of vested interests inimical to integration.

Policy changes initiated by the more radical group involved emphasis on class struggle, ending cooperation with the traditional upper strata, increased reliance on newly trained minorities activists, large-scale abolition of minorities customs and special privileges, and attacks on the autonomous area system[1] as well as immediate adoption of the Han Chinese Communist model of economic and social organization. These measures, embodied in the policies of the Great Leap Forward, resulted in economic hardship, increased awareness of nationality differences, and complications in foreign policy that were particularly noticeable in relations with India and the Soviet Union.

Beginning in early 1959 a great many of these measures were rescinded, largely at the behest of the conservative group. A radical resurgence in the latter half of 1959 and early 1960 showed that the problems of the previous year had not changed the radical group's view on the essential correctness of its policies. By 1961 the conservative group was again in control, and integration was again declared to be a long-term process involving respect for nationalities' special characteristics and support for the autonomous area system. Class struggle was muted, with cooperation with the traditional upper strata again considered necessary, though minorities activists continued to be trained and received incentives not granted to Han. Economic concessions were also made, and emphasis placed on the material benefits that would result from unity and cooperation.

The party's Tenth Plenum in the fall of 1962 saw Mao's return to active participation in politics, a gradual increase in radical propaganda, and renewed emphasis on class struggle. Radicals' efforts to translate propaganda into concrete changes, however, were blunted by conservatives entrenched in the bureaucracy. The radical group countered by launching the Great Proletarian Cultural Revolution to oust the conservatives, do away with vestiges of compromise with minorities' traditional societies, and reintroduce meaningful class struggle to minorities' areas, thus restoring revolutionary purity. The initial vehicle of radical attack was the Red Guards. Administrators, fearing that open suppression of the Guards' attacks on the old societies and powerholders would confirm accusations that they were conservatives, often responded by covertly forming Red Guard groups loyal to themselves. The resulting factionalism mainly concerned urban areas where administrators' headquarters were apt to be, and probably did not seriously affect the rural areas where most of the less assimilated and cohesive minority groups live. While the party's entire apparatus for dealing with minorities' affairs was destroyed and its leading members attacked, an effort to keep factional struggle from affecting the border areas for reasons of national defense mitigated the effects of the Cultural Revolution on many minority groups. In addition, leading members of the Cultural Revolution Group seemed more concerned with changing the values on which minorities policy had been based than in making immediate concrete changes in minorities areas.

Though the Cultural Revolution fell short of radical ideals, its successes included the removal of many entrenched powerholders from office and an upgrading of the level of collectivization in some minorities areas that had lagged furthest behind the Han. A new party constitution eliminated much of the special consideration given to minority groups by its predecessor. However, many symbols of compromise with the traditional minorities upper strata remained, the United Front Work Department reformed, and the treatment of minorities as special groups in these and other organizations continued. On balance, the Cultural Revolution appeared to have resulted in loss of ethnic group cohesion and a concomitant increase in the level of integration of minorities. Increased Han immigration to and military presence in minorities areas and a low-key but steady pressure on minorities to study Han Chinese seemed to portend a continuing diminution of ethnic cultures and group solidarity.

The fall of Lin Piao reversed some aspects of the minorities policy in force in the years immediately following the Cultural Revolution. Minorities' special characteristics again received approval. It became a mark of socialist brotherhood to make minorities' traditional items of food and clothing available to them, and the use of their languages was again encouraged. Education and entertainment were to be adapted to harmonize with unique aspects of minorities life styles. A major campaign began to train more minorities cadres and to promote minority group members to positions of greater responsibility. Just as the Cultural Revolution did not result in a uniformly assimilative policy, the post–Lin Piao era has not seen a return to a uniformly pluralistic policy. While more books and plays are produced in minorities languages, the efforts to teach minorities Han Chinese continue, and the increased assertion of party control over Tibet indicates that recent changes in minorities policy may be tactical rather than stategic. Still, on balance, policy since 1971 has probably increased the salience of ethnic ties and encouraged at least the outward manifestations of minority group identity.

The previous discussion of integration has concerned policymaking as a whole. However, the results of policymaking have differed widely in differing areas: receptivity to efforts at integration has been uneven. In terms of reducing ethnic group resistance to party policies on ethnic grounds and in encouraging members of these groups to participate in party and government structures, the most conspicuous successes have been among the Chuang and agricultural Mongols. Both had been well acquainted with Han Chinese and their life styles before 1949 and had had indigenous communist movements of some strength. A mindset in existence prior to party rule has eased the CCP's task. A moderate success has been scored with the Hui: the Moslem uprisings of the nineteenth and early twentieth centuries have been reduced in number and localized, but at the cost of allowing the Hui community to retain many of its special characteristics of diet, festival days, and the like. A campaign to encourage intermarriage of Hui and Han, if not exactly a success, has at least not touched off a major holy war, as would previously have been the case. Despite the Hui's fierce sense of separatism, party work among them was facilitated by the absence of language barriers, the existence of a small group of assimilated Hui from eastern urban centers who could carry the party's message to more concentrated groups of Hui in the northwest, and an early start in proselytizing from the Yenan base area.

The pastoral Mongols, whose language, customs, and social organization differ radically from those of Han China, and whose way of life had been less affected by Han immigration prior to 1949 than that of the agricultural Mongols, are another example of moderate success. Most of the nomads have been persuaded to adopt at least a partially sedentary life style based on cooperatives and, though there are still reports of Han cadres earnestly haranguing groups of bewildered monolingual herdsmen,[2] many have received instruction in Chinese.

The smaller, more isolated groups of the southwest represent less successful examples of integration. Here, in addition to having to cope with linguistic barriers, great distances, and difficult terrain, party workers were charged with the integration of peoples whose low level of technology and total ignorance of life beyond their own areas gave them no basis for comprehending the economic and political complexities of the modern nation-state. Ethnic identification was strong and cultural differences great; there had been no indigenous communist movement. Efforts at integration were aided by the fact that many small ethnic groups could be more easily penetrated than could one larger unit. In addition, the area's low level of technology not only reduced the level of physical resistance that could be offered, it also allowed the party to associate its clearly superior technology with an allegedly superior economic and social organization, which, party spokesmen would argue, ought therefore to be adopted.

The party's most conspicuous failures have been in Sinkiang and Tibet, where major rebellions occurred in 1962 and 1959, respectively, and where participation of minority group members in party and government organizations has consistently lagged behind that of other minorities. In Sinkiang, long lines of communication from what had traditionally been regarded as China proper combined with strong ethnic group identification, a small Han population, and distinct languages and religion, to intensify the difficulties of integration. The indigenous communist movement had been linked with the Soviet Union rather than with China and had had anti-Han undertones. The only important party member from Sinkiang, Saifudin, had in fact been inherited from the Communist party of the Soviet Union. After 1960 the Soviet Union began to exploit the residue of pro-Soviet and anti-Han feelings increasingly openly. The presence of several nationalities in Sinkiang eased the CCP's task somewhat, since the groups found it difficult to submerge their differences in order to coordinate resistance effectively. Those who had resisted incorporation into China primarily on grounds of anti-communism, or who had hoped to unite their divided nationalities into a separate state, must have felt their position hopeless indeed after 1949, given the combined might of the Soviet Union and China.

In Tibet the population was more ethnically homogeneous than in Sinkiang and shared a common language, culture, and religion distinct from that of China. There were fewer Han residents and, while resistance to Han as Han was probably not as strong as in Sinkiang, the area had become accustomed to self-government. Even more remote from China proper than Sinkiang, Tibet had no indigenous communist movement and had noncommunist nations on its southern border. T'ien Pao, the only important party member of Tibetan origin prior to the Cultural Revolution, was not from the area that subsequently became the Tibetan Autonomous Region.

Examination of the progress of integration since 1949 seems to indicate that its success has been heavily dependent on:

1. the degree of assimilation of an ethnic group to Han Chinese society prior to 1949;
2. lack of cohesiveness of the culture of a given ethnic group;
3. the degree of dispersion of ethnic group members among Han Chinese;
4. the length of an indigenous communist movement among the ethnic group;
5. the physical separation of an ethnic group's territory from Han China;
6. the absence of countervailing pressures from members of the same ethnic group living outside the borders of China.

Though integration in the form sought by CCP policy would seem to imply a reasonable degree of geographical mobility of members of the minority group in the territory of the majority group, the party does not seem to have made efforts toward the encouragement thereof. Reliable statistical data are not available, but it appears fairly certain that members of minority nationalities have not been encouraged to pursue careers outside their nationality's own area. If present in the party-government structure at a national level, they generally serve as spokesmen on minorities affairs. One Szechwan Yi, Wang Ch'i-mei, was chosen to serve on the party work committee in neighboring Tibet, probably on the strength of his knowledge of Tibetan; Liu Ko-p'ing, a Hui, was very briefly chairman of the revolutionary committee in Shansi; and Chi Ya-t'ai, a Mongol, was named ambassador to the Mongolian People's Republic; but they constitute exceptions to the rule. Ironically, efforts have often seemed to go the other way: toward encouraging an awareness of minority origins and a return to the home area. For example, well-known author Lao She, whose pre-1949 novels showed no consciousness of his Manchu forebears, was designated chief spokesman for an all-but-defunct minority group, and Chou Pao-chung, who had served with the Red Army in north China, was sent back to his native Pai area after liberation.

With regard to those trained after 1949, the situation of minority group members remaining in minority areas recurs whatever profession is involved. Tibetan soldiers cited for bravery have invariably performed their meritorious deeds in Tibet; minority group historians and authors write exclusively on their own nationality's history and literature. Cadres who receive training at one of the central or regional minorities institutes have been returned to their native areas as a matter of principle,[3] and one does not find Uighurs assigned to Han or Pai areas, or Mongols serving in south China. It must therefore be concluded that minority group individuals' chances for advancement have been highly circumscribed by geography. This places a limitation on the degree to which integration can be said to have taken place at this time. True integration would, of course, make it necessary for minority group members to stay in or be returned to their native areas to pursue their careers.

As previously stated, disagreements have arisen among party leaders over both the timing and the extent of social changes necessary to bring about complete integration. With regard to timing, the twists and turns of party policy over the past quarter century may be seen as an effort to find a balance between destroying minority group characteristics slowly enough to avoid arousing minorities' antagonism, yet quickly enough to prevent the accretion of vested interests that might become strong enough to halt the destruction in mid-course.

The social changes deemed necessary to bring about a common proletarian culture range from the total abolition of the special characteristics of nationalities and the adoption of Han socialist culture—that is, complete assimilation—to a simple acceptance of Communist economic and social organizations with each minority group retaining much of its own culture. Espousal of the assimilationists' view would lay its proponents open to charges of great-nation chauvinism. The assimilationists would probably point out, however, that adherence to the view favoring retention of a high degree of ethnic forms would, given the overwhelming preponderance of Han in the total population, limit the minority to its own area, cripple its members' social mobility, and make them something less than full citizens of China.

Despite the charges of counterrevolutionary ideology and revisionism that have been hurled back and forth, Marx's ambiguity on the degree of uniformity necessary to the achievement of a common proletarian culture and the speed with which it can be expected to come about gives both sides an equal claim to orthodoxy. Both radical and conservative programs have had their successes and failures. Whereas radicals have seemed unable to distinguish between cultural attachments and political loyalties, conservatives have clung to the status quo with rather more tenacity than necessary. It is clear that a formula for integration acceptable to both radicals and conservatives, and to intermediate gradations of opinion between them, has not yet been found, and further experimentation in policymaking may be expected.

Detailed statistics and personal observation both being denied us, it is difficult to assess the overall successes of party efforts to bring minorities' institutions and social patterns into greater conformity with those of Han China. It is clear that nationalities tensions do still remain, and it would seem that much of the homogeneous culture that has come about exists more because of fear of incurring official displeasure than because it has been internalized. Dances traditionally done around samples of a bounteous harvest or an attractive woman and now done around a picture of Mao, Tai river festival boats now adorned with red pennants, and Buddhist altars which contain plaster images of Mao would probably revert to their original forms if not for party supervision. However, that the party's repeated exhortations to submerge nationalistic particularities for the greater good of the glorious ancestral land have not yet succeeded in creating a homogeneous workers' paradise should not be taken to indicate a failure of the party's efforts. The CCP's own ambitions and expectations notwithstanding, it would be unrealistic to expect that habits and thought patterns developed over thousands of years could be erased in a quarter century. Moreover, the desire to achieve integration on this basis would seem unnecessary as well as unrealistic. Even, or perhaps especially, in nations considered well integrated, unity is maintained less through enforced homogeneity than through what has been called a "vague, intermittent and routine allegiance to a civil state," [4] supplemented by a judicious amount of ideological exhortation and the threat of force held in reserve.

In twenty years the CCP has succeeded in eradicating alternative formal governmental structures among the minorities and in depriving traditional determinants of status of much of their prestige. The futility of revolt has been proven on the relatively few occasions on which it has been attempted. A knowledge of the Han Chinese spoken and written language, while not universalized, seems to be recognized by most minority group members as an important factor in social advancement. Participation in the activities of the party and the governmental structure it has created have come to constitute the only meaningful channel of social mobility. Even those dissatisfied with the treatment of, and/or attitudes toward, nationalities customs and languages have little alternative but to look to party and government for redress of their grievances.

It is to be expected that time will reinforce the directing of activities toward the CCP/CPR structure as a matter of routine, and that from this habit allegiance to party and state will grow. It would appear that a wise course of action for the party would be to encourage this accretion of allegiance by avoiding the disruptive shifts of policy that have worked against routinization in the past.

Probably more by accident than design, CCP policy toward minorities since 1949 has resembled the mechanism of the Marxist dialectic. The rather loosely pluralistic situation of the early 1950's may be conceptualized as thesis, followed by the antithesis of the extreme assimilationism of the Great Leap Forward. The policies of the early 1960's, though a retrogression from the Great Leap period, in no sense represented a return to the loosely pluralistic situation of the early 1950's, and may be considered a synthesis. This synthesis came in time to represent a new thesis, to which radical assimilationists counterposed the antithesis of the Cultural Revolution. The present situation may again be considered a synthesis, with both radical and moderate views represented. It should be pointed out that the swing of the dialectical pendulum of the Cultural Revolution was not nearly as extreme as that which occurred during the Great Leap Forward, and it is interesting to speculate whether future swings of the pendulum may not be smaller yet. Whether this dialectical process will reach an end point acceptable to both radicals and moderates—or indeed to either of the groups—remains to be seen.

It would be unwise to assume that either time or an improving standard of living will solve the nationalities problem. The majority of conspirators in a plot recently uncovered in Tibet had joined their organization in 1964—well after the failure of the 1959 revolt should have shown the futility of such actions, and during a period of rather moderate party policy in Tibet. Moreover, most of the conspirators had been so young when the PLA marched on Tibet that they could not have remembered what life in an independent Tibet had been like.[5] The experience of the Soviet Union has shown that raising living standards may actually encourage the growth of nationalist tendencies, presumably because more affluent groups have more time to devote to an essentially cultural-psychological problem such as nationalism.

It may well be asked whether the large rustication movement now taking place in China may fill minorities areas with young Han settlers to an extent that will render the minorities' cultural and psychological feelings irrelevant. It was indicated in chapter 9 that, owing to the separate facilities provided for most rusticated youth, their impact in changing minorities customs and habits appears to have been minimal thus far. Of course, this separate existence can continue only so long as space and resources permit. The minorities, being exempt from official pressures for birth control, have rapidly growing populations.[6] Given a continuation of the large numbers of Han young people entering the countryside each year, it is highly probable that the needs of their state farms will come into conflict with those of the indigenous population.

The problem is not likely to be confined to that of competition for scarce material resources. The present rather low level of education of most minorities allows a certain number of Han settlers to occupy places as teachers, doctors, skilled workers, and administrators without serious challenge from minorities. However, the current drive to increase educational and employment opportunities open to minorities will almost certainly bring Han settlers into competition with members of the indigenous population in the future, as skilled, ambitious minority individuals seek to capitalize on these opportunities. Moreover, the inducements the party leadership presently holds out to young people in order to make their existence in the countryside more palatable—party and CYL membership and leadership positions—will again bring minority group members into conflict with Han settlers for a limited number of places in these organizations.

Given the extension of current trends, educated young people and indigenous minority group members will be competing for finite amounts of political influence and material resources. It is not inevitable that serious disruptions will result from this situation. A certain amount of inflation in the number of party members would allow both minorities and educated youth to be rewarded with prestigious positions while still maintaining the party's elitist image. And a successful economic policy, including rising living standards, may blunt other resentments. But reconciling the competing claims of rusticated Han and indigenous minorities will constitute a delicate balancing act requiring the party's utmost skill and tact.

In the near future, however, many minority groups are still and will continue to remain far behind the Han in economic level. Sociocultural differences may be expected to continue to impede the development of empathy between members of one group and another. Differences in education and living standards will remain for a long time, hindering minorities from obtaining positions when in competition with Han. Even after a minority group individual decides to opt for the wider opportunities offered by participation in the Han, socialist Chinese system, difficulties may arise. Having sacrificed one's ethnic identity to the degree necessary for this participation, one may find that the system that was presented as universalistic and based on impersonal criteria of merit is in fact discriminatory in practice. In such cases, individuals may well decide that the sacrifice of ethnic identities has been made in vain, and ethnic ties may reintensify.[7] At such a juncture, the social mobilization techniques necessary to bring minorities into the Han Chinese system may be turned against the system. Whereas heretofore minorities had been scattered, poorly organized, and perhaps only dimly aware of other ethnic groups, the party's presence has often resulted in their being more tightly organized into cooperative production groups, factories, and the like. Such groups might well serve as the focal points for channeling and intensifying resentments that might have otherwise remained diffuse minor grievances. Dissatisfaction with one's position in the extant social system is, of course, a problem of a different magnitude from dissatisfaction with the entire system, but it will nonetheless be a difficult problem to deal with and, if not properly handled, a potentially explosive one.

It may be argued that the present policy, which is in essence similar to Stalin's phrase "national in form, socialist in content," will solve this problem of ethnic ties versus participation in the larger society. However, there is a serious question whether the idea "national in form, socialist in content" does not contain an inherent contradiction. That is, might not the nationalist forms contain a political culture of their own that is antithetical to socialism? What, for example, is left of Tibetan national forms once the rule of the Dalai Lama is removed and Lamaist religious practices are regarded as evidence of a feudal mind-set? Even the retention of more superficial manifestations of national identity such as clothing, hair style, and language has been criticized by the party as wasteful of scarce resources and time, or as signs of parochialism and feudalism. So indeed they must seem in a poor country that cannot afford waste, and one in which the minority population totals only 6 percent of the whole.

The Chinese Communist party must be credited with having made sincere, sustained, and often creative efforts to deal with China's minorities. It has set up a framework within which the process of integration might reasonably be expected to take place. However, it is obvious that there is a significant segment in the Chinese leadership group that does not believe that the state of accommodation achieved thus far represents an acceptable fusion of nationalities characteristics or an adequately homogeneous proletarian culture. The nature of the steps necessary to advance this level of accommodation is not clear. Past experience has shown that applying more pressure to induce minorities to adopt majority forms may reduce the degree to which minorities are prepared to accommodate to the majority system. Paradoxically, relaxing pressures on minorities to conform may have the same result. Minorities problems in most societies have proven enormously resistant to easy or rapid "solutions," irrespective of the broad goals enunciated or the concrete policies applied. It is not yet clear that the People's Republic of China constitutes an exception.

Appendix
Notes
Bibliography
Glossary
Index

Appendix

Name	Population	Areas of Chief Distribution
Chuang 僮 after 1965 壯	7,780,000	Kwangsi, Yunnan
Hui 回	3,930,000	Ninghsia, Kansu
Uighurs 維吾尔	3,900,000	Sinkiang
Yi 彝	3,260,000	Szechwan, Yunnan
Tibetans 藏	2,770,000	Tibet, Szechwan, Ch'inghai
Miao 苗	2,680,000	Kweichow, Hunan, Yunnan
Manchus 滿	2,430,000	Liaoning, Kirin, Heilungkiang
Mongols 蒙古	1,640,000	Inner Mongolia, Liaoning
Puyi 布依	1,310,000	Kweichow
Koreans 朝鮮	1,250,000	Kirin
Tung 侗	820,000	Kweichow
Yao 瑤	740,000	Kwangsi, Kwangtung
Pai 白	650,000	Yunnan
T'u-chia 土家	600,000	Hunan, Hupei
Hani 哈尼	540,000	Yunnan
Kazakh 哈薩克	530,000	Sinkiang, Ch'inghai
Tai 傣	500,000	Yunnan
Li 黎	390,000	Kwangtung
Lisu 傈僳	310,000	Yunnan
Wa 佤	280,000	Yunnan
She 畬	220,000	Fukien
Kaoshan 高山	200,000	Taiwan
Lahu 拉祜	180,000	Yunnan
Shui 水	160,000	Kweichow
Tunghsiang 东乡	150,000	Kansu
Nahsi 納酉	150,000	Yunnan
Chingpo 景頗	100,000	Yunnan
Kirghiz[1] 柯尔克孜	68,000	Sinkiang
T'u 土	63,000	Ch'inghai, Kansu
Daguors 达斡尔	50,000	Inner Mongolia, Heilungkiang

Name	*Population*	*Areas of Chief Distribution*
Molao 仏佬	44,000	Kwangsi
Ch'iang 羌	42,000	Szechwan
Pulang 布朗	41,000	Yunnan
Salars 撒拉	31,000	Ch'inghai, Kansu
Maonan 毛难	24,000	Kwangsi
Kelao (Kolao) 仡佬	23,000	Kweichow
Hsi-po (Sibo) 錫伯	21,000	Sinkiang
Tajiks 塔吉克	15,000	Sinkiang
P'u-mi 普米	15,000	Yunnan
A-ch'ang 阿昌	10,000	Yunnan
Nü 怒	13,000	Yunnan
Uzbeks 烏孜別克	11,000	Sinkiang
Russians 俄罗斯	9,700	Sinkiang
Owenk'e 鄂溫克	7,200	Inner Mongolia
Penglung 崩龙	6,300	Yunnan
Pao-an 保安	5,500	Kansu
Yu-ku 裕固	4,600	Kansu
Ching 京	4,400	Kwangtung
Tatars 塔塔尔	4,300	Sinkiang
Menpa (Monba) 門巴	3,800	Tibet
Tulung 独龙	2,700	Yunnan
Olunchun 鄂伦春	2,400	Inner Mongolia
Hol-chih (Heche) 赫哲	600	Heilungkiang
Loyü (Lopa) 珞瑜	?	Tibet

Source: *Jen-min shou-ts'e*, Peking, 1965, except for Loyü (Lopa), listed in *Hsin-hua shu-tien*, Peking, 1971.

1. Usually translated by Chinese Communist sources as "Khalkha"—a grievous error, since the Khalkha are a Mongol people of Lamaist religion, while the Kirghiz are a Turki people of the Islamic faith.

Abbreviations

CB	Current Background
CS	Current Scene
FBIS	Foreign Broadcast Information Service
FEER	Far Eastern Economic Review
HHPYK	Hsin-hua pan-yueh-k'an
HHYP	Hsin-hua yueh-pao
KMJP	Kuang-ming jih-pao
JMJP	Jen-min jih-pao
JPRS	Joint Publications Research Service
MTTC	Min-tsu t'uan-chieh
MTYC	Min-tsu yen-chiu
NCNA	New China News Agency
NYT	The New York Times
NFJP	Nan-fang jih-pao
PA	Pacific Affairs
PR	Peking Review
SCMM	Selections from China Mainland Magazines
SCMP	Survey of China Mainland Press
SWMTT	Selected Works of Mao Tse-tung
TNA	Tibetan News Agency
TSFH	T'ien-shan feng-huo
TR	Tibetan Review

Notes

Introduction

1. This definition is essentially similar to that given in Ernst B. Haas, *The Uniting of Europe* (Stanford, Stanford University Press, 1958), p. 16.

2. Charles Wagley and Marvin Harris, *Minorities in the New World* (New York, Columbia University Press, 1958), p. 10.

3. Quoted in the *New York Times* (hereafter cited as *NYT*), Dec. 19, 1971, sec. 4, p. 2.

4. See, for example, A. Ross Johnson, *Yugoslavia: In the Twilight of Tito* (Beverly Hills, Calif., Sage Papers, 1974), pp. 7–8.

1. The Imperial Legacy

1. The use of the term "Han" to denote a group existing prior to the Han dynasty (206 B.C.–A.D. 6 and 25–220) is of course anachronistic. To circumvent this difficulty Li Chi, in his *Formation of the Chinese People* (Cambridge, Mass., Harvard University Press, 1928), p. 5, refers to the evolving group now known to themselves as the Han as the "we group." What the "we group" called barbarians is termed the "they group." Since the use of the term "we group" by a nonmember is clearly inappropriate, and since the major distinction has come to be made between Han and non-Han, I have chosen to employ these terms instead. The core group of the present-day Han may be traced back to A.D. 722, when a silk-wearing, rice-eating, and city-building people who considered themselves descendants of the Yellow Emperor began to create a civilization that gradually overwhelmed that of their neighbors. Many other ethnic elements were absorbed in the process of expansion, which resulted in the formation of the present-day Han Chinese.

2. Wolfram Eberhard, "Kultur und Seidlung des Randvolkers China," *T'oung Pao*, vol. 38 supplement (Leiden, 1942), pp. 412–419.

3. Hsü Sung-shih, *Yüeh-chiang liu-yü jen-min* (Shanghai, 1939), pp. 177–182, quoted in Herold Wiens,

China's March to the Tropics (Hamden, Conn., Shoestring Press, 1954), p. 128.

4. Eric von Eickstedt, *Rassendynamik von Ostasien* (Berlin, Hauptner, 1944), p. 130.

5. Meaning the adoption of the characteristics of Han Chinese culture. To maintain consistency the word probably should be "hanified." However, in the interests of simplicity, I have chosen to employ the conventional term.

6. Wiens, *China's March*, p. 159.

7. Biography of Chiang T'ung, *chuan* 56, *Shih chi* (1739 edition), quoted in Li Chi, p. 231.

8. This is in fact the origin of the present-day Tunghsiang minority. Members of a Mongol garrison in Kansu province intermarried with the local Han, Hui, and Tibetan inhabitants. After the passage of several hundred years they became barely recognizable in terms of their original component parts. See *Min-tsu t'uan-chieh* (Nationalities solidarity, hereafter cited as *MTTC*), no. 12, 1962, p. 47.

9. For further discussion of the tribute system, see John K. Fairbank and Teng Ssu-yu, "On the Ch'ing Tributary System," in Fairbank and Teng, *Ch'ing Administration: Three Studies* (Harvard Yenching Institute Studies No. 19; Cambridge, Mass., 1961), pp. 107–246.

10. Ennoblement did not necessarily mean that one was confirmed in power. Some of those so honored were simultaneously shorn of administrative power.

11. Charles Bell, *Tibet Past and Present* (Oxford, Clarendon Press, 1924), p. 213.

12. The general Manchu term for a great official, but used with particular reference to imperial residents in these areas.

13. The banner system was a device used to incorporate non-Manchu peoples into the Manchu armies before their conquest of China in and after 1644. Under it, certain Han Chinese soldiers of the Ming dynasty and Mongol warriors who surrendered and adhered to the first two Manchu emperors were enrolled in eight military units modeled and named after the eight Manchu banners. While liable to military service on an hereditary basis, Mongol and Han bannermen received stipends and were eligible for official appointments on a much more favorable basis than other Han or non-Han subjects of the Manchus. They constituted a part of the ruling elite, and none who adhered to the Manchus after 1644 were so well treated.

14. H. S. Brunnert and V. V. Hagelstrom, *Present Day Political Organization of China*, tr. A. Beltchenko and E. E. Moran (Shanghai, Kelly and Walsh, 1912), pp. 438–439.

15. Quoted by Huang Fen-sheng, *Pien-chiang cheng-chiao chih yen-chiu* (A study of frontier political administration; Shanghai, 1947), p. 296.

16. Sun E-tu Zen, *Ch'ing Administrative Terms* (Cambridge, Mass., Harvard University Press, 1961), pp. 32–33.

17. Given the double meanings of the second and fourth Chinese characters, plus the extent of Han contempt for barbarians, it is interesting to speculate that this expression may have had the double entendre "improve the dirt by returning it to the stream" as well as "change from native to regular administration."

18. Hu Nai-an, *Pien-cheng t'ung-lun* (A general discussion of border government, Taipei, 1960), p. 27.

19. Pedro Carrasco, *Land and Polity in Tibet* (Seattle, University of Washington Press, 1959), pp. 25, 223–224; Bell, *Tibet*, pp. 44–45.

20. Tsing Yuan, "Yakub Beg (1820–1877) and the Moslem Rebellion in Chinese Turkestan," *Central Asiatic Journal*, 6.1 (1961), 134–167.

21. Robert H. G. Lee, *The Manchurian Frontier in Ch'ing History* (Cambridge, Mass., Harvard University Press, 1970), pp. 127–128.

22. F. C. Jones, *Manchuria since 1931* (New York, Oxford University Press, 1949), p. 6.

23. Brunnert and Hagelstrom, pp. 165–166.

24. Mary C. Wright, *The Last Stand of Chinese Conservatism* (Stanford, Stanford University Press, 1957), p. 123.

25. The prevailing interpretation is that both Hui (Wright, *The Last Stand*, p. 108) and Miao (Wiens, *China's March*, p. 235) rebellions were due less to enmity against the Confucian state than to local grievances—e.g., discrimination against local people by officials, Han confiscation of local peoples' lands, and the like. According to this interpretation, then, the uprisings had been caused by perversions of the system rather than by dissatisfaction with the system itself.

26. Chu Wen-djang, *The Moslem Rebellion in Northwest China, 1862–1878* (The Hague, Mouton et Cie., 1966), pp. 159–161; Wright, *The Last Stand*, p. 124.

27. Wright, *The Last Stand*, p. 123.

28. Ibid., pp. 130–131.

29. Samuel Pollard, *In Unknown China* (Philadelphia, J. B. Lippincott, 1921), p. 56.

30. Quoted in Wiens, *China's March*, p. 219.

2. The Republican Era

1. H. E. Richardson, *A Short History of Tibet* (New York, Dutton, 1962), p. 103.

2. Mishima Yasuo and Goto Tomio, *A Japanese View of Outer Mongolia*, tr. and condensed by Andrew Grajdanev (New York, Institute of Pacific Relations, 1942), p. 27.

3. Wiens, *China's March*, pp. 254–257; Hugh Tinker, "Burma's Northeastern Borderland Problems," *Pacific Affairs*, 29.4 (Winter, 1956, hereafter cited as *PA*), 334–337.

4. See below, section on Yunnan.

5. See below, section on Kansu-Ninghsia-Ch'inghai.

6. Richard Yang, "Sinkiang under the Administration of Governor Yang Tseng-hsin, 1911–1928," *Central Asian Journal*, 6.1 (1961), 270–316.

7. Sun Yat-sen, *Sun Yat-sen: His Political and Social Ideals*, ed. Leonard Shih-lien Hsü (Los Angeles, University of Southern California Press, 1933), p. 168.

8. Sun Yat-sen, *Memoirs of a Chinese Revolutionary* (Taipei, China Cultural Service, 1953), p. 180.

9. Quoted in *China Handbook, 1937–1945* (New York, Macmillan, 1947), p. 74.

10. Chiang Kai-shek, *China's Destiny*, tr. Wang Chung-hui (New York, Macmillan, 1947), pp. 12–13.

11. *China Handbook, 1937–1945*, p. 99.

12. See, for example, ibid., p. 30.

13. Ibid., p. 74.

14. Ibid.

15. See, for example, Liu En-lan, "Border Tribes of West China," *The China Monthly*, 7.12 (Chungking, Dec. 1946), 441; Wiens, *China's March*, p. 247, quoting Lu-feng hsien magistrate, Yunnan, Dec. 3, 1934.

16. Jones, *Manchuria*, p. 61.

17. Owen Lattimore, *The Mongols of Manchuria* (New York, John Day, 1934), pp. 104–106. However, as discussed in chapter 1 above, the imperial government itself reversed its earlier ban on immigration in hopes that larger population on the frontier would reduce the likelihood of foreign aggression there. Though Lattimore is correct in stating that Mongols bitterly resisted this Han immigration, those Mongols who received a share of the profits from land sales and land taxes often proved willing collaborators. See Lee, *The Manchurian Frontier*, p. 137.

18. Jehol also included part of the former Chihli province.

19. *Fourth Report on Progress in Manchuria* (Dairen, South Manchuria Railway Company, 1934), pp. 248, 250.

20. Not the same five "races" that Sun Yat-sen had distinguished. The five "races" of Manchukuo were Manchu, Han, Mongol, Japanese, and "Chosenese" (Korean). The Manchukuo scheme thus substituted Japanese and Koreans for Tatars and Tibetans.

21. *Answering Questions on Manchuria* (Tokyo, South Manchuria Railway Company, 1936), p. 3.

22. Ibid., p. 7.

23. Jones, *Manchuria*, p. 59.

24. "Local Autonomy in Mongolia," *Chinese Affairs*, 5.16 (Nanking, Jan. 31, 1934), 257–258. Translation of *Chun-hua jih-pao* (China daily) article of Jan. 7. Subsequent issues of *Chinese Affairs* detail the Mongol notes and the Nationalist replies, with editorial emphasis on justifying the Nationalist position.

25. Tê Wang, or "Prince Tê," is the title he inherited from the Chinese imperial system. His Mongol name is Demchukdonggrob.

26. Owen Lattimore, *Nomads and Commissars* (Boston, Little, Brown, 1958), p. 131.

27. Iwamura Shinobu, personal interview, Kyoto, March 28, 1969.

28. Jones, *Manchuria*, p. 67.

29. Ma Ho-t'ien, *Chinese Agent in Mongolia*, tr. John deFrancis (Baltimore, Johns Hopkins University Press, 1949), p. 5.

30. A. Doak Barnett, *China on the Eve of Communist Takeover* (New York, Praeger, 1963), p. 209.

31. *China Handbook, 1937–1945*, p. 30.

32. See Yang, *Central Asian Journal*, 6.1 (1961), 270–316.

33. Allen S. Whiting and Sheng Shih-ts'ai, *Sinkiang: Pawn or Pivot?* (East Lansing, Mich., Michigan State University Press, 1958), p. 11.

34. Ibid., p. 22, quoting *Pravda*, Aug. 15, 1933.

35. Ibid., pp. 193–197.

36. White Russians who had fled to Sinkiang after the Bolshevik revolution.

37. Owen Lattimore, *Pivot of Asia* (Boston, Little, Brown, 1950), p. 75.

38. Ibid.

39. C. C. Ku, "The Economic Development of China's Northwest," *China Quarterly*, 6.2 (Chungking, Spring 1939), 287–288.

40. Whiting and Sheng, *Sinkiang*, pp. 99–100.

41. Lattimore, *Pivot*, p. 75.

42. NYT, Dec. 28, 1948, p. 17.

43. Lattimore *Pivot*, p. 90.

44. See Lattimore, *Pivot*, p. 75; Whiting and Sheng, *Sinkiang*, pp. 99–100.

45. For example, Lung Yun. See below, section on South-Southwest.

46. See, for example, Barnett, *China on the Eve*, p. 256; Lattimore, *Pivot*, p. 90; Whiting and Sheng, *Sinkiang*, p. 114.

47. Lattimore, *Pivot*, p. 103.

48. Barnett, *China on the Eve*, p. 258.

49. Harrison Forman, "China's Moslems," *Canadian Geographic Journal*, 27.9 (Sept. 1948), 134–143.

50. Barnett, *China on the Eve*, p. 182.

51. Ibid., Robert Ekvall, *Cultural Relations on the Kansu-Tibetan Border* (Chicago, University of Chicago Press, 1939), p. 15; Forman, "China's Moslems," p. 135.

52. See Whiting and Sheng, *Sinkiang*, p. 11.

53. See Howard L. Boorman, ed., *Biographical Dictionary of Republican China*, II (New York, Columbia University Press, 1968), 463–464. The Swedish explorer

Sven Hedin gives a more detailed account of the exploits of Ma Chung-ying in his *The Flight of Big Horse* (New York, 1934).

54. Boorman, *Biographical Dictionary*, II, 463–465, 468–478.

55. Ekvall, *Cultural Relations*, p. 15.

56. Forman, "China's Moslems," p. 140.

57. Sun Tso-pin, "Some Opinions on Minority Nationalities Work," *Hsin-hua yüeh-pao* (New China monthly), 1.4 (Peking, 1950, hereafter cited as *HHYP*), 876.

58. Ekvall, *Cultural Relations*, p. 17; Forman, "China's Moslems," p. 140.

59. Ekvall, *Cultural Relations*, p. 24; Forman, "China's Moslems," p. 135.

60. Yang Ching-chih, "Japan—Protector of Islam," *PA*, 15.4 (Dec. 1942), 478. Translation of an article in *Ta-kung pao*, Chungking.

61. Ekvall, *Cultural Relations*, pp. 17–18.

62. Yang Ching-chih, "Japan," p. 479.

63. Whiting and Sheng, *Sinkiang*, p. 63, quoting Japanese Foreign Office archival material.

64. Barnett, *China on the Eve*, p. 189.

65. Ibid., p. 191.

66. Ibid., pp. 233–234.

67. Yang Ching-chih, "Japan," pp. 471–481.

68. Francis L. K. Hsü, *Social Change in Southwest China: Magic and Science in West Yunnan* (New York, Institute of Pacific Relations, 1943), p. 5.

69. Barnett, *China on the Eve*, p. 286.

70. Ibid., p. 294.

71. See, for example, Frank M. Lebar et al., *Ethnic Groups of Mainland Southeast Asia* (New Haven, Conn., Human Relations Area Files, 1964), and Hugo Bernatzik, *Akha and Miao* (New Haven, Conn., Human Relations Area Files, 1970).

72. Liu En-lan, "Border Tribes," p. 441.

73. Wiens, *China's March*, p. 247, quoting Lu-feng hsien magistrate, Yunnan, Dec. 3, 1934.

74. A somewhat unusual case, in that both headmen claimed Han ancestry. They had become assimilated to the tribe with which their forebears had come to live. See ibid., pp. 114–116.

75. Chang Ch'i-yun, "The Four Major Regions of China," *The China Monthly*, 6.1 (Dec. 1944), 7, summarizes these developments.

76. *China Handbook, 1937–1945*, p. 341.

77. J. E. Spencer, "K'ueichou, an Internal Chinese Colony," *PA*, 13.2 (June 1940), 162.

78. Ibid., p. 167.

79. Ibid., p. 171.

80. Hsü, *Social Change in Southwest China*, p. 5.

81. Ibid., p. 46.

82. Li An-che, "China: A Fundamental Approach," *PA*, 21.1 (March 1949), 58; Liu En-lan, "Border Tribes," p. 440; Liu Hsi-fan in Huang Fen-sheng, preface p. 1.

83. Liu En-lan, "Border Tribes," p. 441.

84. Ibid., pp. 441–442.

85. Liu Hsi-fan in Huang Fen-sheng, preface p. 1.

86. *Chung-kuo ku-chin ti-ming ta tzu-tien* (Geographical dictionary of ancient and modern China; Shanghai, Commercial Press, 1931), pp. 353–354.

87. A term to which Younghusband would strongly object. In a letter to his father, he likens negotiating with the Tibetans to throwing butter at a granite rock. Text of the letter may be found in Peter Fleming, *Bayonets to Lhasa* (New York, Harper, 1961), p. 203.

88. See chap. 1, n. 12.

89. Bell, *Tibet*, p. 71; Robert Ford, *Wind between the Worlds* (New York, David McKay, 1957), p. 48.

90. But Chao was apparently not the worst Chinese conqueror the Tibetans had to suffer. Sir Eric Teichman, the British consul at this time, while sympathizing with the Tibetans for the brutalities visited on them by Chao, also expresses the opinion that Chao, once established as an administrator, at least tried to govern fairly. He contrasts this record with that of later governors, finding them both ruthless and corrupt. See Eric Teichman, *Travels of a Consular Officer in Eastern Tibet* (Cambridge, Cambridge University Press, 1922), pp. 36–37, 52.

91. Bell, *Tibet*, pp. 155–156.

92. Ibid., p. 167; Teichman, *Travels of a Consular Officer*, p. 58.

93. George Patterson, *Tibet in Revolt* (London, Methuen, 1960), pp. 47–48.

94. Sir Charles Bell, who conducted the British dealings with Tibet during those years, gives no reason for the decision, which he clearly opposed.

95. The province also contained an important Yi minority.

96. Barnett, *China on the Eve*, p. 224.

97. Ibid., p. 225; Patterson, *Tibet in Revolt*, p. 43.

98. Ford, *Wind between the Worlds*, p. 48; Barnett, *China on the Eve*, pp. 224–225.

99. *Chinese Affairs*, 6.1 (June 15, 1934), 18.

100. Richardson, *A Short History of Tibet*, pp. 141–142.

101. *Chinese Affairs*, 6.8 (Sept. 30, 1934), 186.

102. Richardson, *A Short History of Tibet*, p. 147.

103. See above, section on Sinkiang.

104. Richardson, *A Short History of Tibet*, p. 155. Barnett, *China on the Eve*, p. 216, is in error in saying that this occurred after the installation of the fourteenth Dalai Lama in 1934. The Lama was not installed until 1940, and the office was set up shortly thereafter.

105. Carrasco, *Land and Polity in Tibet*, p. 84.

106. *China Handbook, 1937–1945*, p. 30.

107. Richardson, *A Short History of Tibet*, pp. 159–160.

108. Barnett (*China on the Eve*, pp. 225–226) gives the impression that Liu was successful, while Patterson (*Tibet in Revolt*, p. 51) says he was hated by the Tibetans. Whatever his personal popularity, Liu was able to maintain both himself in power and a reasonable degree of order in Sikang under difficult conditions.

109. In raising living standards, maintaining peace and order, and attempting to deal with outstanding issues raised by minority groups.

110. It is perhaps significant that handling of minorities problems in Sinkiang worsened noticeably after Sheng reached an accommodation with the KMT.

3. Marxist-Leninist Prescriptions and the Soviet Example

1. S. F. Bloom, *The World of Nations: A Study of the National Implications in the Work of Karl Marx* (New York, Columbia University Press, 1941), p. 26.

2. Walker F. Connor, "Minorities in Marxist Theory and Practice" (paper presented to the American Political Science Association Conference, New York, 1969), p. 4.

3. G. Stelkoff, *History of the First International* (New York, Russell and Russell, 1968), p. 85.

4. Julius Braunthal, *History of the International, I, 1864–1914* (New York, Praeger, 1967), 33.

5. S. Shaheen, *The Communist Theory of Self-Determination* (The Hague, W. van Hoeve, 1956), p. 26.

6. Connor, "Minorities," p. 5.

7. V. I. Lenin, *Collected Works* (Moscow, Progress Publishers, 1964), VI, 454–463.

8. Lenin, "The Significance of the Right to Self-Determination and Its Relation to Federation" (1916), in *Collected Works*, XXII, 146.

9. Ibid., p. 146.

10. Lenin, "Report of the Commission on the National and the Colonial Questions" (1920), in *Collected Works*, XXXI, 243.

11. "Theses on the National and Colonial Question," ibid., p. 150.

12. Lenin, "For or against Annexations?" ibid., p. 321.

13. Lenin, "Socialism and the Self-Determination of Nations," ibid., p. 321.

14. Ibid., p. 325. Emphasis added.

15. Lenin, "The Socialist Revolution and the Struggle for Democracy," ibid., p. 144.

16. Lenin, "The Significance of the Right," ibid., p. 146.

17. Lenin, letter to Shaumyan, May 19, 1914, quoted in Bertrand Wolfe, *Three Who Made a Revolution* (Boston, Beacon Press, 1948), p. 585.

18. Lenin, letter to Shaumyan, Dec. 1913, ibid., p. 584.

19. Lenin, "The Question of Nationalities or of 'Autonomization,'" Dec. 31, 1922, in Lenin, *The National Liberation Movement in the East* (Moscow, Foreign Languages Publishing House, 1957), pp. 308–310.

20. Ibid., p. 311.

21. Joseph Stalin, "The October Revolution and the Problem of the Middle Strata" (1923), in *Marxism and the National and Colonial Question* (New York, International Publishers, 1934), p. 185.

22. Stalin, "The Policy of the Soviet Government on the National Question in Russia" (1920), ibid., pp. 79–80.

23. As opposed to Austrian Marxists, who had proposed a plan called "national cultural autonomy." Under this system nationalities, regardless of their place of residence, would be organized under national councils, each of which would have responsibility for its respective group's cultural and educational affairs.

24. Stalin, "Marxism and the National Question" (1913), in *Marxism*, p. 33.

25. Ibid., p. 49.

26. Stalin, "Report on the Immediate Tasks of the Party in Connection with the National Problem" (1921), in *Marxism*, p. 104.

27. Stalin, "Marxism and the National Question," p. 58.

28. Stalin, "Theses on National Factors in Party and State Development" (1923), in *Marxism*, p. 145.

29. Stalin, "Report on National Factors in Party and State Development" (1923), in *Marxism*, p. 149.

30. Stalin, "'Rights' and 'Lefts' in the National Republics and Regions" (1923), in *Marxism*, p. 176.

31. Stalin, "The National Question Presented" (1921), ibid., p. 116.

32. Stalin, "'Rights' and 'Lefts,'" p. 179.

33. Stalin, "Report on National Factors," p. 168.

34. Stalin, "The Policy of the Soviet Government," p. 83; see also Stalin, "Report on the Immediate Tasks," p. 104.

35. Stalin, "Report on the Immediate Tasks," p. 105.

36. Stalin, "The Political Tasks of the University of the Peoples of the East" (1925), in *Marxism*, p. 209.

37. Ibid., p. 210.

38. Ibid., p. 211.

39. Non-Russians constituted a majority of the population of the czarist empire. The secession of Poland put the Russian nationality in a slight majority vis-à-vis the total non-Russian population of the Soviet Union.

40. See Richard Pipes, *The Formation of the Soviet Union: Communism and*

Nationalism 1917–1923 (Cambridge, Mass., Harvard University Press, 1964), chap 1.

41. Ibid., pp. 50–53.
42. See ibid., passim, for a detailed description of the reunification process.
43. Georgian Communist who carried out the invasion.
44. Apparently Russian slang for "oppressors." "Derzha" = "to hold," and "morda" = "snout."
45. Lenin, "The Question of Nationalities," pp. 306–308.
46. Head of the secret police.
47. Lenin, "The Question of Nationalities," p. 311.
48. Yaroslav Bilinsky, "The Rulers and the Ruled," *Problems of Communism,* 16.5 (Sept.–Oct. 1967), 17.
49. Robert S. Sullivant, "The Ukrainians," ibid., p. 54.
50. Bilinsky, "Rulers," p. 17.
51. Vernon R. Aspaturian, "The Non-Russian Nationalities," in Allen Kassof, ed., *Prospects for Soviet Society* (New York, Praeger, 1968), p. 191.
52. Trans. in Walter Batsell, *Soviet Rule in Russia* (New York, Macmillan, 1929), p. 117.
53. Stalin, " 'Rights' and 'Lefts,' " p. 176.
54. Elizabeth Bacon, *Central Asians under Russian Rule* (Ithaca, Cornell University Press, 1966), pp. 119, 147.
55. See Pipes, *Formation,* pp. 26–265, for the details.
56. Sullivant, "The Ukrainians," pp. 48–52.
57. Ibid., p. 52.
58. Aspaturian, "Non-Russian Nationalities," p. 165.
59. *The Anti-Stalin Campaign and International Communism,* ed. Russian Institute, Columbia University (New York, 1956), pp. 57–58.
60. "The Deported Nationalities . . . an Unsavory Story," *Problems of Communism,* 16.5:102–104.
61. "How Russia Is Developing Central Asia," *South China Morning Post* (Hong Kong), Feb. 22, 1968, p. 11.
62. Zvi Gitelman, "The Jews," *Problems of Communism,* 16.5:97.
63. Samuel B. Bloembergen, "The Union Republics: How Much Autonomy?" *Problems of Communism,* 16.5:34.
64. Bilinsky, "Rulers," p. 26.
65. "Half Million Tatars Cleared of Nazi Tie," *NYT,* Sept. 12, 1967, pp. 1, 16.
66. V. Hazners, "Nationalism and Local Tendencies in Occupied Latvia," *Baltic Review,* 19 (March 1960), 43–47.
67. "How Russia Is Developing Central Asia," p. 11.
68. Bilinsky, "The Soviet Education Laws of 1958–59 and Soviet Nationality Policy," *Soviet Studies* (London, Oct. 1962), p. 140.
69. Bilinsky, "Rulers," p. 18.
70. *NYT,* Sept. 12, 1967, pp. 1, 16.
71. Bilinsky, "Rulers," pp. 24–26.
72. Alec Nove and J. A. Newth, *The Soviet Middle East: A Communist Model for Development* (New York, Praeger, 1967), p. 120. See also I. M. Volgin (pseudonym), "The Friendship of Peoples . . . Pages from a Notebook," *Problems of Communism,* 16.5:106.
73. Geoffrey Wheeler, "The Muslims of Central Asia," ibid., p. 75.
74. Gitelman, "The Jews," p. 100.
75. V. Stanley Vardys, "The Baltic Peoples," *Problems of Communism,* 16.5:61.
76. Pipes, " 'Solving' the Nationality Problem," ibid., p. 131.

77. Andrei Amalrik, *Can the Soviet Union Survive until 1984?* (New York, Harper and Row, 1970).

4. Chinese Communist Policy Prior to 1949

1. Chu Ch'i-hua, *Chung-kuo ko-ming yü chung-kuo she-hui ko chieh-chi* (The Chinese revolution and Chinese social classes; Shanghai, Lien-ho shu-tien, 1930), pp. 259–260.

2. Wang Chien-min, *Chung-kuo kung-ch'an-tang shih-kao* (Draft history of the Chinese Communist Party; Taipei, privately printed, 1965), II, 321.

3. C. Brandt, B. Schwartz, and J. Fairbank, *A Documentary History of Chinese Communism* (Cambridge Mass., Harvard University Press, 1952), pp. 219–224.

4. The source either cites the Muslim governor's name erroneously or this is a case of an odd coincidence of names. Ma Liang, same characters, of Kiangsu province was an influential Chinese Catholic known for his mastery of Western science. He lived between 1840 and 1939 and would therefore have been a contemporary of the Shantung governor. See Boorman, *Biographical Dictionary*, II, 470.

5. Han Tao-jen, "Commemorate Revolutionary Martyr Ma Chün," *MTTC*, no. 2 1957, pp. 18–19.

6. Identified in some sources as Li Yu-chih. See, for example, Mao Ao-hai, "The Mongols," in *Jen-min jih-pao* (People's daily, hereafter cited as *JMJP*), May 3, 1953. Revolutionary pseudonyms were popular at this time.

7. In renaming himself Ulanfu, Yun Tse adopted the same character "fu" used to transliterate the Russian suffix *ov*. This would have rendered his name "Ulyanov," which, was, of course, Lenin's family surname. Adoption of an alias in honor of prominent Russian revolutionaries was a not uncommon practice among Chinese Communists at this time. For example, writer Pa Chin is said to have coined his name from those of two Russian authors: the Chinese transliterations of the first syllable of "Bakunin" and the last syllable of "Kropotkin." It is interesting to speculate whether this might have been Ulanfu's motive in choosing his name also. The name would have been doubly meaningful in that "ulan" is the Mongolian word for "red."

8. See chap. 2, n. 25.

9. I am unable to ascertain what percentage of the student body was Tibetan. Possibly it was rather small.

10. See Boorman, *Biographical Dictionary*, I, 7.

11. Chi Ya-t'ai, "Comrade Li Ta-chien and the Beginnings of the Inner Mongolian Autonomous Region," *MTTC*, no. 7 1961, p. 10; see also Yi-tu-ho-shih-ko, "The Mongols," ibid., p. 44.

12. Yi-tu-ho-shih-ko, "The Mongols," p. 45.

13. Boorman, *Biographical Dictionary*, I, 8.

14. Donald Klein files, hereafter cited as DK files; *Who's Who in Communist China* (Hong Kong, 1966; hereafter cited as *Who's Who*), p. 509; "The Establishment and Development of the IMAR," *Min-tsu yen-chiu* (Nationalities research, hereafter cited as *MTYC*), no. 4 1958, trans. in U.S. Department of Commerce, *Joint Publications Research Services* (hereafter cited as *JPRS*), no. 2699, pp. 1–25.

15. *Who's Who*, p. 150.

16. DK files.

17. A pejorative term meaning barbarian in the general sense. Though used as late as 1953, it is now castigated as an insult to the minorities devised by feudal reactionaries. Subsequent allusions to Mao's speech have changed it to read "Mongols, Hui, Tibetans, Miao, Yao, Yi, and Yü." See, for example, Hsieh Ho-ch'ou, "The Great Policy of Regional Autonomy for Nationalities," *MTTC*, no. 1 1960,

p. 3. This clearly unintentional use of an insulting appellation is one indication of the CCP's lack of information on the minorities at this time.

18. Quoted in *JMJP*, Sept. 9, 1953. Emphasis added.

19. Another pejorative term, derived from the Chinese pronunciation of the Yi word for "spirit box," an object that is part of the Yi's shamanistic religion. The CCP later forbade use of the word *Lolo* in deference to Yi feelings.

20. Nym Wales (pseudonym of Helen Foster Snow), *Red Dust* (Stanford, Stanford University Press, 1952), p. 70. A similar account of the trip through Yi territory is contained in Edgar Snow, *Red Star over China* (New York, Grove Press, 1938), pp. 202 –203.

21. Snow, *Red Star*, p. 203.

22. Actually two separate groups, referred to in the sources as "Man" and "Hsi-fan." Again, these are generic terms meaning barbarian and are of course pejorative in connotation. Judging from the geographic area involved and a description of the Man queen, this group was probably Khambas; the Hsi-fan were probably Tibetan as well.

23. Snow, *Red Star*, p. 214.

24. Ekvall, "Nomads of Tibet: A Chinese Dilemma," in Francis Harper, ed., *This Is China* (Hong Kong, Dragonfly Press, 1965), p. 225.

25. Ibid., p. 224.

26. Wales, *Red Dust*, p. 217; *MTTC*, no. 1 1960, p. 3. *Po-pa* is a transliteration of the local word meaning Tibetan.

27. Wales, *Red Dust*, pp. 75, 146; Ekvall, *Cultural Relations*, p. 25.

28. Wales, *Red Dust*, p. 218.

29. Snow, *Red Star*, p. 350.

30. Ibid., p. 348.

31. Mao Tse-tung, "Mu-ch'ien hsing-shih ti fen-hsi" (Analysis of the current situation), quoted in Stuart Schram, *Mao Tse-tung* (New York, Simon and Schuster, 1968), p. 179.

32. Whiting and Sheng, p. 54.

33. Schram, *Mae Tse-tung*, p. 236. Leaders of the Mongolian People's Republic (MPR) apparently still believe China covets their country. Several official protests have been lodged against books and maps published in China which refer to the MPR as "lost territory." Most recently, during a rally celebrating the fiftieth anniversary of the MPR, President Yumjaagiyn Tsedenbal accused Peking of expansionism with regard to Mongolia. See Alan Sanders, "Renewing a Powerful Link with Moscow" *Far Eastern Economic Review* (*FEER*), Dec. 13, 1974, p. 35.

34. Brandt et al., p. 308. I am indebted to Professor Walker Connor for calling this example to my attention.

35. George Moseley, ed. & tr., *The Party and the National Question in China* (Cambridge, Mass, MIT Press, 1966), pp. 53–54; emphasis added.

36. John M. H. Lindbeck, "Communism, Islam and Nationalism in China," *The Review of Politics*, 7.4 (Oct. 1950), 474.

37. *MTTC*, no. 1 1960, p. 4.

38. DK files; *Who's Who*, p. 660.

39. *Who's Who*, p. 444.

40. Snow, *Red Star*, p. 239.

41. Ibid., p. 325.

42. Ibid., pp. 349–350.

43. Ibid., p. 353.

44. Ibid., p. 344.

45. Ibid., p. 348.

46. As expressed in Chalmers Johnson's *Peasant Nationalism and Communist Power* (Stanford, Stanford University Press, 1962).

47. Snow, *Red Star*, p. 348.

48. Wales, "My Yenan Notebooks" (Madison, Conn., mimeographed, 1961), pp. 104–106.

49. See Mao Tse-tung, "A Very Important Policy," Sept. 7, 1942, in *Selected Works of Mao Tse-tung* (Peking, Foreign Languages Publishing House, 1965, hereafter cited as *SWMTT*), III, 99–105, for Mao's explanation of this policy.

50. These include Central Committee member Sang-chi-yüeh-hsi (T'ien Pao) and autonomous chou Party Committee first secretary Cha-hsi-wang-hsü, both Tibetans, Hui Sha Li-shih and Mongol Li Wen-ching, heads of autonomous chou, and Chuang T'an Ying-chi, a deputy secretary of the party committee of the Kwangsi Chuang Autonomous Region.

51. Tsung Ch'un, "Cradle of Minority Nationalities Cadres: Recalling the Yenan Nationalities Institute," *MTTC*, no. 7 1961, pp. 15–19.

52. *SWMTT*, III, 305–306.

53. Barnett, *China on the Eve*, p. 299.

54. See Okada Kenji, *The Li Tribes of Hainan Island* (New Haven, Yale Southeast Asia Translation Series, n.d.), passim.

55. Hainan had a total of sixteen hsien at that time.

56. Feng Pai-chü, "Five Red Clouds on Five Finger Mountain," *MTTC*, no. 2 1957, pp. 20–22.

57. In the interval between these two versions, Feng had been criticized for regarding Hainan as his private kingdom.

58. Literary name for Hainan.

59. Liao Chih-hsiung, "Red Flag Waving over Five Finger Mountain," *MTTC*, no. 6 1961, pp. 39–42.

60. U.S. Consulate General, Hong Kong, *Current Background* (hereafter cited as *CB*), no. 103, p. 1.

61. Robert Rupen, "Partition in the Land of Genghis Khan," in Harper, *This Is China*, p. 206.

62. *JPRS*, no. 2699, pp. 1–25.

63. *MTTC*, no. 1 1960, p. 3.

64. *JPRS*, no. 2699, p. 23.

65. Barnett, *China on the Eve*, p. 213.

66. Rupen, "Partition," p. 206.

67. Professor Iwamura Shinobu recalls that a Japanese Mongolist, Yamasaki Tadashi, served as translator during these negotiations. Since it would seem highly unlikely that Tê Wang, after his years at the Mongolian and Tibetan School, would not speak Chinese, Yamasaki, now deceased, must have played another role apart from interpreting.

68. *NYT*, Sept. 30, 1949, p. 5.

69. Boorman gives a misleading impression by saying that Tê Wang's government was "confronted by Chinese Nationalist forces under the command of Fu Tso-yi's lieutenant Tung Ch'i-wu" and defeated (Boorman, *Biographical Dictionary*, II, 10). Tung had already defected and in fact conquered Tê Wang's state in the name of the CCP, not the KMT.

70. Boorman, *Biographical Dictionary*, II, 10.

71. New China News Agency (hereafter referred to as NCNA), Peking, April 9, 1963.

72. *NYT*, July 1, 1949, p. 5.

73. *NYT*, July 20,1949, p. 13.

74. *NYT*, Aug. 5, 1949, p. 2.

75. *NYT*, Sept. 4, 1949, pp. 1–2.

76. *NYT*, Sept. 21, 1949, p. 17.

77. *NYT*, Sept. 24, 1949, p. 5.

78. Boorman, *Biographical Dictionary*, II, 469–470.

79. See above, chap. 2, section on Sinkiang.

80. *NYT*, Feb. 1, 1949, p. 1; Feb. 2, p. 18; Feb. 6, sec. 4, p. 1.
81. *NYT*, Mar. 22, 1949, p. 22.
82. *NYT*, Sept. 29, 1949, p. 8.
83. DK files.
84. See *NYT*, Jan. 3, 1949, p. 12; Sept. 5, p. 7; Sept. 6, p. 14; Sept. 7, p. 13; Sept. 12, p. 4; Oct. 3, p. 2; Nov. 3, p. 4; Nov. 28, p. 4; Dec. 9, p. 1, for a representative sample of these happenings.
85. Boorman, *Biographical Dictionary*, II, 446–447.
86. *NYT*, Nov. 16, 1949, p. 15; Dec. 7, p. 1; Dec. 15, p. 3.
87. *NYT*, Dec. 16, 1949, p. 1.
88. *NYT*, Dec. 31, 1949, p. 2.
89. On July 2, 1956, NCNA (Lhasa) announced that the first Tibetans from Tibet proper had just been initiated into the CCP. The group numbered seven.
90. NCNA (Peking), Nov. 8, 1950. For a Tibetan view of these events, see Ford, *Wind between the Worlds*, chaps. 1–3.
91. *Wen-hui pao* (Shanghai), Jan. 22, 1950, in HHYP, 4 (Peking, 1950), 879.
92. *HHYP*, 1.4 (1950), 879.
93. See above, chap. 2, section on Tibet.
94. Tibet was virtually snowbound from October to May of each year.
95. Ford, *Wind between the Worlds*, pp. 138–139.
96. U.S. Consulate General, Hong Kong, *Survey of China Mainland Press* (hereafter cited as *SCMP*), no. 1, p. 1; no. 4, p. 5; no. 7, p. 8.
97. Ford, *Wind between the Worlds*, pp. 159, 162.
98. Dalai Lama, *My Land and My People* (New York, McGraw-Hill, 1962), p. 87.
99. Ibid., p. 87.
100. Ibid., p. 88.
101. NCNA, May 27, 1951, in *Tibet, 1950–1967* (Hong Kong, 1968), p. 20.
102. Ibid., pp. 19–23.
103. Leaving only the Kaoshan on Taiwan to be liberated.

5. The Early Years, 1949–1955

1. See below, section on Theory and Practice of Autonomy.
2. Common Program of the Chinese People's Political Consultative Conference, Article 9, in *Min-tsu cheng-ts'e wen-hsien* (Documents on nationalities policy; Peking, n.d.), p. 1.
3. Ibid., Article 51, p. 1.
4. Ibid., Article 53, p. 1.
5. For Mao's explanation of this concept, see *SWMTT*, IV, 421–423.
6. "Party Work among the Minorities of Hainan Island," *Current Scene*, 8.2 (Jan. 15, 1970, hereafter cited as *CS*), 5–6.
7. Pao Ke, "Peiping's Administration of Minority Nationalities," *Chinese Communist Affairs*, 4.3 (Taipei, June 1967), 41–44.
8. Ibid., p. 45.
9. *Min-tsu cheng-ts'e wen-hsien*, pp. 5–7.
10. Pao Ke, "Peiping's Administration," p. 43.
11. Alan Winnington, *Slaves of the Cool Mountains* (London, Lawrence and Wishart, 1959), p. 208.
12. See, e.g., *SCMP*, no. 1, p. 17; no. 70, pp. 20–23; *Nan-fang jih-pao* (Southern daily), Feb. 19, 1951.

13. Shen Chün-ju, "Report to the Ninety-sixth Meeting of the GAC" (Jan. 26, 1951), in *CB*, no. 109, p. 5.

14. See *SCMP*, no. 115, p. 10; *CB*, no. 103, pp. 1–26.

15. As cited in chap. 1. See Pollard, *In Unknown China*, p. 56.

16. Samuel R. Clarke, *Among the Tribes in Southwest China* (London, Morgan and Scott, 1911).

17. Fei Hsiao-t'ung, "Minority Groups of Kweichow," *Hsin Kuan-ch'a* (New observer), no. 3 (March 1951), pp. 2–4; no. 4 (April 1951) pp. 10–12; no. 5 (May 1951) pp. 4–6.

18. Wen-hui pao (Hong Kong), Aug. 9, 1951, in *CB*, no. 109, p. 5.

19. See, e.g., Winnington, *Slaves*, p. 203; Stuart and Roma Gelder, *The Timely Rain: Travels in New Tibet* (London, Hutchinson and Co., 1964).

20. Liu Shao-ch'i, quoted in *Central Asian Review*, 7.4 (1960), 447.

21. See, for example, the story of Mai-mai-t'i-jou-tzu in *SCMP*, no. 798, p. 21.

22. See, e.g., *HHYP*, 1.1 (1950), 876–877.

23. Burhan, "General Report on Five Months' Work in Sinkiang," *HHYP*, 2.4 (1950), 764–765.

24. Translated in *SCMP*, no. 394, pp. 9–20.

25. "Draft Basic Summarization of Experiences in the Promotion of Autonomy in Minority Nationality Organs" (June 15, 1953), *CB*, no. 264, p. 4.

26. NCNA (Huhehot), May 14, 1953.

27. See, e.g., *SCMP*, no. 1484, p. 33; ibid., no. 1517, p. 29.

28. *HHYP*, 1.4 (1950), 376.

29. Winnington, *Slaves*, p. 54.

30. Ma Ta-chün, "Democratic Reforms and the Socialist Transformation in the Nationalities Areas of China," *Chiao-hsüeh yü yen-chiu* (Teaching and research), 6 (June 1958), 62–75.

31. Liu Ko-p'ing, "Unprecedented Unity of China's Nationalities," *Hsin kuan-ch'a*, no. 4 (April 1952), pp. 11-12.

32. See, e.g., "Chairman Mao Has Sent a Very Valuable Person to the Lisu," *MTTC*, no. 8–9 1961, p. 10; "The Nü," *MTTC*, no. 11 1962, pp. 47–48; Winnington, *Slaves*, pp. 141–143.

33. NCNA (Lhasa), Dec. 28, 1965, discussing the period of democratic reforms in 1959.

34. "On the Progress of Establishing Regional Autonomous and Democratic Governments in Minority Areas" (Dec. 15, 1951), *SCMP*, 237, p. 8.

35. *SCMP*, 143, p. 10. The release is dated July 25, 1951.

36. *MTTC*, no. 7 1962, p. 41.

37. Li Liang-chen, "Local Girls Teach Han," *MTTC*, no. 12 1963, pp. 37–38.

38. *MTTC*, no. 8–9 1961, p. 38.

39. *CS*, 8.2 (Jan. 15, 1970), 16–17.

40. See, e.g., "Reader's Forum," *MTTC*, no. 2–3 1964, pp. 16–17, in which cadres are urged to consider these hardships a test of their abilities and reminded that, however harsh conditions are, they are easier than those of the Long March.

41. Quoted in *MTTC*, no. 8 1955, p. 13.

42. *JMJP*, June 14, 1951.

43. Anna Louise Strong, *Tibetan Interviews* (Peking, New World Press, 1959), p. 26.

44. Ibid., p. 102.

45. Ibid., p. 102; Li Wen, "Ssu-lang-pa-mu," *MTTC*, no. 8 1964, pp. 40–41. Given the differences outlined earlier between Lhasa Tibetans and Szechwan Tibetans, using the latter to interpret the party's policies to the former could not have been the best of all possible solutions. In addition, placing the Szechwan Tibetans in positions of authority in Tibet proper would seem likely to cause resentment

among the local population. However, few other alternatives were available to the party. And, at the present time, T'ien Pao, a Szechwan Tibetan, serves as Deputy Party Secretary and Vice-Chairman of the Revolutionary Committee of the Tibet Autonomous Region, without apparent friction.

46. Edgar Snow, *The Other Side of the River* (New York, Random House, 1961), p. 205.

47. Winnington, *Slaves*, p. 85.

48. NCNA (Urumchi), Sept. 27, 1965, in *SCMP*, no. 3549, p. 18.

49. NCNA (Lhasa), Sept. 17, 1963, in *SCMP*, no. 3064, p. 21.

50. *MTTC*, no. 7 1962, p. 20.

51. *JMJP*, July 5, 1959.

52. Ulanfu, "Report on Work in the IMAR" (Dec. 1951), *CB*, no. 190, pp. 21–32.

53. Chang Hung, "Growth of Cultural and Educational Work among the Various Nationalities of Singiang," *Kuang-ming jih-pao* (Bright daily, Peking; hereafter cited as *KMJP*), Sept. 30, 1955.

54. NCNA (Peking), March 12, 1955; *CB*, no.. 332, pp. 8–9.

55. *CB*, no. 332, pp. 16–17.

56. *SCMP*, no. 121, p. 7. Texts of the two documents in *Min-tsu cheng-ts'e wen-hsüan hui-pien* (Collected documents on nationalities policy; Peking, 1953), pp. 6–10.

57. Ibid., pp. 6–8.

58. *CB*, no. 152, p. 1.

59. Ibid., pp. 11–15.

60. Ibid., pp. 6–10.

61. Ibid., pp. 11–15.

62. *HHYP*, 2.4 (1950), 765.

63. "Cultural Work Teams Penetrate Rural Herding Areas," *MTTC*, no. 1 1964, p. 31.

64. *SCMP*, 258, p. 16.

65. Pien Chün, "Great Development of Minority Nationalities Song and Dance Troupe," *MTTC*, no. 7 1959, p. 26–28.

66. *SCMP*, no. 194, p. 20.

67. See above, chap. 4, n. 19.

68. This even necessitated changing the words of Chairman Mao. See above, chap. 4, n. 17.

69. *SCMP*, no. 105, p. 23.

70. See above, chap. 2, section on the Northeast.

71. NCNA (Huhehot), April 28, 1954.

72. *CB*, no. 43, p. 8.

73. NCNA (Peking), Feb. 19, 1953.

74. *SCMP*, no. 129, p. 11.

75. Liu Ko-p'ing, "Achievements in Work among Nationalities during the Past Three Years," *CB*, no. 218, pp. 23–25.

76. NCNA (Peking), Oct. 10, 1953, *SCMP*, no. 666, p. 38.

77. *JMJP*, Oct. 11, 1953; translation in *SCMP*, no. 718, pp. 17–19.

78. Ibid., p. 19.

79. "Implement Thoroughly the Nationalities Policy of the Party, Criticize the Ideology of Pan-Hanism," *JMJP*, Oct. 10, 1953, *SCMP*, no. 666, pp. 34–38; see also *JMJP*, Oct. 11, 1953, translated in *SCMP*, no. 718, pp. 17–19.

80. *CB*, no. 264, p. 8.

81. Ibid., pp. 9–13.

82. *Constitution of the Chinese People's Republic* (Peking, Foreign Languages Press, 1954).

83. *CB*, no. 294, p. 18.

84. Because of reforms instituted under the Japanese occupation, the Korean population of China generally had a higher standard of living than the Han. At the time of liberation, an estimated 84 percent were literate, and their land produced higher per acre yields than that of neighboring Han. During the Great Leap Forward, when Han cooperatives were merged with Korean cooperatives to form communes, this was to cause troubles. See Li Chen-ch'uan, *Economic Geography of the Yenpien Korean Autonomous Chou* (Shanghai, 1957), trans. in *JPRS*, no. 2019-N; also *MTTC*, no. 3 1959, p. 11.

85. "Inner Mongolia: Model Region for Autonomy," *Ta-kung pao* (Hong Kong), Feb. 13, 1954.

86. "Kwangsi Minority Nationality Investigation Team Report," *MTTC*, no. 4 1963, pp. 45–48; see also Hsiang Ta-tu, "General Condition of the Chuang in Kwangsi," *Kwangsi jih-pao* (Kwangsi daily), Feb. 9, 1958, in *CB*, no. 504, p. 27.

87. Personal interview, Mr. Yen Tzer-chung, Hong Kong, July 7, 1968.

88. Wang Chen, "The Past Year in Sinkiang," *JMJP*, Oct. 1, 1950.

89. See *SCMP*, no. 212, p. 13; 220, p. 14.

90. *CB*, no. 190, p. 12.

91. V. F. Kasatkin, "Reshenie natsional'nogo voprosa v Kitaiskoi Narodnoi Respublike," *Sovetskoe vostokvedenie*, no. 4 1956, p. 22, quoted in Arthur C. Hasiotis, Jr., "A Comparative Study of the Political and Economic Policies Pursued by the USSR and Communist China in Their Attempt to Consolidate Their Respective Positions within Russian Central Asia (1917–1934) and Sinkiang (1949–late 1957)," M.A. essay (Columbia University East Asian Institute, 1965), p. 54.

92. Saifudin, "Achievements in Economic Construction in Sinkiang," *JMJP*, Sept. 30, 1955.

93. Ulanfu, "Report on Work in the IMAR," (Dec. 1951), *JMJP*, Jan. 20, 1952.

94. K. I. Kotov, "Autonomy of Local Nationalities in the CPR, Citing as an Example the Sinkiang Uighur Autonomous Region" (Moscow, 1959), trans. in *JPRS*, no. 3547, p. 17.

95. NCNA (Urumchi), April 18, 1952, in *CB*, no. 176, p. 1.

96. Wang Chi-lung, "Sinkiang's Production and Construction Corps," *MTTC*, no. 12 1961, pp. 8–14.

97. Ibid., p. 10.

98. *HHYP*, 2.4 (1950), 767.

99. *SCMP*, 15, p. 14; 74, p. 12.

100. Barnett, *China on the Eve*, pp. 238–239.

101. *JMJP*, Sept. 24, 1955.

102. Winnington, *Slaves*, p. 194.

103. *MTTC*, no. 5 1963, p. 2.

104. Winnington, *Slaves*, pp. 192–193.

105. See Huang Ch'ang-liu, "The Tai," *MTTC*, no. 7 1959, pp. 37–38.

106. Fei Hsiao-t'ung and Lin Yao-hua, "A Study of the Social Nature of the Minority Nationalities," *JMJP*, Aug. 14, 1956.

107. See Wa-cha-mu-chi, "The Yi," *MTTC*, no. 11 1959, p. 26.

108. Winnington, *Slaves*, p. 85.

109. Text of State Council directive in *CB*, no. 346, p. 9.

110. *MTTC*, no. 12 1963, pp. 2–5.

111. *SCMP*, no. 372, p. 22.

112. *SCMP*, no. 108, p. 2.

113. *SCMP*, no. 459, p. 22.

114. *CB*, no. 332, p. 15.

115. Lung interview, May 6, 1968.

116. NCNA (Lhasa), Aug. 22, 1952.
117. *CB*, no. 490, p. 11.
118. Dalai Lama, *My Land*, pp. 64–67.
119. See, e.g., NCNA (Peking), May 19, 1951.
120. *SCMP*, no. 371, pp. 27–28.
121. The remains of their meals. This effort to be sanitary, which would have been laudable in most other contexts, happened to run counter to the Buddhist-lamaist beliefs of Tibetans. Though technically forbidden by their religion to eat meat, many of those of lamaist faith live in cold, arid areas where agriculture is most difficult and animal husbandry is the mainstay of their economy. Though they eat meat, there are often, as in the case of the Lhasa Tibetans, certain acceptable ways to dispose of the remains. To use any other methods, as did these soldiers, was regarded with shock and disgust.
122. Dalai Lama, *My Land*, pp. 92–97.
123. Chuang Kuo-hua, "Report on Work in the Tibet Region," *JMJP*, Sept. 21, 1956.
124. George Ginsburgs and Michael Mathos, *Communist China and Tibet: The First Dozen Years* (The Hague, Martinus Nijhoff, 1964), p. 49.
125. *JMJP*, April 25, 1956.

6. The Radical Experiment and Its Background, 1956–1958

1. Ulanfu, "Success in Nationalities Work and Questions of Policy" (June 20, 1956), *CB*, no. 402, p. 12.
2. Text of State Council directives in *SCMP*, no. 1208, pp. 3–4, 7.
3. *SCMP*, no. 1332, pp. 2–5.
4. NCNA (Peking), July 7, 1956.
5. *SCMP*, no. 1332, p. 50.
6. Fei Hsiao-t'ung and Lin Yüeh-hua, "A Study of the Question of Different Nationalities among the Minority Nationalities of China," *JMJP*, Aug. 10, 1956.
7. *CB*, no. 109, p. 2.
8. Liu Ko-p'ing, "Achievements in Work among Nationalities during the Past Three Years," NCNA (Peking), Sept. 5, 1952.
9. *Hsüeh-hsi* (Study; Peking), no. 7 1952, in *SCMP*, no. 470, p. 22.
10. *Ti-li chih shih* (Geographical knowledge) 4.10 (Peking, April 1953), 10.
11. *Shih-shih shou-ts'e* (Current affairs handbook; Shanghai, 1956), pp. 21–23.
12. *Jen-min shou-ts'e* (People's handbook; Peking, 1957), pp. 623–642.
13. Ibid., 1959, pp. 217–219.
14. Ibid., 1963, pp. 128–129.
15. Ibid., 1965, pp. 115–116.
16. The Loyü or Lopa of southern Tibet. *Gendai Chugoku Jiten* (Encyclopedia of contemporary China; Tokyo, 1969), p. 13, lists as unknown the population size and language and religion of this group.
17. Fei Hsiao-t'ung, *CB*, no. 109, p. 3.
18. Yang Chien-hsin, "The Tunghsiang," *MTTC*, no. 12 1962, pp. 47–48.
19. Wen Ming, "The T'u-chia," *MTTC*, no. 5 1959, p. 37.
20. *MTYC*, no. 2 1958, p. 41. Possibly this is an alternate name for the Hoklo.
21. See the collection of translations from *Sovetskaya Etnografiya* contained in *JPRS*, no. 16431.
22. *CB*, no. 418, p. 18.
23. *SCMP*, no. 1316, pp. 26–27.
24. T'ang Hsien-chih, "Upsurge of Socialism in China's Countryside," Feb. 1956 (pamphlet published by editors of *Hsüeh-hsi*), *CB*, no. 388, p. 13.
25. Hsieh Fu-min, speech to second session of First NPC, *CB*, no. 355, p. 27.

26. Hsiang Ta-yu, "General Condition of the Chuang in Kwangsi," *Kwangsi jih-pao*, Feb. 9, 1958, *CB*, no. 504, p. 28.

27. Chu Tê-hai, speech to second session of First NPC, July 1955, *CB*, no. 355, p. 36.

28. *CB*, no. 402, p. 18.

29. Ibid., p. 18.

30. Chang Chao-lun, "Concerning the Socialist Construction and Transformation in Kweichow Nationality Areas," speech to third session of the Second National Committee of the CPPCC (March 18, 1957), *JMJP*, March 25, 1957.

31. Huang Ch'ang-liu, "The Tai," *MTTC*, no. 7 1959, pp. 37–38.

32. See Winnington, *Slaves*, chap. 4.

33. NCNA (Huhehot), April 4, 1954, *SCMP*, no. 794, p. 41.

34. K'uei Pi, "Mongolian People's Prosperity Is Inseparable from Han People's Help," *JMJP*, Feb. 14, 1958.

35. *CB*, no. 402, p. 18.

36. See *CB*, no. 373 for a discussion of the various targets and revisions in the collectivization drive for Han China at this time.

37. See above, chap. 4, n. 87.

38. A more complete treatment of this campaign may be found in Roderick Mac Farquhar, *The Hundred Flowers Campaign and the Chinese Intellectuals* (New York, Praeger, 1960).

39. "The Building of Socialism Is Impossible without Opposition to Local Nationalism," joint statement of 19 minorities delegates to the fifth session of the First NPC (Feb. 10, 1958), *JMJP*, Feb. 13, 1958. See also Li Hung-fan, "Local Nationalists Are Precisely Those Who Cannot Represent the Nationality's Best Interests," *MTTC*, no. 3 1957, p. 2.

40. *MTTC*, no. 2 1958, p. 7.

41. *MTTC*, no. 6 1958, p. 1.

42. *Nan-fang jih-pao* (Southern daily; Canton). Hereafter cited as *NFJP*. May 5, 1957.

43. *NFJP*, May 5, 1957.

44. Wang Feng, "Report to the Fifth Enlarged Meeting of the First NPC," *MTTC*, no. 2 1958, pp. 2–8.

45. Teng Hsiao-p'ing, report on the rectification campaign, to third enlarged plenary session of the Eighth Central Committee of the CCP, *CB*, no. 477, p. 43.

46. *MTTC*, no. 2 1958, p. 8.

47. *CB*, no. 477, p. 43.

48. *MTTC*, no. 2 1958, p. 8.

49. *CB*, no. 477, p. 42.

50. T. Rakhimov, "The Great Power Policy of Mao Tse-tung on the Nationalities Question," *Kommunist*, 44.7 (May 1967) 114–119.

51. Ma Ta, "Great Victory of the Honan Hui over the Right-Wing Religious Elements within the Nationality," *MTTC*, no. 6 1958, p. 2.

52. "Criticism of Ma Sung-t'ing's So-Called 'Hui Religion, Thus Hui Nationality' Distortion," *MTTC*, no. 2 1957, p. 4; Chen Kuang, "Oppose the Reactionary Religious Elements, Help the Shantung Hui into a New World," *MTTC*, no. 7 1958, p. 16.

53. *MTTC*, no. 7 1958, p. 16.

54. See, e.g., "Taiwan Reports Killing Ten during Raid on Mainland," *NYT*, June 5, 1967, p. 7.

55. *CS*, no. 8.2 (Jan. 15, 1970), 13.

56. Wang Hung-wei, "Is There Nothing to Oppose?" *MTTC*, no. 3 1958, p. 18.

57. *CS*, no. 8.2 (Jan. 15, 1970), 13.

58. *Kansu jih-pao* (Kansu daily), Aug. 16, 1958, *CB* no. 528, p. 1.

59. "People of All Nationalities Criticize Lung Yun," *Hsin-hua pan-yüeh-k'an* (*HHPYK*; New China bimonthly), 17 (Peking, 1957), 108–112; also *SCMP*, no. 1706, p. 6.

60. Reprinted in *Peking Review* (PR), 10.26 (June 23, 1967), 19–20.

61. See the collection of reports from *Hsi-tsang jih-pao* (Tibet daily) for this period carried in *CB*, no. 490.

62. NCNA (Lhasa), April 30, 1958, *SCMP*, no. 1770, p. 21.

63. Wiens (*China's March*, pp. 34–35) cites a study of the 152 clan names found in an unnamed chou of Kwangsi. Not a single clan would admit to being indigenous. Falsification of genealogical records to prove one's Han lineage was common and often imaginatively done. For example, the Wei clan claimed to be descended from a son of Han dynasty general Han Hsing. When his father was executed, the younger Han, to conceal his identity, struck out the radical portion of his surname, leaving a character pronounced Wei.

64. *HHPYK*, 10 (1957), 42–44.

65. See, e.g., "Hui Masses Vehemently Criticize Ma Chen-wu's Monstrous Crimes," *MTTC*, no. 9 1958, pp. 4–5.

66. See *SCMP*, no. 1588, p. 1; 1549, p. 1.

67. Saifudin, "Report to the SUAR Party Committee," *JMJP*, Dec. 26, 1957.

68. Josef Kolmas, "The Minority Nationalities," *Bulletin of the Atomic Scientists*, 22.6 (June 1966), 71. Mr. Kolmas notes that a sign to this effect was posted prominently in the Central Nationalities Institute, where he was a student.

69. *SCMP*, no. 1795, pp. 21–23.

70. Wu Wan-yuan, "Concerning the Ideology of Nationalities Special Characteristics," *MTTC*, no. 6 1958, p. 5.

71. "The Building of Socialism Is Impossible without Opposition to Local Nationalism," *JMJP*, Feb. 13, 1958.

72. Yeh Shang-chih, "Correctly Implement the Autonomous Area Rights and the Nationalization of Minority Nationalities Cadres," *MTTC*, no. 3 1958, pp. 7–8.

73. See, for example, Chao Chien-min, "Reform Funeral Customs, Encourage Thrifty Burials without Coffins, and Graves without Sepulchral Mounds," *JMJP*, June 17, 1958.

74. NCNA (Peking), April 30, 1958.

75. See, for example, *MTTC*, no. 7 1958, pp. 2–3.

76. *MTYC*, no. 5 1959, p. 5.

77. See Yen Fu's brilliant critique of this slogan in Teng Ssu-yu and John Fairbank, *China's Response to the West* (New York, 1965), p. 151.

78. *MTYC*, no. 5 1959, p. 5.

79. Pai-la-ta-cha-pu, "Everyone Asks, 'Do Minorities Cadres Speak for the Local People or Not?' " *MTTC*, no. 3 1958, p. 18.

80. NCNA (Peking), April 19, 1958, *SCMP*, no. 1756, p. 37.

81. *SCMP*, no. 1759, p. 26.

82. Lung interview, Hong Kong, May 15, 1968.

83. *MTTC*, no. 2 1957, p. 8. The figures seem too rounded for statistical accuracy. *JMJP*, in an editorial of Aug. 24, 1957, gave figures of 340,000 minorities cadres and 400,000 minorities party members; it is possible that a printing error occurred in *MTTC*.

84. "Great Victory of Nationalities Policy in Inner Mongolia," *JMJP*, May 1, 1962.

85. *Kwangsi jih-pao*, July 1, 1959.

86. NCNA (Lhasa), July 2, 1956.

87. Yeh Shang-chih, "Some Questions in the Work of Fostering Minority Nationality Cadres," *JMJP*, Feb. 6, 1957. According to KMJP, Dec. 7, 1956, 0.93 percent of the total Han Chinese population served as cadres, but only 0.59 percent of the total minority population, as of the end of 1955.

88. U.S. Department of State, *Biographical Directory No. 271: Directory of Party and Government Officials in Communist China* (Washington, July 20, 1960), pp. 8–11.

89. *MTTC*, no. 4 1958, pp. 7–8.

90. Yang Cheng-wu, "Concerning the Question of Minority Peoples All Studying Han Speech and Writing, and Using the Han Script to Wipe Out Illiteracy," *MTTC*, no. 1 1959, p. 13.

91. *MTTC*, no. 8 1958, pp. 8–11.

92. Chou Lin, "All Peoples Take the Great Road to Socialism," *MTTC*, no. 11 1958, p. 8.

93. Wang Kuo-hsüan, "Fraternal Nationalities of Hunan Province and Elsewhere Vigorously Abolish Decadent Customs," *MTTC*, no. 7 1958, p. 22 and ff.

94. *MTTC*, no. 8 1958, p. 15. See also Liang Chen-feng, "The Urgent Task of Bettering Living Standards," *MTTC*, no. 6 1958, pp. 7–8, and Wu Wan-yuan, "On the Ideology of Nationalities Special Characteristics," *MTTC*, no. 6 1958, p. 5.

95. Chiang Shan, "How Is It That the Lamas of the IMAR Are Engaging in Productive Labor?," *MTTC*, no. 8 1958, p. 18.

96. *MTTC*, no. 12 1958, p. 28.

97. *Chung-kuo ch'ing-nien* (Chinese youth), 2 (Peking, Oct. 1958), 17.

98. Ma-yi-nu-erh, "Implement the Marriage Law," *Sinkiang jih-pao*, Jan. 31, 1959, in *SCMP*, no. 2018, p. 5; Wu-ai-erh-ah-chi, "Temporary Regulations for Marriage Law Are Not Fit for Current Conditions of Sinkiang," ibid.

99. Li Ching-hsien, "Three," *MTTC*, no. 7 1958, p. 26.

100. *MTTC*, no. 5 1958, pp. 24–25.

101. Lung Yu-wu, "Revealing the Reactionary Viewpoint of the Book *Fraternal National Nationalities of Kweichow*," *MTTC*, no. 5 1958, p. 25.

102. NCNA (Peking), April 23, 1958.

103. Su Ko-ch'in, "Great Leap Forward in Nationalities Research Work," *MTTC*, no. 8 1958, p. 7.

104. Yeh Lin, "Great Leap Forward in Nationalities Entertainment Work," *MTTC*, no. 9 1958, pp. 9–10.

105. See, for example, *MTTC*, no. 10 1958, pp. 1–14; "Red Tree on Green Plain," *MTTC*, no. 10 1964, p. 27.

106. *MTTC*, no. 10 1958, p. 26.

107. *MTTC*, no. 11 1958, pp. 7–17.

108. *MTTC*, no. 11 1958, p. 7.

109. *MTTC*, no. 12 1958, p. 2.

110. *MTTC*, no. 12 1958, p. 3.

111. *MTTC*, no. 12 1958, p. 14.

112. *MTTC*, no. 12 1958, p. 22.

113. *MTTC*, no. 12 1958, p. 31.

114. *MTTC*, no. 3 1959, pp. 10–11.

115. *MTTC*, no. 12 1958, p. 9.

116. See collection of articles on this subject from *Hsi-tsang jih-pao* in *CB*, no. 490.

117. See, for example, the speech of Shirob Jaltso, "Pay Attention to Minorities Special Characteristics," to third session of First NPC (June 27, 1956) in *CB*, no. 409, p. 18; also speech of Bando Yanbe to third plenary session of Second CPPCC, in *JMJP*, March 23, 1957.

118. Intermarriage between Tibetans and Han had taken place for many years on a small scale in areas where the two cultures existed in close proximity. Tibetans, very different from the Muslim minorities on this matter, appear to have regarded this sort of intermarriage with equanimity. However, the relatively large influx of young Han males to parts of Tibet where Han-Tibetan contact had been slight seems to have created animosity.

119. Anna Louise Strong, *Tibetan Interviews* (Peking, New World Press, 1959), pp. 88–89.

120. See Chang Kuo-hua's report to the first session of the Preparatory Committee for the Tibet Autonomous Region (April 8, 1959), in *CB*, no. 555, pp. 8–10; Dalai Lama, *My Land*, p. 159.

121. For the Dalai Lama's description of his attempts to cope with the situation, see Dalai Lama, *My Land*, p. 136.

122. Ibid., chap. 10.

123. Ginsburgs and Mathos, *Communist China*, p. 118.

124. NCNA (Peking), March 28, 1959, in *CB*, no. 533.

125. Ibid.

126. For an official view of relations with the Tibetan elite, see *SCMP*, no. 2489, p. 20.

127. *SCMP*, no. 2075, p. 37.

128. *MTTC*, no. 8–9 1961, pp. 23–25.

129. See, for example, International Commission of Jurists, *The Question of Tibet and the Rule of Law* (Geneva, International Commission of Jurists, 1959).

130. *The Tibetan Review*, published twice monthly· in New Delhi.

131. Neville Maxwell, in his careful study *India's China War* (London, Jonathan Cape, 1970), pp. 104–105, presents evidence that certain Indian officials played an active role in planning the revolt. Even after the rebellion was suppressed, remaining Tibetan insurgents were supplied by airdrops made by the China Air Transport, based on Taiwan but funded by the U.S. Central Intelligence Agency (CIA). Allen Whiting, "The Use of Force in Foreign Policy by the People's Republic of China," *The Annals of the American Academy of Political and Social Science*, 402 (July 1972), 58. An ex-CIA agent reports that after the revolt, the agency trained Khamba refugees for guerrilla raids into Tibet. See Victor Marchetti and John Marks, *The CIA and the Cult of Intelligence* (New York, Alfred Knopf, 1974), pp. 115–116.

132. *NYT*, Nov. 16, 1963, p. 2; see also George Moseley, *A Sino-Soviet Cultural Frontier: The Ili Kazakh Autonomous Chou*, Harvard East Asian Monographs no. 22 (Cambridge, Mass., Harvard University Press, 1966), pp. 107–110.

133. T'o-hu-ti Ai-li-mo-fu, "Report on the Work of the Higher People's Court of the SUAR," *Sinkiang jih-pao*, Feb. 3, 1959, *SCMP*, no. 2018, pp. 16, 18. See also *NYT*, April 25, 1959.

134. Chou En-lai, "Report on the Work of the Government," speech to first session of the Third NPC (Dec. 30, 1964), in *SCMP*, no. 3370, p. 12.

135. See, for example, interview with Balkhash Bafin in *Sotsialistik Kazakhstan*, Sept. 27, 1963, trans. in *JPRS*, 21, 735; "Interview with Former Sinkiang Culture Minister" [Zia Samedi], *Kurier* (Vienna), May 8, 1967, in *Foreign Broadcast Information Service: Far East*, hereafter cited as *FBIS*, May 12, 1967; Rakhimov, "The Great Power Policy," pp. 116–118.

136. *MTTC*, no. 9 1958, pp. 14–15.

137. Wu Ching-hua, "Several Problems in the Liangshan Area's Struggle against the Family Branch System," *MTTC*, no. 5 1959, pp. 28–29.

138. Whether or not they were actually intended as assimilative by those who initiated them. It would appear that some of the Great Leap reforms in minority areas were undertaken simply to tighten party control over those areas, but were perceived by minorities as, and often were in fact, assimilative in nature.

7. Reaction and Resurgence, 1958–1965

1. *JMJP*, Feb. 24, 1959.

2. *MTTC*, no. 7 1959, pp. 1–5.

3. NCNA (Huhehot), Dec. 26, 1958, *SCMP* no. 1935, p. 14.

4. Yüan Po, "Seriously Carry Out Socialist-Communist Propaganda Education in Cultural Work among the Nationalities," *Yunnan jih-pao* (Yunnan daily), Dec. 24, 1958. *SCMP* no. 1982, p. 22.

5. Chiang Shan, "The Reform of the Nationalities Habits and Customs Should Be Done according to the Free Will of of the Masses," *MTTC*, no. 2 1959, pp. 5–7.

6. Ibid., p. 3.

7. Yang Ching-jen, "Ideas on Strengthening Planning Work for Minority Nationalities," *MTTC*, no. 2 1959, pp. 2–4.

8. Cheng Hung, "Nationalities Institutes Are Political Schools for Fostering Autonomy," *KMJP*, Dec. 17, 1958.

9. *JMJP*, June 14, 1959.

10. Ulanfu, "Quickly Develop the Livestock Industry," *Hung-ch'i* (Red flag), no. 5 1959, pp. 17–24.

11. *MTTC*, no. 6 1959, p. 15.

12. Ibid., p. 16.

13. Some of these conditions are discussed in Yang Hu-chen, "Let the Youth of the Interior Who Are Participating in the Construction of the Borderlands Take Root, Flower and Produce Fruit," *MTTC*, no. 8 1959, pp. 14–15.

14. Ibid., p. 16.

15. Wang Lien-fang, "On the Correct Attitude toward Minorities' Special Characteristics: Struggle for a Bigger Leap Forward in Border Areas Minorities Districts," *MTTC*, no. 3 1959, pp. 1–4.

16. See *MTTC*, no. 7 1959, p. 38; no. 10 1962, p. 48; no. 8 1959, p. 7.

17. *MTTC*, no. 3 1959, p. 11.

18. Ibid., pp. 10–11.

19. Communiqué of 26 August 1959, in *Eighth Plenary Session of the Eighth Central Committee of the CCP* (Peking, 1959), pp. 1–7.

20. "Overcome Rightist-Inclined Sentiment and Endeavor to Increase Production and Practice Economy," *JMJP*, Aug. 6, 1959, *SCMP* no. 2074, pp. 2–5.

21. NCNA (Peking), Sept. 2, 1959.

22. *MTTC*, no. 9 1959, pp. 1–4.

23. *MTTC*, no. 10 1959, p. 37.

24. *MTTC*, no. 3 1960, p. 10.

25. See ibid., pp. 1–10.

26. *MTTC*, no. 2 1960, pp. 14–15.

27. For example, Chao Chuo-yun, "Northwest Minority Nationality's Situation Is Very Good," *MTTC*, no. 2 1960, pp. 10–11.

28. Ibid.

29. Kao Feng, "Great Victory of the Party's Nationalities Policy in Ch'inghai," *Hung-ch'i*, no. 9 1960, pp. 17–23.

30. Major collections of Chinese Communist materials outside China that do not have these issues include the Harvard, Columbia, and University of Washington libraries in the U.S., the University of British Columbia and University of Toronto libraries in Canada, the Union Research Institute and Hong Kong University libraries in Hong Kong, and the Toyo Bunko and Japanese Diet libraries in Japan.

31. *MTTC*, no. 4 1961, p. 32.

32. See, for example, Wang Lien-fang, "On the Correct Attitude toward Minority Nationalities' Special Characteristics: Struggle for a Larger Great Leap Forward in Border Area Minority Nationality Disticts," *MTTC*, no. 3 1959, pp. 2–4.

33. This policy is discussed in some detail in Yao Hsin, "Correctly Handle Nationality Relations, Continuously Strengthen Nationalities Solidarity," *MTTC*, no. 9 1962, pp. 2–4.

34. See, for example, Hou Fang-yueh, "On the Investigation of Minority Nationalities History," *MTTC*, no. 3 1959, pp. 7–8.

35. *MTTC*, no. 7 1961, pp. 2–9.
36. *MTTC*, no. 4 1961, pp. 2–5; no. 5 1961, pp. 16–18.
37. *MTTC*, no. 6 1961, p. 4.
38. *MTTC*, no. 6 1961, pp. 8–9.
39. *MTTC*, no. 5–6 1962, pp. 2–6.
40. *MTTC*, no. 1 1962, pp. 9–11.
41. Ibid., pp. 13–15.
42. *Ti-li* (Geography), no. 3 1961, pp. 103–117.
43. *MTTC*, no. 1 1962, pp. 9–11; see also ibid., pp. 12–16.
44. Ibid., p. 9.
45. Ibid.
46. Lhasa Radio, April 2, 1961, quoted in *CS*, 1.1 (May 15, 1961), 2.
47. Lhasa Radio, April 4, 1961; quoted ibid.
48. For a complete analysis of this period see ibid., pp. 1–12.
49. Literally, to "turn the body" or "turn over," i.e., to begin a new life, socialist-style. Its connotations include land redistribution, adoption of modern scientific techniques, and abolition of illiteracy.
50. Wang Feng, "Progressively Implement the Party's Nationalities Policy," *MTTC*, no. 10–11 1961, pp. 2–9.
51. Liu Ch'un, "Raise High the Three Red Banners, Struggle to Obtain New Victories in Nationalities Work in 1962," *MTTC*, no. 1 1962, pp. 2–4.
52. Lü Chien-jen, "Continue Good United Front Work with Nationalities Religious and Upper Strata," *MTTC*, no. 2–3 1962, pp. 2–5.
53. *MTTC*, no. 1 1962, pp. 2–4.
54. *SCMP*, no. 2645, p. 46.
55. *SCMP*, no. 2775, p. 16.
56. Chang Chih-yi, "Correctly Know and Carry Out the Party's Policy on Freedom of Religion," *MTTC*, no. 4 1962, pp. 2–5.
57. *MTTC*, no. 9 1962, p. 10.
58. *MTTC*, no. 7 1962, pp. 2–6.
59. *MTTC*, no. 6 1961, pp. 22–23.
60. Fei Hsin, "Correctly Handle Nationality Relations, Continuously Strengthen Nationalities Solidarity," *MTTC*, no. 9 1962, pp. 2–4.
61. *MTTC*, no. 4 1961, pp. 6–9; no. 7 1961, pp. 22–26.
62. *MTTC*, no. 8–9 1961, pp. 1–19 are devoted to material publicizing this campaign.
63. *KMJP*, Nov. 21, 1961, in *SCMP*, no. 2649, p. 11.
64. Su K'o-ch'in, "Report on the Investigation of Minority Nationalities Social History," *MTTC*, no. 5 1961, p. 5.
65. Ibid., p. 8.
66. Ibid., p. 5.
67. Sun Wen-liang, "Liaoning Arranges a Scientific Conference on Manchu History," *MTTC*, no. 12 1961, pp. 33–34.
68. *MTTC*, no. 10–11 1961, pp. 24–25.
69. *MTTC*, no. 9 1962, pp. 30–32.
70. Ch'en Kuo-ch'iang, "Koxinga and the Kaoshan," *MTTC*, no. 1 1962, pp. 5–8.
71. See, for example, Hu Chao-heng, "Development of the Mongolian Spoken and Written Langauge in the IMAR," *MTTC*, no. 8 1962, pp. 6–9.
72. Fu Mou-chi, "An Opinion on Some Questions regarding New Terms and Technical Language in Minority Languages," *MTTC*, no. 3 1962, pp. 25–27; 36–37.
73. See Snow, *Red Star*, pp. 47–48. The term is also used as a generalized form of endearment.
74. *MTTC*, no. 8 1962, pp. 14–15; see also ibid., pp. 16–18, for similar accounts.

75. *MTTC*, no. 3 1962, pp. 18–20.
76. *MTTC*, no. 9 1962, pp. 11–13.
77. *MTTC*, no. 1 1962, pp. 38–40.
78. *MTTC*, no. 9 1962, p. 10.
79. *MTTC*, no. 10 1962, pp. 2–6; English text in *PR*, no. 39 1962.
80. *MTTC*, no. 11 1962, pp. 2–6.
81. See, e.g., *MTTC*, no. 10 1962, p. 6; no. 12 1962, pp. 2–7; no. 1 1963, pp. 2–8; no. 2–3 1963, pp. 2–7.
82. *MTTC*, no. 12 1962, p. 6.
83. *MTTC*, no. 12 1962, pp. 8–9.
84. Ibid., p. 9.
85. *MTTC*, no. 2–3 1963, pp. 8–9.
86. *MTTC*, no. 12 1962, pp. 19–23.
87. *MTTC*, no. 5 1963, p. 2.
88. *MTTC*, no. 11 1963, p. 11.
89. "Strengthen Nationalities Press Work, Put Politics First, Put Quality First," *MTTC*, no. 1 1963, pp. 9–12.
90. Yü Chieh, "Increase Knowledge, Do Nationalities Work Well," *MTTC*, no. 2–3 1963, pp. 8–9.
91. *MTTC*, no. 1 1963, pp. 17–19.
92. *MTTC*, no. 4 1963, pp. 2–5.
93. Ibid., pp. 5–8.
94. *MTTC*, no. 5 1963, pp. 2–4.
95. Text of this directive translated in Richard Baum and Frederick Teiwes, *Ssu-ch'ing: The Socialist Education Movement of 1962–1966* (Berkeley, Center for Chinese Studies, 1968), pp. 58–61.
96. *MTTC*, no. 5 1963, pp. 2–4.
97. *MTTC*, no. 6 1963, pp. 2–21.
98. *MTTC*, no. 5 1963, pp. 5–6.
99. *SCMP* no. 3007, p. 7.
100. *MTTC*, no. 6 1963, pp. 27–32.
101. Huang Ch'eng-liu, "Snow Mountain, Red Pine," *MTTC*, no. 7 1963, pp. 2–10.
102. Ibid., pp. 8–9.
103. *MTTC*, no. 7 1963, pp. 19–20.
104. "Begin Class Education among Minority Nationalities with Great Efforts," *MTTC*, no. 8 1963, pp. 2–5.
105. Ibid., pp. 9–11.
106. Ibid., pp. 12–16.
107. A translation of this directive can be found in Baum and Teiwes, *Ssu-ch'ing*, pp. 72–94.
108. See, for example, Yang Ch'ing-jen, "Commemorate the Fifth Anniversary of the Ninghsia Hui Autonomous Region," *MTTC*, no. 10–11 1963, pp. 2–6; Yang Chih-lin, "Great Victory of the Party's Policy of Nationalities Autonomy in Ch'inghai," *MTTC*, no. 12 1963, pp. 2–5.
109. Huang Lin, "The Road Becomes Broader," *MTTC*, no. 9 1963, pp. 14–17, 48.
110. *MTTC*, no. 9 1963, pp. 36–42.
111. *MTTC*, no. 12 1963, pp. 6–13.
112. *MTTC*, no. 1 1964, p. 24; no. 5 1964, pp. 2–21.
113. As described in the model evolved in the Yenpien Korean Autonomous Chou. See *MTTC*, no. 4 1961, pp. 6–9; above, Chap. V, section on regional progress.
114. See, for example, *MTTC*, no. 4 1964, pp. 12–13.
115. *MTTC*, no. 5 1964, p. 21.

116. Ibid., pp. 2–4.
117. See *MTTC*, no. 5 1964, p. 4.
118. Ibid., p. 21.
119. Liu Ch'un, "The Present-Day Nationalities Question in Our Country and the Class Struggle," *Hung-ch'i*, Dec. 1964; excerpts in *MTTC*, no. 6 1964, pp. 2–9.
120. *MTTC*, no. 10 1964, pp. 2–4.
121. See, for example, *MTTC*, no. 7 1964, p. 2; no. 9 1964, p. 4; no. 11–12 1964, pp. 4–7.
122. *MTTC*, no. 11–12 1964, pp. 3–7.
123. Ibid., p. 7.
124. *MTTC*, no. 1 1965, p. 35.
125. *MTTC*, no. 5–6 1965, p. 35.
126. *MTTC*, no. 2 1965, pp. 25–26.
127. *MTTC*, no. 1 1965, p. 19.
128. *SCMP*, no. 3370, p. 18.
129. *MTTC*, no. 2 1965, pp. 2–11. Emphasis mine.
130. See *MTTC*, no. 3 1965, pp. 2–14.
131. Ibid., pp. 2–4.
132. *MTTC*, no. 5–6 1965, pp. 16–17.
133. "In Memory of Norman Bethune," "Serve the People," and "The Foolish Old Man Who Moved the Mountain."
134. *MTTC*, no. 5–6 1965, pp. 16–17.
135. Ibid., pp. 26–27.
136. *MTTC*, no. 7 1965, pp. 2–9.
137. *MTTC*, no. 8 1965, pp. 35–36.
138. *MTTC*, no. 4 1965, p. 8.
139. *MTTC*, no. 8 1965, pp. 2–34.
140. *SCMP*, no. 3370, p. 27.
141. Marchetti and Marks, *CIA and the Cult*, p. 117.
142. *CB*, no. 775; see also MTTC, no. 9 1965, pp. 1–29.
143. *MTTC*, no. 10 1965, p. 8.
144. Ibid., p. 5.
145. *SCMP*, no. 2889, p. 22.
146. *SCMP*, no. 3757, p. 20.
147. Radio Sining, Nov. 22, 1965; Nov. 30, 1965.
148. *Chinese Communist Who's Who* (Taipei, 1970), II, 159–160.
149. *JMJP*, Nov. 20, 1965.
150. *Hsing-tao jih-pao* (Hong Kong), Nov. 19, 1965.
151. In making this comparison, I am relying on the analysis of the campaign in Han areas given in Baum and Teiwes.

8. The Cultural Revolution, 1966–1969

1. Name withheld by request. The young man and several of his acquaintances had been assigned to an agricultural cooperative in Inner Mongolia after graduation from junior middle school. Among other hardships, he mentioned poor food, cold weather, and lack of recreational facilities.

2. A rather complicated purge, linked with the attacks on Yang Hsien-chien. On Dec. 20, 1964, *JMJP* reprinted, in order to attack it, an article Yang had written in 1941. In it Yang praised Lo Man, which was one of Li Wei-han's pseudonyms (*SCMP* no. 3381, p. 9). By the reasoning "the friend of my enemy is also my enemy," Li seemed to be in trouble. Further confirmation came the next day when Chou En-Lai noted in a speech to the NPC that "quite a number of people" had "actually advocated capitulationism in United Front work" (*SCMP* no. 3370,

pp. 9–12). In March of 1965 it was revealed that Hsü Ping had become head of the UFWD, a post which had been held by Li since 1944.

3. Peking, *Chui ch'iung-k'ou* (Pursue the desperate foe), no. 4, May 20, 1967, in *SCMP* no. 3970, p. 1.

4. "Completely Purge Liu Shao-ch'i for his Counterrevolutionary Revisionist Crimes in the United Front, Nationalities and Religious Work," pamphlet compiled by the Red Army Corps of the K'ang-ta Commune of the Central Nationalities Institute, Peking, April 15, 1967, in U.S. Consulate General, Hong Kong, *Selections from China Mainland Magazines* (hereafter cited as *SCMM*), no. 645, p. 11.

5. For a pre–Cultural Revolution Tibetan view of Prime Minister Lukangwa's relations with the Chinese, see Dalai Lama, *My Land*, pp. 92–97.

6. Canton, *Chih-tien chiang-shan* (Surveying rivers and mountains), Oct. 27, 1967, in *SCMP*, no. 4086, pp. 6–10.

7. *SCMM*, no. 645, p. 17. Emphasis mine.

8. Ibid.

9. Ibid., p. 18.

10. Ibid.

11. Ibid., p. 19.

12. Canton, *Wen-ko feng-yun* (Cultural Revolution wind cloud), no. 2 Feb. 1968, in *SCMP*, no. 4151, p. 3.

13. *Wen-hui pao* (Shanghai), Sept. 6, 1968, *SCMP*, no. 4268, p. 8.

14. *SCMP*, no. 3970, p. 1.

15. Ibid., p. 2.

16. See above, chap. 4, no. 44 and n. 46.

17. Canton, *Chih-k'an nan-yüeh* (Surveying south Kwangtung), no. 3, Oct. 27, 1967, in *SCMP*, no. 4057, pp. 6–7; see also Kansu Radio, Jan. 25, 1968.

18. Huhehot Radio, Aug. 2, 1966.

19. Ibid., Aug. 23, 1966.

20. See, for example, ibid., Sept. 11, 1966.

21. Ibid., Sept. 18, 1966.

22. *The Standard* (Hong Kong), Jan. 27, 1967, p. 1. The report cited the Japanese news agency Kyodo, whose Peking correspondent had photographed the wall newspaper.

23. Peking, *Ts'ai-mao hung-ch'i*, quoted by Radio Sofia, Feb. 18, 1967.

24. Huhehot Radio, March 15, 1967.

25. Ibid., March 18, 1967.

26. Ibid., March 29, 1967.

27. Text in *CB*, no. 852, pp. 118–119.

28. *JMJP*, Jan. 15, 1968.

29. Cf. Wang En-mao's remarks at the SUAR's tenth anniversary celebration, above, chap. VII, section on the 10th Plenum and Socialist Education.

30. *Kung-jen chan-pao* (Workers' combat news), n.d., tr. *JPRS*, 42,933 (Oct. 12, 1967).

31. Certain commentators occasionally list Wu T'ao, a member of the IMAR Revolutionary Committee, as a Mongol. I have been unable to confirm this in any Chinese source. Later, as party committees began to be formed at provincial level, it was customary to list the nationalities of non-Han committee members. See, for example, the name list for Tibet in *SCMP*, no. 4969, p. 31, and for Ninghsia in ibid., p. 41. By contrast, the IMAR name list does not name Wu as a Mongol. Paojihletai, who was later elected a full member of the Tenth Central Committee, was described as having been in the forefront in introducing grain production to a pasturelands commune. Huhehot Radio, Nov. 1, 1967.

32. Ibid., Nov. 17, 1967.

33. Ibid., Nov. 8, 1967.

34. *JPRS*, 42,933 (1967); Huhehot Radio, April 15, 1968.

35. Huhehot Radio, Feb. 26, 1968.

36. See, e.g., ibid., Nov. 11, 1968.

37. Belgrade Radio, October 6, 1966.

38. *T'ien-shan feng-huo* (*TSFH*; T'ien-shan beacon fire), no. 4–5, Jan. 15, 1968, *CB*, no. 855, p. 1.

39. Ibid.

40. Ibid., p. 3.

41. See the description of the Jan. 26 incident, ibid., pp. 5–8.

42. Reprinted in *CB*, no. 852, pp. 54–55.

43. Regulations, dated Feb. 11, 1967, reprinted in *CB*, no. 852, pp. 68–70.

44. Ceteka (Prague), March 1, 1967.

45. One such description may be found in *TSFH*, Jan. 15, 1968, *CB*, no. 855, pp. 5–8.

46. See, for example, "Urgent Notice of the CCP Central Committee and the State Council on the Need for Workers Aiding Construction in the Hinterland and Frontierland to Participate in the Great Proletarian Cultural Revolution in Their Own Localities," dated Feb. 11, 1967, reprinted in *CB*, no. 852, p. 85.

47. *TSFH*, Jan. 15, 1968, *CB*, no. 855, p. 13.

48. Moscow Radio, Dec. 10, 1967.

49. See, for example, *TSFH*, Jan. 15, 1968, *CB*, no. 855, pp. 9–11.

50. Ibid., *CB*, no. 855, p. 15.

51. NCNA Peking, Jan. 1, 1968.

52. See, for example, P. M. H. Jones, "Autonomous Wang," *FEER*, Dec. 28, 1967, pp. 569–570.

53. See, for example, Urumchi Radio, Dec. 28, 1968.

54. Ibid., Sept. 5, 1968.

55. Interview data. The informant, an ethnic Russian in his early thirties, had lived in Ining since childhood. Though he was literate in Russian and could speak Uighur, he knew only a few words of Chinese and had had very little formal education. He left China legally in May of 1972.

56. Reuters, Hong Kong, January 29, 1969.

57. The incident took place on April 30, and Chou En-lai's directive is dated May 2. The directive is referred to in Chiangmen, *Hung-ch'i t'ung-hsün* (Red flag bulletin), no. 14, May 26, 1968, *SCMP*, no. 4201, p. 16, but is not reprinted in full.

58. See, for example, *Wen-hui pao* (Shanghai), May 26, 1968, *SCMP*, no. 4207, pp. 16–17.

59. *CS*, 7.5 (March 19, 1969), 11.

60. William Whitson, *The Chinese High Command* (New York, Praeger, 1973), p. 297.

61. Ibid., p. 118.

62. NCNA Urumchi, Sept. 6, 1968, *SCMP*, no. 4256, pp. 17–20.

63. Urumchi Radio, Dec. 28, 1969.

64. *NYT*, Oct. 9, 1966, p. 27.

65. NCNA Peking, Sept. 29, 1966.

66. *Tibetan News Agency* (hereafter cited as TNA, London), 4.10 (July 6, 1967), 1.

67. Ibid.

68. John Gittings, "Sound and Fury in Tibet," *FEER*, Sept. 12, 1968, p. 519.

69. TNA, July 6, 1967, p. 2.

70. *Lhasa Leaflet*, Jan. 27, 1967, *SCMP*, no. 219 S, p. 23; *Lhasa Leaflet*, Feb. 12, 1967, *SCMP*, no. 204 S, p. 18.

71. Gittings, "Sound and Fury," p. 518.

72. *Lhasa Leaflet,* Jan. 27, 1967, *SCMP,* no. 219 S, p. 23.
73. Sofia Radio, March 16, 1967, quoting *Lhasa Daily,* no date given.
74. Quoted in *NYT,* Sept. 10, 1967, sec. 4, p. 5.
75. See Canton, *Yi-yüeh feng-pao* (January storm), March 23–24, 1968, in *SCMP,* no. 4150, p. 18; Canton, *Kwang-yin hung-ch'i* (Canton printing red flag), March 5, 1958, in *SCMP,* no. 4162, p. 10.
76. *NYT,* Sept. 10, 1967, sec. 4, p. 5.
77. Central Committee directive of Sept. 18, 1967, referred to by Jen Jung in June 1968. *SCMM,* no. 622, p. 2.
78. See Gittings, "Sound and Fury," p. 518; "Important Instructions of Premier Chou En-lai, Ch'en Po-ta, K'ang Sheng and Other Leaders on the Question of Tibet," June 6, 1968, *SCMM,* no. 622, p. 2.
79. Whitson, *Chinese High Command,* p. 197.
80. *CS,* 7.5 (March 19, 1969), 11.
81. Whitson, *Chinese High Command,* p. 332.
82. As Chang Kuo-hua's deputy, Jen had been unacceptable to radicals from the beginning. See, for example, "Cable to Chiang Ching and Others from the United Headquarters of the Tibetan Proletarian Revolutionary Union," *Chinese Communist Affairs: Facts and Features* (Taipei), 1.1 (Nov. 1, 1967), 22–23.
83. NCNA (Lhasa), Sept. 6, 1968, *SCMP,* no. 4256, pp. 13–16.
84. Lhasa Radio, Feb. 19, 1969.
85. *JMJP,* April 12, 1969, *SCMP,* no. 4401, p. 3.
86. *JMJP,* Jan. 16, 1969.
87. *JMJP,* Nov. 16, 1968.
88. Nanning Radio, Jan. 24, 1967.
89. Dated Nov. 18, 1967, text in Chiangmen, *Hung-se tsao-fan-che* (Red rebels), no. 7, Dec. 4, 1967, *SCMP,* no. 4157, pp. 1–3.
90. See, for example, Wuchow, *Shan-ch'eng lieh-huo* (Fierce flames over the mountain country), no. 17, March 1, 1968, *SCMP,* no. 4154, p. 12; Liuchou, *Szu-erh-erh t'ung-hsün* (April 22 Bulletin), no. 6, May 29, 1968, *SCMP,* no. 4202, p. 9; Canton, *Hsi-chiang nu-t'ao* (Angry waves of west river), June 1968, *SCMP,* no. 4213, pp. 4–5; ibid., 4215, pp. 1–6.
91. Personal communication, Mr. Nicholas Platt, United States Consulate General, Hong Kong, July 12, 1968.
92. *Hsi-ch'iang nu-t'ao,* June 1968, *SCMP,* no. 4220, p. 9.
93. NCNA, Nanning, March 1, 1968.
94. Liuchou, *Liuchou kung-tsung* (Workers' summary), no. 7, July 12, 1968, *SCMP,* no. 4227, p. 8.
95. Text of this telegram, marked "specially urgent," and dated June 13, 1968, in *Liuchou kung-tsung,* no. 7, *SCMP,* no. 4226, pp. 1–3.
96. For example, Chou En-lai's telephone call to Kwangsi on June 19, ordering the restoration of railway traffic before June 22. Text in *SCMP,* no. 4226, p. 3.
97. Canton, *Ta-chün pao* (Grand army bulletin), no. 1, July 1968, *SCMP,* 4234, pp. 7–11; ibid., 4235, pp. 5–7; *Hsi-chiang nu-t'ao,* no. 2 (Wuhan edition), July 1968, *SCMP,* no. 4241, pp. 1–5; ibid., 4249, pp. 1–11.
98. Dispatch received by Canton East Wind News Agency, July 3, 1968. No title, name of publisher, or place of publication. *SCMP,* no. 4224, p. 1.
99. NCNA Nanning, Aug. 25, 1967, *SCMP,* no. 4248, p. 15.
100. NCNA Peking, Aug. 27, 1967, *SCMP,* no. 4249, p. 23.
101. NCNA Nanning, Aug. 27, 1967, *SCMP,* no. 4249, pp. 17–19.
102. Tillman Durdin, "Continuing Turmoil in Kwangsi Poses Major Issue for Maoists," *NYT,* July 14, 1968, pp. 1, 5.
103. Though it subsequently attained a foreign border as a result of administrative changes attendant on the reduction in size of Inner Mongolia in 1969.

104. Yinch'uan Radio, Feb. 12, 1968.

105. Yinch'uan Radio, May 4, 1968, discussed the first anniversary of this "victorious struggle."

106. Yinch'uan Radio, April 11, 1968.

107. Kunming Radio, Nov. 30, 1968.

108. Summarized in NCNA (Peking), May 7, 1968.

109. T'ien Pao, "The Counterrevolutionary Revisionist Li Ching-ch'uan's Towering Crimes in Nationality Work in Szechwan," as broadcast by Kweiyang Radio, Oct. 7, 1967.

110. Probably a reference to the Li, the vast majority of whom seem to be surnamed Wang.

111. Haikow Radio, Sept. 23, 1971.

112. Canton Radio, Kwangtung provincial service, April 9, 1968.

113. NCNA (Canton), June 10, 1968, *SCMP*, no. 4199, p. 8.

114. NCNA (Peking), Aug. 18, 1968.

115. Whitson, *Chinese High Command*, p. 219.

116. See, for example, *JMJP*, March 9, 1969, in *CB*, no. 876, pp. 22–24.

117. Compare the minority nationalities members of the NPC mentioned in *Jen-min shou-ts'e's* 1955 edition with those in the 1965 edition, for example.

118. A strange thing to be purged for in 1960, especially in view of the fact that Liu regained power in Shansi during the Cultural Revolution through being championed by a radical Red Guard group. In 1970 he fell from power again, seemingly the victim of a conservative resurgence. It may well be that his purge in 1960 represented an instance of left deviation being declared "rightist in essence."

119. Stuart Schram, *Mao Tse-tung*, p. 236, lists several instances of Mao's desire to win back Outer Mongolia. MPR leaders have recently indicated they feel Mao would still like to do so. *FEER*, Dec. 13, 1974, p. 35.

120. Sining Radio, June 24, 1967.

121. See, for example, Peking Radio, July 10, 1967.

122. Sining Radio, August 13, 1967.

123. *South China Morning Post* (Hong Kong), Oct. 30, 1967, p. 17.

124. See, for example, Sining Radio, Aug. 26, 1966.

125. Sining Radio, May 27, 1967.

126. On June 24, 1967, Sining Radio announced that the party central committee had officially approved the preparatory committee for the provincial revolutionary committee on June 19.

127. NCNA (Lhasa), June 10, 1970.

128. *CS*, 9.10 (Sept. 7, 1971), 14.

129. Lhasa Radio, Feb. 18, 1975. This method of taxation was said to be still in existence as of Feb. 1975.

130. Radio Haikow, Nov. 22, 1970; Radio Kunming, Dec. 11, 1970.

131. *NYT*, June 21, 1970, p. 3.

132. English text in *PR*, 12.18 (April 30, 1969), 36–39.

133. Membership list for the Ninth Central Committee may be found in ibid., pp. 47–48.

134. In August 1969, T'ien Pao was revealed to be a member of the TAR revolutionary committee and subsequently became a secretary of the TAR party committee as well. No reasons were given for his transfer.

135. This draft appeared in Hong Kong in mimeographed form during the fall of 1970. It was said to have been approved at the Second Plenum of the Ninth Central Committee (Aug. 23–Sept. 6, 1970) and was now being circulated so that the masses could study it and make comments. Its authenticity cannot be definitely established, although there are striking similarities with the version actually adopted on Jan. 17, 1975. First, like the 1975 document, it has 30 articles (as opposed to 106 in the 1954 constitution); second, both it and the 1975 document describe

China as a socialist state of the dictatorship of the proletariat (the 1954 constitution had termed China a democratic state); and third, neither 1970 or 1975 documents provide for a chairman of the CPR. The most salient difference between 1970 and 1975 versions is that the 1970 draft names Lin Piao as Mao's successor and the 1975 document, for obvious reasons, does not.

136. Radio Kunming, Aug. 22, 1971, quoted in *CS*, 9.10 (Oct. 7, 1971), 14.

137. *JMJP*, May 22, 1971.

138. Radio Urumchi, Dec. 10, 1970.

139. See, e.g., Wang Ming, *China: Cultural Revolution or Counterrevolutionary Coup?* (Moscow, Novosti Press Agency Publishing House, 1969), pp. 33–34; Radio Peace and Progress (Moscow), Sept. 18, 1968.

140. Saifudin (Uighur), T'ien Pao, Pa Sang, and Yang Tung-sheng (Tibetans), Paojihletai (Mongol), Wei Kuo-ch'ing (Chuang), Wang Chih-ch'iang and Chao Chih-ch'iang (Hui). I am unable to explain the similarity in the given names of the two Hui. Wang had previously held positions in the Kansu government, Chao, a woman, in the Shantung government. Both were named deputy secretaries of the Ninghsia party committee in August 1971. See *SCMP*, no. 4969, p. 41, for complete name list.

141. He subsequently died, aged 74, of heart disease. *JMJP*, Dec. 20, 1968.

142. NCNA (Peking), May 6, 1970, *SCMP*, no. 4656, p. 149.

143. NCNA (Peking), May 1, 1970.

144. NCNA (Peking), Oct. 1, 1970.

145. NCNA (Peking), July 28, 1969.

146. For example, the Bairam festival, as reported by NCNA (Peking), Dec. 22, 1968, *SCMP*, no. 4327, p. 14.

9. After the Cultural Revolution, 1970–1975

1. "Strengthen the Unity of the Masses of Nationalities and Consolidate the Dictatorship of the Proletariat," *JMJP*, Sept. 6, 1969.

2. "If Army and People Are United as One, Who in the World Can Match Them?" NCNA (Peking), July 30, 1969, *SCMP*, no. 4470, p. 18.

3. "Family Study Classes in Mao Tse-tung Thought Thrive in Minority Nationality Production Brigade in Southwest China," NCNA (Kunming), Aug. 1, 1969, *SCMP*, no. 4471, p. 19.

4. Ibid., p. 20.

5. *JMJP*, Feb. 8, 1970.

6. NCNA (Peking), Feb. 10, 1970.

7. Whitson, *Chinese High Command*, charts C and D. Yu had been transferred from Fourth to Second Field Army in 1937.

8. Whitson, *Chinese High Command*, chart E.

9. See chapter 8, n. 82, above.

10. Lhasa Radio, July 2, 1971.

11. Whitson, *Chinese High Command*, chart C.

12. Ibid., p. 130 and chart C.

13. United States Central Intelligence Agency, *Directory of Officials of the PRC*, A 73–35, Jan. 1974, pp. 35, 147.

14. Ibid., pp. 30, 123.

15. Whitson, *Chinese High Command*, p. 122.

16. Whitson, *Chinese High Command*, p. 256.

17. *Chung-fa*, 1972 (12), trans. in *Chinese Law and Government*, 5.3–4 (Fall–Winter, 1972–73), 31–32.

18. Lhasa Radio, April 20, 1971, and June 3, 1971.

19. *PR*, 14.25 (June 18, 1971), 20, 22.

20. *PR*, 15.3 (Jan. 21, 1972), 4.

21. *Hindustan Standard,* Oct. 25, 1973, reprinted in *Tibetan Review* (TR), 8.9–10 (Oct.–Nov. 1973), 21.

22. "Dalai Tribute to Mao," *TR,* 8.9–10 (Oct.–Nov. 1973), 22.

23. "Dalai Lama Hopeful of Return to Tibet," ibid., p. 22.

24. "Tibet and the Superpowers," ibid., p. 4.

25. *The Observer* (London), Oct. 28, 1973.

26. Marchetti and Marks, *CIA and the Cult,* p. 116.

27. See, for example, *TNA* (London), March 31, 1973.

28. For example, *TR,* 8.9–10 (Oct.–Nov. 1973), p. 19.

29. *JMJP,* Nov. 1, 1971.

30. "Use Marxism-Leninism and Mao Tse-tung's Thought to Train Minorities," *KMJP,* Nov. 22, 1971, *SCMP,* no. 5025, p. 117.

31. NCNA (Sining), Nov. 21, 1971, *SCMP,* no. 5026, p. 201.

32. NCNA (Nanning), Oct. 28, 1972, *SCMP,* no. 5252, p. 118.

33. NCNA (Kunming), May 18, 1972, *SCMP,* no. 5143, p. 20.

34. *JMJP,* Aug. 6, 1972.

35. NCNA (Peking), Feb. 13, 1972, *SCMP,* no. 5081, p. 27.

36. *KMJP,* Oct. 19, 1972, *SCMP,* no. 5241, p. 71.

37. NCNA (Peking), Dec. 13, 1972, *SCMP,* no. 5282, p. 173.

38. See, for example, *MTTC,* no. 3 1957, pp. 18–20; *MTTC,* no. 8–9 1961, p. 1.

39. Lhasa Radio, March 16, 1972.

40. Lhasa Radio, Oct. 16, 1972.

41. Kunming Radio, June 12, 1972.

42. *KMJP,* Jan. 29, 1972, *SCMP,* no. 5074, p. 186.

43. Sining Radio, June 15, 1972.

44. *KMJP,* Jan. 29, 1972, *SCMP,* no. 5074, p. 189.

45. *PR,* 17.38 (Sept. 20, 1974), 22.

46. Peking Radio, Aug. 3, 1974.

47. Urumchi Radio, June 15, 1973.

48. Urumchi Radio, Dec. 14, 1974.

49. Peking Radio, Aug. 9, 1974.

50. Urumchi Radio, May 14, 1972.

51. *JMJP,* May 23, 1972.

52. Urumchi Radio, Oct. 9, 1974.

53. Kunming Radio, June 16, 1972.

54. Urumchi Radio, May 14, 1972.

55. *PR,* 15.26 (June 30, 1972), 23.

56. *PR,* 12.25 (June 20, 1969), 28.

57. NCNA (Kunming), May 17, 1972, *SCMP,* no. 5143, pp. 23–24.

58. Lhasa Radio, Aug. 6, 1974.

59. NCNA (Lhasa), July 17, 1972.

60. NCNA (Nanning), May 10, 1974, *SCMP,* no. 5618, p. 71.

61. *PR,* 17.34 (Aug. 23, 1974), 23.

62. *JMJP,* March 22, 1973, *SCMP,* 5346, p. 1.

63. See, for example, NCNA (Nanning), July 23, 1972, *SCMP,* no. 5187, p. 111.

64. NCNA (Urumchi), May 17, 1972, *SCMP,* no. 5143, pp. 22–23.

65. *KMJP,* Oct. 26, 1972, *SCMP,* no. 5252, pp. 151–152.

66. *KMJP,* Nov. 10, 1972, *SCMP,* no. 5259, p. 17.

67. NCNA (Lhasa), March 22, 1973, *SCMP,* no. 5346, pp. 18–19.

68. *KMJP,* Oct. 26, 1972, *SCMP,* no. 5252, pp. 151–152.

69. NCNA (Kunming), June 30, 1972, *SCMP,* no. 5172, p. 101.

70. See, for example, the rehabilitation of a Mongol cadre in Ch'inghai mentioned by Sining Radio, May 18, 1972, and that of a Hui cadre in Kansu discussed

in *KMJP*, Nov. 10, 1972, *SCMP*, no. 5259, p. 17. Wang To, a Mongol who had been a member of the IMAR party committee until 1967, also returned to power at this time.

71. *KMJP*, Nov. 10, 1972, *SCMP*, no. 5259, pp. 17–18.

72. NCNA (Urumchi), May 17, 1972, *SCMP*, no. 5143, pp. 22–23.

73. For example, Ulanfu and Ngapo attended International Labor Day ceremonies in Peking on May 1, 1975 (*PR*, 18.19 [May 9, 1975], 5) while Li and Ngapo attended a rally in Peking the next day to celebrate the liberation of Saigon (ibid., p. 8).

74. *JMJP*, Nov. 6, 1974.

75. Peking Radio, July 27, 1973.

76. *PR*, 16.35–36 (Sept. 7, 1973), 9.

77. See above, chap. 8.

78. *PR*, 14.25 (June 18, 1971), 20, 22.

79. *KMJP*, April 6, 1971.

80. Kunming Radio, Sept. 22, 1974.

81. Peking Radio, Sept. 1, 1973.

82. Nanning Radio, Jan. 10, 1974; Huhehot Radio, Nov. 23, 1974.

83. Lanchow Radio, April 30, 1974.

84. Lhasa Radio, June 6, 1974.

85. *PR*, 17.29 (July 7, 1974), 9–11.

86. Lhasa Radio, Jan. 5, 1975.

87. "People's Communes Set Up in 90 Percent of Tibet's Townships," *PR*, 17.45 (Nov. 8, 1974), 5.

88. NCNA (Lhasa), March 24, 1973, *SCMP*, 5346, p. 103.

89. Peking Radio, Aug. 9, 1974.

90. Peking Radio, May 9, 1974.

91. Lhasa Radio, Aug. 6, 1974.

92. Lhasa Radio, Nov. 20, 1974.

93. Lhasa Radio, Oct. 23, 1974.

94. Lhasa Radio, Nov. 22, 1974.

95. Lhasa Radio, Dec. 1, 1974.

96. Professor Larry W. Moses, Department of Uralic and Altaic Studies, University of Indiana, personal communication, Jan. 2, 1975. Opinions expressed are those of Dr. Moses and Thubten Jigme Norbu. The latter is the brother of the Dalai Lama.

97. See *PR*, 17.33 (Aug. 17, 1974), 22, also Nanking Radio, June 27, 1974; Ch'engtu Radio, July 23, 1974; Lhasa Radio, Dec. 22, 1974.

98. Peking Radio, Oct. 18, 1974.

99. Lhasa Radio, Jan. 4, 1975.

100. Lhasa Radio, Dec. 17, 1974.

101. Lhasa Radio, Dec. 10, 1975.

102. Peking Radio, Oct. 15, 1974.

103. "Analysis of Soviet Revisionists' Policy of 'National Rapprochement,' " *PR*, 17.29 (July 19, 1974), 18.

104. Ibid., p. 19.

105. Ibid.

106. For a timely summary of these charges, see Stephen Osofsky, "Soviet Criticism of China's National Minorities Policy," *Asian Survey*, 14.10 (Oct. 1974), 907–917.

107. Urumchi Radio, Oct. 17, 1974.

108. Urumchi Radio, May 25, 1974.

109. Peking Radio, Oct. 1, 1974.

110. Peking Radio, Oct. 17, 1974.

111. For example, a speech entitled "Do Not Let Lin Piao and Company

Slander the People of Mongol Nationality," made by the Mongol vice-chairman of Ochina Banner's revolutionary committee in Kansu. Lanchow Radio, April 30, 1974.

112. Peking Radio, Jan. 18, 1975.
113. Kunming Radio, Dec. 20, 1974.
114. Kweiyang Radio, Dec. 23, 1974.
115. Urumchi Radio, Dec. 23, 1974.
116. Urumchi Radio, Jan. 10, 1975.
117. Lhasa Radio, May 2, 1974; June 7, 1974; Dec. 28, 1974.
118. Nanking Radio, Nov. 22, 1974.
119. Nanning Radio, Nov. 6, 1974.
120. Peking Radio, Dec. 21, 1974.
121. Shenyang Radio, Dec. 11, 1974.
122. Professor Ivan D. London, Department of Psychology, Brooklyn College, personal communication, Jan. 18, 1975, based on interviewing done in Hong Kong during the summer of 1973.
123. Lhasa Radio, May 3, 1973.
124. NCNA (Peking), June 30, 1973, *SCMP*, no. 5412, p. 106.
125. *MTTC*, no. 2 (Nov.) 1957, p. 8.
126. NCNA (Peking), June 30, 1973, *SCMP*, no. 5412, pp. 106–107.
127. See above, chap. 8.
128. *KMJP*, Aug. 31, 1972, *SCMP*, no. 5213, p. 65.
129. As expressed for example in Yeh Shang-chih, "Some Questions in the Work of Fostering Minority Nationalities Cadres," *JMJP*, Feb. 6, 1957. See also Nichols, "Minority Nationality Cadres," p. 297.
130. *PR*, 18.4 (Jan. 24, 1975), 7.
131. Ibid., p. 6.
132. Ibid., p. 8.
133. *Constitution of the Chinese People's Republic* (Peking, 1954).
134. *PR*, 18.4 (Jan. 24, 1975), 14.
135. Changchun Radio, Jan. 20, 1975.
136. Urumchi Radio, Jan. 23, 1975.
137. Urumchi Radio, Jan. 22, 1975.
138. Lanchow Radio, Nov. 21, 1974.
139. *JMJP*, Nov. 25, 1974.
140. See, for example, "Analysis of Soviet Revisionists' Policy on 'National Rapprochement,'" *PR*, 17.29 (July 19, 1974), 18–19, and "Soviet Revisionists Pursue Policy of Oppressing the Ukraine," NCNA (Peking), Oct. 15, 1974.

10. Minorities Policy: An Overview

1. I can find no evidence that Mao himself encouraged or concurred in an attack on the autonomous area system. It may have come from a group more radical than the chairman, which nonetheless claimed Mao as its leader.
2. See, for example, *JMJP*, Oct. 21, 1968.
3. See, for example, NCNA (Huhehot), Nov. 22, 1969.
4. Clifford Geertz, "The Integrative Revolution: Primordial Sentiments and Civil Politics in the New States," in Claude Welch Jr., ed., *Political Modernization* (Belmont, Calif., Wadsworth, 1967), p. 169.
5. *TR*, 5.10 (May 15, 1971), 2–3, 5–8; see also Lhasa Radio, May 28, 1971. Reports of guerrillas supplied by refugees through Nepal persisted through 1975. See, for example, Peking Radio, Sept. 28, 1974. A 24-year-old Tibetan PLA member who defected to Bhutan in 1974 reported that the ratio of Tibetans to Han in military service in the TAR is minuscule—approximately 20 to 700 in Phari, where he was stationed—indicating that Tibetans are still regarded as politically unreliable ("Tibetan PLA Man Escapes into Bhutan," *TR*, 9.3 [March 1974], 4). This lack

of trust is indirectly confirmed by a Chinese report stating that militia building had been taking place in urban areas and had industrial workers as its mainstay (Lhasa Radio, Dec. 7, 1974). Most of the Han civilian personnel in Tibet are of course industrial workers, and those Tibetans who are permitted to join militia work can be kept under more careful surveillance.

6. "China's Views on Major Issues of World Population," PR, 17.35 (Aug. 30, 1974), 9; Radio Peking, Aug. 25, 1974.

7. This phenomenon is noted by Cynthia Enloe with regard to West Indians who have immigrated to Britain. Cynthia Enloe, *Ethnic Conflict and Political Development* (Boston, Little, Brown, 1973), p. 181.

Bibliography

Amalrik, Andrei. *Can the Soviet Union Survive until 1984?* New York, Harper and Row, 1970.

Answering Questions on Manchuria. Tokyo, South Manchuria Railway Company, 1936.

The Anti-Stalin Campaign and International Communism, ed. Russian Institute, Columbia University. New York, Columbia University Press, 1956.

Aspaturian, Vernon R. "The Non-Russian Nationalities," in Allen Kassof, ed., *Prospects for Soviet Society.* New York, Praeger, 1968.

Bacon, Elizabeth. *Central Asians under Russian Rule.* Ithaca, Cornell University Press, 1966.

Barnett, A. Doak. *China on the Eve of Communist Takeover.* New York, Praeger, 1963.

————. *Cadres, Bureaucracy and Political Power in Communist China.* New York, Columbia University Press, 1967.

Batsell, Walter. *Soviet Rule in Russia.* New York, Macmillan, 1929.

Baum, Richard and Frederick Teiwes. *Ssu-ch'ing: The Socialist Education Movement of 1962–1966.* China Research Monographs 2. Berkeley, Center for Chinese Studies, 1968.

Bell, Charles. *Tibet Past and Present.* Oxford, Clarendon Press, 1924.

Bernatzik, Hugo. *Akha and Miao,* tr. Alois Nagler. New Haven, Human Relations Area Files, 1970.

Bilinsky, Yaroslav. "The Soviet Education Laws of 1958–59 and Soviet Nationality Policy," *Soviet Studies.* London, 14. 2 (Oct. 1962), 138–157.

————. "The Rulers and the Ruled," *Problems of Communism,* 16.5 (Sept.–Oct. 1967), 16–26.

Bitsch, Jørgen. *Mongolia: Unknown Land,* tr. Reginald Spink. London, Allen and Unwin, 1963.

Bloembergen, Samuel. "The Union Republics: How Much Autonomy?" *Problems of Communism,* 16.5 (Sept.–Oct. 1967), 27–35.

Bloom, S. F. *The World of Nations: A Study of the National Implications in the Work of Karl Marx.* New York, Columbia University Press, 1941.

Boorman, Howard, ed. *A Biographical Dictionary of Republican China.* 4 vols. New York, Columbia University Press, 1966, 1968, 1970, 1971.

Brandt, Conrad, Benjamin Schwartz, and John K. Fairbank. *A Documentary History of Chinese Communism.* Cambridge, Mass., Harvard University Press, 1952.

Braunthal, Julius. *History of the International,* tr. Henry Collins and Kenneth Mitchell. 2 vols. New York, Praeger, 1967.

Brunnert, H. S. and V. V. Hagelstrom. *Present Day Political Organization of China,* tr. A. Beltchenko and E. E. Moran. Shanghai, Kelly and Walsh, 1912.

Carrasco, Pedro. *Land and Polity in Tibet.* Seattle, University of Washington Press, 1959.

Casella, Alessandro. "The Pastoral Mongols," *Far Eastern Economic Review* [*FEER*], 52.6 (May 12, 1966), 296–298.

CB, see United States Consulate General, Hong Kong, *Current Background.*

Chang Chi-yun. "The Four Major Regions of China," *The China Monthly,* 6.1 (Chungking, Dec. 1944), 7–10.

Chen Han-seng. "A Critical Survey of Chinese Policy in Inner Mongolia," *Pacific Affairs* [*PA*], 18.4 (Dec. 1936), 557–561.

Ch'en Yuan. *Western and Central Asians in China under the Mongols: Their Transformation into Chinese,* tr. and annotated, Ch'en Hsing-hai and L. Carrington Goodrich. Monumenta Serica Monograph 15, Los Angeles, University of California Press, 1966.

Chiang Kai-shek. *China's Destiny,* tr. Wang Chung-hui. New York, Macmillan, 1947.

China Handbook, 1937–1945. New York, Macmillan, 1947.

Chinese Affairs. Nanking.

Chinese Communist Who's Who. 2 vols. Taipei, Institute of International Relations, Republic of China, 1970, 1971.

Chu Ch'i-hua 朱起華. *Chung-kuo ko-ming yü chung-kuo she-hui ko chieh-chi* 中國革命與中國社會各階級 (The Chinese revolution and Chinese social classes). Shanghai, Lien-ho shu-tien 聯和書店, 1930.

Chu Wen-djang. *The Moslem Rebellion in Northwest China, 1862–1878.* The Hague, Mouton, 1966.

Ch'uan Ju-hsiang 全如向. Manchu nationality, born and raised in Peking; taught music and art at the Central Nationalities Institute, Peking, from 1961 to 1966. Interviewed in Hong Kong, 1968.

Chung-kuo ch'ing-nien 中國青年 (Chinese youth), Peking.

Chung-kuo ku-chin ti-ming ta tz'u-tien 中國古近地名大辭典 (Geographical dictionary of ancient and modern China). Shanghai, Commercial Press, 1931.

Chung-kuo shao-shu min-tsu ti hsin mien-mao 中國小數民族的新面貌 (The new aspects of Chinese minority nationalities). Peking, San-lien shu-tien 三聯書店, 1953.

Clarke, Samuel. *Among the Tribes in Southwest China*. London, Morgan and Scott, 1911.

Clubb, O. E. *Chinese Communist Development Programs in Manchuria*. New York, Institute of Pacific Relations, 1954.

Connor, Walker F. "Minorities in Marxist Theory and Practice," paper presented to American Political Science Association Conference, New York, 1969.

Constitution of the People's Republic of China. Peking, Foreign Languages Press, 1954.

CS, see *Current Scene*.

Current Scene [*CS*]. Hong Kong.

Dalai Lama (Ngawang Lobsang Yishey Tenzing Gyaltso). *My Land and My People*. New York, McGraw-Hill, 1962.

"The Deported Nationalities . . . an Unsavory Story," *Problems of Communism*, 16.5 (Sept.–Oct. 1967), 102–104.

DK files, see Donald Klein files.

Dolfin, John III. "The Process of Reincorporation and Integration in the Tibetan Nationality Areas of China, 1950–1955." M.A. essay, Columbia University East Asia Institute, 1969.

Eberhard, Wolfram. "Kultur und Seidlung des Randvolkers China," *T'oung Pao*, vol. 38 supplement, Leiden, 1942.

von Eickstedt, Eric. *Rassendynamik von Ostasien*. Berlin, Hauptner, 1944.

Eisenstadt, S. N. *Modernization: Protest and Change*. Englewood Cliffs, N. J. Prentice-Hall, 1966.

Ekvall, Robert. *Cultural Relations on the Kansu-Tibetan Border*. Chicago, University of Chicago Press, 1939.

———. "Three Categories of Inmates within Tibetan Monasteries: Status and Function," *Central Asiatic Journal*, 5 (1959), 206–220.

———. "Nomads of Tibet: A Chinese Dilemma," *Current Scene*, Sept. 23, 1961, in Francis Harper, ed., *This is China*. Hong Kong, Dragonfly Press, 1965.

Enloe, Cynthia. *Ethnic Conflict and Political Development*. Boston, Little, Brown, 1973.

Etzioni, Amitai. *Political Unification: A Comparative Study of Leaders and Forces*. New York, Holt, Rinehart and Winston, 1965.

Fairbank, John K. and Teng Ssu-yu. "On the Ch'ing Tributary System," in Fairbank and Teng, *Ch'ing Administration: Three Studies*. Harvard Yenching Institute Studies no. 19. Cambridge, Mass., Harvard University Press 1961.

Far Eastern Economic Review [*FEER*], Hong Kong.

FEER, see *Far Eastern Economic Review*.

Fei Hsiao-t'ung 費孝通. "Minority Groups of Kweichow," *Hsin Kuan-ch'a* 新觀察 (New observer), nos. 3, 4, 5 (March, April, May 1951), pp. 2–4, 10–12, 4–6.

Fleming, Peter. *Bayonets to Lhasa.* New York, Harper, 1961.

Ford, Robert. *Wind between the Worlds.* New York, David McKay, 1957.

Forman, Harrison. "China's Moslems," *Canadian Geographic Journal*, 27.9 (Sept. 1948), 134–143.

Fourth Report on Progress in Manchuria. Dairen, South Manchuria Railway Company, 1934.

de Francis, John. "National and Minority Policies," *Annals of the American Academy of Political and Social Sciences*, 277 (Sept. 1951), pp. 146–155.

Freeberne, Michael. "Changing Population Characteristics in Tibet, 1959 to 1965," *Population Studies*, 19.3 (March 1966), 317–320.

———. "Demographic and Economic Changes in the Sinkiang Uighur Autonomous Region," *Population Studies*, 20.1 (July 1966), 103–124.

Geertz, Clifford. "The Integrative Revolution: Primordial Sentiments and Civil Politics in the New States," in Claude Welch, Jr., ed., *Political Modernization.* Belmont, Calif., Wadsworth, 1967.

Gelder, Stuart and Roma Gelder. *The Timely Rain: Travels in the New Tibet.* London, Hutchinson, 1964.

Ginsburgs, George and Michael Mathos. *Communist China and Tibet: The First Dozen Years.* The Hague, Martinus Nijhoff, 1964.

Gitelman, Zvi. "The Jews," *Problems of Communism*, 16.5 (Sept.–Oct. 1967), 92–101.

Haas, Ernst B. *The Uniting of Europe.* Stanford, Stanford University Press, 1958.

Han Tao-jen 韓道仁. *Min-tsu cheng-ts'e wen-ta* 民族政策問答 (Replying to questions on nationalities policy). Peking, T'ung-su tu-wu ch'u-pan she 通俗讀物出版社, 1957.

Hasiotis, Arthur C., Jr. "A Comparative Study of the Political and Economic Policies Pursued by the USSR and Communist China in Their Attempt to Consolidate Their Respective Positions within Russian Central Asia (1917–1934) and Sinkiang (1949–late 1957)." M.A. essay, Columbia University East Asia Institute, 1965.

Hazners, V. "Nationalism and Local Tendencies in Occupied Latvia," *Baltic Review*, 19 (March 1960), 43–47.

HHPYK, see *Hsin-hua pan-yüeh k'an.*

HHYP, see *Hsin-hua yüeh-pao.*

"How Russia Is Developing Central Asia," *South China Morning Post*, Hong Kong, Feb. 22, 1968, p. 11.

Hsin-hua pan-yüeh k'an 新華半月刊 [*HHPYK*] (New China bimonthly). Peking. Known as *Hsin-hua yüeh-pao* prior to 1956.

Hsin-hua she 新華社 [*NCNA*] (New China news agency), Peking and other locations.

Hsin-hua yüeh-pao 新華月報 [*HHYP*] (New China monthly), Peking. Known as *Hsin-hua pan-yüeh k'an* after 1956.

Hsü, Francis L. K. *Social Change in Southwest China: Magic and Science in Western Yunnan. The Problems of Introducing Scientific Medicine in a Rustic Community.* New York, Institute of Pacific Relations, 1943.

Hu, C. T. *The Education of National Minorities in Communist China.* Washington, Government Printing Office, OE–14146, 1970.

Hu Nai-an 胡耐安. *Pien-cheng t'ung-lun* 邊政通論 (A general discussion of border government). Taipei, 1960.

Huang Fen-shen 黃奮生. *Pien-chiang cheng-chao chih yen-chiu* 邊疆政之研究 (A study of frontier political administration), Shanghai, 1947.

Hudson, G. F. "The Nationalities of China," *St. Antony's Papers*, no. 7, London, 1960.

Hung-ch'i 紅旗 (Red flag). Peking.

International Commission of Jurists. *The Question of Tibet and the Rule of Law.* Geneva, International Commission of Jurists, 1959.

Iwamura Shinobu 岩村忍. Japanese scholar whose focus of research has been the Mongols. In the latter part of the 1930's, sponsored by the Japanese government, he toured Mongolia collecting information which could be used in Japan's policymaking. Interviewed in Kyoto, spring 1969.

Jen-min jih-pao 人民日報 [*JMJP*] (People's daily). Peking.

JMJP, see *Jen-min jih-pao.*

Johnson, A. Ross. *Yugoslavia: In the Twilight of Tito.* Beverly Hills, Calif., Sage Publications, 1974.

Johnson, Chalmers. *Peasant Nationalism and Chinese Power.* Stanford, Stanford University Press, 1962.

Jones, F. C. *Manchuria since 1931.* New York, Oxford University Press, 1949.

JPRS, see United States Department of Commerce, *Joint Publications Research Service.*

Klein, Donald, files. Mr. Klein, research associate of the East Asia Institute, Columbia University, maintains extensive bibliographical data files on CPR leaders.

KMJP, see *Kuang-ming jih-pao.*

Kolmas, Josef. "The Minority Nationalities," *Bulletin of the Atomic Scientists*, 22 (June 1966), 71–75.

Ku, C. C. "The Economic Development of China's Northwest," *China Quarterly*, 6.2 (Chungking, Spring 1939), 287–288.

Kuang-ming jih-pao 光明日報 [*KMJP*] (Bright daily). Peking.

Kunstadter, Peter, ed. *Southeast Asian Tribes, Minorities and Nations.* 2 vols. Princeton, Princeton University Press, 1967.

Kwangsi Chuang-tsu tzu-chih ch'ü chou-pei wei-yüan-hui 廣西僮族自治區 (Preparatory Committee for the Kwangsi Chuang Autonomous Region). *Kwangsi Chuang-tsu tzu-chih ch'ü* 廣西僮族自治区 (The Kwangsi Chuang Autonomous Region). Peking, 1958.

Lattimore, Owen. "The Historical Setting of Inner Mongolian Nationalism," *Pacific Affairs*, 18.3 (Fall 1936), 388–408.

———. *The Mongols of Manchuria.* New York, John Day, 1936.

———. *Pivot of Asia.* Boston, Little, Brown, 1950.

———. *Nomads and Commissars.* Boston, Little, Brown, 1958

Leach, E. R. *Political Systems of Highland Burma*. London, George Bell, 1954.

Lebar, F., G. Hickey, and J. Musgrave. *Ethnic Groups of Southeast Asia*. New Haven, Human Relations Area Files, 1964.

Lee, Robert H. G. *The Manchurian Frontier in Ch'ing History*. Cambridge, Mass., Harvard University Press, 1970.

Lenin, V. I. *Collected Works*. 34 vols. Moscow, Progress Publishers, 1964.

———. *The National Liberation Movement in the East*. Moscow, Foreign Languages Publishing House, 1957.

Li An-che. "China: A Fundamental Approach," *Pacific Affairs*, 21.1 (Spring 1948), 58–63.

Li Chen-ch'uan. *Economic Geography of the Yenpien Korean Autonomous Chou*. Shanghai, April 1957. Tr. in *JPRS*, 2019–N.

Li Chi. *Formation of the Chinese People*. Cambridge, Mass., Harvard University Press, 1928.

Lin Yueh-hua. *The Lolo of Liangshan*. New Haven, Human Relations Area Files, 1960.

Lindbeck, John. "Communism, Islam and Nationalism in China," *The Review of Politics*, 12.4 (Oct. 1950), 473–488.

Liu Ch'un. *The National Question and Class Struggle*. Peking, Foreign Languages Press, 1966.

Liu En-lan. "Border Tribes of West China," *The China Monthly*, 7.12 (Chungking, Dec. 1946), 433–435, 440–441.

Liu Hsi-fan 劉錫蕃. *Ling-piao chi-man* 嶺表紀蠻 (Notes on the barbarians of Kwangsi and Kwangtung). Shanghai, 1935.

Liu Ko-p'ing 劉克平. "Concerning Nationality Autonomous Areas," *Chung-kuo ch'ing-nien*, 70 (July 1951), 20–21.

———. "Unprecedented Unity of China's Nationalities," *Hsin kuan-ch'a*, 4 (April 1952), 11–12.

———. "Progress in Work among the Nationalities," *People's China*, 16 (Oct. 1952), 23–26.

"Local Autonomy in Mongolia," *Chinese Affairs*, 5.16 (Nanking, Jan. 31, 1934), 257–258.

Loewen, Jacob A. "Why Minority Languages Persist or Die," *Practical Anthropology*, 15.1 (Jan.–Feb. 1968), 8–15.

Lung Sheng-te 龍繩德. Yi nationality. Son of Yunnan warlord Lung Yun, Mr. Lung taught history at the Central Nationalities Institute in Peking 1961–1964. Interviewed in Hong Kong, 1968.

Ma Ho-t'ien. *Chinese Agent in Mongolia*, tr. John de Francis. Baltimore, Johns Hopkins University Press, 1949.

Ma Ta-chün 馬達駿. "Democratic Reforms and the Socialist Transformation in Nationalities Areas of China," *Chiao-hsüeh yü yen-chiu* 教學與研究 (Teaching and research), 6 (June 1958), 62–75.

Mac Farquhar, Roderick. *The Hundred Flowers Campaign and the Chinese Intellectuals*. New York, Praeger, 1960.

Mao Tse-tung. *Selected Works of Mao Tse-tung*. 4 vols. Peking, Foreign Languages Publishing House, 1965.

Marchetti, Victor and John Marks. *The CIA and the Cult of Intelligence.* New York, Alfred Knopf, 1974.

Maxwell, Neville. *India's China War.* London, Jonathan Cape, 1970.

Min-tsu cheng-ts'e wen-chien 民族政策文件 (Documents on nationalities policy), Peking, n.d.

Min-tsu cheng-ts'e wen-hsien hui-pien 民族政策文憲滙編 (Collected documents on nationalities policy). Peking, 1953.

Min-tsu t'uan-chieh 民族団結 [*MTTC*] (Nationalities solidarity), Peking.

Min-tsu yen-chiu 民族研究 [*MTYC*] (Nationalities research), Peking.

Mishima Yasuo and Goto Tomio. *A Japanese View of Outer Mongolia*, tr. and cond. Andre Grajdanev. New York, Institute of Pacific Relations, 1942.

Moseley, George. "China's Fresh Approach to the Minority Question," *The China Quarterly*, 24 (Oct.–Dec. 1965), 15–27.

———. *A Sino-Soviet Cultural Frontier: The Ili Kazakh Autonomous Chou.* Harvard East Asian Monographs no. 22. Cambridge, Mass., Harvard University Press, 1966.

———, ed. and tr. *The Party and the National Question in China.* Cambridge, Mass., MIT Press, 1966.

———. *The Consolidation of the South China Frontier.* Berkeley, University of California Press, 1973.

MTTC, see *Min-tsu t'uan-chieh.*

MTYC, see *Min-tsu yen-chiu.*

Nan-fang jih-pao 南方日報 [*NFJP*] (Southern daily), Canton.

NCNA, see *Hsin-hua she.*

The New York Times [*NYT*]. New York, New York.

NFJP, see *Nan-fang jih-pao.*

Nichols, James Lloyd. "Minority Nationality Cadres in Communist China." Ph.D. diss., Stanford University, 1969.

Norins, Martin. "The New Sinkiang: China's Link with the Middle East," *Pacific Affairs*, 15.4 (Dec. 1942), 457–470.

Nove, Alec and J. A. Newth. *The Soviet Middle East: A Communist Model for Development.* New York, Praeger, 1967.

NYT, see *The New York Times.*

Okada, Kenji. *The Li Tribes of Hainan Island.* Yale Southeast Asia Translation Series, New Haven, Yale University Press, n.d.

Orleans, Leo A. "Dealing with Population Problems," *Bulletin of the Atomic Scientists*, 22 (June 1966), 22–26.

PA, see *Pacific Affairs.*

Pacific Affairs [*PA*]

Pao Ke. "Peiping's Administration of Minority Nationalities," *Chinese Communist Affairs*, 4.3 (Taipei, June 1967), 41–44.

"Party Work among the Minorities of Hainan Island," *Current Scene*, 8.2 (Jan. 15, 1970), 1–23.

Pasternak, Burton. "Continuity and Discontinuity in Chinese Policy toward the Southwestern Tribes since 1911." M.A. essay, Columbia University East Asia Institute, 1962.

Patterson, George. *Tibet in Revolt*. London, Methuen, 1960.

Peking Review. Peking.

Pilarski, Laura. "Little Tibet in Switzerland," *National Geographic*, 134.5 (Nov. 1968), 711–727.

Pipes, Richard. *The Formation of the Soviet Union: Communism and Nationalism 1917–1923*. Cambridge, Mass., Harvard University Press, 1964.

———. "'Solving' the Nationality Problem," *Problems of Communism*, 16.5 (Sept.–Oct. 1967), 125–131.

Policy toward Nationalities of the People's Republic of China. Peking, Foreign Languages Press, 1953.

Pollard, Samuel. *In Unknown China*. Philadelphia, J. B. Lippincott, 1921.

Rakhimov, T. "The Great Power Policy of Mao Tse-tung on the Nationalities Question," *Kommunist*, 44.7 (May 1967), 114–119.

Reitlinger, Gerald. *South of the Clouds*. London, Faber and Faber, 1939.

Richardson, H. E. *A Short History of Tibet*. New York, Dutton, 1962.

Rupen, Robert. "Partition in the Land of Genghis Khan," *Current Scene*, Sept. 27, 1962, in Francis Harper, ed., *This Is China*. Hong Kong, Green Pagoda Press, 1965.

Schlesinger, Rudolf. *The Nationalities Problem and Soviet Adminstration: Selected Readings on the Development of Soviet Nationalities Policy*, tr. W. W. Gottlieb. London, Routledge and Kegan Paul, 1956.

Schram, Stuart. *Mao Tse-tung*. New York, Simon and Schuster, 1966.

Schwarz, Henry G. "Language Policies toward Ethnic Minorities," *The China Quarterly*, 12 (Oct.–Dec. 1962), 170–182.

———. "Chinese Migration to Northwest China and Inner Mongolia," *The China Quarterly*, 16 (Oct.–Dec. 1963), 62–74.

SCMM, see United States Consulate General, Hong Kong, *Selections from China Mainland Magazines*.

SCMP, see United States Consulate General, Hong Kong, *Survey of China Mainland Press*.

Senanayake, Ratne Deshapriya. *Inside Story of Tibet*. Peking, Afro-Asian Writers' Bureau, 1967.

Shaheen, S. *The Communist Theory of Self Determination*. The Hague, W. van Hoeve, 1956.

Sheehy, Ann. "The Central Asian Republics," *Conflict Studies*, no. 30 (Dec. 1972), pp. 13–18.

Shih-shih shou-ts'e 时事手册 (Current affairs handbook). Shanghai.

Simpson, George and Milton Yinger. *Racial and Cultural Minorities*. New York, Harper and Row, 1965.

Snow, Edgar. *Red Star over China*. New York, Grove Press, 1938.

———. *The Other Side of the River*. New York, Random House, 1961.

Spencer, J. E. "K'ueichou, an Internal Chinese Colony," *Pacific Affairs*, 23.2 (Summer 1940), 162–169.

Stalin, Joseph. *Marxism and the National and Colonial Question*. New York, International Publishers, 1934.

The Standard. Hong Kong.

Steele, A. T. *The American People and China*. New York, McGraw-Hill, 1966.

Stelkoff, G. *History of the First International.* New York, Russell and Russell, 1968.

Strong, Anna Louise. *Tibetan Interviews.* Peking, New World Press, 1959.

Sullivant, Robert S. "The Ukrainians," *Problems of Communism,* 16.5 (Sept.–Oct. 1967), 46–54.

Sun E-tu Zen. *Ch'ing Administrative Terms.* Cambridge, Mass., Harvard University Press, 1961.

Sun Yat-sen. *Sun Yat-sen: His Political and Social Ideals,* ed. Leonard Shihlien Hsü. Los Angeles, University of Southern California Press, 1933.

———. *Memoirs of a Chinese Revolutionary.* Taipei, China Cultural Service, 1953.

Ta Kung Pao 大公報 (Impartial daily). Hong Kong.

Teichman, Eric. *Travels of a Consular Officer in Eastern Tibet.* Cambridge, Cambridge University Press, 1922.

———. *Journey to Turkestan.* London, Hodder and Stoughton, 1937.

Thompson, Virginia and Richard Adloff. *Minority Problems in Southeast Asia.* Stanford, Stanford University Press, 1955.

Ti-li chih-shih 地理智識 (Geographical knowledge). Peking.

Tibetan Review. New Dehli.

Tinker, Hugh. "Burma's Northeastern Borderland Problems," *Pacific Affairs,* 29.4 (Winter 1956), 324–346.

Tomson, Edgar, ed. *Dokumente: die Volksrepublik China und das Recht nationaler Minderheiten.* Frankfurt, Alfred Metzner, 1963.

Tsing Yuan. "Yakub Beg (1820–1877) and the Moslem Rebellion in Chinese Turkestan," *Central Asiatic Journal,* 6.1 (1961), 134–167.

United States Consulate General, Hong Kong. *Current Background* [*CB*].

———. *Selections from China Mainland Magazines* [*SCMM*].

———. *Survey of China Mainland Press* [*SCMP*].

United States Department of Commerce. *Joint Publications Research Service* [*JPRS*].

United States Department of State. *Biographical Directory No. 271: Directory of Party and Government Officials in Communist China.* Washington, D.C., July 20, 1960.

Volgin, I. M. (pseudonym). "The Friendship of Peoples . . . Pages from a Notebook," *Problems of Communism,* 16.5 (Sept.–Oct. 1967), 106.

Wagley, Charles and Marvin Harris. *Minorities in the New World.* New York, Columbia University Press, 1958.

Wales, Nym (pseudonym of Helen Foster Snow). *Red Dust.* Stanford, Stanford University Press, 1952.

———. "My Yenan Notebooks." Madison, Conn., mimeographed, 1961.

Wang Chien-min 王建民. *Chung-kuo kung-ch'an-tang shih-kao* 中國共產黨史稿 (Draft history of the Chinese Communist Party). 3 vols. Taipei, privately printed, 1965.

Wang Ming. *China: Cultural Revolution or Counterrevolutionary Coup?* Moscow, Novosti Press Agency Publishing House, 1969.

Weng Tu-chien. "China's Policy on National Minorities," *People's China,* 1.7 (April 1, 1950), 6.

Wheeler, Geoffrey. "The Muslims of Central Asia," *Problems of Communism*, 16.5 (Sept.–Oct. 1967), 72–81.

Whiting, Allen and Sheng Shih-ts'ai. *Sinkiang: Pawn or Pivot?* East Lansing, Michigan State University Press, 1958.

Whiting, Allen. "The Use of Force in Foreign Policy by the People's Republic of China," *The Annals of the American Academy of Political and Social Science*, 402 (July 1972), 55–66.

Whitson, William. *The Chinese High Command: A History of Communist Military Politics, 1927–1971.* New York, Praeger, 1973.

Wiens, Herold J. *China's March toward the Tropics.* Hamden, Conn., Shoestring Press, 1954.

———. "Some of China's Thirty-Five Million Non-Chinese," *Journal of the Hong Kong Branch of the Royal Asiatic Society*, 2.1 (1962), 21.

Winnington, Alan. *The Slaves of the Cool Mountains.* London, Lawrence and Wishart, 1959.

Wolfe, Bertrand. *Three Who Made a Revolution.* Boston, Beacon Press, 1948.

Wright, Mary C. *The Last Stand of Chinese Conservatism.* Stanford, Stanford University Press, 1957.

Yakhontoff, Victor. "Mongolia: Target or Screen," *Pacific Affairs*, 18.1 (Spring 1936), 13–23.

Yang Ching-chih. "Japan—Protector of Islam," *Pacific Affairs*, 15.4 (Winter 1942), 471–481.

Yang Chün-sheng 楊俊生, ed. *Chung-kuo ko min-tsu fu-nü fu-shih* 中国各民族妇女服飾 (Women's costumes of China's nationalities). Shanghai, 1963.

Yang, Richard. "Sinkiang under the Administration of Governor Yang Tseng-hsin, 1911–1928," *Central Asian Journal*, 6.1 (1961), 270–316.

Yen Tzer-chung 嚴則中. Pai nationality. Presently a businessman in Hong Kong. Mr. Yen left his home in the Tali area of Yunnan in 1949, but has maintained close contact with family and friends. Interviewed in Hong Kong in 1968.

Glossary

Amban 安班
an yuan-ts'e pan-shih 按原則办事
cha-ken k'ai-hua chieh-kuo 扎根开花結果
cha-sa (Yasa) 扎撒
cheng-feng 正风
ch'i 旗
chia (pao-chia) 甲
chien-ch'uan ho ch'ung-shih 建全和充实
ch'ien-wu wan-wu tseng-chia sheng-ch'u shih ti-yi t'iao 千条万条增加牲畜是第一條
Chih-pien hsüeh-t'ang 殖邊學堂
ch'in-wu yüan 勤务員
chü t'i ti shih-shih ch'iu shih 具体的实事求是
Chueh-wu she 覚悟社
chung-nung ch'ing-mu 重農輕牧
chung-tsu 種族
fan 蕃
fan-shen 翻身
ho-feng hsi-yü 和风細雨
ho-p'ing ma-pi ssu-hsiang 和平痲痺思想
hou-ku po-chin 厚古薄今
Hsi-fan 西蕃
hsia-fang 下放
Hsü-min 胥民
huan-ch'ing 还清
huan ho 緩和
jen-chung 人種
jen-shen yi-fu 人身袾附
jung-ho 融合
kai-t'u kuei-liu 改土歸流
kung-t'ung hsing 共同性
kuo-shih 过时
Li-fan yüan 理藩院
li-mao 礼帽
Li-pu 禮部
Lolo 猪猪
lung-tzu ti erh-tuo 聾子的耳杂
Ma Liang 馬良
man 蠻
Man, Yi, Jung, Ti 蠻夷戎氏
meng 盟
Meng-Tsang shih-wu ch'u 蒙藏事務局
Meng-Tsang wei-yüan hui 蒙藏委員會
Meng-Tsang yüan 蒙藏院
min-tsu-hua 民族化
ming-tuo shih-shao 名多实少
pang 邦
pao (pao-chia) 保
p'ei pu-shih 賠不是
Po-pa 博巴

san-pao yi-chiang 三包一奖
sheng 生
shih-pan 試办
shih pu-neng tang chen-t'ou, Han pu-neng tso p'eng-yu 石不能当枕头，汉不能作朋友
shu 熟
ssu-ku-ting 四固定
Tan-chia 艇家
tsung-tsu 宗族
t'u 土
t'u-kuan 土官
t'u-ssu 土司
t'un-t'ien 屯田

t'ung-hua 同化
tzu-chih chou 自治州
tzu-chih ch'ü 自治區 or 区
tzu-chih hsiang 自治鄉 or 乡
tzu-chih hsien 自治縣
tzu-wu tao-yu 自無到有
Ulanfu 鳥兰夫
Ulanmuchi 鳥兰牧冀
wantao (wang-tao) 王道
yi-chih 移植
yin-shih chih-yi 因时制宜
yin-ti chih-yi 因地制宜
yüan 院

1. The form of the characters, whether simplified or unsimplified, depends on the form current in the period when the phrases were current.

Index

HARVARD EAST ASIAN SERIES